PARALLEL PROCESSING

From Applications to Systems

PARALLEL PROCESSING

From Applications to Systems

Dan I. Moldovan

Morgan Kaufmann Publishers
San Mateo, California

Senior Editor: Bruce M. Spatz
Production Manager: Yonie Overton
Editorial Coordinator: Douglas Sery
Cover Designer: Rebecca Evans & Associates
Copy Editor: Judith Abrahms
Proofreader: Fran Taylor
Postscript conversion/output: Superscript Typography
Printer: R.R. Donnelley & Sons

This book has been author-typeset using laTEX macros, with technical assistance
provided by the publisher.

Morgan Kaufmann Publishers
Editorial Offices:
2929 Campus Drive, Suite 260
San Mateo, CA 94403

Library of Congress Cataloging-in-Publication Data

Moldovan, Dan I.
        Parallel processing from applications to systems / Dan
  I. Moldovan.
              p.   cm.
        Includes bibliographical references and index.
        ISBN 1-55860-254-2
        1. Parallel processing (Electronic computers)   I. Title.
QA76.58.M65   1993
004'.35--dc20   92-44256
                                                        CIP

To my children,
Nicole and Gregory,
and my wife Ileana

Contents

Preface

Parallel Processing

Parallel processing is a fast growing technology that permeates many areas of computer science and engineering. It is only natural that the concurrencies which abound in many application domains start to reflect in computer systems. We live in a concurrent and complex universe, and as we master computer technology better, we tend to bring this concurrency to our computers. Supercomputers as well as smaller computers rely more and more on parallel processing methods. Parallelism brings unprecedented speed and cost effectiveness, but also raises a new set of complex and challenging problems to solve. Most of these problems are software related.

Parallel processing comprises algorithms, computer architecture, programming, and performance analysis. There is a strong interaction among these aspects and it becomes even more important when we want to implement systems. A global understanding of these aspects allows programmers and designers to make trade-offs in order to increase overall efficiency. The book emphasizes the relation between parallel algorithms and computer architectures via program transformations.

Motivation for writing this book

The main motivation for writing this book was to offer instructors and students a comprehensive presentation of the rapidly expanding field of parallel processing. Parallel processing is becoming a mature subject area and courses are offered at most universities. Although there are several books on various aspects of parallel processing, there is no textbook covering this area in a comprehensive way. The book is intended to save you from having to read separate books on parallel algorithms, computer architecture, programming, and performance. It presents a broad background with sufficient depth.

This book is intended for anyone interested in the wonders of parallel processing, from students learning about these things for the first time to practitioners with many years of experience in conventional computers currently with a need to understand techniques for designing and building efficient parallel computer systems.

This book has evolved from class notes for a graduate level course in parallel processing originated by the author at the University of Southern California in 1982. The text has been continously upgraded to the present form.

Approach to material presented

This book is called *Parallel Processing from Applications to Systems* mainly because of the approach taken. The reason why one wants to use the parallel processing technology is supposedly that one has a computationally demanding application which calls for large processing power. A first step that one may take is to understand the nature of computations in that application domain. A second step is to design a parallel algorithm or parallelize an existing sequential algorithm. The next step is to either map the parallel algorithm into suitable computer architectures or design algorithmically specialized architectures.

The book provides ample techniques and examples for mapping problems into parallel computers. An efficient mapping takes into consideration matching an algorithm's data dependencies to the interconnection network, creating processes suitable for the size of processors and allocating data to memories.

The book presents both parallel processing applied to scientific and engineering applications, as well as to artificial intelligence. Many problems from signal processing, communication, automatic control, and other engineering areas lead to numeric algorithms. Applications from artificial intelligence such as rule-based systems, natural language processing, and others, lead to algorithms involving knowledge representation and reasoning.

Organization

The book is divided into eight chapters. Chapter 1 is an introduction
to parallel processing containing basic computer models, performance,
and applications. Chapter 2 is a basic chapter introducing the concept
of dependencies and techniques for parallelism analysis in algorithms.
Fairly complex examples of numeric and nonnumeric algorithms are
given. Chapter 3 contains techniques for transforming programs from
sequential to parallel forms. Such techniques are used in parallel compilers. Chapter 4 presents a major class of parallel computer architectures: array processors. Examples of modern supercomputers of this
class are given. Systolic processors and associative processors are also
presented as part of array processors. Chapter 5 combines some of the
ideas from Chapters 3 and 4 and discusses the mapping of algorithms
into array processors. Chapter 6 is dedicated to multiprocessors. These
parallel computers are the most flexible, yet most difficult to use. In
Chapter 7, data-flow computers are described. Finally, Chapter 8 is
dedicated to parallel knowledge processing. It contains material on
parallel rule-based systems and semantic networks. The design of parallel computer architectures for artificial intelligence is discussed.

Features

Some of the book's most distinctive features are

- It covers the majority of the important topics in parallel processing. The book is self-contained and is adaptable to professors
  with different requirements.

- Each chapter has two sets of problems: the set A problems have
  solutions and the set B problems are without solutions. The problems are medium to difficult and are stimulating. Many of them
  have been given as exams in the parallel processing course at the
  University of Southern California.

- Each chapter has a short bibliographical note, as well as references
  which point to major results in the field, for further studies.

- The book contains material on numeric as well as artificial intelligence parallel processing. As application systems become more

and more "intelligent," there is a need to build computer systems incorporating both numeric and knowledge processing capabilities. The same approaches are used for these two types of applications in an attempt to unify the field of parallel processing. The subject of parallel processing applied to artificial intelligence is rather new and has not been covered yet in any other textbook. There are, however, some edited books containing a collection of papers on the subject.

- The book presents parallel processing from applications to systems emphasizing a mathematical treatment of the mapping problem. The author believes that this is a better approach than exposing students to facts about existing parallel machines. The book has, however, sufficient material on some case studies of supercomputers, allowing students to link theory with reality.

- The book raises a number of research issues as yet unsolved. In this sense, the book may serve as a source of inspiration for students and young reserchers who want to engage in parallel processing research. Chapter 1 presents a list of such issues. Hopefully, this book will provoke and help the reader to identify meaningful research challenges.

Teaching from this book

The material in this book is suitable for a course of approximately 45 to 60 hours. The field of parallel processing is expanding rapidly and new, improved results become available every year. Current parallel supercomputers are only briefly described; their design details and programming may be supplemented with recent technical reports made available by manufacturers. The instructor may emphasize one area or another by augmenting the text with results from current research papers.

The book does not cover some forms of parallelism such as pipelining and vector processing. These topics have been omitted because of the size limitations and also because in many universities they are part of computer architecture courses.

The prerequisites for this book are: general knowledge about computer structure and operation, and some knowledge about discrete mathematics and graph theory, normally acquired in undergraduate courses. Although the last chapter dealing with parallelism in AI is self-contained, for a deeper understanding and possible extensions of the results, greater AI knowledge is helpful.

Acknowledgements

Part of the material in this book stems from research performed at USC by the author and his students. I express my gratitude and appreciation for the following former and current doctoral students who have contributed many ideas to the book during long years of research:

Jose A.B. Fortes	Yu Wen Tung	Fernando Tenorio
Tsair-Chin Lin	Chung I. Wu	Vish Dixit
Steve Sen-Hao Kuo	Wing Lee	Ronald F. DeMara
Eric Changhwa Lin	Minhwa Chung	Seungho Cha
Juntae Kim	Sanghwa Chung	Steve Kowalski
Ken Hendrickson	Adrian Moga	Traian Mitrache
Sanda Harabagiu	Chin-Yew Lin	Hasan Akhter

During 1987-88, I spent a sabbatical year working at the National Science Foundation in Washington, D.C. A good part of this book was written in my spare time throughout this sabbatical year. I am deeply indebted to Bernard Chern and John Lehmann who have provided a most pleasant working environment and much encouragement.

My stay at NSF has overlapped with Professor Ben Wah. Is addition to being a truly wonderful individual, Ben has been a fountain of knowledge, who has provided me with feedback regarding many technical aspects of this book. I am also thankful to John Hennessy, Larry Wittie, Mark Franklin, John Hayes and the anonymous reviewers for suggestions made to improve the manuscript.

On the production side, I have benefitted by the diligence and help of Dawn Ernst, who has typeset the last few versions of the book. Dawn has also produced the figures in the book. I am grateful for her highly professional work. Eric Lin has acted as a LaTeX and computer consultant whenever tough problems occured. His valuable assistance made it possible for us to put the book in production form.

I express my gratitude to the staff at Morgan Kaufmann Publishers for an excellent job with editing and production of the book. Bruce Spatz has suggested many improvements regarding the content of the book and provided valuable guidelines. Yonie Overton has contributed with the production of the book. Judith Abrahms has done an outstanding job editing the text. I thank them all.

Finally, I want to acknowledge the support of the National Science Foundation, Joint Services Electronics Program, Defence Advanced Research Projects Agency, Shell Foundation, AT&T, and Texas Instruments for the research funding I received during the last ten years. This financial support of our research made possible the graduation of many talented individuals and has produced numerous research results, many of which appear in the book.

Dan I. Moldovan
Los Angeles

Chapter 1

INTRODUCTION

Parallelism is a general term used to characterize a variety of simultaneities occurring in modern computers. The main advantage offered by parallelism is improved speed. This first chapter is an introduction to parallel processing. We start with some models of parallel computation, which either are extensions of the von Neumann model or are developed especially for parallel computations. Parallel processing has great flexibility, which causes many programming problems, but which permits parallelism to be analyzed at several levels of complexity.

The growing importance of parallel processing is reflected by the large number of applications that embrace it. Some of these are discussed below. At present, parallel processing permeates almost all aspects of computer science and engineering. It includes the study of parallel algorithms and architectures and much more. Many factors contribute to the performance of parallel systems: understanding the interaction among software, hardware architectures, technology, theory, and applications is of great importance.

Rather than focus on the history of parallel processing, we will concentrate on identifying some of the main unresolved issues in the field. Much progress has been made in many areas, but much more remains to be done.

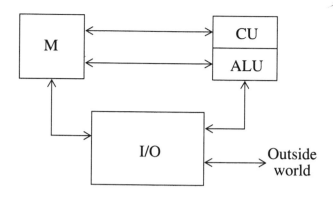

Figure 1.1 Von Neumann computer model.

1.1 PARALLELISM AS A CONCEPT

1.1.1 Models of Parallel Computations

Sequential Von Neumann Model

For more than 40 years, the *von Neumann principles* have dominated computer architectures. This computational model was first used to build uniprocessors. It was natural that the first efforts in parallel processing were extensions of the von Neumann model. A classical von Neumann computer consists of a program control unit (CU), an arithmetic logic unit (ALU), an input/output unit (I/O), and memory (M), as shown in Figure 1.1. The CU and the ALU collectively make up the processing element.

The von Neumann model is based on the following principles:

- A single processing element separated from memory by a communication bus;

- Linear organization of fixed-size memory cells;

- Low-level machine language with instructions performing simple operations on elementary operands; and

- Sequential centralized control of computations.

These principles are simple and well understood; considerable progress has been made with them and confidence in this model has grown over the years. One reason for the success of the von Neumann computer is the flexibility of its implementation. For example, communication between processor and memory may be achieved with separate or multiplexed data and address buses. Also, the von Neumann model leaves room for a variety of processor and memory organizations, such as hierarchical memory. While the hardware performs low-level arithmetic and logic operations, the programs are usually written in high-level languages. This gap between low-level hardware operation and high-level software is detrimental, on the one hand, because it requires the use of compilers and other software tools; but, on the other hand, it enables programs from a wide range of software to run efficiently on machines with a wide range of hardware.

RAM Model

The conventional uniprocessor can be abstracted as a random-access machine (RAM) model, as shown in Figure 1.2. This theoretical model is useful for algorithm development and for complexity studies. It also constitutes the starting point for theoretical parallel models.

A RAM consists of a program, a memory, a read-only input tape, and a write-only output tape. The program is a sequence of instructions addressed by a program counter. The input tape contains symbols i_1, i_2, ..., read by the program. After a read operation, the tape head moves one step. The output is a write-only tape. Initially blank, this tape is filled with symbols o_1, o_2, ... as the result of program execution. The memory contains a number of locations 0, 1, 2, ..., used as read/write scratch memory during program execution.

The main ways used to extend the sequential von Neumann model to parallel architectures are by employing the concepts of *pipelining, vector processors, array processors,* and *multiprocessors.* These are described below.

Pipelining

The process of pipelining divides a task T into subtasks T_1, T_2, ..., T_k and assigns them to a chain of processing stations. These stations are

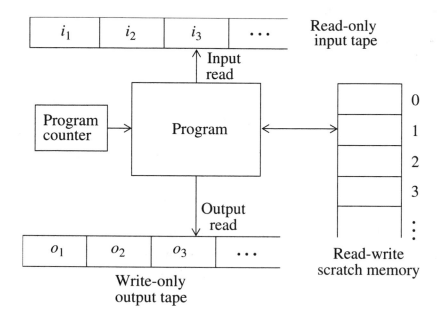

Figure 1.2 A random-access machine.

called pipeline segments. Parallelism is achieved when several segments operate simultaneously. It is possible to use the principle of pipelining either at the *instruction* level or at the *arithmetic* level. As shown in Figure 1.3, in instruction-level pipelining, the control unit (CU) consists of several stages organized as a pipeline; in arithmetic-level pipelining, the arithmetic logic unit (ALU) is organized in several stages, and operations inside the ALU are pipelined.

Vector Processors
Vector processors are specially designed to handle computations formulated in terms of vectors. A vector processor has a set of instructions that treat vectors as single operands. For example, the subtraction of two vectors of n elements each may be performed simultaneously for all n elements. The vector processor could conceivably be implemented by replicating the number of scalar ALUs to the size of a vector. This requires considerable hardware, so pipelining is used instead. Since vectors are one-dimensional arrays and the same sequence of operations is

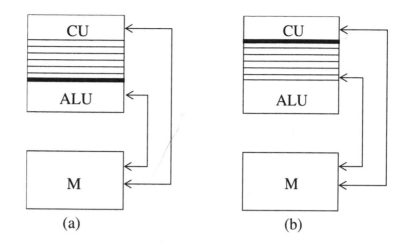

Figure 1.3 (a) CU pipelining; (b) ALU pipelining.

repeated for every vector element, vector processing is ideally suited to pipeline arithmetic. One or more pipelined ALUs may be used. Figure 1.4 shows a set of vector registers that hold vector elements, and illustrates the way they supply data to the pipelined ALUs.

Often uniprocessor computer systems are equipped with vector coprocessors in order to speed up vector computations. Sequential code can sometimes be vectorized. This simple and inexpensive technique usually provides significant speed improvements over a purely scalar operation.

Array Processors

The term *array processor* refers to a synchronous parallel computer, which consists of multiple ALUs under the supervision of a single control unit, as shown in Figure 1.5. The control unit synchronizes all the ALUs by broadcasting control signals to them. The ALUs perform the same instruction, but on different data that each of them fetches from its own memory. This is why this model is sometimes called *data parallel*. The interconnection network (IN) facilitates data communication among the processing units and among processing units and memories (M). This type of computer is also called a single-instruction multiple-data (SIMD) computer. The source of parallelism in SIMD computers

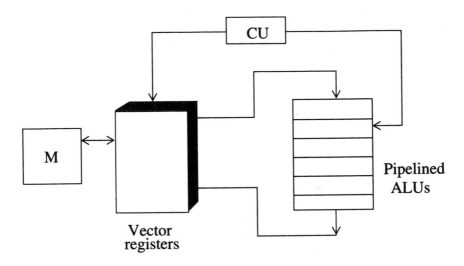

Figure 1.4 Vector processor.

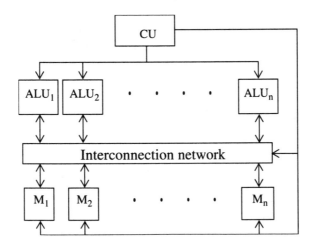

Figure 1.5 Array processor organization.

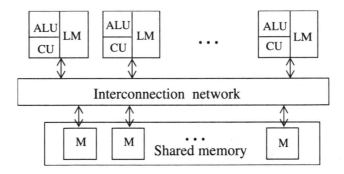

Figure 1.6 Multiprocessor organization.

is that one instruction operates on several operands simultaneously rather than on a single one.

Shared-memory Multiprocessors

Another way of introducing parallelism in the sequential von Neumann model is to use several processors, each including a CU, an ALU, and several memory and I/O modules.

Two distinct possibilities exist regarding the way processors communicate with each other: (1) *shared-memory* communication, in which processors communicate via a common memory; and (2) *message-passing* communication, in which processors communicate via communication links. The shared-memory organization is shown in Figure 1.6. Each processor operates on its own instruction stream, fetched either from the local memory (LM) or from the shared memory. The shared-memory multiprocessor is usually composed of independent modules, each connected to a port of the interconnection network. Since processors operate more or less independently of each other, this is an asynchronous architecture. It is obviously more flexible and can be more widely utilized than the array processor organization. The interconnection network facilitates exchanges between processors, and between processors and the shared memory.

PRAM Model

The parallel random-access machine (PRAM) model is an abstraction of the shared-memory multiprocessor in the same way as the RAM is an abstraction of the conventional uniprocessor. As shown in Figure 1.7, a PRAM consists of: p separate programs; p accumulators, one for each program; a single read/write memory that is accessible to all programs; a read-only input tape; and a write-only output tape.

Each program can access the input and output tapes. The programs are different from each other; however, it is assumed that all instructions take the same amount of time to execute. Because of this assumption, the PRAM is a synchronous machine, unlike the actual shared-memory multiprocessor. Another simplifying assumption is that there is no interconnection network; in other words, the communication time is zero.

The common memory is available to all programs. Four distinct possibilities exist regarding the collective reads and writes:

1. EREW (exclusive read, exclusive write). The programs cannot simultaneously access the same memory cell.

2. ERCW (exclusive read, concurrent write). The programs cannot simultaneously read the same memory cell, but can simultaneously write to the same memory cell.

3. CREW (concurrent read, exclusive write). The programs can simultaneously read the same memory cell, but cannot simultaneously write to the same memory cell.

4. CRCW (concurrent read, concurrent write). The programs can simultaneously read and write to the same memory cell.

The PRAM model is useful for designing parallel algorithms for shared-memory systems and for studying their properties.

Message-Passing Multiprocessor

In this model, the memory is distributed among the processors such that each processor has its own program and data memory. Figure 1.8 illustrates this model. The communication of shared data is achieved

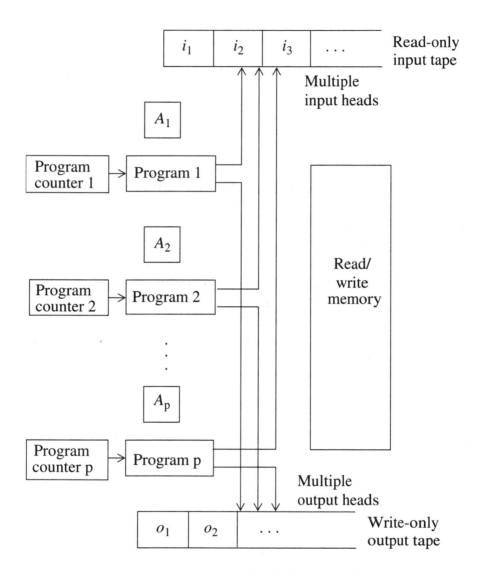

Figure 1.7 A parallel random-access machine.

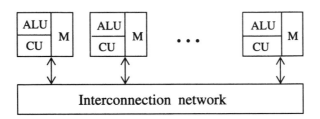

Figure 1.8 Message-passing multiprocessor.

via messages exchanged directly between processors through an interconnection network. This mode of operation differs from the shared-
memory mode, and this affects the architecture design as well as the
type of problems suitable for message-passing multiprocessors.

Another natural extension of the von Neumann model is to use a
network of computers. In this scheme, each node in the network is a
self-contained computer, which can be considerably complex and which
operates completely autonomously from the other nodes. A computer
network may be geographically dispersed.

In addition to these natural extensions of the von Neumann model,
it is possible to take a more fundamental approach and to design new
computation models exclusively for parallel processing. These models
include *systolic processors, data-flow models, logic-inference models, reduction models, neural networks,* and others. Systolic processing and
data-flow concepts are briefly discussed in the sections that follow; some
other non–von Neumann models will be presented later.

Systolic Processing

Systolic arrays are pipelined array processors consisting of identical cells
that perform simple arithmetic functions. Data travels from one cell
to the next cell, where it is updated, and finally the result comes out.
Parallelism is achieved because all the cells operate concurrently. Let
us consider as an example a matrix-vector multiplication algorithm

$$
\begin{bmatrix} y_1 \\ y_2 \\ y_3 \end{bmatrix} = \begin{bmatrix} a_{11} & a_{12} & a_{13} \\ a_{21} & a_{22} & a_{23} \\ a_{31} & a_{32} & a_{33} \end{bmatrix} \begin{bmatrix} x_1 \\ x_2 \\ x_3 \end{bmatrix} + \begin{bmatrix} y_1^0 \\ y_2^0 \\ y_3^0 \end{bmatrix}
$$

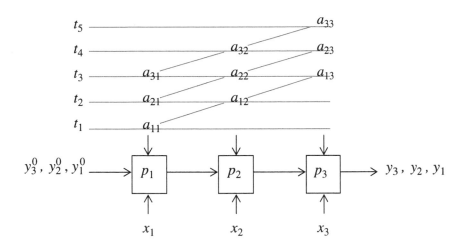

Figure 1.9 A systolic computation for matrix-vector multiplication.

This algorithm can be computed on three processing cells pipelined as in Figure 1.9. Five time steps are necessary. The inputs are fed to the cells and partial results travel from one cell to the next cell. The correct results are obtained by sending the proper inputs to the proper cells at the right times. Each cell computes a single inner product, as indicated in Figure 1.10.

Systolic arrays need to be attached to a host computer that provides storage for input and output data and control signals for the cells' hardware. Systolic arrays are characterized by simple and regular interconnections, which makes them suitable for very large-scale integration (VLSI) implementations. More complex algorithms may be mapped into systolic arrays, as will be seen later.

Data-Flow Computations

The data-flow model of computation was suggested as an alternative to the rigid von Neumann model. In the data-flow scheme, computations take place when operands become available. This eliminates the need for a program counter. The result produced by an instruction is used as *pure data* or *tokens,* which travel directly to the operands of the next instructions. The data-flow model does not need addresses for storing

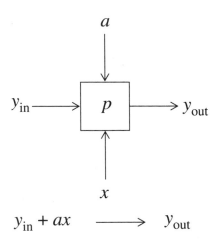

Figure 1.10 A systolic processing cell.

variables; thus, it is free of side-effects. This is in contrast to the von Neumann model, where storing, fetching, and some other operations do not directly contribute to the result and are sometimes called side-effects.

Abundant parallelism may be achieved. Let us consider the expression $z = y(x + 1)$. This computation can be represented by a *data-flow graph* that indicates the interdependencies between operations, as shown in Figure 1.11. The graph consists of nodes, or *actors,* and arcs linking the actors. The presence of a data value on an arc is marked by a token. For example, x has value 4 and y has value 5. One way to execute a data-flow graph is to allow each actor to *fire* only when tokens are present on all of its input arcs and there is no token on its output arc. In Figure 1.11(a), the "plus" operator is eligible to fire, whereas the "multiplication" operator is not. In Figure 1.11(b), the "plus" operator has already fired, which now enables the "multiplication" operator to fire. Finally, in Figure 1.11(c), the result is $z = 25$. In Chapter 7 we will elaborate on the data-flow model and other non–von Neumann models and show how these models can be implemented in hardware.

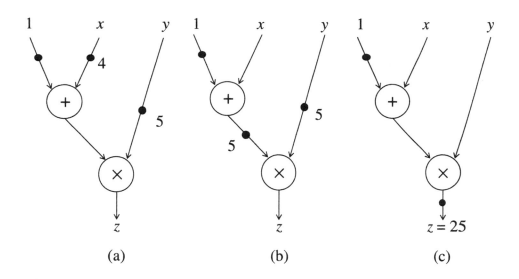

Figure 1.11 Snapshots of data-flow graphs for $z = y(x + 1)$.

1.1.2 Levels of Parallelism

Parallelism in computations may be examined at several levels, depending on the desired complexity. These are the *job, task, process, variable,* and *bit* levels. Each level is briefly described below.

- *Job level.* As an example, consider a professor who teaches two classes, one undergraduate and one graduate. The professor uses two unrelated computer programs to calculate the final scores and to assign grades to students. Each program may be regarded as a job, and obviously these two jobs can be processed in parallel if computing resources exist.

- *Task level.* Consider a robot with arms and legs. A computer program may be written to process the information provided by sensors and to move the arms and legs. The entire program may be considered as a job that can be partitioned into tasks. A task may be responsible for the sensors and movement of each arm or leg, or it may consist of some software maintenance procedure. It is possible to perform in parallel several tasks, or parts of them, even though interaction between them may exist.

- *Process level.* Each task is divided into several processes. Each process is an entity performing a specific function. The partitioning of tasks into processes is not unique, and is done either by the user or automatically by the compiler. Consider, for example, the following loop:

for $i = 1, 5$

$$P_1(i) \begin{cases} x(i) = x(i-1) + y(i-1) \\ \\ y(i) = x(i-2) * y(i-1) \end{cases}$$

$$P_2(i) \begin{cases} s(i) = x(i) + y(i) \\ \\ \text{if } s(i) \geq 100 \\ \qquad \text{then } a = a + 1 \\ \text{else } b = b + 1 \end{cases}$$

The loop body is separated into two processes $P_1(i)$ and $P_2(i)$, where i is the current iteration. $P_1(i)$ and $P_2(i)$ cannot be performed in parallel because variables $x(i)$ and $y(i)$ are generated in $P_1(i)$ and then used in $P_2(i)$. However, $P_1(i)$ and $P_2(i-1)$ can be performed in parallel. The interdependence between these two processes is shown in Figure 1.12. This can be seen if the expression in P_2 is rewritten as $s(i-1) = x(i-1) + y(i-1)$. It is clear that both $x(i)$ and $s(i-1)$ depend on previously calculated $x(i-1)$ and $y(i-1)$, thus $x(i)$ and $s(i-1)$ can be done in parallel. This is depicted in Figure 1.12 by the wave-front lines. The nodes in the graph, which belong to the same line, can be performed in parallel. Note that each line is such that all dependencies traverse it in one direction only. In this case, the line rests on the tips of dependence arrows.

- *Variable level.* A process consists of several instructions, each of which computes an output variable by operating on some input variables. Parallelism may exist within a process; that is, several

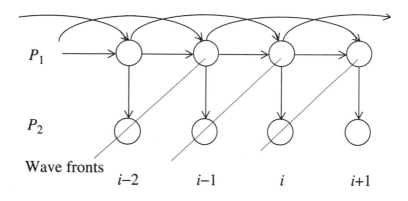

Figure 1.12 Process-level parallelism.

variables may be computed simultaneously. For example, consider process $P_1(i)$ in the preceding algorithm. Variables $x(i)$ and $y(i+1)$ can be computed in parallel, because, as shown in Figure 1.13, both depend on variables computed in previous iterations.

- *Bit level.* All computers, with very few exceptions, use bit-parallel arithmetic; that is, the processing elements are built to operate simultaneously on all the bits that make up a word. This is the lowest level of parallelism.

The implementation of these levels on parallel computers varies with the type of computer. This should become clear later.

1.2 APPLICATIONS OF PARALLEL PROCESSING

Our society demands more and more computation power every year. A strong high-performance computer industry is essential for a successful modern economy. Critical security areas and a broad range of private-sector activities depend on high-performance computers.

Most of the computer performance improvements made so far have been based on *technological* developments. In fact, the so-called first

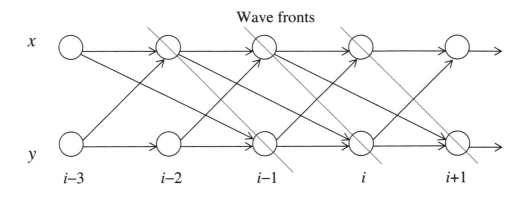

Figure 1.13 Variable-level parallelism.

four generations of computers are defined by improved technologies, namely vacuum tubes, transistors, integrated circuits, and large-scale integrated circuits. Semiconductor technology already has reached a point of maturity beyond which no significant switching-speed improvements are possible. The fundamental limitation is the speed of light (300,000 km/s), because electrons cannot move faster than this speed limit. The switching speed of electronic devices is so fast that processing time is related to the communication time between processors: it takes approximately 1 ns for electrons to travel 30 cm. Thus, the source

for increasing computing power must be looked for in areas other than technology.

Semiconductor-based performance enhancements, which have delivered on the average a tenfold performance increase every 7 years over the last 40 years, have been falling off recently. This has forced designers to embrace parallel processing and to look for new architectural concepts that have the capability of providing orders-of-magnitude performance increases. It is in this context that parallel processing plays a growing role in the computer industry. Right now, uniprocessor supercomputers are running neck-and-neck with parallel machines for the best speed performance, but it is easy to see that parallel machines will soon outperform uniprocessors.

In this section, we identify some computation-intensive applications for which parallel processing makes or will make a significant difference. These are only a few of the large number of applications waiting to embrace parallel processing. As we will see, many applications require 10^{15} operations per second, and the fastest uniprocessor today delivers only 10^9 operations per second.

Weather Forecasting

Weather prediction relies on simulation of future atmospheric conditions evolving from observed initial states. Currently, weather-forecasting centers around the world use supercomputers such as the Cray X-MP and CDC 205, which are dedicated full-time to data assimilation, numerical prediction, and model development. With the computing power available today, these weather forecasts are accurate for 5 days. Their accuracy is determined by the number of initial states and the geographic distribution. Through increased resolution and improved observations, including data from polar-orbiting and geosynchronous satellites, the U.S. National Weather Service hopes to extend the forecast to 8 to 10 days. Supercomputers with parallel processing capabilities may be able to provide sufficient power for modeling thunderstorms and other nonlinear systems that require tremendous computational power.

Other challenging applications include modeling the interactions between the atmosphere and the oceans and creating models of three-dimensional oceanic currents. With enough computing power it may become possible to develop a model that will simulate the evolution of the earth's entire system over a large interval of time. The components of the earth's system evolve nonlinearly and interact in nonlinear ways with other components. It is known that the accuracy of such complex models depends a great deal upon resolution, which may be handled through parallel processing.

Engineering

High-speed computing is essential to modern engineering research and development. We rely more and more on computational approaches instead of analytical theory and laboratory experiments. In addition to increasing productivity, parallel processing is an enabling technology that permits advances that are not otherwise obtainable.

Fluid equations and turbulence models, for example, are some of the most computation-intensive engineering applications. The computation of a single data point in the entire flow space involves hours of Cray supercomputer time. Recent theoretical advances in this area suggest that realistic turbulence models should take into account the complete space flow. In order to obtain quantitative data on full space flow, new experimental methods based on advanced techniques such as laser sheet scanning, nuclear magnetic resonance, and electronic spin resonance must be used. These new experimental methods require tremendous computer power that is unavailable today.

Recently there has been a great deal of planning for the design of a superfast airplane capable of flying from the continental U.S. to Japan in less than one hour. Its design would be based on complex computations, and it has been predicted that this design will be feasible using the next generation of supercomputers built with parallel processing.

Materials Science

The application of high-performance computing to material science is still in an early stage. However, it has already had a significant impact in numerous areas. The future will bring even greater progress as more scientists rely on high-speed simulations as a cost-effective method. Simulations have been conducted of electronic transport in semiconductor devices. Two- and three-dimensional device and process simulations have been successfully applied to silicon technology. Transient effects related to impact ionization and hot electron emissions into silicon dioxides have been simulated using Monte Carlo techniques. The simulation of gallium arsenide (GaAs) devices is amenable to vector and parallel computing because of the inherent complexity of the equations of motion of this material. Also, simulation of semiconductor crystal growth, which is done by calculating atomic trajectories using classical molecular dynamics and interatomic potentials, requires considerable computing power. In the future, parallel processing will allow scientists to design materials with innovative and useful properties based on the predictions of computer simulations.

Plasma Physics

Plasmas are high-temperature ionized gases. Their study is complex because they are subject to electric and magnetic forces as well as pressure forces. Plasmas display nonlinear properties, and their study requires high-performance computing. Plasma physics was discovered through the use of computer modeling. Through computations it was shown that there is a possibility of using plasmas in high-energy physics as an accelerating structure and as focusing elements. Computer modeling has proved to be a powerful and inexpensive method for investigating the physics involved, replacing complex and expensive experimental equipment. In the area of space plasma physics, studies are performed to understand the interaction of the solar wind with the earth's magnetic field. This is extremely important because it provides an understanding of the earth's magnetosphere, where many satellites operate. By using large-scale computer models, it is possible to understand the formation and the effects of magnetic storms, the aurora borealis, and other interactions of the solar wind with the earth's magnetosphere.

Economics

The nature of economic modeling and forecasting is different from much of natural science research, in which the challenge is to implement theories known to be true. In economics there are no theories known to be true in the sense of predicting the results of experiments with high accuracy. However, complex computer models are useful to interpret, in the context of theoretical ideas, the large amounts of data available. Such models are currently used to guide economic decision-making and to test various hypotheses. For example, the Congressional Budget Office uses several models in making its economic projections; the Federal Reserve Board relies on several models in its formulation of monetary policy. In the private sector, computer models are currently used to predict the stock market and to do financial planning. Such models include databases of hundreds of thousands of economic time series, which are regularly forecast with the aid of nonlinear models involving tens of thousands of equations. These models are imperfect because of the complexity of economic systems. Consider, for example, the uncertainties caused by individual behavior or expectations. Some recent developments in economic modeling use new techniques such as stochastic dynamic optimization, computable general equilibrium, nonparametric and semiparametric econometrics, Bayesian multivariate time series, and others. Although large-scale computing in economics is in its early stages, many believe that in the future more complex models, coupled with a better theoretical understanding, can increase the accuracy of economic forecasting.

Artificial Intelligence (AI)

As many application areas demand more and more "intelligent processing," future generations of computer systems will undoubtedly incorporate more and more knowledge-processing capabilities. Historically, numerical processing has received more attention than knowledge processing. The motive is simple: number crunching is much easier to do than knowledge processing.

Consider, for example, *automated reasoning*—computer programs that reason in order to prove theorems from mathematics, design logic circuits, verify computer codes, solve puzzles, and perform other tasks. Today the main obstacle to automated reasoning remains the same as years ago when this field started; that obstacle is computer time. Automated reasoning is well suited to parallel treatment. The basic procedures on which automated reasoning programs rely—forming a hypothesis, drawing a conclusion, rewriting each conclusion into some canonical form, testing it for significance, comparing it with background information, and integrating it into a knowledge base—are essentially independent of one another. At the coarse level, a separate processor could be used for each of these procedures and corresponding actions taken in parallel. Moreover, a large number of hypotheses can be pursued in parallel. Additional parallelism is available at lower granularity levels.

Reasoning is by far the most complex of all activities connected to problem solving. To design and implement an automated reasoning program that takes full advantage of parallel processing is a major undertaking. Because of the huge size of the knowledge base and the complexity of the problem, it is believed that only through the use of parallel processing will major achievements be possible in this area. The potential of these applications is so great that undoubtedly society will spend much effort striving for results in automated reasoning. Other areas of AI, such as computer vision, robotics, natural language processing, and speech processing, may all benefit from this progress.

National Defense

In the United States, the national defense complex is a prime promoter and user of parallel processing technology. Much of the research and development in advanced computer technology has been funded under national defense programs. In 1983, the Defense Advanced Research Project Agency (DARPA) initiated the Strategic Computing Program, whose main goal was to stimulate national research in machine intelligence and to advance computing technologies. Parallel processing was an important ingredient of this program. The following three main projects were part of the Strategic Computing Program:

- The *Autonomous Land Vehicle* program aimed to demonstrate the feasibility of autonomous navigation and tactical decision-making. Among the research areas it explored were computer vision, expert systems, robotics, numerical computation, and others. The program's initial capabilities were demonstrated in the mid-1980s when the Autonomous Land Vehicle traversed terrain and avoided obstacles. This proved that real-time image understanding can be achieved by using parallel processing technology.

- The *Navy Battle Management* program was intended to demonstrate the feasibility of automated systems that can deal consistently and accurately with the complex situations inherent in battle management during combat and crisis situations. Expert system technologies, natural language interfaces, programs for reasoning on large knowledge bases, allocation, and scheduling were only some of the research areas explored in this program. Again, parallel processing was the main technology in all these areas.

- The *Pilot's Associate* program goal was to stimulate research for developing automated systems to assist combat pilots making split-second, life-or-death decisions based on rapidly changing and often incomplete information. The role of such systems was to integrate and prioritize large amounts of information based on the situation at hand. Advances in expert systems, parallel processing of sensor data, speech processing, and predictive processing for trajectory planning were needed for this program.

The High Performance Computing and Communication (HPCC) program, initiated by the United States government in 1992, aims at investigating and solving a wide range of scientific and engineering "grand challenge" problems. Parallel processing is a key technology for the HPCC program.

1.3 RELATION BETWEEN PARALLEL ALGORITHMS AND ARCHITECTURES

Parallel processing includes both *parallel algorithms* and *parallel architectures*. A parallel algorithm can be viewed as a collection of independent task modules, some of which can be executed simultaneously. Modules communicate with each other during the execution of an algorithm. Since algorithms run on parallel hardware, which basically consists of processing modules that are exchanging data, it is natural to be concerned with the way in which the algorithm space relates to the hardware space. The more we know about the interaction between these two spaces, the better we can design parallel processing systems. H. T. Kung [Kung 1980] was one of the first to study the relation between parallel algorithms and architectures. He has identified some of the features of algorithms and architectures and has shown their correlation. These are summarized in Table 1.1.

The main criteria that may be used to characterize *algorithms* are module granularity, concurrence control, data mechanism, communication geometry, and algorithm size.

- *Module granularity* refers to the number of computations contained in a typical module. The modules may be jobs, tasks, processes, or instructions, depending upon the level at which the parallelism is expressed. Often there is abundant parallelism at low granularity, which may not be exploited. This is because working with small granularity increases the amount of data communication between modules, in addition to increasing software complexity. The fastest overall speed is achieved through a compromise between granularity and communication.

Parallel algorithms	Parallel architectures
Module granularity	Processor complexity
Concurrence control	Mode of operation
Data mechanism	Memory structure
Communication geometry	Interconnection network
Algorithm size	Number of processors, memory size

Table 1.1: Relation between features of parallel algorithms and parallel architectures.

- *Concurrence control* refers to the scheme of selecting modules for execution. The control scheme must satisfy data and control dependencies so that the overall execution of algorithms is correct. Some possible control schemes are executed on the basis of data availability (data-flow), central control (synchronized), or demand (demand-driven). Algorithms with a high degree of regularity, such as matrix multiplications, are more suitable for synchronized control and will map well into systolic and other array processors. Algorithms that incorporate conditional transfers and other irregularities are better suited to asynchronous architectures such as multiprocessors or data-flow.

- *Data mechanism* refers to the way in which instruction operands are used. The data generated by an instruction either can be used as "pure data," as in the data-flow model, or can be put in a storage location and then be referred to by its address, as in the von Neumann model and its extensions.

- *Communication geometry* refers to the interconnection pattern between computational modules. The communication geometry of an algorithm is said to be regular when the interconnection pattern repeats over the set of computations, and irregular when the communications are random. Regular interconnections may resemble trees, arrays, cubes, or other patterns often seen in nature.

- *Algorithm size* refers to the total number of computations the algorithm must perform. The size can be small, medium, or large. For example, manipulation of 1000×1000 matrices is considered to be a large problem. Algorithm size affects the number of processors and the size of computer memory.

Parallel computer *architectures* may be characterized using the following criteria: processor complexity, mode of operation, memory structure, interconnection network, and number of processors and memory size.

- *Processor complexity* refers to the computing power and the internal structure of each processing element. Homogeneous systems are those in which all processors have identical capabilities. Heterogeneous systems are those in which the processors are not identical, as for instance when they are specialized for performing certain functions. Processor complexity varies from one architecture to another. For example, in systolic processors the cells are simple, and the data is only processed, not stored. In array processors some memory may be associated with the processing element for storing data, and in multiprocessors each processor may incorporate local memory, cache module, memory management, and so on. Processor complexity is related to algorithm granularity. We distinguish between large-grain, medium-grain, and small-grain architectures. Large-grain architectures have few, but powerful, processors. The best known example is the Cray X-MP, which has from one to four extremely powerful processors. Medium-grain architectures have an intermediate number of processors, with intermediate processing power. For example, a Cedar multiprocessor employs eight clusters of Alliant FX-8; each cluster has eight processors. Fine-grain architectures employ a large number of smaller processors. The Connection Machine has

65,536 bit-serial processor. Clearly, processor complexity relates to algorithm granularity.

- *Mode of operation* is a general term referring to both instruction control and data handling. The traditional mode of operation is command-flow, so called because the flow of events is triggered by commands derived from instruction sequences. Another method is to trigger operations as soon as their operands become available, as in data-flow operations. In this case, the control is determined by the availability of data. Yet another mode of control is demand-flow, in which computations take place only if their results are requested by other computations. Combinations of these control modes are also possible. The architecture mode of operation is related to the mode of algorithm concurrency control.

- *Memory structure* refers to the mode of operation and the organization of computer memory. Memories can be accessed by using either addresses or data content (as in associative memories). In some new computer models, such as connectionist architecture and neural networks, memory consists of interconnection weights that indicate how easily connections can be made. In ordinary computers, memory organization and the size of memory files are closely related to data structure.

- *Interconnection network* refers to the hardware connections among processors and between processors and memories. The architecture interconnection network should match the algorithm communication geometry as closely as possible. Computers with simple interconnection networks are efficient only for a small number of algorithms, whereas complex interconnection networks can be configured for a broad range of applications. Of course, the price paid in this case is increased cost and extra switching time.

- *Number of processors and memory size* simply indicates how many processors the parallel system contains and how large the main memory is. Systems with 1 to 100 processors are considered small; systems with 100 to 1,000 processors are considered medium; systems with over 1,000 processors are considered large and very large. Many people foresee parallel systems with a million processors in the near future. In general, more processors provide more computing power, which enables the system to approach more complex problems. When the size of the algorithm is greater than the size of the system, algorithm partitioning is required. This means that the algorithm needs to be folded into processors and memory and intermediate results must be stored. Algorithm partitioning may have undesired side-effects, so ideally the number of processors should match the size of the algorithm.

1.4   PERFORMANCE OF PARALLEL COMPUTATIONS

1.4.1   Need for Performance Evaluation

Currently, one of the most important issues in parallel processing is how to effectively utilize parallel computers that have become increasingly complex. It is estimated that many modern supercomputers and parallel processors deliver only 10 percent or less of their peak-performance potential in a variety of applications. Yet high performance is the very reason why people build complex machines.

The causes of performance degradation are many. Performance losses occur because of mismatches among application, software, and hardware. The main steps leading to loss of parallelism, ranging from problem domain to hardware, are shown in Figure 1.14. The *degree of parallelism* is the number of independent operations that may be performed in parallel. In complex systems, mismatches occur even among software modules or hardware modules. For example, the communication network bandwidth may not correspond to the processor speed or that of the memory.

Consider, for example, the matrix multiplication problem $C = AB$, where the size of each matrix is $n \times n$. The parallel computational complexity for this problem is $O(\log n)$. All multiplications can be done in parallel, and $\log n$ time steps are necessary to add n partial products to produce one element of matrix C. Suppose now that we use an algorithm according to which the addition of n terms is done sequentially.

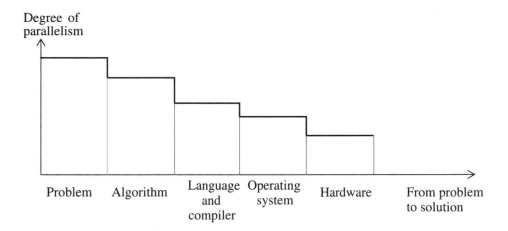

Figure 1.14 Main steps leading to loss of parallelism.

This implies a complexity of $O(n)$ for such a matrix multiplication algorithm. This is the first step where parallelism is lost. More parallelism is lost when an algorithm is actually implemented as a program, because of the inability of many languages to express parallelism. Some of the parallelism lost through the language may sometimes be recovered by using parallelizing compilers. Additional parallelism is lost when a program is executed on a particular parallel machine. The operating system that schedules and synchronizes tasks, and manages memory and other resources, imposes restrictions that hinder parallelism. At the hardware level, the number of available processors may not match the size of the problem, the processor granularity may be larger than required and waste resources, or the bandwidth and topology of an interconnection network may not correspond to algorithm requirements. All these and other mismatches contribute to performance degradation.

Mapping applications to parallel computers and balancing parallel processors is indeed a very difficult task, and the state of understanding in this area is quite poor. Moreover, small changes in problem size while using different algorithms or different applications may have undesirable effects and can lead to performance degradation.

The study of performance evaluation is motivated by the following needs:

- Evaluation of new computers when they enter the market;

- Increase of efficiency in utilization resulting from better matching of algorithms and architectures; and

- Acquisition of information for the design of new computer systems.

In general, computer performance can be studied by *analytical* means, and by *measurements* and *analysis*.

Because of the complexity of parallel computers, many attempts to use analytical models based on queuing models have not succeeded. Too many simplifying assumptions had to be made, so the end results hardly resembled the operation of parallel computers. There is a large range of applications and distribution events. While queuing models for uniprocessors exist and are used, queuing models for parallel computers are not good enough. Analytical models of global performance are seldom of much use in complex systems. At present, empirical results are the only ones that can be relied upon to assess the performance of parallel computer systems.

Another approach is to perform measurements on software and hardware over a large number of applications and to analyze the results. Some benchmarks using single-value performance matrices have been used to assess the performance of commercially available systems. While benchmarks have been useful, such work does not address the problem of how to tune the architecture, hardware, system software, and applications algorithms to improve the performance. We have to move away from the concept of *which* machine is best for a single benchmark to the more important question of *how* a machine performs across a wide range of benchmarks and, perhaps even more important, *why* it behaves that way.

1.4.2   Performance Indices of Parallel Computation

Some performance indices have been defined over the years for measuring the "goodness" of parallel computation. Because of the level of complexity involved, no single measure of performance can give a truly accurate measure of a computer system's performance. Different indices are needed to measure different aspects. Some indices for global measurements follow.

1. *Execution Rate.* The execution rate measures the machine output per unit of time. Depending on how machine output is defined, several execution rate measurements can be used. The concept of instructions per second, measured in *mips* (millions of instructions per second), is often used. While this measurement is meaningful for uniprocessors and multiprocessors, it is inappropriate for SIMD machines, in which one instruction operates on a large number of operands. Moreover, it does not differentiate between true results and overhead instructions. Another measure used is *mops* (millions of operations per second). However, this measure does not take word length into consideration. A good measure for arithmetic operations is megaflops, or Mflops (millions of floating point operations per second). While this measure is appropriate for many numeric applications, it is not very useful for AI programs. A measure used for logic programs and sometimes appropriate for AI is the number of logic inferences per second, or *lips.*

2. *Speedup (S_p).* The speedup factor of a parallel computation using p processors is defined as the ratio

$$S_p = \frac{T_1}{T_p} \qquad (1.1)$$

where T_1 is the time taken to perform the computation on one processor, and T_p is the time taken to perform the same computation on p processors. In other words, S_p is the ratio of the sequential processing time to the parallel processing time. Normally, the sequential algorithm is the best algorithm known for this computational problem. The speedup shows the speed gain of parallel computation; the higher the S_p, the better. Note that T_1, the sequential time, usually cannot be obtained from T_p by setting $p = 1$. The speedup factor is normally less than the number of processors because of the time lost to synchronization, communication time, and other overheads required by the parallel computation

$$1 \leq S_p \leq p \tag{1.2}$$

However, it is interesting to mention that speedups larger than the number of processors, called superlinear speedups, have been reported for nondeterministic AI computations, especially search operations. Because of parallel processing in a number of branches, some paths leading to wrong results may be eliminated earlier than with sequential processing. Thus, by avoiding some unnecessary computations, the speedup may increase by more than the number of processors.

3. *Efficiency (E_p)*. The efficiency of a parallel computation is defined as the ratio between the speedup factor and the number of processors:

$$E_p = \frac{S_p}{p} = \frac{T_1}{pT_p} \tag{1.3}$$

The efficiency is a measure of the cost-effectiveness of computations.

4. *Redundancy (R_p)*. The redundancy of a parallel computation is the ratio between the total number of operations O_p executed in performing some computation with p processors and the number of operations O_1 required to execute the same computation with a uniprocessor.

$$R_p = \frac{O_p}{O_1} \tag{1.4}$$

R_p is related to the time lost because of overhead, and is always larger than 1.

5. *Utilization (U_p).* The utilization factor is the ratio between the actual number of operations O_p and the number of operations that could have been performed with p processors in T_p time units.

$$U_p = \frac{O_p}{pT_p} \tag{1.5}$$

1.4.3 Striving Toward Teraflops Performance

A wide variety of new high-performance computers is emerging. There are machines today capable of delivering hundreds of Gflops peak performance (G, or Giga, means 10^9). This, coupled with numerous research and development efforts, makes many expect that in the mid-1990s Tflops (T, or Tera, means 10^{12}) machines will become reality. In this section, we briefly survey the front-running high-performance computers and speculate on their evolution over the next few years.

An important factor to consider is the fast-growing power of uniprocessors. Built around simple RISC (reduced instruction set computer) architectures, these uniprocessors will continue to advance computer performance. They can be used as building blocks for large multiprocessor systems. The addition of attached vector processors can boost their performance significantly. Using ECL gate arrays, it is possible to build processors that operate at over 200 MHz (or 5 ns clock).

The relative capabilities of some high-performance computers are shown in Figure 1.15. In the Cray family, the Cray Y-MP, built with eight processors operating at 50 percent more than the X-MP processors, is capable of 1-Gflops performance when operating on a 100×100 Linpack. The Cray 3, available around 1991, has 16 processors operating at twice the speed of the Cray 2 processors, and delivers approximately a 50-Gflops performance. The Cray 4 will have 64 complex processors and will deliver 125 Gflops at peak performance. Since Cray supercomputers base their high performance on advanced uniprocessor architectural concepts and technology, it remains to be seen how they will be able to make use of advances in software for parallel processors.

Hypercubes and mesh-connected message-passing multiprocessors are strong contenders in the race toward Tflops performance. The Touchstone Delta computer is made by an Intel Corporation subsidiary. Equipped with 528 microprocessors, it delivered approximately

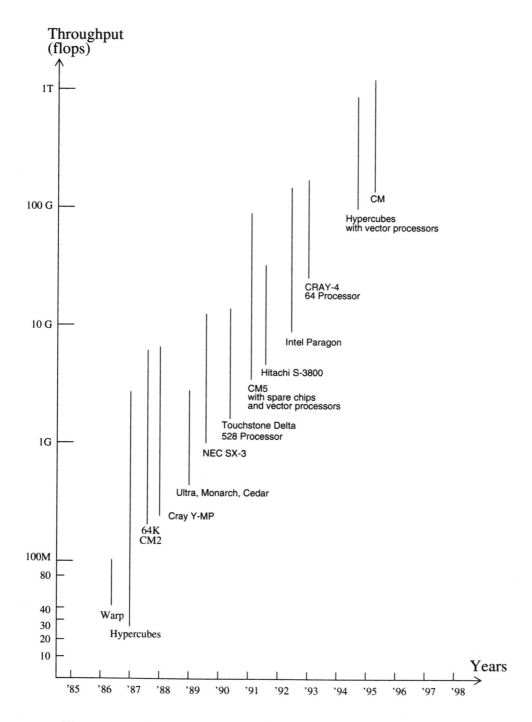

Figure 1.15 Evolution of some high-performance computers.

10 Gflops in 1991. Hypercubes with 1K processors will be available; these will reach 100-Gflops performance. Moreover, the future 4K hypercube, with vector-processing capabilities, may very well be capable of Tflops performance.

Shared-memory multiprocessors, such as the RP3, Monarch, Ultracomputer, and Cedar, have over 1-Gflops performance.

The Connection Machine (CM), built at Thinking Machines Corporation, was originally intended for semantic network processing. In practice, it was used more for numeric applications, such as image processing, computational fluid dynamics, circuit and logic simulations, text searching, and so on. Equally important is the applicability of CM computers to AI applications. Built with simple processors in large numbers, the CM family has the capability of Tflops performance. The CM1, the first Connection Machine, delivered around 1986, was capable of 100 Mflops. The subsequent CM2 model provides 64K processing elements and operates at 10 Gflops. The CM5, available since late 1991, has a peak performance of 40 Gflops. Future CM designs will deliver hundreds of Gflops and perhaps even Tflops.

1.4.4 Mathematical Models

In this section, some basic mathematical models of parallel computation are presented. These are useful for understanding the limits of parallel computation. These analytical models have the benefit of variables that can be manipulated to investigate a large number of special instances. Specifically, they can be used to investigate the limits of the domain to which multiprocessors apply.

Weighted Harmonic Mean Principle
This principle relates the execution rate to a weighted harmonic mean. Let T_n be the time required to compute n tasks of k different types. Each type consists of n_i tasks requiring t_i seconds each, such that

$$T_n = \sum_1^k n_i t_i \qquad (1.6)$$

and

$$n = \sum_{1}^{k} n_i \tag{1.7}$$

By definition, the execution rate R is the number of events or operations in unit time, so

$$R_n = \frac{n}{T_n} = \frac{n}{\sum_{1}^{k} n_i t_i} \tag{1.8}$$

Let us define f_i as the fraction of results generated at rate R_i, and $t_i = 1/R_i$ as the time required to generate a result. Then

$$R_n = \frac{1}{\sum_{1}^{k} f_i t_i} = \frac{1}{\sum_{1}^{k} f_i / R_i} \tag{1.9}$$

where

$$f_i = n_i/n$$
$$\sum_{i} f_i = 1$$
$$R_i = 1/t_i$$

Equation (1.9) represents a *basic principle in computer architecture* sometimes called "bottleneckology," or the weighted harmonic mean principle. The importance of Equation (1.9) is in the fact that it indicates that a single rate that is out of balance (lower than others) dominates the overall performance of the machine.

Amdahl's Law

Introduced by Amdahl in 1967, this law is a particular case of the above principle. Two rates are considered: the high- (or parallel-) execution rate R_H and the low- (or scalar-) execution rate R_L. If f denotes the fraction of results generated at the high rate R_H and $1-f$ is the fraction generated at the low rate R_L, then Equation (1.9) becomes

$$R(f) = \frac{1}{f/R_H + (1-f)/R_L} \tag{1.10}$$

This formula is called *Amdahl's law*. It is useful for analyzing system performance that results from two individual rates of execution, such as vector and scalar operations or parallel and serial operations. It is also useful for analyzing a whole parallel system in which one rate is out of balance with the others. For example, the low rate may be caused by the I/O, or communication operations, and the high rate may be caused by vector, memory, or other operations.

Limits of Parallel Computation

Jack Worlton [Worlton 1986] has studied the limits of parallel computations using a model that approximates a multiprocessor operation. He assumed that a parallel program typically consists of repeated instances of synchronization tasks followed by a number of actual computational tasks distributed over processors. Because of various overheads, the execution time of computational tasks on a parallel system is longer than it would be if they were executed on a single processor. Let us define the following variables:

$$
\begin{aligned}
t_s &= \text{synchronization time} \\
t &= \text{task granularity, defined as average task execution time} \\
t_0 &= \text{task overhead caused by parallel execution} \\
N &= \text{number of tasks between synchronization points} \\
P &= \text{number of processors}
\end{aligned}
$$

The sequential execution time of N tasks, each taking time t, is

$$T_1 = Nt$$

In a parallel environment, each task requires $(t + t_0)$ time units rather than just t. For N tasks executed on P processors, the number of parallel steps is the ceiling ratio $\lceil N/P \rceil$. The parallel execution time may be approximated as

$$T_{N,P} = t_s + \lceil N/P \rceil (t + t_0)$$

Metrics	$P \to \infty$ N fixed	$N \to \infty$ P fixed
$S_{N,P}$	$N/(1 + (t_s + t_0)/t)$	$P/(1 + t_0/t)$
$E_{N,P}$	0	$1/(1 + t_0/t)$

Table 1.2: Limits of parallel computation.

If N is an exact multiple of P, there is no load-balancing penalty at the end of the calculation; otherwise, one or more processors must execute one final task while the rest of the processors are idle. Using the speedup definition,

$$
\begin{aligned}
S_{N,P} &= \frac{T_1}{T_{N,P}} = \frac{Nt}{t_s + \lceil N/P \rceil (t + t_0)} \\
&= \frac{1}{t_s/(Nt) + (1/N)\lceil N/P \rceil (1 + t_0/t)}
\end{aligned}
\qquad (1.11)
$$

To increase the speedup, we need to minimize the denominator of this expression by reducing the effects of *synchronization, overhead,* and the *number of steps.*

The *synchronization effect* caused by $t_s/(Nt)$ may be reduced either by decreasing the synchronization time t_s or by increasing the product Nt, meaning larger intervals between synchronizations.

The *overhead effect* caused by t_0/t may be reduced by decreasing the overhead time t_0 or by increasing the task granularity t. Note that large task granularity helps to reduce the effects of both synchronization and overhead.

The number of *computation steps* $\lceil N/P \rceil$ can obviously be decreased by using more processors and by making the number of tasks an exact multiple of the number of processors.

We can use now the concepts of speedup and efficiency (defined as $E_{N,P} = S_{N,P}/P$) to investigate the limits of parallel computation, as summarized in Table 1.2. The first column of the table shows that the speedup improvements that result from increasing the number of processors are constrained by the number of tasks, and that efficiency approaches zero for large P. The second column shows that a speedup equal to the number of processors can be attained by performing a large number of tasks, provided that the overhead is negligible relative to the task granularity.

1.4.5 Performance Measurement and Analysis

To understand the complex interactions of many factors contributing to the performance of parallel processors, performance measurement and analysis must be done. These are achieved with specialized hardware and software. The traditional approach for measuring the performance of a program running on a parallel computer is to time its execution from the beginning to the end and compute megaflops (Mflops). However, timing alone is inadequate to fully characterize the program's behavior. It is also necessary to detect and record data related to the dynamic occurrences of hardware, system software, and application programming events and interactions. Next, we examine hardware- and application/software-type measurements and static versus dynamic measurements.

Hardware and Software Measurements

Hardware measurements focus on the physical events taking place within various machine components. They are usually made with hardware monitors connected directly to hardware devices, and are triggered by certain signals. Measuring devices need to be designed such that they do not interfere with the systems being measured. For example, when designing processor chips, it is important to make critical signals accessible for measurement. Measurement instrumentation has been integrated into the design of a few parallel systems. For example, the Cm* multiprocessor, designed at Carnegie-Mellon University, had an integrated instrumentation environment; the Erlangen general-purpose array processor had a monitor; the Cray X-MP has special-purpose counters for tracking events such as floating-point operations, instruction buffer fetch, I/O and memory references, vector operations, and others; and the Cedar multiprocessor, designed at the University of Illinois, has a number of hardware monitors.

Software measurements are directed more toward logical events that occur during program execution. These include individual timing of routines or tasks, and observation of events related to loop-level parallelism, synchronization, and other measurements. Special software is needed to start, accumulate, and interpret records.

Static and Dynamic Analysis

The goal of *static analysis* is to extract, quantify, and analyze various characteristics of benchmark code and its mapping to a particular architecture *at compile time* without actually executing the code. Through static analysis we can measure the effectiveness of the compiled portion of a system. In general, the purpose is to detect whether or not the software component of the system is responsible for poor performance. Conclusions may be reached about the appropriateness of the hardware model, load algorithms, code restructuring, mapping, allocation, and so on. The Paraphrase compiler, developed at the University of Illinois, illustrates how static analysis tools are used to perform tradeoffs. It extracts code characteristics such as data dependence information and evaluates static metrics in order to make decisions concerning code transformations, synchronizations, scheduling, and resource allocation.

Another set of static measurements is related to the resources of each processor. For example, instruction timing, operation chaining, and internal data path limitations may be of interest. These performance measurements may be useful in determining the tradeoffs involved in implementing code in terms of scalar or vector instructions.

The goal of *dynamic analysis* is to monitor the hardware and software while the application program is running. Many performance losses are associated with inefficiencies in processor scheduling, load balancing, data communication, and so on.

1.5   MAIN ISSUES FOR FUTURE RESEARCH IN PARALLEL PROCESSING

In this section, a number of critical unsolved issues in parallel processing are identified. The first question that comes to mind is "Unsolved in what sense?" In other words, what should be the goal in parallel processing research? Since different designers have different goals, it is rather difficult to specify a general goal for the field. For example, one goal may be to solve large and new problems, but how large? A related goal may be to build parallel supercomputers capable of performing 10^{12} operations per second, but why only 10^{12}? Many believe that Tflop performance will provide enough brute force for addressing a new set of important applications.

Since such goals tend to be time-dependent, we suggest here that the goal should be to build *efficient parallel systems*. By this we mean the ability to build large or small computers capable of exploiting greater or smaller degrees of parallelism, as desired, without wasting resources. At present, as we have noted, it is estimated that supercomputers deliver no more than 10 percent of their peak performance when applied to a wide range of problems. This is why we take the position that the level of understanding in parallel processing should be raised to the point at which system efficiency can be controlled regardless of size.

The term *unsolved* also refers to the fact that solutions to some problems are thought to exist, but have not yet been demonstrated. Parallel processing research is highly experimental, and often it is not sufficient to use simplified models. Implementation of concepts and ideas reveals hidden aspects that must be overcome to solve a problem completely.

Parallel processing permeates the entire spectrum of computer science and engineering research. The areas that we consider important and discuss in this section are shown in Figure 1.16. There are two main possibilities:

- The computer is fixed in terms of hardware and software resources. In this case the main issue is how to use the computer efficiently for a large range of problems, and we face the so-called *mapping problem*.

- The computer is to be designed; it can be either a special-purpose or a general-purpose system. In this case we face a *design problem*.

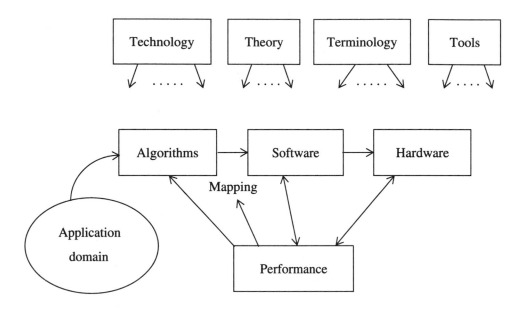

Figure 1.16 Main areas of parallel processing.

1.5.1   Understand the Influence of Technology on Parallel Computer Design

Technology is undoubtedly the driving factor that makes parallel processing possible. Of course, technology is relevant to a much broader class of systems than parallel processing. Very large-scale integrated (VLSI) technology is used to build most of the components in today's computers. Significant work has been done in studying the models and limitations of this technology. At present, we are witnessing the emergence of new technologies such as analog (as opposed to digital), optical, superconductivity, biotechnology, and neural networks. While semiconductor technology will continue to be used, these new technologies will sooner or later be available to parallel processor designers.

Because of these rapid technological advances, it is not too early to seek computer architecture improvements related to:

- Processing in three-dimensional space;

- Wireless computers;

- Parallel access to memories;

- Self-adapting architectures;

- Specialized architectures for exotic applications; and so on.

Some of the research issues to be addressed are:

- Development of new models for the emerging new technologies;

- Study of the fundamental limitations imposed by these technologies on parallel processors;

- Study of performance factors and design tradeoffs;

- Study of mixtures of technologies in relation to problem domains; and so on.

1.5.2   Develop Models for Large Parallel Computer Systems

Another result of technological advances is that for the first time we can build very large-scale systems (VLSS). These are systems with millions of processors, capable of enormous computing power. These VLSS are expensive and complex, and because of this, modeling becomes an important means to study their features and predict their performance. Today, we lack realistic models for VLSS. Some research goals should be to:

- Identify what to model and at what level to model it;

- Develop modeling techniques and tools;

- Find out which computing structures are scalable;

- Study fundamental limits on size and performance;

- Find out whether there is an optimal size imposed by the design space;

- Identify relations between efficiency and design parameters;

- Identify partitioning techniques for reducing VLSS to manageable size and performance; and so on.

1.5.3   Define the Fundamental Parallel Architectures

Most existing parallel processing systems are extensions of the von Neumann model. Since this model is more applicable to uniprocessors, it is appropriate to study what some of the fundamental parallel architectures are. Some research goals should be to:

- Study new non–von Neumann models of computation;

- Find ways to physically intermix processors and memories;

- Reduce the semantic gap between low-level hardware operations and high-level software;

- Identify new processor architectures especially suitable for parallel systems;

- Study interconnection networks for massively parallel systems;

- Study highly parallel I/O operations;

- Improve the human-machine interface;

- Identify ways to build reliable parallel computers, including reconfigurable and fault-tolerant systems; and so on.

1.5.4   Develop a System-Level Design Theory

One of the main obstacles to understanding the behavior of parallel machines is the lack of a system-level design theory. While there are many procedures, tools, and even theoretical results that facilitate the design of VLSI chips, design at the system level is still an ad hoc process. Especially in parallel processing, the system-level design must deal with hierarchical levels of abstractions. The development of such a theory requires efforts ranging from heuristics to new mathematics. A system-level design theory might make it possible to:

- Compare computers and computer performances;

- Match computer features with applications;

- Perform design tradeoffs;

- Balance design and eliminate bottlenecks;

- Relate computer design to principles of physics, energy, ecology, and other disciplines; and

- Facilitate rapid prototyping.

1.5.5   Develop Theory and Practices for Designing Parallel Algorithms

Two basic approaches are used for designing parallel algorithms: either parallelize existing sequential algorithms developed for a computation problem, or directly design new parallel algorithms by taking a fresh look at the problem. The first approach is preferable when considerable effort has been spent to develop the sequential algorithm, and when it will probably be difficult to develop a new algorithm. However, the second approach is likely to produce a more efficient algorithm and it is advocated here. Some research goals should be to:

- Develop methods for designing new parallel algorithms;

- Address new application areas;

- Integrate numeric and knowledge processing;

- Develop a taxonomy of parallel algorithms; and

- Automate the algorithm design process.

1.5.6   Develop Techniques for Mapping Algorithms and Programs into Architectures

The mapping problem can be generally stated as one of matching the algorithm with hardware resources. It is an important and difficult problem. Related to the mapping problem is the transformation of algorithms from one form to another form more suitable to the computer on hand. Algorithms can be transformed from sequential to parallel forms, or from one parallel form to another. An algorithm transformation is valid only when it maintains the algorithm equivalence. As a result of handling the mapping problem one can answer questions such as these: (1) Which computer is more suitable for a given application? (2) With what efficiency can an application run on a given computer? Some research goals should be to:

- Create automatic modification of dependencies;

- Develop transformation techniques;

- Understand partitioning, allocation, and scheduling;

- Understand static and (especially) dynamic load balancing; and

- Study the effect of algorithm variations on performance; for example, how changes in granularity, vector size, and so on affect performance and other aspects of the system.

1.5.7   Develop Languages Specific to Parallel Processing

One of the main obstacles we face in using parallel machines is the lack of truly parallel languages. The concurrent languages now used are extensions of languages used for uniprocessors. Often they miss essential constructs for parallel processors, such as synchronization, communication protocols, granularity changes, network control, performance tradeoffs, masking (for SIMD), parallel I/O, and others. Figure 1.17 outlines some of the most popular programming styles and languages.

Style	Language
Procedural programming Conventional concurrent	Fortran, Pascal
Shared-memory Message-passing	Ada OCCAM
Object-oriented programming	SMALL-TALK
Functional programming Applicative data flow	LISP ID, LUCID
Logic programming	PROLOG
Knowledge-based programming	OPS5

Figure 1.17 Styles of programming.

More work needs to be done in order to develop parallel languages capable of handling problems specific to parallel processing.

1.5.8   Develop Parallel Compilers for Commonly Used Languages

Parallelizing compilers are necessary to transform sequential programs into parallel code. Much work has been done toward developing compilers for code vectorization and some compilers for multiprocessors. Future research may improve our understanding of issues such as:

- How to control the parallelism explosion;

- How to handle synchronization in multiprocessors;

- How to develop compilers for a larger number of languages; and

- How to develop compilers for knowledge processing languages.

A related area that also needs attention is the development of operating systems for parallel computers. Work has already been done in this area at CMU and other research laboratories, but this work is not yet applicable to all parallel machines.

1.5.9 Develop the Means to Evaluate Performance of Parallel Computer Systems

In parallel processing many factors contribute to performance. There is a need to change the emphasis:

- From peak-performance to average, global-performance measurements;

- From a few benchmarks to a library of benchmarks; and

- From one algorithm performance to that of a collection of applications performance.

Some of the main research goals in this area should be to:

- Include hardware and software measurements tools early in the design process;

- Develop procedures to analyze performance measurements and create feedback mechanisms for algorithm design, mapping, and so on;

- Develop debugging hardware and software tools;

- Understand the effect of individual components on overall performance; and

- Understand performance limitations.

1.5.10 Develop Taxonomies for Parallel Processing Systems

The main reason that taxonomies are useful is that they tend to stimulate research by showing gaps and opportunities. Also, established taxonomies and commonly used terminology and definitions reflect the maturity of a field. There are some taxonomies for parallel architectures, such as Flynn's or Handler's, but they are either incomplete or too complicated to be used. Moreover, there are almost no taxonomies for software or parallel algorithms.

1.5.11 Develop Techniques for Parallel Knowledge Processing

One can distinguish between the following classes of computations: analog, numeric, word, relation, and meaning. Much of today's processing consists of numeric and word processing. Database processing deals to a certain extent with relations, but very little is done today in the area of semantic processing. Knowledge processing is a large, important application area. Parallel processing has the potential to overcome one of the main limiting factors in today's knowledge processing, namely speed. Some research goals should be to:

- Develop parallel languages for knowledge processing;

- Study forms of knowledge representation as they relate to parallelism;

- Study new architectures for AI;

- Develop parallel algorithms for AI;

- Experiment with existing parallel computers; and so on.

1.6 BIBLIOGRAPHICAL NOTES AND FURTHER READING

Among the basic textbooks in computer architecture are [Hayes 1978] and [Kuck 1978]. A more recent book in this area, which discusses many practical design aspects, is [Patterson and Hennessy 1990]. Many aspects of parallel algorithms and interconnection networks are thoroughly presented in [Leighton 1992]. There are several books covering various aspects of parallel processing. [Hockney and Jesshope 1981] includes a brief history of early parallel computers and ably presents array processor architectures, languages, and algorithms. [Hwang and Briggs 1984] presents a large body of material on pipeline, vector, array, and multiprocessor architectures, with many examples of real machines. A book dedicated to the design of parallel algorithms is [Quinn 1987]; [Chandy and Misra 1988] focuses on the design of parallel programs. [Almasi and Gottlieb 1989] is a more recent book on parallel processing, which discusses parallel models of computations, hardware, and software; it includes examples of several modern parallel computers. Another recent book on parallel architectures is [DeCegama 1989].

The material on interrelation between parallel algorithms and architectures follows the work of [Kung 1980]. The PRAM model of computation and a survey of parallel algorithms for shared memory machines are presented in [Karp and Ramachandran 1990]. A recent book on parallel algorithms that extensively uses the PRAM model is [JaJa 1992]. The material on performance measurements presented in this chapter follows the work of [Malony 1986], [Kuck and Sameh 1987], and [Carpenter 1987]. The discussion of basic limitations of parallel computers is from [Worlton 1986].

The need for parallel computers for scientific applications was the topic of a workshop sponsored by the National Science Foundation in 1987. The conclusions of this workshop, indicating the main application areas that may benefit from the new parallel supercomputers, have been documented in [Raveche, Lawrie, and Despain 1987]. The section on applications of parallel processing mentions some of these areas.

1.7 PROBLEMS

1.1.A. *(a)* Propose a taxonomy of parallel architectures based on two principles: concurrency in instruction control and execution.

(b) How does Flynn's taxonomy relate to the taxonomy you derived in *(a)*? Flynn's taxonomy refers to single-instruction single-data

Type of instruction	(a, b)	Examples
Scalar	$(1, 1)$	$A = B + C$
Vector	$(1, N)$	$A_i = B_i + C_i, \qquad i = 1, N$
Systolic	$(M, 1)$	Matrix operations with data from rows and columns used repeatedly
VLIW	(M, N)	Multiple operations per instruction, each with own address field

Table 1.3: Generic instruction types.

(SISD), single-instruction multiple-data (SIMD), multiple-instruction single-data (MISD), and multiple-instruction multiple-data (MIMD).

Solution [Worlton 1986].

(a) We distinguish three main levels of concurrence in instruction control: serial, with one instruction stream being executed; parallel, with multiple instruction streams being executed; and clustered, with several independent sets of multiple instruction streams being executed. These three levels constitute a hierarchy: parallel control is a generalization of serial control and clustered control is a generalization of parallel control.

We distinguish four basic instruction types by defining the number pair (a, b), where a specifies the number of different operations to be performed and b specifies the number of operands (or pair of operands) on which the operations are performed. Table 1.3 shows the four resulting instruction types. By matching these two taxonomic principles, we create a more generalized taxonomy, as shown in Table 1.4.

(b) Each entry in this taxonomy is itself a root of a taxonomic tree. For example, the "serial" entry in Flynn's taxonomy has two branches, SISD and SIMD; and scalar execution has two branches, pipelined and nonpipelined. Thus, the upper-left corner contains a four-way classification. The box below this also has four categories: MISD and MIMD for parallel control, and two types for scalar operation. Flynn's taxonomy is a subset of this taxonomy. The other columns also can be

	Generic instruction types			
Level of concurrence	Scalar	Vector	Systolic	VLIW
Serial				
Parallel				
Clustered				

Table 1.4: A generalized taxonomy for computer architectures.

subdivided. For example, vector processing may be memory-to-memory and register-to-register; systolic operations may be programmable and non-programmable; VLIW (very large instruction words) operations are homogeneous and nonhomogeneous. Finally, clustering may be of two forms, $n \times (MISD)$ and $n \times (MIMD)$. Thus, the 12-way taxonomy may be extended to a 48-way taxonomy.

1.2.A. Consider the matrix multiplication problem

$$Z = XY$$

where X and Y are $n \times n$ matrices.

Indicate in words (or in any other better way you know) how to compute Z on the following types of computers: SIMD, MIMD, and systolic array. In each case assume that p processing elements are available, with $p = n$.

Solution.

SIMD. Assume the structure shown in Figure 1.5. Matrices X, Y and Z are mapped into memories as shown in Figure 1.18. The CU fetches each x_{ij} in row order and broadcasts it to all PEs where $x_{ij}y_{jk}$ is computed. The results z_{ik} are the summations of respective partial products.

MIMD. Assume the multiprocessor organization shown in Figure 1.6. Matrices Y and Z may be stored in processor local memories, similarly to the SIMD case, and matrix X is stored in the shared-memory processor. The elements x_{ij} are fetched individually by all processors.

	M_1	M_2	M_3
	x_{11}	x_{12}	x_{13}
	x_{21}	x_{22}	x_{23}
	x_{31}	x_{32}	x_{33}
	y_{11}	y_{12}	y_{13}
	y_{21}	y_{22}	y_{23}
	y_{31}	y_{32}	y_{33}
	z_{11}	z_{12}	z_{13}
	z_{21}	z_{22}	z_{23}
	z_{31}	z_{32}	z_{33}

Figure 1.18 Memory mapping for the SIMD case.

Systolic Array. A one-dimensional systolic array solution is shown in Figure 1.19. The elements of matrix X are input to the array in row-wise order and move from left to right. They meet (at the "right time") the elements of matrix Y and produce partial products that are summed together to produce the elements of matrix Z.

1.3.A. A multiprocessor is capable of a 100-Mflop peak execution rate. Scalar code is processed at a 1-Mflop rate. What is the performance of this machine when 10 percent of the code is scalar and 90 percent of the code is fully parallel?

Solution.
   Use Amdahl's law:

$$R = \frac{1}{\frac{f}{R_H} + \frac{1-f}{R_L}}$$

$$= \frac{1}{\frac{0.9}{100} + \frac{0.1}{1}}$$

$$= \frac{1}{0.109} = 9.17 \text{ Mflops}$$

1.4.A. (Extension of Amdahl's Law.) One way to extend Amdahl's law, expressed by Equation (1.10), is to study R as a function of R_H/R_L when f is defined over an interval $f \in [a, b]$ where $0 < a < b < 1$.

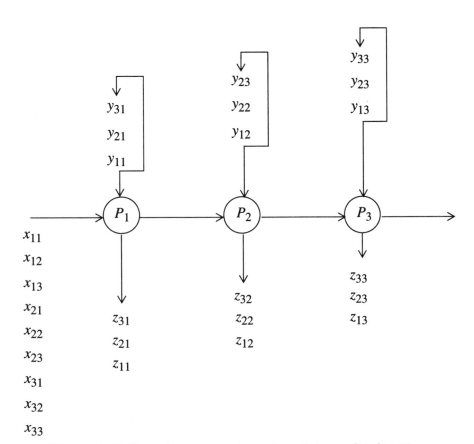

Figure 1.19 Systolic processing of matrix multiplication.

(a) Derive the expression for the average ratio and interpret the results.

(b) Do you observe any connection with Minsky's conjecture?

Solution [Worlton 1986].

    (a) Let $R_{HL} = R_H/R_L$.

$$R_{ave} \;\; = \;\; \frac{1}{(b-a)} \int_a^b R(f)d(f) = \frac{1}{(b-a)} \int_a^b \frac{df}{f(1-R_{HL}) + R_{HL}}$$

$$R_{ave} = \frac{R_H}{(b-a)(1-R_{HL})} \ln \frac{b(1-R_{HL})+R_{HL}}{a(1-R_{HL})+R_{HL}}$$

This function is approximately log X/X. For a = 0 and b = 1:

$$R_{ave} = R_H \frac{\ln R_{HL}}{(R_{HL}-1)}$$

Clearly, R_{ave} approaches zero when R_{HL} becomes large.

(b) Minsky's conjecture states that the performance of a parallel system increases at most as a logarithmic function with the number of processors. In the expression above, by dividing both sides by R_L, we obtain that relative growth in performance, $R_{ave}/R_l = ln R_{HL}$. Thus, performance is limited to logarithmic improvement as R_{HL} increases.

1.5.A. A sequential algorithm for performing a decomposition of a square matrix of size $n \times n$ into its lower and upper triangular matrices takes $n^3/3 - n^2/3$ time units to execute. Given p processors, the time needed to execute the parallel algorithm is $(n^2 - 1)(n/2)/p$.

(a) Calculate the speedup factor. Show the curve representing the speedup factor as a function of n.

(b) What is the efficiency of this algorithm as $n \to \infty$? For what size n is the algorithm within 5 percent of the highest efficiency?

Solution.

(a) The speedup graph is shown in Figure 1.20.

$$S_p = \frac{\frac{n^3}{3} - \frac{n^2}{3}}{(n^2-1)\frac{n}{2}} p = \frac{2pn}{3} \frac{n-1}{n^2-1} = \frac{2p}{3} \frac{n}{n+1}$$

(b)

$$E_p = \frac{S_p}{p} = \frac{\frac{2p}{3}\frac{n}{n+1}}{p} = \frac{2}{3}\frac{n}{n+1}$$

$$\lim_{n\to\infty} E_p = \frac{2}{3}$$

$$\frac{n}{n+1} = \frac{95}{100} \Rightarrow n = 19$$

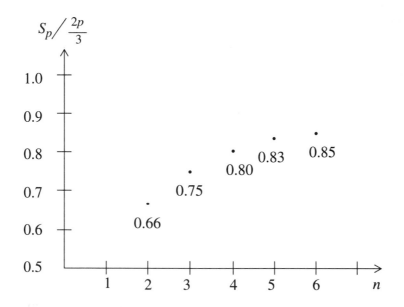

Figure 1.20 Speedup graph for solution to Problem 1.5.A.

1.1.B. Show an abstract model for the message-passing multiprocessor similar to the PRAM model that abstracts a shared-memory multiprocessor. What are the differences between this model and the PRAM for shared memory? Which of the two models is more general? In other words, is shared memory more powerful than message passing or vice versa?

1.2.B. *(a)* Fill in Table 1.4 from Problem 1.1.A with as many computers as you can.

(b) Propose some other principles for expanding the taxonomy of parallel architectures.

1.3.B. *(a)* Propose a taxonomy of parallel software systems (compilers, operating systems). Carefully select the principles and fill in the boxes with examples.

(b) Do the same for parallel algorithms.

1.4.B. Elaborate on the principles of parallel processing.

1.5.B. "Rapid prototyping" is a term recently coined to describe a short design-and-implementation cycle of computer systems. One approach to rapid prototyping is to simply assemble previously designed modules ("off-the-shelf" modules). Different applications call for different modules.

(a) Name and briefly describe up to 10 types of modules that can be used to assemble complete and efficient parallel systems. One type of module can be used repetitively. The applications intended for this system are signal processing, image processing and understanding, robotics, database processing, and computer graphics.

(b) Sketch an approach for correlating application space with processing modules.

1.6.B. Choose a specific array processor and a multiprocessor. (If you do not know any, find them in the literature).

Use Table 1.1 to identify for each machine at least one algorithm that matches each of the selected architectures in terms of module granularity, concurrence control, and communication geometry.

1.7.B. Consider the problem of matrix-vector multiplication $\mathbf{y} = \mathbf{Ax}$, where matrix A is of size 8×8. Assume that a message-passing multiprocessor with two Intel 80286 processors is available for this computation. Identify specifically the causes of the loss of parallelism at the algorithm level, the program level, the level of data assignment in memory, and the hardware execution level.

1.8.B. Figures 1.12 and 1.13 show lines representing computational wave fronts, such that the computations on each line can be performed in parallel. Is it possible to change the slopes of the computational fronts? Explain why or why not.

1.9.B. For each of the following two loops, answer the two questions below. Ignore memory access and communication and assume that addition and multiplication each require one step.

```
DO I = 1, N
    X(I) = A(I) * B(I) + C(I)
END DO
```

```
DO I = 1, N
    X(I) = A(I) − B(I−1) * C(I)
    Y(I) = X(I−1) + X(I−2)
END DO
```

(a) What is the minimum time required to execute each loop? What is the speedup over sequential processing?

(b) What is the smallest number of processors p required to achieve the fastest processing time?

1.10.B. Perform an analysis of limits of parallel computation similar to the one described in Section 1.4.4 by taking into consideration the communication time between computation steps.

1.11.B. Repeat problem 1.2.A for the case in which $p < n$.

Chapter 2

ANALYSIS OF PARALLELISM IN COMPUTER ALGORITHMS

An *algorithm* is a procedure consisting of a finite set of unambiguous rules that specify a finite sequence of operations leading to the solution of a problem or a class of problems. Algorithms are expressed in several forms; the most common are English-like statements, programs, and graphs. In this discussion, we will consider algorithms written as programs.

This chapter focuses on the analysis of parallelism, meaning the detection of parallelism. Parallelism detection involves finding sets of computations that can be performed simultaneously. The approach to parallelism is based on the study of *data dependencies*. The presence of a dependence between two computations implies that they cannot be performed in parallel; the fewer the dependencies, the greater the parallelism. An important problem is determining the way to express dependencies. Many algorithms have regular data dependencies; that is, dependencies that repeat over the entire set of computations in each algorithm. For such algorithms, dependencies can be concisely described mathematically and can be manipulated easily. However, there are algorithms for which dependencies vary from one computation to another, and these algorithms are more difficult to analyze. Dependencies may be used to form classes of parallel algorithms, because when two or more algorithms have similar dependencies, it means that they display the same parallelism properties.

In this chapter we concentrate on parallelism analysis and do not focus on data communication aspects. For this reason, the parallelism analysis is done regardless of the computer architecture; however, the data communication aspects are extremely important and will be considered in later chapters.

The analysis of parallelism in algorithms is essential for designing new parallel algorithms, transforming sequential algorithms into parallel forms, mapping algorithms into architectures, and, finally, designing specialized parallel computers. We will consider both numeric and nonnumeric algorithms.

2.1   DATA AND CONTROL DEPENDENCIES

The basic structural features of algorithms are dictated by their data and control dependencies. These dependencies refer to the precedence relations of computations that need to be satisfied in order to compute a problem correctly. The absence of dependencies indicates the possibility of simultaneous computations.

The study of dependence analysis, which is essential for parallel processing, was originated at the University of Illinois in the early 1970s by a group led by David Kuck [Kuck, Muraoka, and Chen 1972, Towle 1976]. Dependencies can be studied at several distinct levels: the blocks-of-computation level, the statement (or expression) level, the variable level, and even the bit level. For instance, the study of dependencies between larger blocks of computation is more useful when applied to multiprocessor computers. At the other extreme, the study of dependencies at bit level is useful in designing efficient ALUs (adders, multipliers, and so on). In the discussion that follows, we will concentrate on dependencies between statements and variables.

Consider a FORTRAN loop structure of the form

$$\text{DO } 10 \ I^1 = l^1, \ u^1$$
$$\vdots$$
$$\text{DO } 10 \ I^n = l^n, \ u^n$$
$$\text{S}_1 \ (\mathbf{I})$$
$$\text{S}_2 \ (\mathbf{I})$$
$$\vdots$$

$$S_N \; (\mathbf{I})$$

10   CONTINUE

where l^j and u^j are integer-value linear expressions involving $I^1, \ldots, I^{j-1}$ and $\mathbf{I} = (I^1, I^2, \ldots, I^n)$. $S_1, S_2, \ldots, S_N$ are assignment statements of the form $X_0 = E(X_1, X_2, \ldots, X_k)$ where X_0 is an output variable produced by an expression E operating on some input variables $X_1, X_2, \ldots, X_k$. The input variables of a statement are produced by other statements, and sometimes even by the same statement during previous iterations.

When this loop is executed, indices $\mathbf{I}$ are ordered *lexicographically*. As the name suggests, this ordering is performed similarly to the way words are ordered in a dictionary: the first letter is the most important; for entries with the same first letter the next letter is used for ordering; and so on. For example, if $\mathbf{I}_1 = (I^1, I^2, I^3) = (2, 4, 1)$ and $\mathbf{I}_2 = (I^1, I^2, I^3) = (4, 3, 1)$, we say that $\mathbf{I}_2 > \mathbf{I}_1$ in the lexicographical sense, since their first components are respectively 4 and 2, and $4 > 2$. This ordering is induced by the programmer, and often it may be modified, provided that data dependencies are satisfied. Dependencies occur between generated and used variables.

Example 2.1. Consider first a simple sequence of statements without indices, a degenerate case of the loop discussed above.

$$
\begin{aligned}
S_1 : \quad & A = B + C \\
S_2 : \quad & B = A + E \\
S_3 : \quad & A = A + B
\end{aligned}
$$

A careful analysis of this simple example reveals many dependencies. If one wishes to execute the three statements in parallel, instead of sequentially as they now are listed, one must become aware of the dependencies. The *data dependence graph*, or DDG, is shown in Figure 2.1. Statement S_1 produces the variable A that is used in statements S_2 and S_3 (dependencies d_1 and d_2, respectively); statement S_2 produces the variable B that is used in statement S_3 (dependence d_3), and the previous value of B was used in statement S_1 (dependence d_4); both statements S_1 and S_3 produce variable A (dependence d_5); statement S_3 produces variable A, previously used in statement S_2 and in S_3 itself (dependencies d_6 and d_7, respectively). All these must be taken into

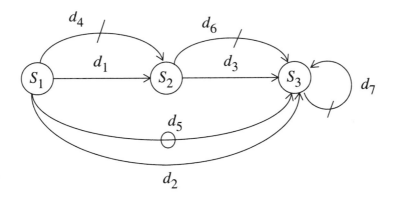

Figure 2.1 Data dependence graph (DDG) for Example 2.1.

consideration when parallelism is analyzed. Three types of dependencies can be identified in this example.

Dependencies d_1, d_2, and d_3 indicate that the value of a variable produced in a statement will be used in a subsequent statement; thus, statements cannot be performed in parallel. They are called *data-flow dependencies* and are indicated by the symbol $\longrightarrow$.

Dependencies d_4, d_6, and d_7 indicate that the value produced in one statement has been previously used in another statement or in the same statement. These dependencies prevent the parallelism, because if they are violated, it is possible to overwrite some variables before they are used. They are called *data antidependencies* and are indicated by the symbol $\not\longrightarrow$.

Dependence d_5 indicates that two statements produce the same variable. Clearly, if executed simultaneously, they overwrite the same memory location. This dependence is called *data-output dependence* and is indicated by the symbol $\multimap\rightarrow$.

The data dependence graph is a directed graph $G(V, E)$ with vertices V corresponding to statements in a program, and edges or arcs E representing data dependencies between statements. As will be seen in Chapter 3, the antidependencies and output dependencies can be eliminated at the cost of introducing new redundant variables and using more memory locations.

Next, dependencies are described formally for the general case; that is, as programs with loops. Let f and g be two integer functions defined on the set of indices $\mathbf{I}$ such that $X(f(\mathbf{I}))$ is an output variable and $X(g(\mathbf{I}))$ is an input variable. Consider two statements $S(\mathbf{I}_1)$ and $S(\mathbf{I}_2)$.

Definition 2.1 *Data-Flow Dependence.* Statement $S(\mathbf{I}_2)$ is data-flow dependent on statement $S(\mathbf{I}_1)$, and their relationship is written $S(\mathbf{I}_1) \longrightarrow S(\mathbf{I}_2)$, if:

1. $\mathbf{I}_1 \leq \mathbf{I}_2$

2. $f(\mathbf{I}_1) = g(\mathbf{I}_2)$

3. $X(f(\mathbf{I}_1))$ is an output variable in statement $S(\mathbf{I}_1)$ and $X(g(\mathbf{I}_2))$ is an input variable in statement $S(\mathbf{I}_2)$.

This is equivalent to saying that variable $X(g(\mathbf{I}_2))$ is dependent on variable $X(f(\mathbf{I}_1))$. Data-flow dependence is illustrated by the following:

$$S(\mathbf{I}_1): \ X(f(\mathbf{I}_1)) = (\qquad)$$

$$S(\mathbf{I}_2): \ (\qquad) = (\ , X(g(\mathbf{I}_2)), \ )$$

The data-flow dependence indicates a *write-before-read* ordering that must be satisfied. This dependence cannot be avoided and limits possible parallelism.

Definition 2.2 *Data Antidependence.* Statement $S(\mathbf{I}_2)$ is data antidependent on statement $S(\mathbf{I}_1)$, and their relationship is written $S(\mathbf{I}_1) \nrightarrow S(\mathbf{I}_2)$, if:

1. $\mathbf{I}_1 \leq \mathbf{I}_2$

2. $g(\mathbf{I}_1) = f(\mathbf{I}_2)$

3. $X(g(\mathbf{I}_1))$ is an input variable in statement $S(\mathbf{I}_1)$ and $X(f(\mathbf{I}_2))$ is an output variable in statement $S(\mathbf{I}_2)$.

Data antidependence is illustrated by the following:

$$S(\mathbf{I}_1):\ (\qquad\ ) = (\ ,\ X(\ g(\mathbf{I}_1)),\ )$$

$$S(\mathbf{I}_2):\ X(\ f(\mathbf{I}_2)) = (\qquad\ )$$

The data antidependence indicates a *read-before-write* ordering that should not be violated when performing computations in parallel. However, as we will see, there are techniques for avoiding this dependence.

Definition 2.3 *Output Dependence.* Statement $S(\mathbf{I}_2)$ is data-output dependent on statement $S(\mathbf{I}_1)$, and their relationship is written $S(\mathbf{I}_1) \ \multimap\!\rightarrow\ S(\mathbf{I}_2)$, if:

1. $\mathbf{I}_1 \leq \mathbf{I}_2$

2. $f_1(\mathbf{I}_1) = f_2(\mathbf{I}_2)$

3. $X(f_1(\mathbf{I}_1))$ is an output variable in statement $S(\mathbf{I}_1)$, and $X(f_2(\mathbf{I}_2))$ is an output variable in statement $S(\mathbf{I}_2)$.

Output dependence is illustrated by the following:

$$S(\mathbf{I}_1):\ X(\ f(\mathbf{I}_1)) = (\qquad\ )$$

$$S(\mathbf{I}_2):\ X(\ f(\mathbf{I}_2)) = (\qquad\ )$$

The data-output dependence indicates a *write-before-write* ordering. As in the case of antidependence, there are techniques for eliminating output dependencies.

Notice that data dependencies are directed from a generated variable to a used variable, whereas data antidependencies are directed from a used variable toward a generated variable.

Definition 2.4 *Dependence Vector.* The dependence vector $\mathbf{d}$ is defined as $\mathbf{d} = \mathbf{I}_2 - \mathbf{I}_1$, and results from the equalities $f(\mathbf{I}_i) = g(\mathbf{I}_j)$ given in the definitions above.

The dependence vectors indicate the number of iterations, or loops, between the generated variables and the used variables. In Example 2.1 there are no indices, and the value of the dependence vectors is zero; this means that there are no dependencies between different iterations, although dependencies exist between statements of the same iteration.

The procedure for finding dependence vectors is as follows:

1. Identify all pairs of generated-used variables.

2. Equate their index functions $f(\mathbf{I})$ and $g(\mathbf{I})$ and derive dependence vectors $\mathbf{d}$ as in Definition 2.4.

As discussed above, dependence relations can be represented by a dependence graph. For large programs, or programs with loops, it is not practical to display all dependencies for all index points. Often, dependence vectors may be assembled as matrices. This is a compact representation that allows the user to benefit from an ability to handle matrices. Its disadvantage, however, is that sometimes dependence vectors are variable functions on index sets, which lead to variable matrices.

Example 2.2. Consider the following loop program:

$$
\begin{aligned}
&\text{DO } 10 \quad I = 1, 20 \\
&S_1 : A(I) = X(I) - 3 \\
&S_2 : B(I+1) = A(I) * C(I+1) \\
&S_3 : C(I+4) = B(I) + A(I+1) \\
&S_4 : D(I+2) = D(I) + D(I+1) \\
&S_5 : C(I+3) = X(I) \\
&10 \quad \text{CONTINUE}
\end{aligned}
$$

The dependence graph is shown in Figure 2.2; the dependence vectors are listed in Table 2.1. The dependence vectors (scalars in this case) are derived as outlined in the procedure given above. Notice the difference between dependence d_1 and all other dependencies: d_1 is the result

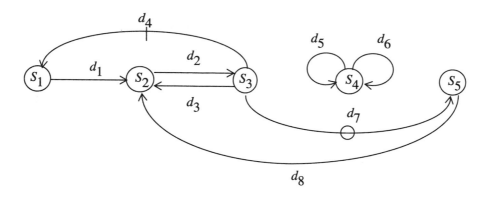

Figure 2.2 Dependencies for Example 2.2.

Variable	Functions f,g	$d = I_2 - I_1$	Type
A	$I_1 = I_2$	$d_1 = 0$	flow dependence
B	$I_1 + 1 = I_2$	$d_2 = 1$	flow dependence
C	$I_1 + 4 = I_2 + 1$	$d_3 = 3$	flow dependence
A	$I_1 + 1 = I_2$	$d_4 = 1$	data antidependence
D	$I_1 + 2 = I_2$	$d_5 = 2$	flow dependence
D	$I_1 + 2 = I_2 + 1$	$d_6 = 1$	flow dependence
C	$I_1 + 4 = I_2 + 3$	$d_7 = 1$	output dependence
C	$I_1 + 3 = I_2 + 1$	$d_8 = 2$	flow dependence

Table 2.1: Dependencies for Example 2.2.

of the way statements were originally ordered inside the loop, namely S_1 before S_2. It is a dependence between statements within the same iteration. All other dependencies are between iterations, and the value of each dependence indicates the number of iterations apart from what its generated and used variables are.

Programs with nested loops involve as many indices as loops, and in this case, dependencies become vectors defined on the index space. The dependence vectors of an algorithm can be written collectively as a *dependence matrix* $\mathbf{D} = [\mathbf{d}_1, \mathbf{d}_2, \ldots, \mathbf{d}_m]$.

Example 2.3.

$$
\begin{array}{ll}
\text{DO 10} & I^1 = 1 \text{ to } 5 \\
\text{DO 10} & I^2 = 1 \text{ to } 10 \\
\text{DO 10} & I^3 = 1 \text{ to } 20 \\
S_1: & A(I^1, I^2, I^3) = A(I^1 - 1, I^2, I^3 + 1) + B(I^1, I^2, I^3) \\
S_2: & B(I^1, I^2, I^3 + 1) = B(I^1, I^2 - 1, I^3 - 1) + 3 \\
\end{array}
$$

10   CONTINUE

The dependence vectors for this program are found using the procedure given above. There are three pairs of generated-used variables:

$$
\begin{array}{l}
A(I^1, I^2, I^3); \; A(I^1 - 1, I^2, I^3 + 1) \\
B(I^1, I^2, I^3 + 1); \; B(I^1, I^2, I^3) \\
B(I^1, I^2, I^3 + 1); \; B(I^1, I^2 - 1, I^3 - 1)
\end{array}
$$

The respective dependencies for these pairs are d_1, d_2, d_3 and are written as columns of matrix $\mathbf{D}$:

$$
\mathbf{D} = [\mathbf{d_1} \; \mathbf{d_2} \; \mathbf{d_3}] =
\left[
\begin{array}{rrr}
1 & 0 & 0 \\
0 & 0 & 1 \\
-1 & 1 & 2
\end{array}
\right]
\begin{array}{l}
I^1 \\
I^2 \\
I^3
\end{array}
$$

$\mathbf{D}$ is an alternative way of expressing dependencies in algorithms with multiple indices. As we will see, dependence matrices are useful in mathematical manipulations involving parallelism transformations.

In addition to the three dependencies already defined, there is one more type of dependence, which occurs in programs with conditional jumps.

Definition 2.5 *Control Dependence.* A control dependence exists between a statement S_i with a conditional jump and another statement S_j if the conditional jump statement controls the execution of the other statement. It is written as $S_i \; \text{-} \; \text{-} \; \rightarrow S_j$.

For the purpose of parallelism analysis in conditional statements, assign some variables to the boolean expression (condition); in this way, new statements are created. Then proceed with the analysis as you have done for other dependencies.

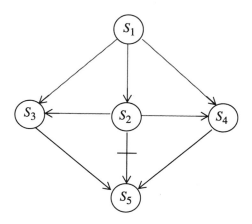

Figure 2.3 Dependence graph for Example 2.4.

Example 2.4. Consider the following program:

$$\text{if } A > 1 \text{ then go to } S_4; \text{ end if}$$
$$\text{if } B > 0 \text{ then } D = 3$$
$$\text{go to } S_4;$$
$$\text{else go to } S_5;$$
$$\text{end if;}$$

S_4: $E = 5$
S_5: $B = E + D$

This program can be written in the following equivalent form:

S_1 : $b_1 : A > 1$
S_2 : $b_2 : B > 0$ when not b_1
S_3 : $D = 3$ when not b_1 and b_2
S_4 : $E = 5$ when b_1 or b_2
S_5 : $B = E + D$

The dependence graph is shown in Figure 2.3. In the rest of this chapter, it is shown how dependencies play an important role in the analysis of parallelism.

2.2 PARALLEL NUMERICAL ALGORITHMS

2.2.1 Algorithms Without Loops

There are some algorithms or portions of algorithms without explicit loop statements (such as DO, FOR) or conditional loop statements (such as WHILE). These programs do not take a long time to run. In the most general case, these algorithms consist of sequences of assignment statements (or expressions). The absence of loops also eliminates indices and dependence vectors. Parallelism may be analyzed by simply using dependence graphs. There are two main sources of parallelism in these programs: parallelism within a statement and parallelism between statements.

Parallelism Within a Statement

Parallelism within expressions may be exploited by taking advantage of the associative, commutative, and distributive properties of arithmetic expressions. An expression is defined as a well-formed string of atoms and operators. An atom is a constant or a variable, and the operators are the normal dyadic arithmetic operations ($+$, $\times$, $-$) or logic operations (OR, AND). If only one processor is used, then the evaluation of an expression containing n operands requires $n - 1$ units of time. On the other hand, if we use as many processors as needed, then the expression may be evaluated in $\log n$ units of time. This is a lower bound. The communication time is neglected. For example, consider the addition of eight numbers as shown in Figure 2.4. At least three steps are necessary. There are four processors, but not all are used in every step.

Tree-Height Reduction

The *tree height* of a parallel computation is the number of computing steps it requires. A minimum is often achieved simply by rewriting the expression in a more convenient form. The goal is to reduce the tree height and increase parallelism. Consider the expression $(((a+b) \times c) \times d)$. The tree height for this expression is shown in Figure 2.5. By using the *associativity law* the tree height can be reduced to only two steps, as shown in the figure. The height of a tree may also be reduced by using the *commutativity law,* as shown in Figure 2.6. In addition, the

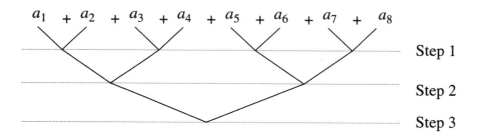

Figure 2.4 Example of the addition of eight numbers.

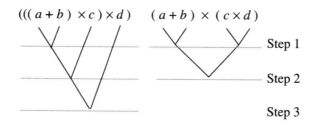

Figure 2.5 Parallelism provided by associativity.

height of the tree may be reduced by using the *distributivity law*. In the example shown in Figure 2.7, the distributivity property is applied through factorization.

These observations are useful not only for analyzing parallelism in existing statements, but also for coding mathematical expressions. Theorem 2.1 [Brent 1973] gives bounds for the processing time and for the number of processors required by transformed expressions. Define, using T_p, the parallel processing time of an arithmetic expression when p processors are used. The expression is defined by $E(e)$ where e represents the number of atoms or elements on the right-hand side. For instance $E(3) : d = a + b + c$. Also, define, using O_p, the number of parallel operations, including overhead.

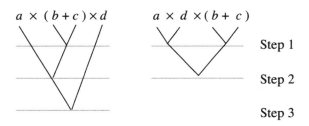

Figure 2.6 Parallelism provided by commutativity.

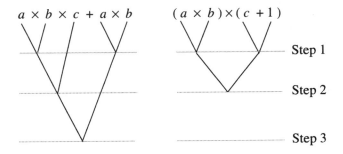

Figure 2.7 Tree-height reduction provided by factorization.

Theorem 2.1 [Brent 1973]. Given any expression $E(e)$, by proper use of associativity, commutativity, and distributivity laws, $E(e)$ can be transformed such that for the processing time T_p,

$$T_p[E(e)] \leq \lceil 4\log(e-1) \rceil - 1$$

and

$$O_p < 10e$$

with $p < 3e$.

The conclusion is that if assignment statements contain expressions of e atoms, then, by tree-height reduction methods, the expression can be evaluated in $O(\log e)$ steps. Similarly, if a conditional expression contains e possible outcomes, then it can be transformed for evaluation in $O(\log e)$ steps.

Parallelism Between Statements

Parallelism in programs with statements can be analyzed by constructing data dependence graphs between statements, as discussed in Section 2.1. Even when there are dependencies between statements, it is sometimes possible to increase the parallelism by rewriting the statements. Statement substitution is sometimes useful, as will now be explained. Consider the statements

$$S_1: x = a + bcd$$
$$S_2: y = ex + f$$
$$S_3: z = my + x$$

The dependence graph in Figure 2.8 shows the relationship among the statements. If parallelism is analyzed at the statement level, one concludes that there is no parallelism due to the dependencies between statements (a total of seven steps). However, parallelism may be exploited at the variable level. By substituting the expressions of x and y in S_3, a new statement is obtained. Figure 2.8 shows that only five steps are needed.

2.2.2   Matrix Multiplication

Matrix multiplication is a basic operation in many computer science and engineering algorithms. Let $\mathbf{A}$ and $\mathbf{B}$ be two $n \times n$ matrices. Their product is defined as $\mathbf{C} = \mathbf{AB}$, where each element of $\mathbf{C}$ is

$$c_{ij} = \sum_{k=1}^{n} a_{ik} b_{kj}$$

This formula may be put in a nested loop program:

```
for i = 1 to n
    for j = 1 to n
        for k = 1 to n
        c_ij^k = c_ij^{k-1} + a_ik b_kj
        end k
    end j
end i
```

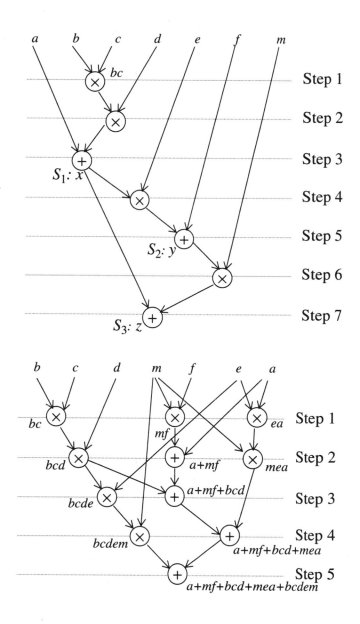

Figure 2.8 Parallelism through statement substitution.

In order to analyze the parallelism, let us first identify dependencies. For this, we rewrite the above program into an equivalent form in which the flow of a's and b's is specified. Let us first rewrite

$$a(i,j,k) = a_{ik}^j$$

$$b(i,j,k) = b_{kj}^i$$

$$c(i,j,k) = c_{ij}^k$$

```
for i = 1 to n
    for j = 1 to n
        for k = 1 to n
        a(i, j, k) = a(i, j - 1, k)
        b(i, j, k) = b(i - 1, j, k)
        c(i, j, k) = c(i, j, k - 1) + a(i, j, k)b(i, j, k)
        end k
    end j
end i
```

The statement $a(i,j,k) = a(i, j - 1, k)$ was introduced to indicate that variable a has the same value for all j indices. This was the missing index in the original program. Similary, the statement $b(i,j,k) = b(i - 1, j, k)$ was introduced to indicate that the same value of b is used for all i indices.

Figure 2.9 shows the flow of data and dependencies corresponding to the above program. This figure also helps us visualize the computational complexity of the matrix multiplication algorithm that is measured by the number of multiplications performed. In the sequential case, the *time complexity* required to perform the algorithm is $O(n^3)$. Note that this corresponds to the number of nodes in the cube. In the sequential algorithm, there are three dependencies, one for each variable. These dependencies are summarized as

$$\mathbf{D} = [\mathbf{d_1} \ \mathbf{d_2} \ \mathbf{d_3}] = \begin{bmatrix} 1 & 0 & 0 \\ 0 & 1 & 0 \\ 0 & 0 & 1 \end{bmatrix} \begin{matrix} i \\ j \\ k \end{matrix}$$
$$\qquad\qquad\qquad\qquad\quad b \quad a \quad c$$

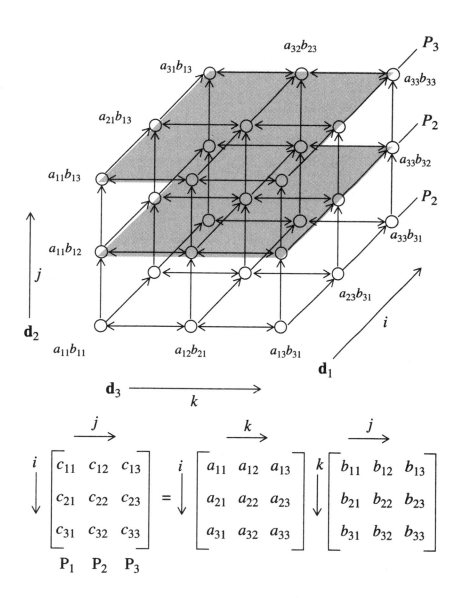

Figure 2.9 Data dependencies in matrix multiplication.

Dependence $\mathbf{d}_1$ corresponds to variable b, dependence $\mathbf{d}_2$ to variable a, and dependence $\mathbf{d}_3$ to variable c. These dependencies that occur in the sequential algorithm do not necessarily exist in the matrix multiplication formula.

Case 1. Suppose that n processors are used. One processor can be assigned to compute one column (row) of matrix $\mathbf{C}$. This means that each horizontal (vertical) layer of the three-dimensional cube is done in one processor. Note that in this case loop j is performed in parallel. This means that dependence $\mathbf{d}_2$, which corresponds to loop j, is an induced dependence in the sequential algorithm. The same can be said, respectively, about dependence $\mathbf{d}_1$ and loop i. The parallel time complexity in this case is $O(n^2)$.

Case 2. Suppose that n^2 processors are used. Each processor may be assigned to compute an element c_{ij}, and the time complexity is $O(n)$. This corresponds to the number of multiplications in each horizontal row of the cube. In this case both loops i and j are performed in parallel. This means that both $\mathbf{d}_1$ and $\mathbf{d}_2$ may be collectively eliminated. Note that for the sequential case and for these two cases of limited parallelism,

$$(\text{number of processors}) \times (\text{time complexity}) = O(n^3)$$

Case 3. Suppose that n^3 processors are used. Can the time complexity be reduced to a constant? The lower bound of a matrix multiplication algorithm is $O(\log n)$, and no parallel algorithm can perform below this theoretical bound. Note that this is also the lower bound for adding n numbers. Dependence $\mathbf{d}_3$ cannot be totally eliminated. However, it can be transformed to provide the lower bound.

Thus, in general, it is important to notice that an algorithm implementing some mathematical formula introduces *artificial dependencies*. The best (the fastest) parallel algorithms are those that do not introduce unnecessary dependencies. However, when algorithms are executed on parallel computers, it is possible that the interconnection network may not match the algorithm's natural dependencies, and this is a primary source of performance loss.

2.2.3 Relaxation

Relaxation is a method used in solving partial differential equations (PDE), image processing, and other engineering problems. Basically, it consists of updating a variable at a particular point by finding the average of the values of that variable at neighboring points. The following loop contains a relaxation expression:

for $i = 1$ to l
  for $j = 1$ to m
    for $k = 1$ to n
      $u(j,k) = 1/4[u(j+1,k) + u(j,k+1) + u(j-1,k) + u(j,k-1)]$
    end k
  end j
end i

In the loop statement, index i is omitted but it is implied that

$$u(i,j,k) = 1/4[u(i-1,j+1,k) + u(i-1,j,k+1) + u(i,j-1,k)+$$
$$+u(i,j,k-1)]$$

Because of its simplicity, this relaxation program was one of the first algorithms subjected to parallelism analysis. Leslie Lamport [Lamport 1974] has studied parallel relaxation and has introduced the idea of the *hyperplane*. As we will see, a hyperplane contains a set of index points (often lying on a plane) that can be processed in parallel. This is a powerful concept in parallel processing, on which other techniques such as algorithm transformations are based.

The loop is executed lmn times, once for each point (i,j,k) in the index set. We want to see what parallelism exists in such nested loops and what the parallel processing time is. Consider the computation of $u(2,4)$ when $(i,j,k) = (8,2,4)$. $u(2,4)$ is the average of its four neighboring array elements, $u(2,5)$, $u(3,4)$, $u(1,4)$, and $u(2,3)$. The values of $u(2,5)$ and $u(3,4)$ were calculated during the execution of the loop body for iterations (7,2,5) and (7,3,4), respectively. These iterations occurred in the previous i loop, namely $i=7$. The values of $u(1,4)$ and $u(2,3)$ were calculated during the current execution of the outer i loop, $i = 8$. This is shown in Figure 2.10. Hence, the

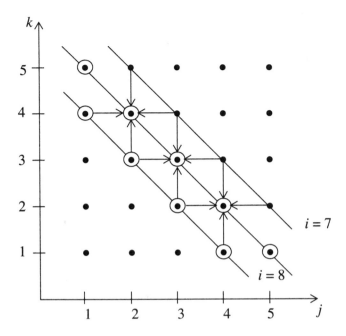

Figure 2.10 Index plane and dependencies for relaxation equation.

computation at (8,2,4) is dependent on the results computed at (7,2,5), (7,3,4), (8,1,4), and (8,2,3). It is easy to see from the equation that the last four index points are independent of each other, and thus can be performed in parallel. Similarly, notice that the computation at (8,3,3) is dependent on the results computed at (7,3,4), (7,4,3), (8,2,3), and (8,3,2), and the computation at (8,4,2) is dependent on the results at (7,4,3), (7,5,2), (8,4,2), and (8,3,2).

$$
\left.\begin{array}{ccc}
7 & 3 & 4 \\
7 & 2 & 5 \\
8 & 2 & 3 \\
8 & 1 & 4
\end{array}\right\} \rightarrow 8\,2\,4
\qquad
\left.\begin{array}{ccc}
7 & 3 & 4 \\
7 & 4 & 3 \\
8 & 2 & 3 \\
8 & 3 & 2
\end{array}\right\} \rightarrow 8\,3\,3
\qquad
\left.\begin{array}{ccc}
7 & 4 & 3 \\
7 & 5 & 2 \\
8 & 4 & 2 \\
8 & 3 & 2
\end{array}\right\} \rightarrow 8\,4\,2
$$

Notice now that points (8,2,4), (8,3,3), and (8,4,2) can be computed simultaneously. These three points are on the line $j + k = 6$ for $i = 8$. All points on this line can be computed simultaneously. Similarly,

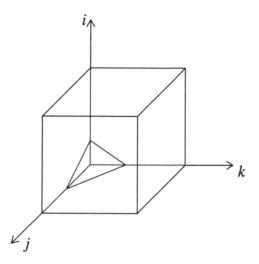

Figure 2.11 Index set intersected by plane $2i + j + k = constant$.

observe now that points (7,2,5), (7,3,4), (7,4,3), and (7,5,2), which are on the line $j + k = 7$ for $i = 7$, can be computed simultaneously and so can the other points on this line. The points on line $i = 8$ can be computed simultaneously. Moreover, the points on both lines can be computed simultaneously because they depend on points computed previously. The commonality among points (7,2,5), (7,3,4), (7,4,3), (7,5,2), (8,1,4), (8,2,3), (8,3,2), and (8,4,1) is that they all belong to a plane whose equation is $2i + j + k = 21$. The intersection of this plane with the three-dimensional index set is shown in Figure 2.11. This is the equation of a hyperplane, and indicates that the nested loop can be executed in parallel for all points (i, j, k) lying on this plane.

It is tedious to analyze parallelism this way. A simpler way is to use dependence vectors. The dependence matrix for this program is

$$\mathbf{D} = [\mathbf{d}_1 \ \mathbf{d}_2 \ \mathbf{d}_3 \ \mathbf{d}_4] = \begin{bmatrix} 1 & 1 & 0 & 0 \\ -1 & 0 & 0 & 1 \\ 0 & -1 & 1 & 0 \end{bmatrix} \begin{matrix} i \\ j \\ k \end{matrix}$$

It is easy now to see that the point (8,2,4) is dependent on points (7,3,4), (7,2,5), (8,2,3), and (8,1,4) through dependencies $\mathbf{d}_1, \mathbf{d}_2, \mathbf{d}_3,$

$\mathbf{d}_4$, respectively. The dependence vectors are useful for finding out how all points in the index set interrelate. The interpretation of the plane $(2i+j+k) = constant$ is that all dependence vectors traverse the plane in the same direction. In other words, all computations on one side of the plane are done before the computations on the other side of the plane. This guarantees that no dependence lies on this plane, and thus that no two points on the plane are interdependent.

The *parallel processing time* can also be determined from the structure of dependence vectors in the index space. It it sufficient to find the longest path of dependencies, called the *critical path*, the link between the first index point $(1, 1, 1)$ and the last point (l, m, n). This path may not be unique. Since no two points on the path can be computed simultaneously, the length of this path indicates the minimum parallel processing time. In this example the time is $O(l + m + n)$, and is thus a significant speedup over the sequential time lmn. Notice that the length of the critical path is related to the number of distinct planes $(2i + j + k) = constant$ crossing the index space. Finally, notice that many valid hyperplanes can be found for this program; for example, $4i + j + k = constant$ is another possibility. Thus we face several questions: How can we find valid hyperplanes? Which one leads to the shortest parallel time? The answers to these questions will be provided in Chapter 3.

2.2.4   Recurrence Relations

A recurrence relation specifies a dynamic procedure for computing scalars or vectors. Recurrences are frequently found in numerical analysis, signal processing, computer programming, and many other applications. For example,

$$x_i = a_1 x_{i-1} + a_2 x_{i-2} + c$$

is a linear recurrence of the second order, describing the behavior of a digital filter with constant coefficients. The order of a recurrence is given by the number of previous iterations needed to compute the current value. In their most general form, recurrences may have variable coefficients.

Definition 2.6 An mth-order linear recurrence system of n equations, denoted as $R(n, m)$, is defined as

$$x_i = 0 \quad \text{for} \quad i \leq 0$$

$$x_i = c_i + \sum_{j=i-m}^{i-1} a_{i,i-j} x_j \quad \text{for} \quad 1 \leq i \leq n, \quad 1 \leq m \leq n$$

In matrix notation, $R(n, m)$ can be written as

$$\mathbf{x} = \mathbf{c} + \mathbf{A}\mathbf{x}$$

where $\mathbf{A}$ is a strictly lower triangular band matrix.

$$(\mathbf{I} - \mathbf{A})\mathbf{x} = \mathbf{c}$$

For example, $R(8, 2)$ is

$$
\begin{bmatrix}
1 & & & & & & & \\
-a_{21} & 1 & & & & & & \\
-a_{32} & -a_{31} & 1 & & & & & \\
& -a_{42} & -a_{41} & 1 & & & & \\
& & -a_{52} & -a_{51} & 1 & & & \\
& & & -a_{62} & -a_{61} & 1 & & \\
& & & & -a_{72} & -a_{71} & 1 & \\
& & & & & -a_{82} & -a_{81} & 1
\end{bmatrix}
\begin{bmatrix}
x_1 \\ x_2 \\ x_3 \\ x_4 \\ x_5 \\ x_6 \\ x_7 \\ x_8
\end{bmatrix}
=
\begin{bmatrix}
c_1 \\ c_2 \\ c_3 \\ c_4 \\ c_5 \\ c_6 \\ c_7 \\ c_8
\end{bmatrix}
$$

Recurrence processing seems inherently sequential because x_i is by definition a function of previous m values. Nevertheless, it is possible to transform recurrence systems into parallel forms.

One way to accomplish this is to partition $R(n, m)$ into smaller systems $R^l(p, m)$, where $1 \leq l \leq \lceil n/p \rceil$. Each smaller system is such that its corresponding matrix is in a column format, instead of a band diagonal format as before. This allows the computation of all variables in parallel. By selecting $p = 5$, we can transform $R(8, 2)$ from the example above into

$$
\begin{bmatrix}
1 & & & & & & & \\
-b_{21} & 1 & & & & & & \\
-b_{32} & -b_{31} & 1 & & & & & \\
-b_{42} & -b_{41} & & 1 & & & & \\
-b_{52} & -b_{51} & & 0 & 1 & & & \\
& & & -b_{62} & -b_{61} & 1 & & \\
& & & -b_{72} & -b_{71} & & 1 & \\
& & & -b_{82} & -b_{81} & & & 1
\end{bmatrix}
\begin{bmatrix}
x_1 \\ x_2 \\ x_3 \\ x_4 \\ x_5 \\ x_6 \\ x_7 \\ x_8
\end{bmatrix}
=
\begin{bmatrix}
d_1 \\ d_2 \\ d_3 \\ d_4 \\ d_5 \\ d_6 \\ d_7 \\ d_8
\end{bmatrix}
$$

It is easy to verify that the new coefficients, the b's and d's, are obtained as follows:

$l = 1$

$$
i = 1 \quad (b_{11}\ b_{12}\ d_1) = (a_{11}\ a_{12}\ c_1)
\begin{pmatrix}
1 & 0 & 0 \\
0 & 1 & 0 \\
0 & 0 & 1
\end{pmatrix}
$$

$$
i = 2 \quad (b_{21}\ b_{22}\ d_2) = (a_{21}\ a_{22}\ c_2)
\begin{pmatrix}
1 & 0 & 0 \\
0 & 1 & 0 \\
0 & 0 & 1
\end{pmatrix}
$$

$$
i = 3 \quad (b_{31}\ b_{32}\ d_3) = (a_{31}\ a_{32}\ c_3)
\begin{pmatrix}
1 & 0 & 0 \\
0 & 1 & 0 \\
0 & 0 & 1
\end{pmatrix}
$$

$$
i = 4 \quad (b_{41}\ b_{42}\ d_4) = (a_{41}\ a_{42}\ c_4)
\begin{pmatrix}
b_{31} & b_{32} & d_3 \\
1 & 0 & 0 \\
0 & 0 & 1
\end{pmatrix}
$$

$$
i = 5 \quad (b_{51}\ b_{52}\ d_5) = (a_{51}\ a_{52}\ c_5)
\begin{pmatrix}
b_{41} & b_{42} & d_4 \\
b_{31} & b_{32} & d_3 \\
0 & 0 & 1
\end{pmatrix}
$$

$l = 2$

$$
i = 1 \quad (b_{61}\ b_{62}\ d_6) = (a_{61}\ a_{62}\ c_6)
\begin{pmatrix}
1 & 0 & 0 \\
0 & 1 & 0 \\
0 & 0 & 1
\end{pmatrix}
$$

$$
i = 2 \quad (b_{71}\ b_{72}\ d_7) = (a_{71}\ a_{72}\ c_7)
\begin{pmatrix}
b_{61} & b_{62} & d_6 \\
1 & 0 & 0 \\
0 & 0 & 1
\end{pmatrix}
$$

$$i = 3 \quad (b_{81} \; b_{82} \; d_8) = \; (a_{81} \; a_{82} \; c_8) \begin{pmatrix} b_{71} & b_{72} & d_7 \\ b_{61} & b_{62} & d_6 \\ 0 & 0 & 1 \end{pmatrix}$$

$$i = 4 \quad (b_{91} \; b_{92} \; d_9) = \; (a_{91} \; a_{92} \; c_9) \begin{pmatrix} b_{81} & b_{82} & d_8 \\ b_{71} & b_{72} & d_7 \\ 0 & 0 & 1 \end{pmatrix}$$

Figure 2.12 shows the form of matrix $\mathbf{A}$ corresponding to a recurrence system $R(n, m)$ and the form of matrix $\mathbf{B}$ corresponding to the transformed system $R^l(p, m)$. The speed advantage is derived from the fact that the computation of matrix $\mathbf{B}$ is done simultaneously for all $\lceil n/p \rceil$ blocks. Within each block, sequential order must be respected. Once matrix $\mathbf{B}$ is computed, the computation of x_i may start. Because of the column format of blocks in matrix $\mathbf{B}$, the computation of all x_i corresponding to each block requires only the availability of the last mx_i of the previous block. Since the order in which the x_i within each block are computed is not important, it is possible to start each block from the last row up. This is another source of parallelism.

Daniel Gajsky [Gajsky 1981] has developed an algorithm for partitioning an $R(n, m)$ into $\lceil n/p \rceil$ subsystems $R^l(p, m)$. We will derive dependencies and analyze the parallel timing for this algorithm.

Let $\mathbf{a}_i = (a_{i1}, a_{i2}, ..., a_{im}, c_i)$ and $\mathbf{b}_i = (b_{i1}, b_{i2}, ..., b_{im}, d_i)$. The unit vector $\mathbf{e}_i$ has a 1 in the ith position. Then $\mathbf{b}_i$ is defined recursively as

$$\mathbf{b}_i = \mathbf{a}_i \mathbf{B}_{i-1}$$

where matrix $\mathbf{B}_{i-1} = (\mathbf{b}_{i-1}, \mathbf{b}_{i-2}, ..., \mathbf{b}_{i-m}, \mathbf{e}_{m+1})^T$. The initial conditions, $\mathbf{b}_0, \mathbf{b}_{-1}, ..., \mathbf{b}_{-m+1}$, equal $\mathbf{e}_1, \mathbf{e}_2, ..., \mathbf{e}_m$. In what follows, $\mathbf{x}_0 = (x_0, x_{-1}, ..., x_{-m+1})$ are the initial conditions.

A linear recurrence system $R(n, m)$ is transformed into $\lceil n/p \rceil$ subsystems $R^l(p, m)$ by the following algorithm:

Recurrence Transformation Algorithm [Gajsky 1981].

1.   begin
2. $\mathbf{x}_p^0 = \mathbf{x}_0$
3.   for $l = 1$ until $\lceil n/p \rceil$ do

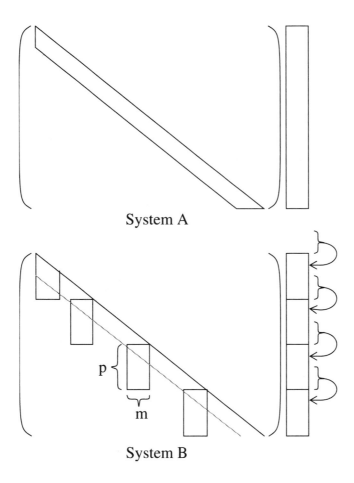

Figure 2.12 Partitioning of a recurrence system.

4.   begin
5. $\mathbf{B}_0^l$ = identity matrix
6.   for $i = 1$ until p do $\mathbf{b}_i^l = \mathbf{a}_i^l \mathbf{B}_{i-1}^l$
7.   end
8.   for $l = 1$ until $\lceil n/p \rceil$ do
9.   for $i = 1$ until p do $x_i^l = \mathbf{b}_i^l \, (\mathbf{x}_p^{(l-1)})^T$
10.   end

The main processing occurs in lines 6 and 9. In line 6, the coefficients of matrix $\mathbf{B}$ are computed. The dependencies are caused by the relation between $\mathbf{b}_i^l$ and $\mathbf{B}_{i-1}^l$. It can be seen that these dependencies do not cross l loops; in other words, both $\mathbf{b}_i^l$ and $\mathbf{B}_{i-1}^l$ refer to the same l iteration. This means that $\mathbf{b}_i^l$ can be computed in parallel for all l iterations. We also see that there are dependencies between i iterations because of the difference between i and $i - 1$. Thus, loop i needs to be done serially. The number of time steps taken by line 6 is $O(pm)$; that is, p, the number of iterations in loop i, times $m + 1$, the size of vector $\mathbf{a}_i$. Note that the elements of vector $\mathbf{b}_i^l$ can all be done simultaneously.

The processing in line 9 computes the values of the recurrence variable x_i. The dependencies derive from the fact that x_i^l depends on $\mathbf{x}_p^{l-1}$. We can observe two things: (1) the iterations in loop l cannot be done in parallel because the result x_i^l, computed for loop l, requires values computed in the previous loop $l - 1$; and (2) there are no dependencies for loop i, which means that all iterations in loop i can be done in parallel. The parallel processing time for line 9 is $O(mn/p)$; that is, the number of blocks $\lceil n/p \rceil$ times the size of vector $\mathbf{b}_i$, which is $m + 1$. It follows that overall parallel time is $O(pm + n/pm)$. Figure 2.13 illustrates this result.

The time analysis for this example did not take into account the communication time; that is, the time required by variables to move from where they are computed to where they will be used next. In the case of the matrix multiplication example in Section 2.2.2, we added two extra lines that specified how a and b moved. We could have done the same for this recurrence example and, in this case, obtained specific dependence vectors.

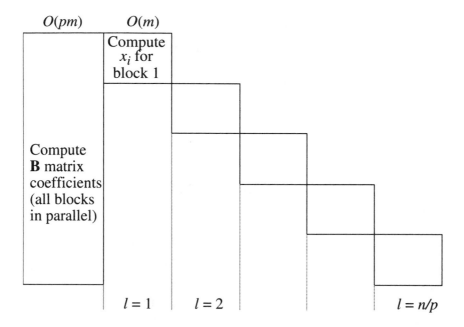

Figure 2.13 Parallel processing time for recurrence systems.

2.2.5   QR Algorithm

A widely accepted method for computing the eigenvalues of an $n \times n$ matrix $\mathbf{A}$ is first to transform $\mathbf{A}$ into an upper Hessenberg form and then to apply iteratively a QR algorithm to this Hessenberg matrix. A Hessenberg matrix has zero elements in the lower part, starting with the second line below the main diagonal. If $\mathbf{Q}_k$ is an orthogonal matrix, that is $\mathbf{Q}_k\mathbf{Q}_k^T = \mathbf{I}$, then after a similar transformation

$$\mathbf{A}_{k+1} = \mathbf{Q}_k^T\mathbf{A}_k\mathbf{Q}_k = \mathbf{R}_k\mathbf{Q}_k$$

the eigenvalues of $\mathbf{A}_{k+1}$ are the same as the eigenvalues of $\mathbf{A}_k$. $\mathbf{Q}_k$ is chosen such that $\mathbf{R}_k = \mathbf{Q}_k^T\mathbf{A}_k$ is upper triangular. The QR algorithm, applied directly to a full matrix $\mathbf{A}$, leads to $O(n^4)$ multiplications. This is the reason it is preferable first to transform $\mathbf{A}$ into an upper Hessenberg form by a sequence of elementary reflectors transformations, which require $O(n^3)$ multiplications. Then the application of the QR algorithm to the Hessenberg form requires only $O(kn^3)$ operations, where k is the average number of iterations for one eigenvalue. If $\mathbf{A}$ is symmetric, then the upper Hessenberg form reduces to a tridiagonal matrix, and a repeated QR algorithm applied to such a matrix diagonalizes the matrix, leaving eigenvalues as diagonal elements. QR algorithms have remarkable numerical stability.

The QR algorithm follows. In this algorithm, the input matrix $\mathbf{A}$ is upper Hessenberg of order n and the shift scalar is x. The algorithm overwrites $\mathbf{A}$ with $\mathbf{Q}^H \mathbf{A} \mathbf{Q}$ where the orthogonal matrix $\mathbf{Q} = \mathbf{P}_{12}^T, \mathbf{P}_{23}^T,$ ..., $\mathbf{P}_{n-1,n}^T$, where $\mathbf{P}_{k,k+1}$ is a plane rotation in the $(k, k+1)$ plane.

QR Algorithm [Stewart 1974].

$$
\begin{aligned}
&\text{begin} \\
&\quad a_{11} \leftarrow a_{11} - x; \\
100:\quad &\quad \text{for } k \leftarrow 1 \text{ step } 1 \text{ until } n \text{ do} \\
&\quad \text{begin} \\
&\qquad \text{if } k = n \text{ then go to 200;} \\
&\qquad (r_k, \sigma_k, v_k) \leftarrow \text{rot } (a_{kk}, a_{k+1,k}); \\
&\qquad a_{kk} \leftarrow v_k; \\
&\qquad a_{k+1,k} \leftarrow 0; \\
&\qquad a_{k+1,k+1} \leftarrow a_{k+1,k+1} - x; \\
&\qquad \text{for } j \leftarrow k + 1 \text{ step } 1 \text{ until } n \text{ do} \\
&\qquad\quad \begin{bmatrix} a_{kj} \\ a_{k+1,j} \end{bmatrix} \leftarrow \begin{bmatrix} r_k & \sigma_k \\ \sigma_k & v_k \end{bmatrix} \begin{bmatrix} a_{kj} \\ a_{k+1,j} \end{bmatrix}; \\
&\qquad \text{if } k = 1 \text{ then go to 100;} \\
200:\quad &\qquad \text{for } i \leftarrow 1 \text{ step } 1 \text{ until } k \text{ do} \\
&\qquad\quad [a_{i,k-1}, a_{ik}] \leftarrow [a_{i,k-1}, a_{ik}] \begin{bmatrix} r_{k-1} & -\sigma_{k-1} \\ \sigma_{k-1} & r_{k-1} \end{bmatrix}; \\
&\qquad a_{k-1,k-1} \leftarrow a_{k-1,k-1} + x; \\
&\quad \text{end; } k \\
&\quad a_{nn} \leftarrow a_{nn} + x; \\
&\text{end}
\end{aligned}
$$

The parallelism analysis of this algorithm follows the work of Moldovan [Moldovan 1984]. As for any complex algorithm, it is advantageous to break the analysis down into the following steps:

1. Write the algorithm in a form in which each variable has all indices.

2. Find data dependencies.

3. Correlate index points with elements of matrix **A**.

4. Find out how index points are linked by data dependencies.

5. Determine the parallel processing time by finding the length of the critical path.

Step 1. Pipelined QR Algorithm.

$$
\begin{array}{ll}
 & \text{begin} \\
1: & \qquad a_{11}^{0} \leftarrow a_{11}^{0} - x; \\
2: & 100: \quad \text{for } k \leftarrow 1 \text{ step } 1 \text{ until } n \text{ do} \\
 & \qquad \text{begin} \\
3: & \qquad\qquad \text{if } k = n \text{ then go to } 200; \\
4: & \qquad\qquad (r_{k}^{k+1}, \sigma_{k}^{k+1}, v_{k}^{k+1}) \leftarrow \text{rot } (a_{kk}^{k}, a_{k+1,k}^{k}); \\
5: & \qquad\qquad a_{kk}^{k} \leftarrow v_{k}^{k+1}; \\
6: & \qquad\qquad a_{k+1,k}^{k} \leftarrow 0; \\
7: & \qquad\qquad a_{k+1,k+1}^{k} \leftarrow a_{k+1,k+1}^{k-1} - x; \\
8: & \qquad\qquad \text{for } j \leftarrow k + 1 \text{ step } 1 \text{ until } n \text{ do} \\
 & \qquad\qquad\qquad \text{begin} \\
9: & \qquad\qquad\qquad i \leftarrow k; \\
10: & \qquad\qquad\qquad a_{ij}^{k} \leftarrow a_{ij}^{k-1} r_{k}^{j} + a_{i+1,j}^{k-1} \sigma_{k}^{j}; \\
11: & \qquad\qquad\qquad a_{i+1,j}^{k} \leftarrow a_{ij}^{k-1} \sigma_{k}^{j} + a_{i+1,j}^{k-1} v_{k}^{j}; \\
12: & \qquad\qquad\qquad r_{k}^{j+1} \leftarrow r_{k}^{j}; \\
13: & \qquad\qquad\qquad \sigma_{k}^{j+1} \leftarrow \sigma_{k}^{j}; \\
 & \qquad\qquad \text{end } j; \\
14: & \qquad\qquad \text{if } k = 1 \text{ then go to } 100; \\
15: & 200: \quad \text{for } i \leftarrow k \text{ step } -1 \text{ until } 1 \text{ do} \\
 & \qquad\qquad \text{begin} \\
16: & \qquad\qquad j \leftarrow k; \\
17: & \qquad\qquad a_{i,j-1}^{k} \leftarrow a_{i,j-1}^{k-1} r_{k-1}^{i} + a_{i,j}^{k-1} \sigma_{k-1}^{i}; \\
18: & \qquad\qquad a_{i,j}^{k} \leftarrow -a_{i,j-1}^{k-1} \sigma_{k-1}^{j} + a_{ij}^{k-1} r_{k-1}^{i}; \\
19: & \qquad\qquad \sigma_{k-1}^{i-1} \leftarrow \sigma_{k-1}^{i};
\end{array}
$$

20: $\qquad\qquad r_{k-1}^{i-1} \leftarrow r_{k-1}^{i};$
$\qquad\qquad$ end $i;$

21: $\qquad\qquad a_{k-1,k-1}^{k+1} \leftarrow a_{k-1,k-1}^{k} + x;$
$\qquad\qquad$ end $k;$

22: $\qquad\qquad a_{nn} \leftarrow a_{nn} + x;$

23: $\quad$ end; QR-pipelined

Step 2. The algorithm index set is $J^3 : 1 \leq k \leq n,\ 1 \leq i \leq k,\ k+1 \leq j \leq n$. A data dependence vector is easily picked as the difference between the index points where a variable is used and the index point where that variable was generated, i.e., $\mathbf{d} = (k^2, i^2, j^2)^T - (k^1, i^1, j^1)^T$. We find $\mathbf{d}_1 = (1,0,0)^T$ from statements 10, 11, and 17; $\mathbf{d}_2 = (1,-1,0)^T$ from line 10; $\mathbf{d}_3 = (1,1,0)^T$ from line 11; $\mathbf{d}_4 = (0,0,1)^T$ from lines 12 and 13; $\mathbf{d}_5 = (1,0,-1)^T$ from line 17; $\mathbf{d}_6 = (1,0,1)^T$ from line 18; and $\mathbf{d}_7 = (0,-1,0)^T$ from lines 19 and 20. Notice that $\mathbf{d}_7 \leq 0$ because we have changed the direction of loop i; it is ordered from the upper limit toward the lower limit. It results the data dependence matrix

$$\mathbf{D} = [\mathbf{d}_1\ \mathbf{d}_2\ \mathbf{d}_3\ \mathbf{d}_4\ \mathbf{d}_5\ \mathbf{d}_6\ \mathbf{d}_7] = \begin{bmatrix} 1 & 1 & 1 & 0 & 1 & 1 & 0 \\ 0 & -1 & 1 & 0 & 0 & 0 & -1 \\ 0 & 0 & 0 & 1 & -1 & 1 & 0 \end{bmatrix} \begin{matrix} k \\ i \\ j \end{matrix}$$

Step 3. Figure 2.14 shows a Hessenberg matrix. The premultiply operations are between corresponding row terms coupled by dependencies $\mathbf{d}_2$ and $\mathbf{d}_3$, and the postmultiply operations are between corresponding column terms coupled by dependencies $\mathbf{d}_5$ and $\mathbf{d}_6$. Figure 2.15 shows the correlation between the elements of the matrix and the index points for premultiply and postmultiply.

Step 4. The interdependencies between index points are shown in Figure 2.16.

Step 5. The critical path is shown in Figure 2.16. We see that for the first $(n-2)k$ iterations two time steps are needed, and for the $(n-1)$th iteration one time step is needed. Finally, the last iteration requires n steps. Thus, the parallel processing time is:

$$\text{Time} = 2(n-2) + 1 + n = 3n - 3$$

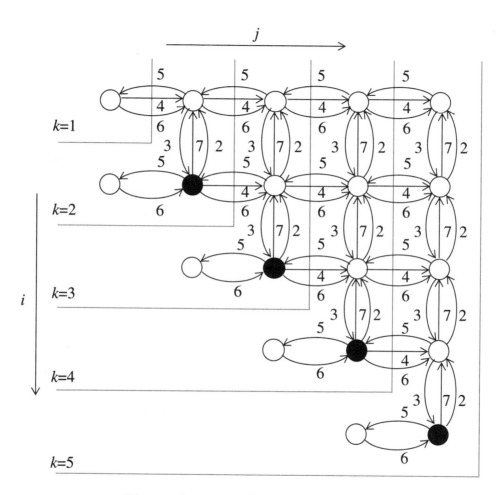

The numbers near the arcs indicate the
dependence number; i.e., 5 means $\mathbf{d}_5$.

Figure 2.14 A 5 × 5 Hessenberg matrix used in the QR Algorithm.

112	113	114	115	223	224	225	334	335	445
a_{12}	a_{13}	a_{14}	a_{15}	a_{23}	a_{24}	a_{25}	a_{34}	a_{35}	a_{45}
a_{22}	a_{23}	a_{24}	a_{25}	a_{33}	a_{34}	a_{35}	a_{44}	a_{45}	a_{55}

a_{11} a_{12} 212	a_{12} a_{13} 313	a_{13} a_{14} 414	a_{14} a_{15} 515
a_{21} a_{22} 222	a_{22} a_{23} 323	a_{23} a_{24} 424	a_{24} a_{25} 525
	a_{32} a_{33} 333	a_{33} a_{34} 434	a_{34} a_{35} 535
		a_{34} a_{44} 444	a_{44} a_{45} 545
			a_{54} a_{55} 555

Figure 2.15 Computations in the QR algorithm.

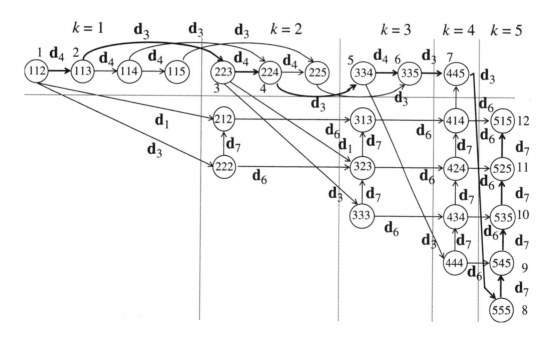

Figure 2.16 Data dependencies in the QR algorithm ($n = 5$).

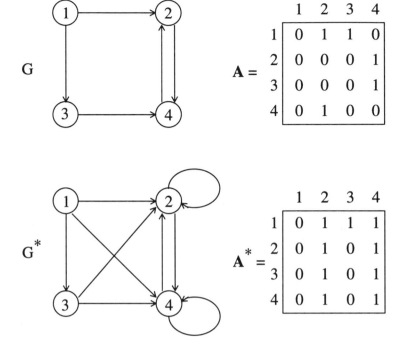

Figure 2.17 Example of transitive closure.

2.3 PARALLEL NON-NUMERICAL ALGORITHMS

2.3.1 Transitive Closure

Given a directed graph $G = (V, E)$, it is sometimes necessary to know whether or not there is a connecting path between any two vertices. Let $\mathbf{A} = [a_{ij}]$ be the adjacency matrix of G, where $a_{ij} = 1$ if there is an edge $(i, j) \in E$ and $a_{ij} = 0$ if not. We want to compute the connectivity matrix $\mathbf{A}^* = [a_{ij}^*]$, defined by $a_{ij}^* = 1$ if there is a path in G from i to j, and $a_{ij}^* = 0$ if not. $\mathbf{A}^*$ is the adjacency matrix for the graph $G = (V, E^*)$, in which E^* is the *transitive closure* of the binary relation E. Figure 2.17 displays a graph G with its adjacency matrix $\mathbf{A}$ and its transitive closure.

A well-known algorithm for computing $\mathbf{A}^*$ is *Warshall's algorithm*. An example follows.

Transitive Closure Algorithm [Aho, Hopcroft, and Ullman 1974].

```
for k=1 to n
    for i = 1 to n
        for j = 1 to n
            a_{ij}^k ← a_{ij}^{k-1} ∪ (a_{ik}^{k-1} ∩ a_{kj}^{k-1})
        end j
    end i
end k
```

The dependencies are

$$\mathbf{D} = [\mathbf{d}_1 \ \mathbf{d}_2 \ \mathbf{d}_3] = \begin{bmatrix} 1 & 1 & 1 \\ 0 & 0 & i-k \\ 0 & j-k & 0 \end{bmatrix} \begin{matrix} k \\ i \\ j \end{matrix}$$

Dependence $\mathbf{d}_1$ is constant, but dependencies $\mathbf{d}_2$ and $\mathbf{d}_3$ are variable; that is, they have elements that are dependent on the iteration point where they originate. The parallelism analysis of this algorithm is extremely simple. It is sufficient to notice that all dependencies have a 1 in the first row, meaning that the dependencies are between successive k loops and no dependence lies on the (i,j) planes. We conclude that all operations on the (i,j) plane can be done in parallel, and the k coordinate becomes the parallel time coordinate. Thus the total time required is $O(n)$. Figure 2.18 illustrates the flow of dependencies between successive (i,j) planes.

It is interesting to look at dependencies from another viewpoint; that is, as they project on the (i,j) plane. This view may help us understand the communication requirements of this algorithm. Figure 2.19 depicts dependencies between the elements of matrix $\mathbf{A}$ in the (i,j) plane for four k iterations. In this figure, the arrows represent actual dependencies given by the dependence matrix, with the understanding that each dependence has a 1 component along the k coordinate (not shown). Provided that there are sufficient interconnections in the parallel computer, all computations for each iteration k can be done in one time step.

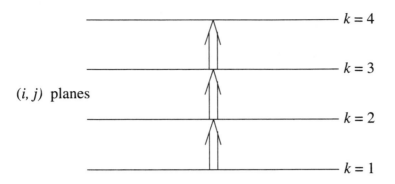

Figure 2.18 The critical path for a transitive closure algorithm $(n = 4)$.

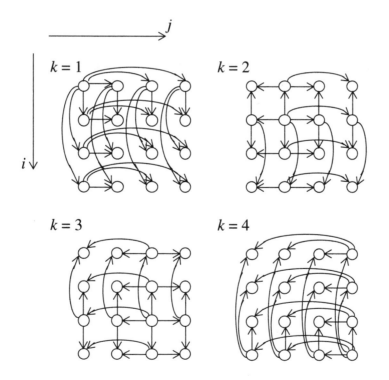

Figure 2.19 Data dependencies for transitive closure algorithm $(n = 4)$.

There are other important combinatorial problems with the same computational structure. Most notable are the shortest-path problem and the graph isomorphism problem.

2.3.2   Dynamic Programming

Many problems in computer science and engineering can be solved by the use of dynamic programming technique. Here we consider the parallel implementation of an optimal parenthesization algorithm based on dynamic programming. A string of n matrices is multiplied:

$$\mathbf{M} = \mathbf{M}_1 \times \mathbf{M}_2 \times \cdots \times \mathbf{M}_n$$

The cost of computing $\mathbf{M}$ depends on the order in which multiplications are performed. Let r_0, r_1, ..., r_n be the dimensions of the n matrices and r_{i-1} and r_i be dimensions of $\mathbf{M}_i$. Denote by m_{ij} the minimum cost of computing the product $\mathbf{M}_i\mathbf{M}_{i+1} \cdots \mathbf{M}_j$. The algorithm that finally produces m_{1n} is shown below.

Dynamic Programming Algorithm [Aho, Hopcroft, and Ullman 1974].

```
for i ← 1 to n do mᵢᵢ ← 0
for l ← 1 to n − 1 do
    for i ← 1 to n − l do
        begin
            j ← i + l
            mᵢⱼ ← minᵢ≤ₖ<ⱼ (mᵢₖ + mₖ₊₁,ⱼ + rᵢ₋₁rₖrⱼ)
        end
```

The analysis of parallelism in this algorithm was done by Moldovan [Moldovan 1983b]. Particularly interesting for this algorithm is the detection of data dependencies. In order to find dependencies and analyze parallelism, the algorithm is first transformed as shown below.

```
for i ← 1 to n do mᵢᵢ ← 0
for l ← 1 to n − 1 do
    for i ← 1 to n − l do
```

Pairs of generated-used variables	Data dependencies			
	$(l-l')$	$(i-i')$	$(k-k')$	Type
$< m_{i'k'}^{l'} \, , \, m_{ik}^{l-1} >$	1	0	0	$\mathbf{d}_1$
$< m_{k'+1, \, i'+l'}^{l'} \, , \, m_{k+1, \, i+l}^{l-1} >$	1	-1	0	$\mathbf{d}_2$
$< m_{i', \, i'+l'}^{l'} , \, m_{ik}^{l-1} >$	1	0	f	$\mathbf{d}_3$
$< m_{i', \, i'+l'}^{l'} , \, m_{k+1, \, i+l}^{l-1} >$	1	-1	g	$\mathbf{d}_4$

Table 2.2: Data dependencies for the dynamic programming algorithm.

$$
\begin{aligned}
&\text{for } k \leftarrow i \text{ to } i + l - 1 \text{ do} \\
&\quad \text{begin} \\
&\qquad m_{ik}^{l} \leftarrow m_{ik}^{l-1} \\
&\qquad m_{k+1,i+l}^{l} \leftarrow m_{k+1,i+l}^{l-1} \\
&\qquad m_{i,i+l}^{l} \leftarrow \min_k (m_{ik}^{l-1} + m_{k+1,i+l}^{l-1} + r_{i-1} r_k r_{i+l}) \\
&\quad \text{end}
\end{aligned}
$$

The data dependencies derived from the above algorithm are shown in Table 2.2. There are only four possible distinct pairs of generated-used variables.

The data dependence vectors for the first two pairs of generated-used variables are easily derived in the same manner as for the previous examples. The last two dependencies, however, require more attention. Consider, first, the pair $(m_{i',i'+l'}^{l'}, m_{ik}^{l-1})$; it yields that

$$
\begin{aligned}
l - l' &= 1 \\
i - i' &= 0 \\
k &= i' + l'
\end{aligned}
$$

From the program, k' takes values between i' and $i' + l' - 1$. It follows that

$$
k - k' = l - 1, l - 2, \ldots, 1
$$

Similarly, the pair $(m_{i',i'+l'}^{l'}, m_{k+1,i+l}^{l-1})$ yields

$$l - l' = 1$$
$$i' + l' = i + l$$
$$i' = k + 1$$

From the first two equalities it follows that

$$i - i' = -1$$

and finally, since

$$k' = i', \ldots, i' + l' - 1$$

it follows that

$$k - k' = -1, -2, \ldots, -l + 1$$

Therefore, for both $\mathbf{d}_3$ and $\mathbf{d}_4$, $k - k'$ can take many possible values

$$f = l - 1, l - 2, \ldots, 1$$
$$g = -1, -2, \ldots, -l + 1$$

The difference $k - k'$ is not fixed because the order in which the minimization in loop k is performed is not specified. For instance, in the program, if $m_{i,i+l}^l$ is generated when k takes the largest value, then $f = 1$ and $g = -l + 1$. When the minimization procedure in loop k is performed sequentially, then either f or g will depend on the value of l.

Figure 2.20 shows the dependencies between the iteration elements for $n = 6$. Each circle is marked with a number indicating the value of (l, i, k) to which it corresponds. A column corresponds to a single value of l and each group in the column corresponds to a different loop k, in which the order is not yet specified. For example, element 512 receives data from elements 412 and 422, but element 511 receives m_{26}, the result of elements 422, 423, 424, and 425.

From the dependence graph, we can see that this algorithm is symmetric and has considerable parallelism. There are many critical paths. The numbers outside the circles represent possible time instances when iterations may be performed. For now, we can say that the timing was chosen arbitrarily such that the ordering of indices does not violate the

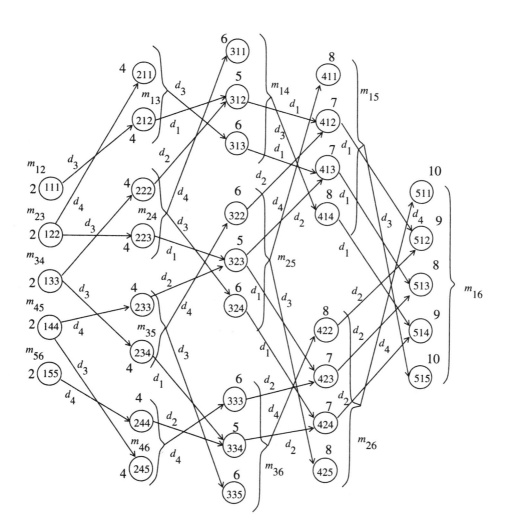

Figure 2.20 Data dependencies for the dynamic programming
algorithm ($n = 6$) [Moldovan 1983b].

ordering imposed by dependencies. Later, in Chapter 3, we will be able to determine this timing with a mathematical formula. A time unit consists of computation of partial results and comparison with two other terms. For example, the operations performed at some timing instances are:

t_8 Compute partial result for index point 513.

t_9 Compute partial result for index points 512 and 514 and take the minimum between these and the one at t_8.

t_{10} Compute partial results for points 511 and 515 and take the minimum between these and the one at t_9.

As can be seen in the data dependence graph, parallel processing time increases linearly with l, thus

$$\text{Time} = O(n)$$

2.3.3 Optimal Binary Search Trees

Binary search is a fast search method used in many applications. Let S be a set of elements $S = \{a_1, a_2, \ldots, a_n\}$ ordered by a relation; for example, numbers ordered by $>$, or names ordered lexicographically. A binary search tree over these elements is a labeled tree in which each vertex is a unique element a_j such that there are at most two branches from each vertex, and for each vertex i to the left of j, $a_i < a_j$, and for each vertex k to the right, $a_j < a_k$. To minimize the search of the tree, the depth of an element is dependent on the probability that there will be a search for that element. The desired element to be placed at each root or vertex of the tree is the element that will give the minimum search cost of the tree leading to the optimal tree. The search cost of a tree is determined by the root element. An element's search cost is a function of the probability that there will be a search for that root element plus the cost of the elements deeper in the tree.

The optimal binary search algorithm is based on applying dynamic programming technique to the costs of subsets of elements. In the algorithm below, p_i is the probability that a search for element a_i occurs and q_i is the probability that a search for $a_i < a < a_{i+1}$ occurs. Thus p_i and q_i are, respectively, successful and unsuccessful probabilities.

The subtree for a subset of elements $(a_{i+1}, a_{i+2}, ..., a_j)$ is denoted as T_{ij}. The subtree T_{ij} has an average cost w_{ij} taken over all successful and unsuccessful searches, plus a cost that depends on its root. The algorithm minimizes the cost c_{ij} of subtree T_{ij} over all possible roots a_k with $i < k \le j$, then applies dynamic programming to these costs. The minimum-cost search tree is constructed recursively based on the minimized values of c_{ij}.

Optimal Binary Search Tree Algorithm [Aho, Hopcroft, and Ullman 1974].

```
begin
        for i = 0 to n do
           begin
                   w_ii ← q_i;
                   c_ii ← 0
           end;
        for l ← 1 to n do
           for i ← 0 to n − l do
              begin
                      j ← i + l;
                      w_ij ← w_{i,j−1} + p_j + q_j;
                      let m be a value of k, i < k ≤ j,
                         for which c_{i,k−1} + c_kj is minimum;
                      c_ij = w_ij + c_{i,m−1} + c_mj;
                      r_ij ← a_m
              end
   end
```

The first loop initializes the cost of each leaf to zero. It also sets the average cost, or weight, of each leaf to the probability of choosing that leaf; this weight represents an element that is not in the tree's original set of elements. The next two cyclic loops equate the weight of the next higher level root or vertex in the tree to the previous weight and to the probability of choosing that root element. Next, the best minimum cost for the root is found. Only the smallest cost is added to the weight, resulting in the search cost of the tree with that root. The minimum cost defines which elements at which vertices would give the optimal binary search tree. Once the root is determined, the next higher level or root in the tree is found. When the program is completed, an optimal binary search tree can be constructed from the given elements.

In order to identify dependencies and to analyze the parallelism, the algorithm is transformed into an equivalent form as shown below. The initialization loop is omitted. The variable j is replaced with its equivalent $i + l$. The values of p and q are brought forward for each iteration of loop k to make those values available for the entire loop. Statement 6 represents the minimum cost as k varies. Each iteration k compares the current cost to the minimum cost found within loop k. The lower of the two costs is forwarded to the next iteration k. Statement 8 retains the value of k that produced the minimum cost. That value of k defines the root element a_k that will create the optimal tree.

Modified Optimal Binary Search Tree Algorithm [Moldovan 1987].

for $l = 1$ to n do
    for $i = 0$ to $n - l$ do
        init b
        for $k = i + 1$ to $i + l$

1:            $p_{i+l}^{k+1} = p_{i+l}^{k}$
2:            $q_{i+l}^{k+1} = q_{i+l}^{k}$
3:            $w_{i,i+l}^{k} = w_{i,i+l-1}^{k} + p_{i+l}^{k} + q_{i+l}^{k}$
4:            $c_{i,k-1}^{l} = c_{i,k-1}^{l-1}$
5:            $c_{k,i+l}^{l} = c_{k,i+l}^{l-1}$
6:            $b_{i,i+l}^{k} = \min(b_{i,i+l}^{k-1};\ (c_{i,k-1}^{l-1} + c_{k,i+l}^{l-1}))$
7:            $c_{i,i+l}^{l} = w_{i,i+l}^{k-1} + b_{i,i+l}^{k}$
8:            if $b_{i,i+l}^{k} \neq b_{i,i+l}^{k-1}$ then $m = k$
9:            $r_{i,i+l} = a_m$
        end k
    end i
  end l

Pairs of generated-used variables	Data dependencies			
	$(l-l')$	$(i-i')$	$(k-k')$	Type
$<p_{i'+l'}^{k'+1},\ p_{i+l}^{k}>$ $<q_{i'+l'}^{k'+1},\ q_{i+l}^{k}>$ $<b_{i',\,i'+l'}^{k'},\ b_{i,\,i+l}^{k-1}>$	0	0	1	$\mathbf{d}_1$
$<w_{i',\,i'+l'}^{k'},\ w_{i,\,i+l-1}^{k}>$ $<c_{i',\,k'-1}^{l'},\ c_{i,\,k-1}^{l-1}>$	1	0	0	$\mathbf{d}_2$
$<c_{i',\,i'+l'}^{l'},\ c_{i,\,k-1}^{l-1}>$	1	0	f	$\mathbf{d}_3$
$<c_{i',\,i'+l'}^{l'},\ c_{k,\,i+l}^{l-1}>$	1	-1	g	$\mathbf{d}_4$
$<c_{k',\,i'+l'}^{l'},\ c_{k,\,i+l}^{l-1}>$	1	-1	0	$\mathbf{d}_5$

Table 2.3: Dependencies for optimal binary search tree.

The dependencies derived from the algorithm are shown in Table 2.3. The first dependence $\mathbf{d}_1$ was introduced when the algorithm was transformed; thus it can be modified if necessary. The last four dependencies are inherent in the algorithm and must be dealt with. Dependencies $\mathbf{d}_3$ and $\mathbf{d}_4$ vary as a function of k. They are derived below. By equating the indices of generated and used variables we have

$$l - 1 = l' \quad \text{or} \quad l - l' = 1$$
$$i = i' \quad \text{or} \quad i - i' = 0$$
$$k - 1 = i' + l \quad \text{or} \quad k = l' + i' + 1$$

Since k' varies from $i' + 1$ to $i' + l'$, it follows that

$$k - k' = f \quad \text{where} \quad f = (l - 1, l - 2, ..., 1)$$

For dependence $\mathbf{d}_4$,

$$l - 1 = l' \quad \text{or} \quad l - l' = 1$$
$$i + l = i' + l' \quad \text{or} \quad i - i' = -(l - l') = -1$$
$$k = i'$$

and again, since k' varies from $i' + 1$ to $i' + l'$,

$$k - k' = g \quad \text{where} \quad g = (-1, -2, \ldots, 1 - l)$$

They are written as:

$$\mathbf{D} = [\mathbf{d}_1 \ \mathbf{d}_2 \ \mathbf{d}_3 \ \mathbf{d}_4 \ \mathbf{d}_5] = \begin{bmatrix} 0 & 1 & 1 & 1 & 1 \\ 0 & 0 & -1 & 0 & -1 \\ 1 & 0 & g & f & 0 \end{bmatrix} \begin{matrix} l \\ i \\ k \end{matrix}$$

A data dependence graph is shown in Figure 2.21. Notice the similarity to the data dependence graph for the dynamic programming algorithm shown in Figure 2.20. Ignore for a moment dependence $\mathbf{d}_1$. A timing order, marked by numbers near the index points, is selected such that the ordering imposed by $\mathbf{d}_2$, $\mathbf{d}_3$, $\mathbf{d}_4$, and $\mathbf{d}_5$ is not violated. It can be seen that the groups representing the search-cost calculations can be processed in parallel over all i iterations. The major dependencies are between the l loops. However, within the cost calculations for the group, there are dependencies $\mathbf{d}_1$ between k iterations. The time ordering shown in Figure 2.21 violates dependence $\mathbf{d}_1$.

Next we explain how this time ordering can be maintained and how dependence $\mathbf{d}_1$ can be transformed. Recall that we introduced $\mathbf{d}_1$ in statements 1, 2, and 6 when a certain movement of variables p, q, and b was determined along index k. In fact, the entire loop k was introduced and it was specified that the ordering of k would be from $i + 1$ to $i + l$. This does not necessarily have to be so. Now that we realize that the induced dependence $\mathbf{d}_1$ tends to slow down the parallel algorithm, we look for a better ordering of k iterations. Such an ordering causes each k loop to execute from the center toward the extremes, as indicated in the figure. This new ordering of k is acceptable because it produces the same results as the original algorithm. Meanwhile, the new ordering

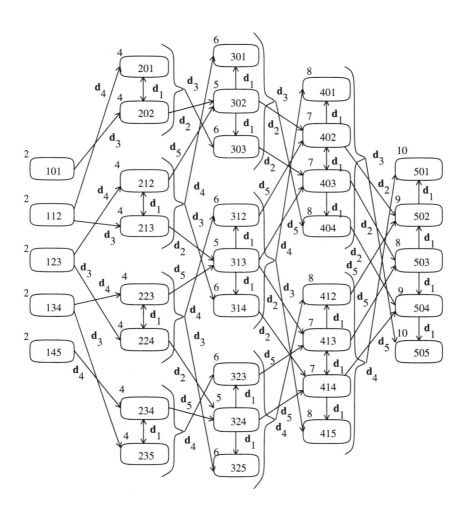

Figure 2.21 Data dependence graph for optimal binary search tree algorithm ($n = 4$) [Moldovan 1987].

changes dependence $\mathbf{d}_1$ from $(0, 0, 1)$ into two dependencies: $(0, 0, 1)^T$ from the center down, and $(0, 0, -1)^T$ from the center up.

This is an example of an algorithm in which examination of the dependence graph reveals an induced dependence that increases the parallel time unnecessarily. In such cases, one can go back and reexamine the original algorithm or formula and find ways to change that dependence.

Because of its symmetry, this algorithm has several equally long critical paths. If the computations are followed along a critical path, the result is that the parallel processing time of this algorithm is $O(n)$.

2.3.4 Subgraph Isomorphism

Consider two graphs $G_a = (V_a, E_a)$ and $G_b = (V_b, E_b)$ where for each graph V denotes the set of vertices (or points) and E denotes the set of edges (or lines). The adjacent matrices for the two graphs are, respectively, $\mathbf{A} = [a_{ij}]$ and $\mathbf{B} = [b_{ij}]$. Two graphs G_a and G_b are said to be *isomorphic* to each other if there exists a 1:1 correspondence between the points of G_a and G_b that preserves adjacency. This definition implies that the two graphs have the same number of points and the same number of lines. If the numbers of points in the two graphs are not the same, it may be that the smaller graph is isomorphic to a part of the larger graph. This is the problem of *subgraph isomorphism*; it is more general, and includes the graph isomorphism as a particular case. Here, we will assume that G_a is the smaller graph (i.e., $n_a \leq n_b$, where n is the number of nodes).

Many possible algorithms for subgraph isomorphism can be devised. One approach is to verify whether adjacent matrix $\mathbf{A}$ can be made identical to a submatrix of the larger adjacent matrix $\mathbf{B}$ by permuting the rows and columns of $\mathbf{B}$. The complexity of this operation is $O(n_b!)$. Algorithms with such exponential complexity are inefficient. An acceptable algorithm for subgraph isomorphism should be $O(n_b^k)$.

The algorithm for subgraph isomorphism is based on manipulations of adjacent matrices. Performing the permutations of rows and columns of one adjacent matrix is equivalent to a tree search. Let us first formulate the mathematical condition for isomorphism and then examine a refinement that will improve on the brute-force method.

Define an $n_a \times n_b$ permutation matrix $\mathbf{M}^* = [m_{ij}]$ whose elements are 1's and 0's. This boolean matrix is such that each row contains one 1 and no column contains more than one 1. Define a new matrix $\mathbf{C} = [c_{ij}]$ that is obtained by permuting the rows and columns of $\mathbf{B}$. If it is true that

$$(\forall i \forall j)(a_{ij} = 1) \Rightarrow (c_{ij} = 1) \qquad (2.1)$$

for $1 \leq i \leq n_a$ and $1 \leq j \leq n_a$, then $\mathbf{M}^*$ specifies an isomorphism between G_a and a subgraph of G_b. In matrix form,

$$\mathbf{C} = \mathbf{M}^*(\mathbf{M}^*\mathbf{B})^T \qquad (2.2)$$

Thus the isomorphism problem is to identify all possible permutation matrices $\mathbf{M}^*$ that will lead to $\mathbf{A} = \mathbf{C}$. The brute-force solution to this problem is to perform a tree search on an initial matrix $\mathbf{M}^0 = [m_{ij}]$ that contains all existing isomorphisms, if any. Such an $\mathbf{M}^0$ can be constructed as follows:

$$m_{ij}^0 = \begin{cases} 1 & \text{if the number of vertices of the } j\text{th point} \\ & \text{in } G_b \text{ is greater than or equal} \\ & \text{to the degree of the } i\text{th point} \\ & \text{in } G_a \\ 0 & \text{otherwise} \end{cases}$$

Subgraph Isomorphism with Refinement

J. R. Ullmann [Ullmann 1976] has studied subgraph isomorphism and has proposed a refinement procedure for the tree-search method that significantly reduces the computation time. This refinement procedure tests the following *necessary condition*: if node i in graph G_a corresponds through an isomorphism to node j in graph G_b, then all nodes in G_a adjacent to i must have corresponding nodes in graph G_b that are adjacent to j. This observation translates into the following mathematical condition:

$$(\forall x)((a_{ix} = 1) \quad \Rightarrow \quad (\exists y)(m_{xy} \cdot b_{yj} = 1)) \qquad (2.3)$$
$$\text{for} \qquad 1 \leq x \leq n_a$$
$$1 \leq y \leq n_b$$

The computational power introduced by this condition resides in the fact that for any $m_{ij} = 1$ in matrix $\mathbf{M}$ for which this condition is not satisfied, $m_{ij} = 1$ is changed to $m_{ij} = 0$. It is convenient to define a boolean matrix $\mathbf{R} = [r_{xj}]$ as

$$r_{xj} = (\exists y)(m_{xy} \cdot b_{yj}) \tag{2.4}$$

Equation (2.4) is a logical implication of the form $P \rightarrow Q$. This means that P implies Q, or Q is implied by P, or if P is true then Q is true. The truth table for the implication statement is

P	Q	$P \rightarrow Q$
F	F	T
F	T	T
T	F	F
T	T	T

(where T means *true* and F means *false*). From the truth table we see that $P \rightarrow Q$ is equivalent to $\bar{P} \vee Q$. Thus condition 2.3 can now be written as

$$m_{ij} = m_{ij} \cdot (\forall x)(\bar{a}_{ix} \vee r_{xj}) \tag{2.5}$$

which can be manipulated to yield

$$m_{ij} = m_{ij} \cdot (\forall x)(\overline{a_{ix} \cdot \bar{r}_{xj}}) \tag{2.6}$$

These equations can now be written compactly as boolean matrix equations:

$$\begin{aligned} \mathbf{R}_i &= \mathbf{M}_i \times \mathbf{B} \\ \mathbf{S}_i &= \mathbf{A} \times \bar{\mathbf{R}}_i \\ \mathbf{M}_{i+1} &= \mathbf{M}_i \cdot \bar{\mathbf{S}}_i \end{aligned} \tag{2.7}$$

where $\times$ indicates the boolean product and $\cdot$ indicates logical AND.

These equations contain a high degree of parallelism because it is possible to test the necessary condition at all nodes simultaneously. The algorithm uses the equations above in an iterative manner; $\mathbf{M}_i$ is simplified to $\mathbf{M}_{i+1}$ during iteration i. Notice that $\mathbf{M}_{i+1}$ does not have more 1's than $\mathbf{M}_i$; it can only have fewer 1's or be identical to $\mathbf{M}_i$.

The subgraph isomophism presented here is summarized in the flow chart in Figure 2.22. The algorithm starts by inputting adjacency matrices $\mathbf{A}$ and $\mathbf{B}$. It follows the creation of $\mathbf{M}^0$, the initial boolean matrix from which all isomorphisms are generated. $\mathbf{M}^0$ and all subsequent matrices generated from $\mathbf{M}^0$ may be pushed into a last-in-first-out (LIFO) stack. The refinement procedure is applied to the matrix pulled out of the stack.

As a result of the refinement procedure, only one of the following possibilities exists:

1. $\mathbf{M}_{i+1}$ has fewer 1's than $\mathbf{M}_i$, but $\mathbf{M}_{i+1}$ is not yet an isomorphism. In this case, repeat the refinement procedure:

$$\mathbf{M}_i \leftarrow \mathbf{M}_{i+1}$$

2. $\mathbf{M}_{i+1} = \mathbf{M}_i$ (i.e., no change made). In this case, split $\mathbf{M}_{i+1}$ into $\mathbf{M}'_{i+1}$ and $\mathbf{M}''_{i+1}$ such that $\mathbf{M}'_{i+1}$ has one more row with only one 1 than does $\mathbf{M}_{i+1}$:

$$\mathbf{M}_{i+1} = \mathbf{M}'_{i+1} + \mathbf{M}''_{i+1} \qquad (+ \text{ indicates the logical OR})$$
$$\mathbf{M}_{i+1} \leftarrow \mathbf{M}'_{i+1}$$
$$\text{LIFO} \leftarrow \mathbf{M}''_{i+1}$$

3. $\mathbf{M}_{i+1}$ has a row of zeroes or two or more identical rows with only one 1. In this case, fetch a new matrix from the LIFO:

$$\mathbf{M}_{i+1} \leftarrow \text{LIFO}$$

4. $\mathbf{M}_{i+1}$ is an isomorphism. In this case, send $\mathbf{M}_{i+1}$ to output because it is an isomorphism:

$$\text{Output} \leftarrow \mathbf{M}_{i+1}$$

The algorithm consists of a sequence of computations, tests, and actions. The computations refer to the refinement procedure in the equations above. These equations are highly parallel. The tests are as follows: test $\mathbf{M}_{i+1}$ if at least one row has 0's, test if there are two identical rows having only one 1 and the rest 0's, test if $\mathbf{M}_{i+1} \neq \mathbf{M}_i$, and test if $\mathbf{M}_{i+1}$ is an isomorphism.

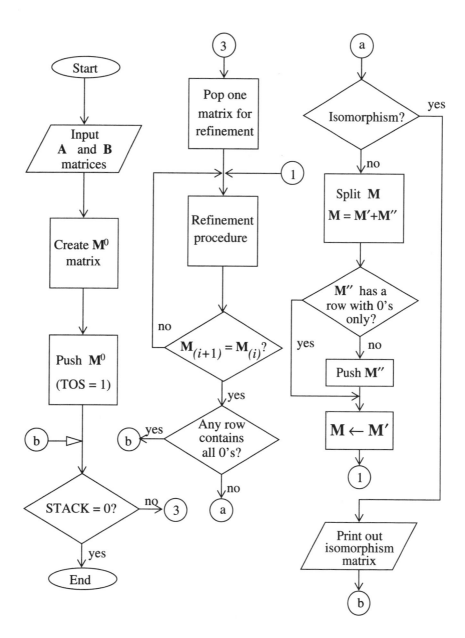

Figure 2.22 Flow chart for subgraph isomorphism.

Example 2.5. Consider two graphs G_a and G_b whose adjacency matrices $\mathbf{A}$ and $\mathbf{B}$ are as shown in Figure 2.23. For these graphs, an initial matrix $\mathbf{M}^0$ can be constructed as indicated above.

$$
\mathbf{M}^0 = \begin{array}{c|cccc}
 & 1 & 2 & 3 & 4 \\
\hline
1 & 1 & 1 & 0 & 0 \\
2 & 1 & 1 & 1 & 1 \\
3 & 1 & 1 & 0 & 0 \\
4 & 1 & 1 & 1 & 1
\end{array}
$$

In Figure 2.24, the search tree that normally results for two fourth-order graphs is shown. The refinement procedure systematically eliminates those branches which do not lead to any isomorphism. The algorithm first splits $\mathbf{M}^0$ into $\mathbf{M}_1$ and $\mathbf{M}_2$:

$$
\mathbf{M}^0 = \begin{bmatrix}
1 & 1 & 0 & 0 \\
1 & 1 & 1 & 1 \\
1 & 1 & 0 & 0 \\
1 & 1 & 1 & 1
\end{bmatrix}
$$

$$
\mathbf{M}_1 = \begin{bmatrix}
1 & 0 & 0 & 0 \\
1 & 1 & 1 & 1 \\
1 & 1 & 0 & 0 \\
1 & 1 & 1 & 1
\end{bmatrix}
\qquad
\mathbf{M}_2 = \begin{bmatrix}
0 & 1 & 0 & 0 \\
1 & 1 & 1 & 1 \\
1 & 1 & 0 & 0 \\
1 & 1 & 1 & 1
\end{bmatrix}
$$

$\mathbf{M}_2$ is stored in LIFO, and the refinement procedure is applied to $\mathbf{M}_1$. After the refinement procedure, $\mathbf{M}_1$ is changed to

$$
\mathbf{M}_1' = \begin{bmatrix}
1 & 0 & 0 & 0 \\
0 & 1 & 1 & 1 \\
0 & 1 & 0 & 0 \\
0 & 1 & 1 & 1
\end{bmatrix}
$$

Then $\mathbf{M}_1'$ is split into $\mathbf{M}_{12}$ and $\mathbf{M}_{12}'$.

$$
\mathbf{M}_{12} = \begin{bmatrix}
1 & 0 & 0 & 0 \\
0 & 1 & 0 & 0 \\
0 & 1 & 0 & 0 \\
0 & 1 & 1 & 1
\end{bmatrix}
\qquad
\mathbf{M}_{12}' = \begin{bmatrix}
1 & 0 & 0 & 0 \\
0 & 0 & 1 & 1 \\
0 & 1 & 0 & 0 \\
0 & 1 & 1 & 1
\end{bmatrix}
$$

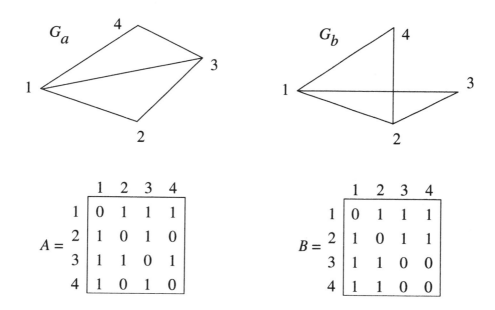

Figure 2.23 Two isomorphic graphs.

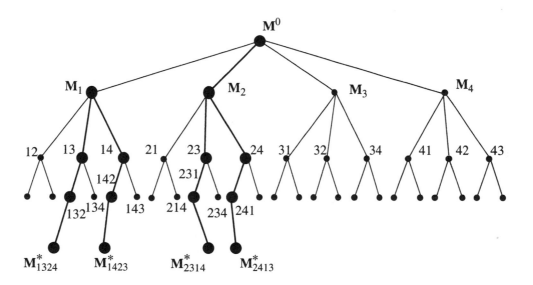

Figure 2.24 Tree search for Example 2.5.

G_a	G_b	G_b	G_b	G_b
1	1	1	2	2
2	3	4	4	3
3	2	2	1	1
4	4	3	3	4

Number of pushes/pops: 4

Number of refinements: 10

Figure 2.25 Isomorphisms for the graphs in Figure 2.24.

The refinement procedure is applied to M_{12}, while M'_{12} is stored. It is found that M_{12} does not lead to any isomorphism, and then M'_{12} is fetched from the LIFO. The process continues, and eventually it is found that four isomorphisms exist for these two graphs. The paths from M^0 to these isomorphisms are marked with heavy lines in Figure 2.24. The isomorphisms found are shown in Figure 2.25. The algorithm presented in this section has a fast rate of convergence because the refinement procedure reduces the tree search. Moreover, the refinement procedure, consisting of boolean matrix operations, is highly parallel and can be implemented with simple gates. Another advantage of this algorithm is its reduced storage requirement. Subgraph isomorphism is used in other graph operations, including *clique detection* (a clique is a maximal complete subgraph), directed graphs, and others.

2.3.5   Parallel Sorting

Sorting is the process of ordering a set of values in ascending or descending order. Sorting is one of the most important operations performed in computers today, because it is used in compilers, editors, memory management, and so on. Algorithms for sorting may be classified under internal sorting or external sorting. Sorting done in main memory is called *internal sorting*. Sorting of large files of data records, stored in mass storage devices, is done outside of main memory, and is therefore called *external sorting.* In this section, we discuss internal sorting only.

Many results are available for serial sorting, as well as for parallel sorting. The optimal algorithm for sorting n elements requires $O(n \log n)$ comparisons. This is the best sequential time. The optimal speedup would be achieved by a parallel algorithm, using n processors, that sorts n elements in $O(\log n)$ time. Several algorithms are known to achieve this optimal parallel time, but often the number of processors used is larger than n.

Some of the first fast algorithms for parallel sorting were designed using *network sorting,* in which a network of processors performs comparisons and exchanges in parallel. Some networks that sort n elements in $O(\log^2 n)$ comparison exchanges are presented in this section.

A powerful method of sorting is the use of *shared-memory* models. Several such algorithms exist that can sort n elements in $O(\log n)$ time. These algorithms generally use enumeration to compute the rank of each element, then route the element to the location specified by its rank. The shared-memory sorting algorithms differ in the ways they handle read and write conflicts.

In the two models discussed above, the number of processors is at least $O(n)$. Often it becomes necessary to sort a very large number of elements, for which the number of processors is insufficient. To handle such situations, block-sorting algorithms have been developed which, by selecting the size of the block, can use an arbitrarily small number of processors.

Odd-Even Sorting.

A network for odd-even sorting is illustrated in Figure 2.26. The first stage has $n/2$ comparators. Each comparator sorts two numbers. The numbers at the end of the first stage are grouped in ordered pairs. The second stage consists of $n/4$ boxes, each box sorting four numbers. Each box is implemented with two levels of two input comparators. The iterative process continues until the current stage contains only one box; thus, the outputs are sorted.

The name *odd-even* comes from the interconnections between stages. The inputs to each box in stage $i+1$ combine two sorted sequences from two modules in stage i. The connections are such that the respective *odd* outputs of each sequence become the inputs of the same comparator,

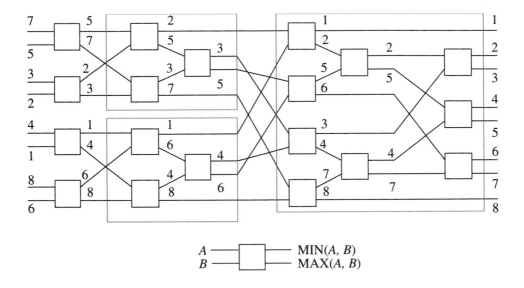

Figure 2.26 Odd-even network sorting.

and the respective *even* outputs from each sequence are combined as inputs of the same comparator. This network has $\log n$ stages; each stage has one more level of comparators than the previous one. The total time is equivalent to the number of levels of comparators; that is,

$$1 + 2 + \ldots + \log n = \log n (\log n + 1)/2$$

Thus the time is $O(\log^2 n)$.

The total number of comparators is the number of levels $O(\log^2 n)$ times the number of comparators per level $O(n)$; thus, a total of $O(n \log^2 n)$.

Bitonic Sorting

Bitonic sorting is similar in performance to odd-even network sorting. An example is shown in Figure 2.27. For bitonic sorting, a different iterative rule is used. A bitonic sequence is obtained by concatenating two monotonic sequences, one ascending and one descending. For example, the sequences (5, 7, 3, 2) and (5, 3, 2, 7) are bitonic, but (5, 3, 7, 2) is not. Bitonic sorting is based on performing comparison-exchange operations on bitonic sequences. In Figure 2.27, the first stage of comparators provides two bitonic sequences of four elements each. In the second stage, these two sequences are combined into one bitonic sequence, and in the third stage a single monotonic sequence is formed. This sorting procedure works because of the following property: A bitonic sequence of n elements can be split by comparison exchanges into two bitonic sequences half its length, such that the first sequence contains the $n/2$ lower elements of the original sequence and the second sequence contains the $n/2$ higher elements. Then it becomes possible to form a monotonic sequence of n elements by merging two such bitonic sequences. This idea can be seen in the second stage of Figure 2.27.

Bitonic sorts can be implemented with multistage networks and recirculating networks (see Problem 4.5.A).

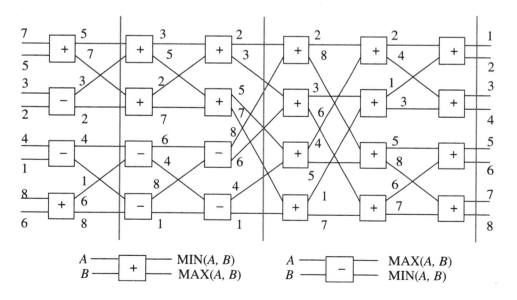

Figure 2.27 Bitonic sorting network.

2.4   BIBLIOGRAPHICAL NOTES AND FURTHER READING

The section on data and control dependencies is based on the work done in the 1970s at the University of Illinois: [Kuck, Muraoka, and Chen 1972], [Towle 1976], and others. Some of the early work on parallelism analysis in algorithms started with parallelism in arithmetic expressions: [Brent 1973] and [Kuck and Maruyama 1975]. Parallelism in resolving systems of equations was studied in [Sameh 1971], [Sameh and Brent 1977], and [Kuck and Sameh 1971]. Parallelism in QR algorithms and eigenvalue problems was studied in [Sameh and Kuck 1977]. The analysis of parallelism in relaxation problems was done in [Lamport 1974]. Parallelism analysis in recurrence relations was studied in [Chen and Kuck 1975] and others. The parallel algorithm for recurrence relations is from [Gajski 1981].

[Kung 1979] considered the parallelism for dynamic programming and other problems and proposed VLSI structures. The parallelism analysis for dynamic programming is from [Moldovan 1983b]. The parallelism in optimal binary search tree is from [Moldovan 1987].

The highly parallel algorithm for subgraph isomorphism was first formulated in [Ullmann 1976]. The example is taken from [Moldovan and Nudd 1984].

Much work has been done in parallel sorting. Some of the early results are in [Batcher 1968], [Stone 1971], [Knuth 1973], [Muller and Preparata 1976], [Preparata 1978], and others. The material in the last section follows the tutorial presented in [Bitton, DeWitt, Hsiao, and Menon 1984].

Some excellent presentations of parallel algorithms are the recent books by Leighton [Leighton 1992] and JaJa [JaJa 1992]. For futher reading on parallelism in differential equations see [Franklin 1978], and for parallel graph algorithms see [Quinn and Deo 1984].

2.5 PROBLEMS

2.1.A. (Product of Polynomials.) Consider two polynomials

$$P(x) = a_{n-1}x^{n-1} + a_{n-2}x^{n-2} + \cdots + a_1 x + a_0$$

$$Q(x) = b_{n-1}x^{n-1} + b_{n-2}x^{n-2} + \cdots + b_1 x + b_0$$

(a) Write a sequential algorithm to perform the product $P(x)Q(x)$.

(b) Analyze parallelism in the sequential algorithm developed in *(a)*.

(c) Construct a parallel algorithm for the product of polynomials directly from the problem definition and compare the speed of this algorithm with the results in *(b)*. What is the lower-bound complexity for the product of polynomials and how far are your results from it? Why?

Solution.
   (a) One can rewrite $P(x)$ in another form to facilitate serial program execution:

$$P(x) = ((a_{n-1}x + a_{n-2})x + \ldots + a_1)x + a_o$$

A serial program to calculate the product might be:

$P_0 = a_{n-1}$
$Q_0 = b_{n-1}$
for $i := n - 2$ down to 0 do
begin
$\qquad P_{n-1-i} = P_{n-2-i}x + a_i$
$\qquad Q_{n-1-i} = Q_{n-2-i}x + b_i$
end;
Product $= P_{n-1} * Q_{n-1}$

The time complexity for this serial program is $O(n)$.
   (b) The data dependence matrix $\mathbf{D}$ for the above serial program is:

$$\mathbf{D} = \begin{bmatrix} 1 & 1 \\ P & Q \end{bmatrix}$$

The dependence matrix $\mathbf{D}$ indicates that there is no dependence between calculations of $P(x)$ and $Q(x)$, which means that $P(x)$ and $Q(x)$ can be done in parallel. Within the calculation for $P(x)$ and $Q(x)$, a dependence vector equal to 1 exists; this means that only serial operations are possible for this algorithm. Thus, if we want to increase parallelism we have to change the algorithm.

(c) Let us start from the problem definition and find out what needs to be done to calculate the product $P(x)Q(x)$. To calculate $P(x)$ one needs:

    (i) $x^{n-1}, x^{n-2}, \ldots, x, x^0$

    (ii) $a_i x^i$ for $0 \leq i \leq n-1$

    (iii) $P(x) = \sum_{i=0}^{n-1} a_i x^i$

The time to calculate x^i, $i \leq n$, is $t = \log n$. Given n PEs, $a_i x^i$, $0 \leq i \leq n-1$, multiplication takes one time unit. The summation

$$P(x) = \sum_{i=0}^{n-1} a_i x^i$$

takes only $\log n$ steps.

It follows that the total time to calculate the product is $O(\log n)$, which is also the lower bound.

2.2.A. The problem given below represents a convolution algorithm frequently used in digital signal processing.

```
for k = 1, m
    for i = 1, n
        x^{k+1}(k + i − 1) = x^k(k + i − 1)
        w^{k+1}(i) = w^k(i)
        y^{i+1}(k) = y^i(k) + w^k(i)x^k(k + i − 1)
    end i
end k
```

Find the data dependence matrix. Indicate which vector corresponds to which variable.

Solution.

$$\mathbf{D} = \begin{bmatrix} 1 & 1 & 0 \\ -1 & 0 & 1 \end{bmatrix} \begin{matrix} k \\ i \end{matrix}$$
$$\phantom{\mathbf{D} = }\; x \;\; w \;\; y$$

2.3.A. Generalization of dependence vectors.

```
do I = l, u
S₁: A(c * I + j)= ...
S₂:    ...     = A(d * I + k)
end do
```

where c, d, j, and k are integers.
   Under what condition is there a data dependence in the loop above?

Solution. A dependence exists whenever

$$c * x + j = d * y + k$$

Thus, the condition for the existence of dependence is:
the greatest common divisor of c and d, $gcd(c, d)$, must divide $k - j$.

2.4.A. Consider the following algorithm:

```
for i = 1 to 9
   for j = 2 to 20
      for k = 5 to 9
         s₁: a(i, j, k) = a(i − 1, j + 1, k) + b(i, j, k)c(i, j, k − 1)
         s₂: b(i + 2, j + 1, k + 2) = a(i − 1, j + 3, k)c(i, j, k)
         s₃: c(i + 1, j, k − 3) = c(i, j + 1, k) + a(i, j, k − 2)c(i − 1, j, k)
      end k
   end j
end i
```

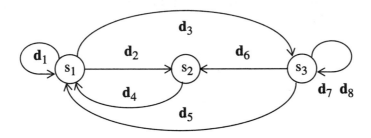

Figure 2.28 Dependence graph for Problem 2.4.A.

(a) For each pair of used and generated variables find the data dependence vectors.

(b) Draw the dependence graph between statements s_1, s_2, and s_3. Are there any antidependencies or output dependencies? Explain.

Solution.

  (a)

$$\mathbf{D} = \begin{array}{c} \begin{array}{cccccccc} \mathbf{d}_1 & \mathbf{d}_2 & \mathbf{d}_3 & \mathbf{d}_4 & \mathbf{d}_5 & \mathbf{d}_6 & \mathbf{d}_7 & \mathbf{d}_8 \end{array} \\ \left[\begin{array}{cccccccc} 1 & 1 & 0 & 2 & 1 & 1 & 1 & 2 \\ -1 & -3 & 0 & 1 & 0 & 0 & -1 & 0 \\ 0 & 0 & 2 & 2 & -2 & -3 & -3 & -3 \end{array} \right] \\ \begin{array}{cccccccc} a & a & a & b & c & c & c & c \end{array} \end{array}$$

(b) The dependence graph is shown in Figure 2.28. There are no antidependencies; there are no output dependencies. The generated variables are unique for one iteration.

2.5.A. (The Cholesky Algorithm [O'Leary and Stewart 1985].) The Cholesky algorithm is used for factoring a symmetric positive matrix $\mathbf{A}$ of order n into the product $\mathbf{LL}^T$ of the lower triangular matrix and its transpose. The following overwrites the lower half of $\mathbf{A}$ with $\mathbf{L}$ and the upper half with $\mathbf{L}^T$:

```
        for k := 1 to n loop
sqrt:       a[k, k] := sqrt(a[k, k]);
```

```
           for i := k + 1 to n loop
cdiv:          a[i, k] := a[i, k]/a[k, k];
           end loop;
           for j := k + 1 to n loop
rdiv :         a[k, j] := a[k, j]/a[k, k];
           end loop;
           for i := k + 1 to n loop
               for j := k + 1 to n loop
elim:              a[i, j] := a[i, j] − a[i, k] * a[k, j];
               end loop;
           end loop;
       end loop;
```

Analyze the parallelism and compute the parallel time.

Solution. The algorithm can be rewritten as follows:

for $k := 1$ to n loop
    $i \leftarrow k$;
    $j \leftarrow k$;
$S1$: $a_{ij}^k := \text{sqrt}(a_{ij}^{k-1})$;
    for $i := k + 1$ to n loop
       $j \leftarrow k$;
$S2$: $a_{ij}^k := a_{ij}^{k-1}/a_{jj}^k$;
    end loop;
    for $j := k + 1$ to n loop
       $i \leftarrow k$;
$S3$: $a_{ij}^k := a_{ij}^{k-1}/a_{ii}^k$
    end loop;
    for $i := k + 1$ to n loop
       for $j := k + 1$ to n loop
$S4$: $a_{ij}^k := a_{ij}^{k-1} - a_{ik}^k \times a_{kj}^k$;
       end loop;
    end loop;
end loop;

The dependencies for this algorithm are:

$S1, S2, S3, S4 : \ <a_{ij}^k, a_{ij}^{k-1}>$
$$\mathbf{d}_1 = (1, 0, 0)^t$$

$S2 :$
$$<a_{ij}^k, a_{jj}^k>$$
$$i = k + 1 \text{ to } n$$
$$j = k$$
$$\mathbf{d}_2 = (0, f, 0)^t \text{ where } f = 1 \text{ to } n - k$$

$S3 :$
$$<a_{ij}^k, a_{ii}^k>$$
$$j = \ k + 1 \text{ to } n$$
$$i = k$$
$$\mathbf{d}_3 = (0, 0, g)^t \ \text{ where } g = 1 \text{ to } n - k$$

$S4 :$
$$<a_{ij}^k, a_{kj}^k>$$
$$i = \ k + 1 \text{ to } n$$
$$k = k$$
$$\mathbf{d}_2 = (0, f, 0)^t$$

$S4 :$
$$<a_{ij}^k, a_{ik}^k>$$
$$j = \ k + 1 \text{ to } n$$
$$k = k$$
$$\mathbf{d}_3 = (0, 0, g)^t$$

$$\mathbf{D} = \begin{bmatrix} 1 & 0 & 0 \\ 0 & f & 0 \\ 0 & 0 & g \end{bmatrix}$$

As can be seen from Figure 2.29, for each k iteration, three time units are required, except for the last one, for which only one time unit is needed. Thus, the total parallel computation time is $3(n - 1) + 1$.

2.6.A. [Prasanna 1991] Show how to compute the maximum of n numbers on an EREW PRAM using p processors in $O(n/p + \log p)$ time. Assume that $n = 2^k$, with k an integer and $1 \le p \le n$.

Solution. Assume we have n PEs; use the shared memory to simulate the computations of a complete binary tree on n leaf nodes. This can

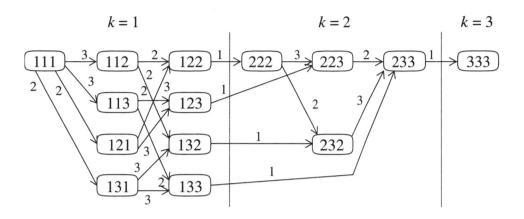

Figure 2.29 Dependencies for the Cholesky algorithm.

be done in $O(\log p)$ time. If $p < n$, then divide the input into p disjoint sets whose size is at most n/p. Use a serial algorithm to compute the maximum of each set in $O(n/p)$ time. This can be done in parallel for each of the sets. We now have p outcomes, the maximum of which can be computed in $O(\log p)$ time using the binary tree simulation in the case in which $p = n$.

2.7.A. Show how to compute the maximum of n numbers on a CRCW PRAM using n^2 PEs in $O(1)$ time. Assume a concurrent write model in which if more than one PE writes to a memory location during a clock cycle, one of these values is arbitrarily written into it. Assume that $n = 2^k$, with k an integer.

Solution. Construct an $n \times n$ array $\mathbf{A}$ such that $\mathbf{A}(i, j) = 1$ if input $x_i \geq$ input x_j, $1 \leq i$, $j \leq n$. Using n^2 PEs, this array can be built in $O(1)$ time. Note that x_i is the maximum if $\mathbf{A}(i, j) = 1$, $1 \leq j \leq n$. Using n PEs, this condition can be checked for x_i in $O(1)$ time.

2.1.B.

$$f(x) = \frac{x^2 - 3x + 2}{x(x - 3)(x - 4)}$$

(a) How many time steps and processors are required to evaluate this expression?

(b) Is it possible to find an equivalent form for $f(x)$ that could be processed faster than your answer to *(a)*?

2.2.B. Show the dependence graph for the following program:

$A = B + 1$
if $A < 5$ then $C = A + 1$; go to S_5
$\quad$ else $D = A + 1$; go to S_6
end if
$S_5 : E = A + 1$
$S_6 : F = A + 1$

2.3.B. Draw the dependence graph for the following program:

$\quad$ do S_3 $i_1 = 1, 10$
$\quad$ do S_3 $i_2 = 1, 10$
S_1: if $i_1 > i_2$ then $(S_2$:) $a(i_1, i_2) \leftarrow a(i_1 - 1, i_2 - 2) + a(i_1 - 3, i_2 - 4)$
S_3: if $i_1 < i_2$ then $(S_4$:) $b(i_1, i_2) \leftarrow b(i_1 - 1, i_2) + b(i_1, i_2 - 1)$
S_5: if $i_1 = i_2$ then $(S_6$:) if $\mod(i_1, 2) = 0$ then
$\quad\quad (S_7$:) $c(i_1, i_2) \leftarrow c(i_1 - 1, i_2 - 1)$

2.4.B. Consider the following two programs:

(a) for $I := 1$ step 1 until N do
$\quad$ begin
$\quad$ $A(I) := B(I) + A(I - 1)$;
$\quad$ $B(I + 1) := C(I)$
$\quad$ end
(b) for $I := 1$ step 1 until N do
$\quad$ for $J := 1$ step 1 until N do
$\quad$ $A(I, J) = A(I - 1, J) + A(I, J - 1)$
$\quad$ end

Analyze the parallelism in these programs. What is the minimum computation time in each case? How many processors are needed to achieve this in each case?

2.5.B. Are there any dependencies in the following program?

for $i = 1, n$
S1: $a(6i + 3) = 2 * a(4i + 6)$
S2: $b(8i + 1) = a(2i + 7)$
end i

Indicate how to test for their existence. If they do exist, express them.

2.6.B. (Computation of costs between vertices [Aho, Hopcroft and Ullmann 1974].)

For a given directed graph $G = (V, E)$, where $V = v_1, v_2, \ldots, v_n$, and a labeling function l, an algorithm to compute the cost $c(v_i, v_j)$, which is equal to the sum over all paths v_i to v_j for all i and j between 1 to n, is given below:

```
        begin
1.          for i ← 1 until n do C⁰ᵢᵢ ← 1 + l(vᵢ, vᵢ);
2.          for 1 ≤ i, j ≤ n and i ≠ j do C⁰ᵢⱼ ← l(vᵢ, vⱼ);
3.          for k ← 1 until n do
4.            for 1 ≤ i, j ≤ n do
5.                Cᵏᵢⱼ ← Cᵏ⁻¹ᵢⱼ + Cᵏ⁻¹ᵢⱼ · (Cᵏ⁻¹ₖₖ)*· Cᵏ⁻¹ₖⱼ;
6.            for 1 ≤ i, j ≤ n do c(vᵢ, vⱼ) ← Cⁿᵢⱼ
        end
```

For this algorithm:
    (a) Find the data dependence matrix.
    (b) Find the parallel execution time.

2.7.B. (Parallelism in Strassen's Matrix Multiplication Algorithm [Kronsjo 1979].)

Strassen suggested an algorithm for computing the product of two square matrices $\mathbf{A}$ and $\mathbf{B}$ of order n in $O(n^{\log 7})$ arithmetic operations.

$$\mathbf{A} = \begin{bmatrix} \mathbf{A}_{11} & \mathbf{A}_{12} \\ \mathbf{A}_{21} & \mathbf{A}_{22} \end{bmatrix}; \mathbf{B} = \begin{bmatrix} \mathbf{B}_{11} & \mathbf{B}_{12} \\ \mathbf{B}_{21} & \mathbf{B}_{22} \end{bmatrix}; \mathbf{C} = \begin{bmatrix} \mathbf{C}_{11} & \mathbf{C}_{12} \\ \mathbf{C}_{21} & \mathbf{C}_{22} \end{bmatrix}$$

The algorithm is:

Compute

$$
\begin{aligned}
\mathbf{Q}_1 &= (\mathbf{A}_{11} + \mathbf{A}_{22})(\mathbf{B}_{11} + \mathbf{B}_{22}) \\
\mathbf{Q}_2 &= (\mathbf{A}_{21} + \mathbf{A}_{22})\mathbf{B}_{11} \\
\mathbf{Q}_3 &= \mathbf{A}_{11}(\mathbf{B}_{12} - \mathbf{B}_{22}) \\
\mathbf{Q}_4 &= \mathbf{A}_{22}(-\mathbf{B}_{11} + \mathbf{B}_{21}) \\
\mathbf{Q}_5 &= (\mathbf{A}_{11} + \mathbf{A}_{12})\mathbf{B}_{22} \\
\mathbf{Q}_6 &= (-\mathbf{A}_{11} + \mathbf{A}_{21})(\mathbf{B}_{11} + \mathbf{B}_{12}) \\
\mathbf{Q}_7 &= (\mathbf{A}_{12} - \mathbf{A}_{22})(\mathbf{B}_{21} + \mathbf{B}_{22})
\end{aligned}
$$

Then

$$
\begin{aligned}
\mathbf{C}_{11} &= \mathbf{Q}_1 + \mathbf{Q}_4 - \mathbf{Q}_5 + \mathbf{Q}_7 \\
\mathbf{C}_{21} &= \mathbf{Q}_2 + \mathbf{Q}_4 \\
\mathbf{C}_{12} &= \mathbf{Q}_3 + \mathbf{Q}_5 \\
\mathbf{C}_{22} &= \mathbf{Q}_1 + \mathbf{Q}_3 - \mathbf{Q}_2 + \mathbf{Q}_6
\end{aligned}
$$

(a) What is the parallel time and the number of processors?

(b) How does your parallel scheme compare with the example in Section 2.2.2?

2.8.B. Design parallel algorithms to compute:

(a) $e^{\mathbf{A}}$, where $\mathbf{A}$ is an $n \times n$ matrix. (This problem occurs frequently in automatic control, for example in the solution of the matrix Riccati Equation.)

(b) $\mathbf{A}!$

(c) $\mathbf{A}^{-1}$

2.9.B. (Givens' Algorithm.) Givens' algorithm triangularizes $\mathbf{A}$ with a sequence of plane rotations

$$
\begin{bmatrix} \cos\theta & -\sin\theta \\ \sin\theta & \cos\theta \end{bmatrix} \begin{bmatrix} \text{row } r \\ \text{row } i \end{bmatrix} \quad \text{with } i > r
$$

One merit of this algorithm is that in addition to possessing numerical stability, it does not require pivoting. Denote by a_{ij} the (i, j)th element of $\mathbf{A}$ and let n be the order of $\mathbf{A}$. The following sequential program details the operations performed by the algorithm:

for $r = 1$ to n
  for $i = r + 1$ to n
    compute $\theta_{ri} = -\tan_{-1} a_{ir}/a_{rr}$ and
    $$a_{rr} \leftarrow \sqrt{a_{rr}^2 + a_{ir}^2}$$
    for $j = r + 1$ to n
      compute $\begin{bmatrix} a_{rj} \\ a_{ij} \end{bmatrix} \leftarrow \begin{bmatrix} \cos\theta_{ri} & -\sin\theta_{ri} \\ \sin\theta_{ri} & \cos\theta_{ri} \end{bmatrix} \begin{bmatrix} a_{rj} \\ a_{ij} \end{bmatrix}$
    end j-loop
    compute $\begin{bmatrix} b_r \\ b_i \end{bmatrix} \leftarrow \begin{bmatrix} \cos\theta_{ri} & -\sin\theta_{ri} \\ \sin\theta_{ri} & \cos\theta_{ri} \end{bmatrix} \begin{bmatrix} b_r \\ b_i \end{bmatrix}$
  end i-loop
end r-loop

The j-loop (minor step) performs the rotation on the two rows r and i that zeros out a_{ir}; the i-loop (major step) repeats this operation to zero out all the elements a_{ir} below a_{rr}. Study the parallelism and find the parallel time of computation.

2.10.B. For the recurrence algorithm in Section 2.2.4:

(a) Rewrite statements 6 and 9 to specify the exact order of each operation and the movement of variables from one operation to the next. Then derive the data dependence vectors.

(b) Show the dependence graph between iterations, and determine the parallel processing time by tracing the longest dependence path.

2.11.B. Design a parallel algorithm to compute

$$f(x) = x^{31} + x^{30} + x^{28} + x^{16}$$

(a) Express your algorithm as a computational graph.

(b) Compute the speedup of your parallel algorithm over the fastest sequential algorithm for this polynomial function that you know. Explain your answer.

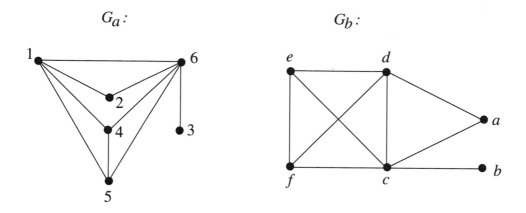

Figure 2.30 Graphs for Problem 2.13.B.

2.12.B. A program for solving a system of equations $\mathbf{Ax} = \mathbf{b}$, where $\mathbf{A}$ is a lower triangular matrix, is as follows:

$$
\begin{aligned}
&\text{do } 20 \ i = 1, 6 \\
&\quad y(i, 0) = 0 \\
&\text{do } 10 \ k = 1, i - 1 \\
&\quad y(i, k) = y(i, k - 1) + a(i, k) \cdot x(k) \\
&10 \ \text{continue} \\
&\quad x(i) = (b(i) - y(i, i - 1))/a(i, i) \\
&20 \ \text{continue}
\end{aligned}
$$

Show all the index points and the dependence vectors among them.

2.13.B. Find all the isomorphisms, if any, between the graphs in Figure 2.30.

Chapter 3

PROGRAM TRANSFORMATIONS

Program transformations are a powerful concept for studying and exploiting parallelism. It is useful for a broad range of computers ranging from multiprocessors to algorithmically specialized architectures. In general, programs may be said to consist of *computations* and *control*. The control part determines the order of computations. *Program transformations* are operations that change the structure of computations and the execution order while maintaining the equivalence of the program. There are many types of transformations, depending upon the equivalence criterion used. The simplest, but weakest, criterion is *input-output equivalence,* in which a set of input variables is mapped into the same set of output variables for all input-output equivalent programs. Stronger equivalence criteria are often necessary to retain some built-in features of the original programs.

The need for program transformations arises in many areas of computer science: compiler design, program correctness proofs, automatic programming, and others. In this chapter, we explore program transformations that speed up processing time. This is why the transformations discussed in this chapter are called *time transformations.* In later chapters, we will be more interested in transforming algorithms for the purpose of mapping them onto various computer structures. These mappings are called *space transformations.*

The approach taken here toward program transformations is based on the analysis of data dependencies. In many programs, there are dependencies that are introduced artificially by the programmer and that may be eliminated. Many other dependencies are inherent, and cannot be removed. However, they may be modified, provided that the ordering of computations imposed by them is maintained.

One simple technique for achieving some degree of parallelism is to perform *local transformations;* that is, to point out the inherent concurrency of some particular task while taking into account the semantics of the program. Often this can be done during the execution of tasks. A more complex technique is to achieve a *global transformation;* that is, to perform a syntactical analysis of a sequential algorithm and to modify its control structure in order to allow concurrent execution of instructions.

3.1 REMOVAL OF OUTPUT DEPENDENCIES AND ANTIDEPENDENCIES

Often, when programmers code algorithms they introduce dependencies that do not exist in the original algorithms. Output dependencies and antidependencies are among these false dependencies. They occur not because data is passed from one statement to another, but because the same memory location is used in more than one place. These dependencies can be removed without impairing the equivalence of the algorithm. It is useful to eliminate unnecessary dependencies in order to expose more parallelism and to allow more tradeoff options. Some techniques for eliminating dependencies, proposed in [Padua, Kuck, and Lawric 1980], are *variable renaming, scalar expansion,* and *node splitting.*

Variable Renaming
One possibility for removing dependencies is to rename some of the variables. If some of the recurrences of old variables are replaced with new variables, output dependencies and antidependencies disappear.

Example 3.1. The following program has several dependencies, as shown in the dependence graph given in Figure 3.1:

$$S_1 : A = B * C$$

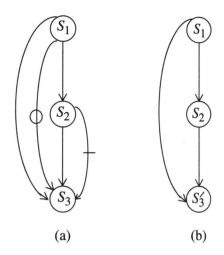

(a)   (b)

Figure 3.1 (a) Initial dependence graph for Example 3.1;
(b) simplified dependence graph.

$$S_2 : D = A + 1$$
$$S_3 : A = A * D$$

This program does not change if statement S_3 is replaced with

$$S_3' : AA = A + D$$

If this change is made, the antidependence and output dependence arcs
are removed. Variable renaming can also be applied to arrays, but it is
more difficult.

Scalar Expansion
Another technique for removing dependence arcs, called *scalar expansion,* is to associate indices with scalars occurring repeatedly in loop
iterations. This technique is illustrated in the next example.

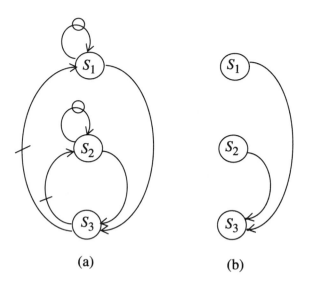

(a)   (b)

Figure 3.2 (a) Initial dependence graph for Example 3.2;
(b) simplified dependence graph for Example 3.2.

Example 3.2. Consider the loop

> for $i = 1$ to n do
> $S_1 : b = B(i) - 2$
> $S_2 : c = C(i) * B(i)$
> $S_3 : A(i) = b + c$
> end

This loop corresponds to the dependence graph shown in Figure 3.2(a).
If we replace all occurrences of b with $b(i)$, and of c with $c(i)$, the output
dependencies and antidependencies are eliminated and a new simpler
dependence graph results, as shown in Figure 3.2(b). All loop iterations
are now independent.

Node Splitting
Some loops contain data dependence cycles that can be easily eliminated by introducing temporary variables.

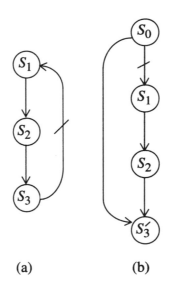

(a)   (b)

Figure 3.3 (a) Initial dependence graph for Example 3.3;
(b) dependence graph without a data dependence cycle.

Example 3.3. The loop

$$\text{DO } I = 1, N$$
$$S_1 : A(I) = B(I) + C(I)$$
$$S_2 : D(I) = A(I) + 2$$
$$S_3 : F(I) = D(I) + A(I + 1)$$
$$\text{END DO}$$

results in the data dependence graph shown in Figure 3.3(a). There
is a data dependence cycle, which indicates dependencies between loop
iterations. However, one of the arcs in the cycle corresponds to an
antidependence; if this arc is removed, the cycle will be broken. The
antidependence relation can be removed from the cycle by inserting a
new temporary variable as follows:

$$\text{DO } I = 1, N$$
$$S_0 : AA(I) = A(I + 1)$$
$$S_1 : A(I) = B(I) + C(I)$$
$$S_2 : D(I) = A(I) + 2$$

$$S_3' : F(I) = D(I) + AA(I)$$
END DO

The modified loop has the data dependence graph shown in Figure 3.3(b). The data dependence cycle has been eliminated by splitting the S_3 node in the data dependence graph into S_0 and S_3'. The loop iterations are now independent and can be performed simultaneously for all I from 1 to N in the following way:

$$S_0 : AA(1 : N) = A(2 : N + 1)$$
$$S_1 : A(1 : N) = B(1 : N) + C(1 : N)$$
$$S_2 : D(1 : N) = A(1 : N) + 2$$
$$S_3 : F(1 : N) = D(1 : N) + AA(1 : N)$$

3.2   PROGRAMS WITH LOOPS

Since loops represent a rich source of parallelism, parallel loop transformations are some of the most important techniques in parallel processing. In this section, we present several forms of parallel loops and identify transformations for achieving these forms.

3.2.1   Forms of Parallel Loops

Loop Vectorization

Vector parallelism is a low-level form of parallelism, which usually occurs within a processor. Vector instructions allow a single processor to operate with a single instruction on multiple data entries. Loops without dependence cycles can be vectorized, meaning that for each instruction in the loop body, all iterations can be executed simultaneously.

Example 3.4. The loop

DO $I = 1, N$
$$S_1 : A(I) = B(I + 1) + C(I)$$
$$S_2 : B(I) = A(I) + 5$$
END DO

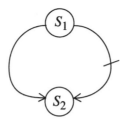

Figure 3.4 Data dependencies for Example 3.4.

has a data dependence and antidependence between S_1 and S_2, as shown in Figure 3.4. Because the data dependence graph has no cycles, it can be *completely vectorized*. The vector instructions are written in the form

$$A(1:N) = B(2:N+1) + C(1:N)$$
$$B(1:N) = A(1:N) + 5$$

Example 3.5. Now we consider a loop that contains a data dependence cycle that cannot be removed. As we will see, it is possible to vectorize some of the loop body that is not part of the cycle.

> DO $I = 1, N$
> $S_1 : D(I) = A(I + 1) + 3$
> $S_2 : A(I) = B(I - 1) + C(I)$
> $S_3 : B(I) = A(I) - 5$
> END DO

As shown in Figure 3.5, statements S_2 and S_3 are connected in a cycle in the data dependence graph; the other statement is not. It is possible to vectorize the statement that is outside the cycle. Thus, the previous loop may be *partially vectorized,* as follows:

> $S_1 : D(1:N) = A(2:N + 1) + 3$
> DO $I = 1, N$
> $S_2 : A(I) = B(I - 1) + C(I)$
> $S_3 : B(I) = A(I) - 5$
> END DO

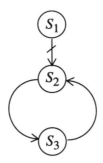

Figure 3.5 Data dependencies for Example 3.5.

Some vector operations transform a vector into a scalar; an example is the dot product of two vectors.

DO $I = 1, N$
$S_1 : A(I) = B(I) * C(I)$
$S_2 : \text{DOT} = \text{DOT} + A(I)$
END DO

This loop can be vectorized as

$S_1 : A(1{:}N) = B(1{:}N){*}C(1{:}N)$
$S_2 : \text{DOT} = \text{DOT} + \text{SUM}(A(1{:}N))$

The SUM function computes the summation of its arguments.

DOALL Loop

DOALL is a construct in parallel Fortran that indicates that all iterations of a DO loop are performed in parallel. Other high-level languages have similar constructs. Each loop iteration is transformed into an independent process. The condition for the existence of DOALL is that there are no dependencies across iterations. Because there is no ordering between iterations, it is possible to assign each iteration to a different processor for execution. Or, if it is advantageous, sets of iterations may each be assigned to one processor. The test for independent iterations is based on data dependencies. If the data dependence matrix has one row with only zero elements, then the iterations over that index are independent.

Example 3.6. The loop

```
DO I = 1, N
S1:  A(I) = B(I) + C(I)
S2:  D(I) = A(I) + 2
END DO
```

has no cross-iteration dependencies and can be transformed into

```
DOALL I = 1, N
S1: A(I) = B(I) + C(I)
S2: D(I) = A(I) + 2
END DOALL
```

Provided there are N processors, the processing time is reduced by a factor of N because all iterations are done in parallel.

DOACROSS Loop

DOACROSS is another construct of parallel languages for performing loops in parallel. Each loop iteration becomes a process; however, these processes are not completely independent. DOACROSS is used when there are dependencies between iterations. These dependencies may be obeyed by either implicit or explicit synchronization.

Example 3.7. The loop

```
DO I = 1, N
S₁ : A(I) = B(I) + C(I)
S₂ : D(I) = B(I − 1) + C(I)
S₃ : E(I) = A(I − 1) + D(I − 2)
END DO
```

$$S_1 : A(I) = B(I) + C(I)$$
$$S_2 : D(I) = B(I - 1) + C(I)$$
$$S_3 : E(I) = A(I - 1) + D(I - 2)$$

has two dependencies, $d_1 = 1$ and $d_2 = 2$. (The dependence graph is shown in Figure 3.6.) It can be executed in parallel using DOACROSS as follows:

```
DOACROSS I = 1, N
S₁ : A(I) = B(I) + C(I)
S₂ : D(I) = B(I − 1) + C(I)
synchronization d₁
```

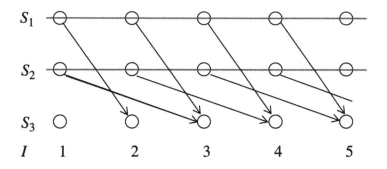

Figure 3.6 Data dependencies for Example 3.7.

synchronization d_2
$S_3 : E(I) = A(I-1) + D(I-2)$
END DO

Each iteration may be assigned to a different processor. The synchronization statements constrain the execution of S_3 until dependencies have been satisfied. Notice that parallelism exists in DOACROSS loops because of some overlapped execution of successive iterations. There is a partial execution order across iterations, in the sense that iterations are forced to wait for the execution of some of the instructions from previous iterations.

Often a reordering of statements inside the loop is necessary in order to increase the parallelism, as can be seen in the following example.

Example 3.8. Consider the two equivalent loops given below.

Program a:
```
        DO I = 1, N
        S₁ : B(I) = A(I − 2) + 2
        S₂ : A(I) = D(I) + C(I)
        S₃ : C(I) = A(I − 1) + 3
        END DO
```

This loop has a dependence d_1 between statement S_2 and S_1 and a dependence d_2 between statement S_2 and S_3, both caused by variable A. Another form of this loop is:

Program b:

> DOACROSS $I = 1$, N
> $S_2 : A(I) = D(I) + C(I)$
>   synchronization d_1
>   synchronization d_2
> $S_1 : B(I) = A(I - 2) + 2$
> $S_3 : C(I) = A(I - 1) + 3$
> END DOACROSS

The loop in *Program a* is not appropriate for DOACROSS transformation because one dependence is upward, and iteration I cannot start until the previous iteration $(I - 2)$ has ended. By simply interchanging the order of the statements S_1 and S_2 in *Program a,* it is possible to achieve parallelism. The loop in *Program b* still has dependencies between iterations, but they are oriented downward, from the first statement to the second statement. This can be seen in Figure 3.7. Each loop iteration (statements S_1, S_2, and S_3) becomes a process and is assigned to an independent processor. As shown in the time-processor chart in Figure 3.8, processes need to communicate while being executed.

Next, consider an example of a DOACROSS transformation applied to a nested loop.

Example 3.9.

> DO $I = 1$, N
>   DO $J = 1, N$
> $S_1 : A(I, J) = B(I, J - 1) + 2$
> $S_2 : B(I, J) = A(I, J) + B(I - 1, J - 1)$
>   END DO
> END DO

This loop has three dependencies, as shown by the dependence matrix

$$\mathbf{D} = \begin{bmatrix} 0 & 0 & 1 \\ 0 & 1 & 1 \end{bmatrix} \begin{matrix} I \\ J \end{matrix}$$

The first dependence is caused by variable A between statements S_1 and S_2, and dependencies $\mathbf{d}_2$ and $\mathbf{d}_3$ are caused by variable B. This

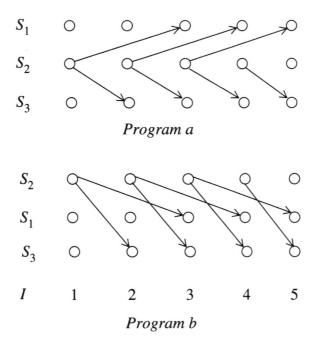

Figure 3.7 Data dependencies for Example 3.8.

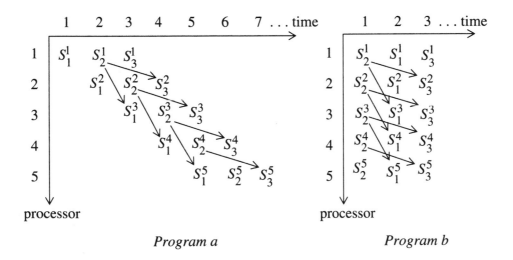

Figure 3.8 Time-space diagram for Example 3.8.

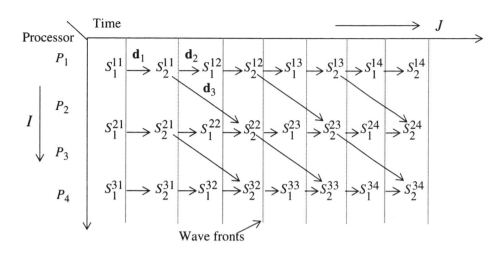

Figure 3.9 Dependencies for Example 3.9.

program can be executed in DOACROSS format by parallelizing the outer loop I. The time-space diagram for this loop is shown in Figure 3.9. Each row represents a process assigned to a separate processor. Notice that dependencies must be satisfied; this is usually achieved with a synchronization mechanism.

$$
\begin{aligned}
&\text{DOACROSS } I = 1, N \\
&\quad \text{DO } J = 1, N \\
&S_1 : \ A(I, J) = B(I, J - 1) + 2 \\
&S_2 : \ B(I, J) = A(I, J) + B(I - 1, J - 1) \\
&\quad \text{END DO} \\
&\text{END DOACROSS}
\end{aligned}
$$

One synchronization is required because of the dependence $\mathbf{d}_3$ between I iterations. From the dependence matrix, we can see that $\mathbf{d}_1$ and $\mathbf{d}_2$ have zero components along index I and do not require any synchronization, whereas $\mathbf{d}_3$ has a nonzero entry along I and does require synchronization.

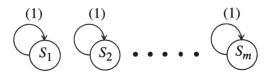

Figure 3.10 Dependence graph for Example 3.10.

Pipelining

The pipelining transformation consists of distributing a loop to several processors; that is, assigning independent statements to independent processors and then chaining iterations in time. This is shown in the next example.

Example 3.10.

$$\text{DO } I = 1, N$$
$$S_1; S_2; ...; S_m$$
$$\text{END DO}$$

Assume that the dependence graph for this loop is as shown in Figure 3.10. The dependence vectors have value 1 as shown. This means dependencies between two consecutive iterations for each statement. Suppose that $m = 3$ and $N = 4$.

The time-space diagram for pipelining is shown in Figure 3.11(a) for $m = 3$ and $N = 4$. All statements in the loop can be performed simultaneously using m processors. This corresponds to distributing the statements in space (i.e., to processors), then pipelining the iterations in time. The total execution time is N.

The time-space diagram for this example, using the DOACROSS transformation, is shown in Figure 3.11(b). The statements in the loop are executed sequentially, and the N iterations are chained in space. A certain overlap results in this case, such that the total processing time is $N + m - 1$. Notice that for large m and small N, pipelining is much faster than DOACROSS and, for this example, does not require any interprocessor communication. The DOACROSS transformation requires near-neighbor interprocessor links.

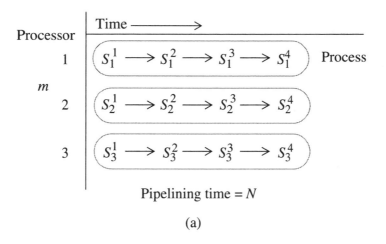

(a)

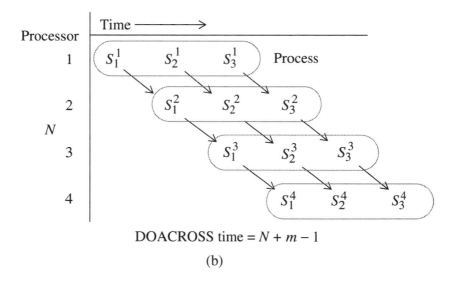

DOACROSS time $= N + m - 1$

(b)

Figure 3.11 (a) Time-space diagram using the pipelining transformation; (b) time-space diagram using the DOACROSS transformation.

3.2.2   Loop Transformations

Often transformations are required in order to put loops into one of the parallel forms presented above. In this section, a variety of such transformations are presented.

Cycle Shrinking

This transformation is applicable in cases when the dependence cycle of a loop involves dependencies between loops that are far apart. It transforms a serial DO loop into two nested loops: an outer, serial loop and an inner, parallel loop. Cycle shrinking extracts the dependence-free instances of the statements inside a loop, and creates an inner parallel loop. This is illustrated in the next example.

$$\text{DO } I = 1, N, \text{step } 1$$
$$A(I + K) = B(I) - 1$$
$$B(I + K) = A(I) + C(I)$$
$$\text{END DO}$$

This loop has a constant dependence cycle with each dependence $d = K$. Because the size of the dependence is larger than 1, the loop can be transformed into an equivalent nested loop with faster processing time.

$$\text{DO } I1 = 1, N, \text{step } K$$
$$\text{DOALL } I = I1, I1 + K - 1$$
$$A(I + K) = B(I) - 1$$
$$B(I + K) = A(I) + C(I)$$
$$\text{END DOALL}$$
$$\text{END DO}$$

In the case in which the loop has several constant dependencies, the cycle can be reduced by a factor that is the minimum distance between iterations. For example, the loop

$$\text{DO } I = 1, N$$
$$X(I) = Y(I) + Z(I)$$
$$Y(I + 3) = X(I - 4) * W(I)$$
$$\text{END DO}$$

has two dependencies, one of size 3 and another of size 4. It is possible to shrink the dependence cycle by a factor of 3 as follows:

DO $J = 1$, N, step 3
    DOALL $I = J, J + 2$
        $X(I) = Y(I) + Z(I)$
        $Y(I + 3) = X(I - 4) * W(I)$
    END DOALL
END DO

Next we consider the case of multidimensional iteration space and try to find ways to shrink several loops. For example:

DO $I = 3$, N
    DO $J = 5$, M
        $A(I, J) = B(I - 3, J - 5)$
        $B(I, J) = A(I - 2, J - 4)$
    END DO
END DO

This loop has the dependence matrix

$$\mathbf{D} = \begin{bmatrix} 2 & 3 \\ 4 & 5 \end{bmatrix} \begin{matrix} I \\ J \end{matrix}$$

Cycle shrinking can be applied to each index separately; that is, to each row of the dependence matrix. The outer loop can be shrunk by a factor of $2 = \min(2, 3)$ and the inner loop by a factor of $4 = \min(4, 5)$. This yields

DO $I_1 = 3, N, 2$
    DO $J_1 = 5, M, 4$
        DOALL $I = I_1, I_1 + 1$
            DOALL $J = J_1, J_1 + 3$
                $A(I, J) = B(I - 3, J - 5)$
                $B(I, J) = A(I - 2, J - 4)$
            ENDOALL
        ENDOALL
    END DO
END DO

The transformed loop can execute eight iterations at a time in parallel, resulting in a speedup of 8.

A more careful examination of the dependence matrix allows us to improve the execution time by performing only *selective shrinking*. This means that often it is sufficient to apply cycle shrinking only to the outer loop and to transform the loops inside to DOALL. In the example above, it is sufficient to perform cycle shrinking on loop I, and to execute in parallel all J iterations. This is possible because the cycle shrinking of loop I automatically takes care of the dependencies.

$$\text{DO } I_1 = 3, N, \text{ step } 2$$
$$\quad \text{DOALL } I = I_1, I_1 + 1$$
$$\quad\quad \text{DOALL } J = 5, M$$
$$\quad\quad\quad A(I, J) = B(I - 3, J - 5)$$
$$\quad\quad\quad B(I, J) = A(I - 2, J - 4)$$
$$\quad\quad \text{ENDOALL}$$
$$\quad \text{ENDOALL}$$
$$\text{END DO}$$

The speedup factor for this case is $2(M - 5 + 1)$.

Loop Interchanging

This technique consists of performing a valid interchange of the order of indices (loops) for the purpose of increasing parallelism. For example, in the program above, by first making the J loop the outer loop and the I loop the inside loop, we increase the shrinking factor from 2 to 4, which results in more parallelism. An interchange is permissible when the new dependence vectors remain positive. For example, indices in the following loop are not interchangeable:

Example 3.11.

$$\text{DO } I = 1, N$$
$$\quad \text{DO } J = 1, N$$
$$\quad\quad A(I, J) = A(I - 1, J + 1) + B(I - 2, J)$$
$$\quad \text{END DO}$$
$$\text{END DO}$$

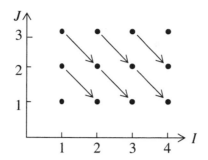

Figure 3.12 Dependence graph for Example 3.11.

The dependence vector is

$$\mathbf{d} = \begin{bmatrix} 1 \\ -1 \end{bmatrix} \begin{matrix} I \\ J \end{matrix}$$

When loop I is interchanged with loop J, this dependence vector becomes negative. This in turn will violate the correct execution ordering. Dependencies are shown in Figure 3.12.

In the next example, the loops are interchangeable.

Example 3.12.

```
DO J = 1, N
    DO I = 1, N
        A(I, J) = A(I − 1, J) + B(I − 2, J)
    END DO
END DO
```

is equivalent to the following loop:

```
DO I = 1, N
    DO J = 1, N
        A(I, J) = A(I − 1, J) + B(I − 2, J)
    END DO
END DO
```

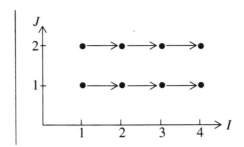

Figure 3.13 Data dependencies for Example 3.12.

The dependencies are shown in Figure 3.13. The gain achieved in this case is that index J can now be vectorized, whereas in the original loop it cannot. If parallelism is achieved through a vector processor, then this transformation is useful.

Example 3.13. Next we consider an example of a loop with three indices.

$$
\begin{aligned}
&\text{DO 2 } I_1 = 0,\ 9 \\
&\text{DO 2 } I_2 = 0,\ 9 \\
&\text{DO 2 } I_3 = 0,\ 9 \\
&A(I_1, I_2) = A(I_1, I_2) + B(I_1, I_3) * C(I_2, I_3) \\
2\quad &\text{CONTINUE}
\end{aligned}
$$

In this program loop I_3 cannot be executed in parallel, but loops I_1 and I_2 can be. The reason for this is easier to see if we rewrite the statement by completing the missing index:

$$A(I_1, I_2, I_3) = A(I_1, I_2, I_3 - 1) + B(I_1, I_2, I_3) * C(I_1, I_2, I_3)$$

Clearly, there is only one data dependence vector $\mathbf{d} = (0,\ 0,\ 1)^t$. By interchanging the order of I_1 and I_3, it becomes clear that the new inner loops, namely I_2 and I_1, can both be executed in parallel, and a speedup factor of 100 is achieved. To understand these claims, it is instructive to visualize the three-dimensional index space.

Loop Fusion

This is a technique that transforms two adjacent loops into a single loop. The condition for performing such a transformation is that the ordering imposed by the data dependencies may not be violated. For example, the loops

$$
\begin{aligned}
&\text{DO } I = 1, N \\
S_1: \quad &A(I) = B(I) + C(I + 1) \\
&\text{END DO} \\
&\text{DO } I = 1, N \\
S_2: \quad &C(I) = A(I - 1) \\
&\text{END DO}
\end{aligned}
$$

can be fused, because the data dependence relation is not violated.

$$
\begin{aligned}
&\text{DO } I = 1, N \\
S_1: \; &A(I) = B(I) + C(I + 1) \\
S_2: \; &C(I) = A(I - 1) \\
&\text{END DO}
\end{aligned}
$$

Loop fusion is not possible when dependencies are violated, as in this example:

$$
\begin{aligned}
&\text{DO } I = 1, N \\
S_1: \quad &A(I) = B(I) + C(I + 1) \\
&\text{END DO} \\
&\text{DO } I = 1, N \\
S_2: \quad &C(I) = A(I + 2) \\
&\text{END DO}
\end{aligned}
$$

If fusion were performed, the new loop would introduce an antidependence directed from S_2 to S_1. This is not allowed because $A(I + 2)$ would use values not produced by $A(I)$.

$$
\begin{aligned}
&\text{DO } I = 1, N \\
S_1: \; &A(I) = B(I) + C(I + 1) \\
S_2: \; &C(I) = A(I + 2) \\
&\text{END DO}
\end{aligned}
$$

Loop fusion is used in conventional compilers to reduce the overhead of loops. Likewise, fusion helps to reduce startup costs for DOALL loops.

Loop Collapsing

This transformation combines two nested loops into a single one for the purpose of increasing the vector length for vector machines. Again, this operation is permissible when dependencies are not violated. For example, loop collapsing is possible whenever the data dependence matrix has a row containing zeros. That index can be attached to another index without affecting dependencies. Under loop collapsing transformation, the loop

$$
\begin{aligned}
&\text{DO } I = 1, 4 \\
&\quad \text{DO } J = 1, 5 \\
&\qquad A(I, J) = A(I, J - 1) - 3 \\
&\quad \text{END DO} \\
&\text{END DO}
\end{aligned}
$$

becomes

$$
\begin{aligned}
&\text{DO } IJ = 1, 20 \\
&\quad I = \lceil IJ/5 \rceil \\
&\quad J = IJ \bmod 5 \\
&\quad A(I, J) = A(I, J - 1) - 3 \\
&\text{END DO}
\end{aligned}
$$

Loop Partitioning

Some programs can be partitioned into independent (or almost independent), smaller problems. Such clever partitioning usually leads to a considerable improvement in processing time. The partitioning strategy can be derived from an analysis of dependencies between computational blocks. The fewer the dependencies between blocks, the better the partitioning is.

$$
\begin{aligned}
&\text{DO } I = 1, M \\
&A(I) = A(I - 2) - 3 \\
&\text{END DO}
\end{aligned}
$$

There is a dependence $d = 2$. Since the greatest common divider (gcd) of all dependencies (here only one dependence) is gcd > 1, it is possible to form two independent processes. The loop can be split (partitioned) into two loops without violating the dependencies. The new limits must be computed carefully.

Process 1

$$\text{DO } I = 1, \lfloor (M - 1)/2 \rfloor * 2 + 1, \text{ step } 2$$
$$A(I) = A(I - 2) - 3$$
$$\text{END DO}$$

Process 2

$$\text{DO } I = 2, \lfloor M/2 \rfloor * 2, \text{ step } 2$$
$$A(I) = A(I - 2) - 3$$
$$\text{END DO}$$

A loop may be split into g independent loops, where g is the gcd of the dependence vectors.

3.3   TRANSFORMATION OF INDEX SETS AND DEPENDENCIES

This technique consists of the modification of nested loop index sets and data dependencies via some mathematical function. It is a powerful tool, which may be regarded as *global transformation* because it rearranges the entire index set and, subsequently, the dependencies. As we will see, this transformation subsumes some of the transformations presented earlier. The only restriction, of course, is that an execution order must still be maintained that does not violate the original dependencies. The questions are how such transformations are found, and, if more than one exist, which one should be used.

3.3.1   The Basic Idea

Algorithms with nested loops occur in almost all programs. In order to introduce the *transformation of index sets,* we will first discuss what we mean by index set and how dependence vectors are defined on an index set.

Index set: Denote by $\mathbf{J}^n$ the nth-dimensional index set of an algorithm with n nested loops. Each point in this nth-cartesian space is a distinct instantiation of the algorithm indices. The geometrical form of the index space is a function of the indices' lower and upper limits. For example, a nested loop containing three indices with constant limits has a parallelepipedic index space.

Dependence vectors: The dependence vectors forming matrix $\mathbf{D}$ are defined on the index space; their sources and destinations are points in the index space. Formally, to each index point, we can associate the dependence vectors starting at that point, as well as variables produced at that point. It is useful to notice that while most index points receive input data from other index points through dependencies, there are points where input variables are used, and points where output variables are produced.

Execution ordering: An important concept underlying the performance of an algorithm is the order in which its index points are executed. A correct execution order is one that satisfies the data dependencies. Many execution orderings are possible. In sequential algorithms, index points are visited one at a time; in parallel algorithms, groups of compatible index points are formed, and each group is processed concurrently.

The idea of transformation of index sets and dependencies and its matrix formulation was presented in [Moldovan 1983b] and [Moldovan and Fortes 1986]. It was first used for mapping algorithms into systolic arrays, but it soon became clear that this is a powerful technique that is useful in compiler design and other aspects of parallel processing.

The essence of index set transformation is to find a function that transforms a sequentially ordered index set into another index set, on which a parallel-execution ordering exists.

Example 3.14. [Moldovan and Fortes 1986] Consider the following algorithm:

$$\text{for } j_0 = 1 \text{ to } N$$
$$\quad \text{for } j_1 = 1 \text{ to } N$$

$$\text{for } j_2 = 1 \text{ to } N$$

$S_1:$ $a(j_0, j_1, j_2) = a(j_0 - 1, j_1 + 1, j_2) * b(j_0 - 1, j_1, j_2 + 1)$

$S_2:$ $b(j_0, j_1, j_2) = b(j_0 - 1, j_1 - 1, j_2 + 2) + b(j_0, j_1 - 3, j_2 + 2)$

$$\text{end } j_2$$
$$\text{end } j_1$$
$$\text{end } j_0$$

The index set space is

$$\mathbf{J}^3 = \{(j_0, \ j_1, \ j_2) \quad 1 \le j_0, \ j_1, \ j_2 \le N\}$$

In this example, for every point in the index space, a multiplication and an addition take place. Dependencies are found between pairs of generated and used variables. Four dependence vectors exist:

$\mathbf{d}_1 = (1, -1, 0)^t$ for pair $< a(j_0, j_1, j_2), a(j_0 - 1, j_1 + 1, j_2) >$

$\mathbf{d}_2 = (1, 0, -1)^t$ for pair $< b(j_0, j_1, j_2), b(j_0 - 1, j_1, j_2 + 1) >$

$\mathbf{d}_3 = (1, 1, -2)^t$ for pair $< b(j_0, j_1, j_2), b(j_0 - 1, j_1 - 1, j_2 + 2) >$

$\mathbf{d}_4 = (0, 3, -2)^t$ for pair $< b(j_0, j_1, j_2), b(j_0, j_1 - 3, j_2 + 2) >$

The dependence matrix may be written as

$$\mathbf{D} = [\mathbf{d}_1\mathbf{d}_2\mathbf{d}_3\mathbf{d}_4] = \begin{bmatrix} 1 & 1 & 1 & 0 \\ -1 & 0 & 1 & 3 \\ 0 & -1 & -2 & -2 \end{bmatrix} \begin{matrix} j_0 \\ j_1 \\ j_2 \end{matrix}$$
$$\quad\quad\quad\quad\quad\quad\; a \quad b \quad b \quad b$$

Notice that the index points in the original program are ordered lexicographically. This is an artificial ordering and can be modified for the purpose of parallelism extraction. By definition, $\mathbf{d} = \mathbf{j} - \mathbf{j}^* > 0$ means that computations indexed by $\mathbf{j}^*$ must be performed before those indexed by $\mathbf{j}$. Often we desire to change the features of an algorithm while preserving its equivalence in computations. Two algorithms A and $\hat{A}$ are equivalent if, given any set of input variables, they map it into the same set of output variables.

Next, we define a transformation that, under certain conditions, transforms A into $\hat{A}$.

Definition 3.1 T is a valid transformation function of algorithm A into $\hat{A}$ if:

1. Algorithm $\hat{A}$ is input-output equivalent to A;

2. T is a bijection and monotonic function defined on the index set $\mathbf{J}^n$;

3. The index set of $\hat{A}$ is the transformed index set of A, namely $\hat{\mathbf{J}}^n = T(\mathbf{J}^n)$; and

4. Dependencies of $\hat{A}$ are the transformed dependencies of A, written $\hat{\mathbf{D}} = T(\mathbf{D})$.

The main purpose of looking for such a T is the hope that the execution time of $\hat{A}$ is much shorter than the execution time of A. Often, many such transformations exist. We are interested in transformed algorithms for which the ordering imposed by the first coordinate of the index set is an execution ordering. The motivation is that if only one coordinate of the index set preserves the correctness of the computation by maintaining an execution ordering, then the rest of the index coordinates can be selected by the algorithm designer to meet some communication requirements. In the discussion that follows, it is shown how such a transformation T can be found.

Since, by definition, T is a bijection and a monotonic function on the index set,

$$\mathbf{d} > 0 \text{ implies that } \hat{\mathbf{d}} = T(\mathbf{d}) > 0 \qquad (3.1)$$

This simply means that the transformation T preserves the sense of the data dependencies. Let us partition the transformation T into two functions such that the first deals with the first k indices and the second deals with the rest of the $n - k$ indices, as follows:

$$T = \begin{bmatrix} \Pi \\ S \end{bmatrix} \qquad (3.2)$$

where the mapping Π is defined as

$$\Pi : \mathbf{J}^n \rightarrow \hat{\mathbf{J}}^k \text{ or } \Pi(I^1, I^2, \dots, I^n) = (\hat{I}^1, \hat{I}^2, \dots, \hat{I}^k) \qquad (3.3)$$

and the mapping S is defined as

$$S : \mathbf{J}^n \to \hat{\mathbf{J}}^{n-k} \text{ or } S(I^1, I^2, \ldots, I^n) = (\hat{I}^{k+1}, \hat{I}^{k+2}, \ldots, \hat{I}^n) \qquad (3.4)$$

The dimensionality of functions Π and S is marked by k, and k is selected as the minimum value such that Π alone establishes the execution ordering of $\hat{A}$, or in other words ensures the input-output equivalence of the transformed algorithm. Under these conditions, it is possible now to think of the first k coordinates, or indices of $\hat{\mathbf{J}}^n$, as *time coordinates* and of the rest of the $n - k$ coordinates as *space coordinates*. The time coordinates are used for speed performance, and the space coordinates are used for communication performance.

All elements $\mathbf{I}$ of the index set $\mathbf{J}^n$, i.e., $\mathbf{I} \in \mathbf{J}^n$, for which $\Pi(\mathbf{I}) = constant$ can be performed in parallel. This is true because $\Pi(\mathbf{I}) = constant$ implies that their first k transformed coordinates, namely $(\hat{I}^1 \ldots \hat{I}^k)$, are also constant, and we have said that these coordinates represent time. It follows that all such points $\mathbf{I}$ can be processed concurrently. $\Pi(\mathbf{I}) = constant$ represents hypersurfaces with the property of containing elements which are not data dependent.

The freedom of selecting $(\hat{I}^{k+1}, \ldots, \hat{I}^n)$ can be used to great advantage to satisfy data communication requirements, as we will see in Chapter 5. In the next section, the space of transformations is restricted to linear transformations, namely matrices.

3.3.2 Linear Transformations

Consider the case in which a program with n nested loops provides m constant data dependence vectors. They are grouped in a matrix $\mathbf{D} = [\mathbf{d}_1, \mathbf{d}_2, \ldots, \mathbf{d}_m]$, of order $n \times m$. A linear transformation $\mathbf{T}$ is sought such that $\hat{\mathbf{I}} = \mathbf{T}\mathbf{I}$. Since $\mathbf{T}$ is linear, $\mathbf{T}(\mathbf{I} + \mathbf{d}_j) - \mathbf{T}(\mathbf{I}) = \mathbf{T}\mathbf{d}_j = \hat{\mathbf{d}}_j$ for $1 \le j \le m$. These equations can be written as

$$\mathbf{T}\mathbf{D} = \hat{\mathbf{D}} \qquad (3.5)$$

where $\hat{\mathbf{D}} = [\hat{\mathbf{d}}_1, \hat{\mathbf{d}}_2, \cdots, \hat{\mathbf{d}}_m]$ represents the modified data dependencies in the new index space $\hat{\mathbf{J}}^n$.

Suppose now that we want to select $\hat{\mathbf{D}}$ such that the new algorithm meets some predetermined requirements. The interesting question now is: Under what conditions does such a $\mathbf{T}$ exist? Equation (3.5) represents $n \times m$ diophantine equations with n^2 unknowns. $\mathbf{T}$ exists if Equation (3.5) has a solution and the solution consists of integers. The next theorem indicates the necessary and sufficient conditions for valid linear transformations, and it can be used as a tool to preselect $\hat{\mathbf{D}}$.

Definition 3.2 *Congruence.* If the difference between two integers a and b is divisible by a number p, then a is said to be *congruent* to b for modulus p and is written

$$a \equiv b \bmod p$$

For example, $7 \equiv 2 \bmod 5$, and $13 \equiv -3 \bmod 8$.

In the case when $\mathbf{a}$ and $\mathbf{b}$ are vectors, congruence is defined as follows: Let c be the greatest common divisor of the elements of $\mathbf{b}$; i.e., $c = \gcd(b_1, b_2, ..., b_n)$. Then $\mathbf{a}$ is congruent to $\mathbf{b}$ modulo c, written

$$\mathbf{a} \equiv \mathbf{b} \bmod c$$

if $a_i \equiv b_i \bmod c$ for $i = 1, ..., n$. In other words, each component a_i is a multiple of c.

Theorem 3.1 [Moldovan 1983b] For an algorithm with a constant set of data dependencies $\mathbf{D}$, the necessary and sufficient conditions that a valid transformation $\mathbf{T}$ exists are:

1. The new data dependence vectors $\hat{\mathbf{d}}_j$ are congruent to dependence $\mathbf{d}_j$ modulo c_j, where c_j is the greatest common divisor (gcd) of the elements of $\mathbf{d}_j$, for all dependencies $1 \leq j \leq m$.

$$\hat{\mathbf{d}}_j \equiv \mathbf{d}_j \bmod c_j$$

2. The first nonzero element of each vector $\hat{\mathbf{d}}_j$ is positive.

Proof.

Sufficient: Condition 1 indicates that the elements of $\hat{\mathbf{d}}_j$ are multiples of the gcd of the elements of the respective $\mathbf{d}_j$. This is a necessary and sufficient condition for each of the $n \times m$ diophantine equations to be solved for integers. Equation (3.5) has a solution. Since the first nonzero elements of $\hat{\mathbf{d}}_j$ are positive, it follows that $\Pi\mathbf{d}_j > 0$; thus $\mathbf{T}$ is a valid transformation.

Necessary: Transformation $\mathbf{T}$ is a bijection and consists of integers; hence conditions 1 and 2 are required conditions. Because $\mathbf{T}$ preserves the ordering of the transformed algorithm, $\hat{\mathbf{d}}_j > 0$, and this implies that the first nonzero element is positive, the proof is complete.

As an example, consider a loop with

$$\mathbf{D} = [\mathbf{d}_1, \mathbf{d}_2] = \begin{bmatrix} 3 & 4 \\ 2 & 2 \end{bmatrix}$$

The gcd for the first column is $c_1 = 1$; the gcd for the second column is $c_2 = 2$. A congruent of $\mathbf{d}_1$ is a vector $\hat{\mathbf{d}}_1$ whose components are any combination of elements in the first and second rows of

$$\begin{pmatrix} \cdots & -2 & -1 & 0 & 1 & 2 & 3 & \cdots \\ \cdots & -2 & -1 & 0 & 1 & 2 & 3 & \cdots \end{pmatrix}$$

Similarly, a congruent of $\mathbf{d}_2$ is a vector $\hat{\mathbf{d}}_2$ found by combining any two elements in the rows

$$\begin{pmatrix} \cdots & -4 & -2 & 0 & 2 & 4 & 6 & \cdots \\ \cdots & -4 & -2 & 0 & 2 & 4 & 6 & \cdots \end{pmatrix}$$

We select $\hat{\mathbf{d}}_1$ and $\hat{\mathbf{d}}_2$ as

$$\hat{\mathbf{D}} = \left[\hat{\mathbf{d}}_1, \hat{\mathbf{d}}_2\right] = \begin{bmatrix} 1 & 2 \\ 1 & 0 \end{bmatrix}$$

In the relation $\hat{\mathbf{D}} = \mathbf{T}\mathbf{D}$, $\mathbf{D}$ and $\hat{\mathbf{D}}$ are known, and it follows that

$$\mathbf{T} = \begin{bmatrix} 1 & -1 \\ -1 & 2 \end{bmatrix}$$

Note that many $\hat{\mathbf{D}}$ are possible, which means that many transformations $\mathbf{T}$ are possible. Normally, one wants to find a valid transformation that minimizes parallel processing time and data communication. For this purpose, when selecting $\hat{\mathbf{D}}$, one should choose the smallest possible integers for its elements. The optimization of processing time is discussed in Section 3.4; the relation between transformation and data communication is discussed in Chapter 5.

3.4   OPTIMAL TIME TRANSFORMATIONS

3.4.1   Parallel Computation Time

In this section, the steps taken to express the parallel time as a function of the transformation Π are shown. Then we discuss an optimization technique that leads to the optimum (shortest) computation time when Π is linear. In a parallel algorithm one can think of computations as grouped into sets, such that all computations in one set are done at the same time. We say that each set represents a time step. It follows that the number of sets, or time steps, represents the parallel execution time. In algorithms for which a transformation exists it is possible to express the parallel time as a function of the transformation. The parallel time, or the number of time steps, is

$$\text{time} = \frac{(\text{end time} - \text{start time})}{\text{displacement}} + 1 \tag{3.6}$$

This can be seen in Figure 3.14. The displacement is the minimum time required between two consecutive time steps. It includes the computation time at a time step and the propagation of variables to the next step.

Equation (3.6) can be expressed mathematically as follows: For the purpose of simplicity we assume that only the first coordinate of the transformed algorithm, $\hat{I}^1$, is associated to time; that is, $k = 1$. This indicates that the transformation Π is $1 \times n$.

A correct execution ordering, called a linear ordering, of the new algorithm is achieved if

$$\Pi \mathbf{d}_j > 0 \quad j = 1, ..., m \tag{3.7}$$

For a variable with dependence $\mathbf{d}_j$, the time increment between the generation and the use of that variable is exactly $\Pi \mathbf{d}_j$. Each dependence may lead to a different time increment. The displacement of the algorithm, defined as the smallest time step between any two consecutive computations, is

$$\text{disp}\Pi = \min\{\Pi \mathbf{d}_j\} \quad \text{for} \quad j = 1, ..., m \tag{3.8}$$

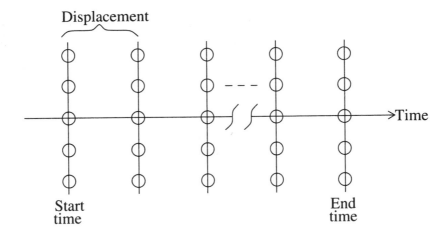

Figure 3.14 Parallel computation time.

The difference between the end time and the start time is simply

$$\max(\mathbf{\Pi I_2}) - \min(\mathbf{\Pi I_1}) = \max \mathbf{\Pi}(\mathbf{I_2} - \mathbf{I_1}) \qquad (3.9)$$

where $\mathbf{I_2}$ is an index point processed at the latest time and $\mathbf{I_1}$ is an index point processed at the earliest time.

It follows that the parallel computation time is

$$t_{\mathbf{\Pi}} = 1 + \left\lceil \frac{\max \mathbf{\Pi}(\mathbf{I_2} - \mathbf{I_1})}{\operatorname{displ} \mathbf{\Pi}} \right\rceil \qquad (3.10)$$

3.4.2 Selection of Optimal Time Transformation

An optimal time transformation $\mathbf{\Pi}$ is achieved if $t_{\mathbf{\Pi}}$ is minimized over all possible $\mathbf{\Pi}$ that satisfy Equation (3.7). This minimization problem is a difficult one.

Example 3.15. Let us derive an optimum $\mathbf{\Pi}$ for the algorithm in Example 3.14. We search for a transformation

$$\mathbf{T} = \begin{bmatrix} \mathbf{\Pi} \\ \mathbf{S} \end{bmatrix} = \begin{bmatrix} t_{11} & t_{12} & t_{13} \\ t_{21} & t_{22} & t_{23} \\ t_{31} & t_{32} & t_{33} \end{bmatrix}$$

In this chapter we focus only on finding the time transformation $\mathbf{\Pi}$; in Chapter 5 we will continue this example and find the space transformation S. When the transformation $\mathbf{T}$ is applied to the program, the new indices are $\hat{\mathbf{j}} = \mathbf{Tj}$, or

$$\hat{j}_0 = t_{11}j_0 + t_{12}j_1 + t_{13}j_2$$
$$\hat{j}_1 = t_{21}j_0 + t_{22}j_1 + t_{23}j_2$$
$$\hat{j}_2 = t_{31}j_0 + t_{23}j_1 + t_{33}j_2$$

From Equation (3.7) we derive conditions for elements t_{ij}:

$\mathbf{\Pi d}_1 > 0$	$t_{11} - t_{12} > 0$
$\mathbf{\Pi d}_2 > 0$	$t_{11} - t_{13} > 0$
$\mathbf{\Pi d}_3 > 0$	$t_{11} + t_{12} - 2t_{13} > 0$
$\mathbf{\Pi d}_4 > 0$	$3t_{12} - 2t_{13} > 0$

As we can see, a large number of transformations $\mathbf{\Pi} = [t_{11}\ t_{12}\ t_{13}]$ can be found to satisfy the given relations. Let us arbitrarily limit their number by imposing the condition

$$\sum_{i=1}^{3} |t_{1i}| \leq 3$$

This condition is consistent with our desire to keep the coefficients of the transformation matrix small. The computations in this example can be done by hand, or by using a computer program. The results are summarized in Table 3.1. The first column lists the five transformations found. The second column lists the first row of each transformed dependence matrix. For each case, the displacement is the smallest integer in the set, namely 1 for the first four transformations and 2 for the last one. The next two columns in the table show the start points and the end points of the index set that are touched by the respective hyperplane transformation $\mathbf{\Pi}$. Here X signifies "don't care," meaning that there is more than one point. The last column shows the parallel time achieved with each transformation $\mathbf{\Pi}$. By inspection one can see that $\mathbf{\Pi}_5$ is the best time transformation. This time results from Equation (3.10).

$$t = \frac{(2N-1) - (2-N)}{2} + 1 = \frac{3N-3}{2} + 1 = \frac{3N-1}{2}$$

Π	$\Pi\,\mathbf{D}$	Start Point	End Point	Parallel Time
$\mathbf{\Pi}_1 = [2\ 1\ 0]$	$(1\ 2\ 3\ 3)$	$1\ 1\ X$	$N\ N\ X$	$3N - 2$
$\mathbf{\Pi}_2 = [1\ 0\ -1]$	$(1\ 2\ 3\ 2)$	$1\ X\ N$	$N\ X\ 1$	$2N - 1$
$\mathbf{\Pi}_3 = [1\ 0\ -2]$	$(1\ 3\ 5\ 4)$	$1\ X\ N$	$N\ X\ 1$	$3N - 2$
$\mathbf{\Pi}_4 = [0\ -1\ -2]$	$(1\ 2\ 3\ 2)$	$X\ N\ N$	$X\ 1\ 1$	$3N - 2$
$\mathbf{\Pi}_5 = [2\ 0\ -1]$	$(2\ 3\ 4\ 2)$	$1\ X\ N$	$N\ X\ 1$	$(3N - 1)/2$

Table 3.1: Five time transformations for Example 3.15.

Figure 3.15 shows the cube index set and the family of planes $\mathbf{\Pi}_5$ moving inside the cube from start points to end points.

Thus the speedup obtained is $2N^3/(3N-1)$. All index points $\mathbf{I}$ that are contained in one plane, $\mathbf{\Pi}_5$, at a given moment can be processed in parallel because they obey the equation $\mathbf{\Pi}_5\mathbf{I} = constant$.

3.5   NONLINEAR TRANSFORMATIONS

For many algorithms, it is not possible to find linear transformations that will improve their processing time or communication time. Sometimes a nonlinear transformation does exist for such an algorithm. This section presents examples that illustrate a few different types of nonlinear transformations.

Example 3.16. Consider again the dynamic programming example in Section 2.3.2. For convenience, the data dependence graph is reproduced in Figure 3.16. The data dependencies are

$$\mathbf{D} = \begin{bmatrix} 1 & 1 & 1 & 1 \\ 0 & -1 & 0 & -1 \\ 0 & 0 & f & g \end{bmatrix} \begin{matrix} l \\ i \\ k \end{matrix}$$
$$\quad\ \ \mathbf{d}_1\ \ \mathbf{d}_2\ \ \mathbf{d}_3\ \ \mathbf{d}_4$$

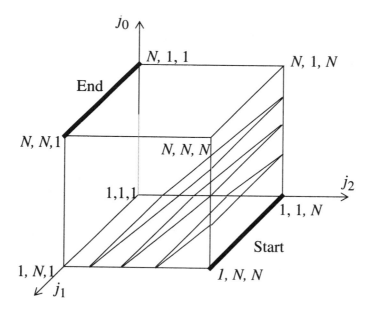

Figure 3.15 Index set and hyperplane $\mathbf{\Pi}$.

Dependencies $\mathbf{d}_1$ and $\mathbf{d}_2$ are fixed over the index set, but $\mathbf{d}_3$ and $\mathbf{d}_4$ vary with the index point where they are computed. The functions f and g take values

$$f = l - 1, l - 2, ..., 1$$
$$g = -1, -2, ..., -l + 1$$

While it is easy to find a linear transformation $\mathbf{\Pi}$ to satisfy the fixed dependencies $\mathbf{d}_1$ and $\mathbf{d}_2$, it is not possible to find a linear transformation to satisfy both $\mathbf{\Pi}\mathbf{d}_3 > 0$ and $\mathbf{\Pi}\mathbf{d}_4 > 0$. This means we have to try nonlinear functions that may compensate for the fact that the signs of the functions f and g are different. It is difficult to devise a procedure for finding nonlinear transformations, mainly because of the large number of candidates. A good way to start is to look carefully at the dependence graph and then to propose simple nonlinear functions that provide a satisfactory parallel execution ordering. This will

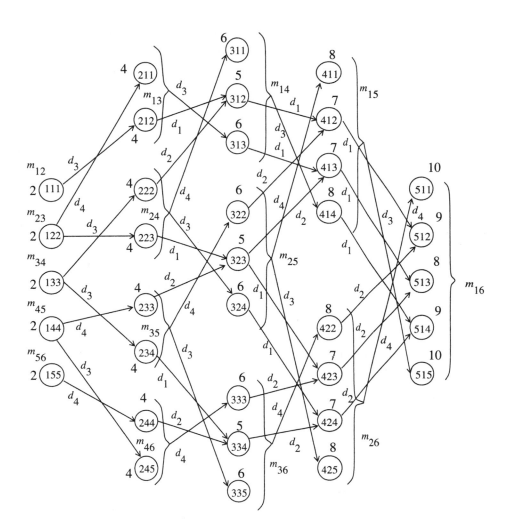

Figure 3.16 Data dependencies for the dynamic programming
algorithm $(n = 6)$ [Moldovan 1983b].

be an ordering that does not violate the dependencies, thus implicitly satisfying the condition $\Pi \mathbf{d}_i > 0$.

For example, for the dependence graph in Figure 3.16 an execution ordering is provided by the numbers near the index points. These numbers indicate the time at which we want each index point to be executed. Note that all dependencies are satisfied because an index point at the tip of a dependence arrow is executed after the index point at the source of that arrow.

Next, we have to find a mathematical function that provides this timing. One such function is

$$\Pi(l, i, k) = \max \begin{cases} \Pi_1(l, i, k) = 2l + i - k \\ \Pi_2(l, i, k) = l - i + k + 1 \end{cases}$$

Function Π_1 is meant to satisfy dependence $\mathbf{d}_4$ and Π_2 is meant to satisfy dependence $\mathbf{d}_3$.

The next example illustrates a type of transformation that modifies the structure of algorithm expressions in order to speed up processing.

Example 3.17. Consider the algorithm described by the program

$$\begin{aligned}
&\text{for } j_1 = 0 \text{ to } N - 1 \\
&\quad \text{for } j_2 = 0 \text{ to } N - 1 \\
&\qquad x(j_1, j_2) = x(j_1 - 1, j_2) + x(j_1 - 4, j_2 + 1) \\
&\quad \text{end } j_2 \\
&\text{end } j_1
\end{aligned}$$

which has the dependence matrix

$$\mathbf{D} = \begin{bmatrix} 1 & 4 \\ 0 & -1 \end{bmatrix}$$

The optimal time transformation is $\mathbf{\Pi} = [1\ 0]$ and disp $\mathbf{\Pi} = 1$. The resulting execution time is N units; each unit corresponds to the time taken to execute one addition. Using back-substitution twice, we can replace $x(j_1 - 1, j_2)$ with $x(j_1 - 3, j_2) + x(j_1 - 5, j_2 + 1) + x(j_1 - 6, j_2 + 1)$ to obtain a new algorithm, described as follows:

```
for j₁ = 0 to N − 1
    for j₂ = 0 to N − 1
        x(j₁, j₂) = x(j₁ − 3, j₂) + x(j₁ − 4, j₂ + 1) +
        x(j₁ − 5, j₂ + 1) + x(j₁ − 6, j₂ + 1)
    end j₂
end j₁
```

The dependence matrix $\mathbf{D}$ is

$$\mathbf{D} = \begin{bmatrix} 3 & 4 & 5 & 6 \\ 0 & -1 & -1 & -1 \end{bmatrix}$$

The optimal time transformation for this dependence matrix is $\mathbf{\Pi} = [1 \ 0]$, disp $\mathbf{\Pi} = 3$. The three additions can be executed in two steps and the execution time is

$$2\frac{N}{\text{disp } \Pi} = \frac{2N}{3}$$

The speedup achieved by the modified parallel algorithm over the original parallel algorithm is

$$\frac{N}{\frac{2N}{3}} = \frac{3}{2}$$

This speed improvement is achieved at the cost of increased data communication.

This example shows that when the internal structure of an algorithm is modified, a different data dependence matrix is obtained, which may lead to an improved parallel processing time. It is clear now that "optimal" time transformation is achieved only in the context of a specific data dependence matrix, which in turn is algorithm-dependent. Different, but equivalent, algorithms may lead to different execution times.

3.6 BIBLIOGRAPHICAL NOTES AND FURTHER READING

The compiler techniques for removing dependencies and loop transformations follow the work done at the University of Illinois around the Paraphrase compiler, [Padua, Kuck, and Lawrie 1980] and [Padua and

Wolfe 1986]. [Polychronopoulos 1988] is a comprehensive treatment of algorithm transformations and parallel compiler design.

The concept of transformation of index sets and dependencies and its matrix formulation was presented in [Moldovan 1983b]. Subsequent work at the University of Southern California considered optimal time transformations [Fortes and Parisi-Presicce 1984], nonlinear transformations [Fortes 1983], and algorithm partitioning [Moldovan and Fortes 1986].

3.7   PROBLEMS

3.1.A.

for $I = 1, 10$
  for $J = 1, 10$
    for $K = 1, 10$
    $A(I, J, K) = A(I, J, K - 1)A(I - 1, J + 1, K - 2) +$
                $+ A(I - 1, J, K - 1)$
    end K
  end J
end I

Hint:

(i) When we say "in parallel" with respect to one index, we mean that some iterations along that index can be done in parallel, but not necessarily all of them.

(ii) Whenever possible, try to derive the largest speedup factor.

For this algorithm:

(a) Find the data dependence matrix D.

(b) Can this algorithm be executed with loops I and J in parallel and loop K serially? Why or why not? If yes, what is the speedup factor that is achieved?

(c) Can this algorithm be executed with loop I serially and loops J and K in parallel? Why or why not? If yes, what is the speedup factor that is achieved?

(d) Can this algorithm be executed with loops I and K serially and loop J in parallel? Why or why not? If yes, what is the speedup factor that is achieved?

(e) Can this algorithm be executed in parallel with respect to I, J, and K? Why or why not? If yes, what is the speedup factor that is achieved?

Solution.

(a)

$$\mathbf{D} = \begin{bmatrix} 1 & 0 & 1 \\ 0 & 0 & -1 \\ 1 & 1 & 2 \end{bmatrix} \begin{matrix} I \\ J \\ K \end{matrix}$$
$$\quad\ \ \mathbf{d}_1\ \ \mathbf{d}_2\ \ \mathbf{d}_3$$

(b) There is no dependence lying on the (I, J) plane. Thus all points on the (I, J) plane for $K = constant$ can be processed in parallel. Performing the loop serially provides an execution ordering that satisfies all dependencies. The speedup factor, representing the ratio between the sequential time and parallel time, is:

$$S = \frac{10 \times 10 \times 10}{10} = 100$$

(c) Dependence $\mathbf{d}_2$ lies on the (J, K) plane. It is not possible to perform in parallel all points on the (J, K) plane for $I = constant$. However, loop J alone can be performed in parallel, and there are many possibilities for performing some points (J, K) in parallel. A possible $\mathbf{\Pi}$ is

$$\mathbf{\Pi} = \begin{bmatrix} 1 & 0 & 0 \\ 0 & 1 & 1 \end{bmatrix}$$

This means I serially, and (J, K) points along line $J + K = constant$ in parallel. The speedup factor in this case is:

$$S = \frac{1000}{10 \times ((10 - 1) + (10 - 1) + 1)} = \frac{1000}{10 \times 19} \approx 5.26$$

(d) Yes, because there are no dependencies lying along coordinate J.

$$S = \frac{1000}{100} = 10$$

(e) Yes. The best time is achieved when I and J are processed in parallel, i.e., $\mathbf{\Pi} = (0, 0, 1)$. The speedup factor is 100.

3.2.A. The following program performs a multiplication of two 3×3 matrices:

$$
\begin{aligned}
&\text{for } i = 1,\ 3 \\
&\quad \text{for } j = 1,\ 3 \\
&\quad\quad \text{for } k = 1,\ 3 \\
&\quad\quad\quad c_{ij}^k = c_{ij}^{k-1} + a_{ik} b_{kj} \\
&\quad\quad \text{end } k \\
&\quad \text{end } j \\
&\text{end } i
\end{aligned}
$$

This problem is transformed into a parallel form by the linear transformation

$$
\mathbf{T} = \begin{bmatrix} \mathbf{\Pi} \\ \mathbf{S} \end{bmatrix} = \begin{bmatrix} 1 & 0 & 1 \\ 0 & 1 & 0 \\ \text{--} & \text{--} & \text{--} \\ 0 & 1 & 1 \end{bmatrix}
$$

Here $\mathbf{\Pi}$ is a 2×3 matrix, and S is a 1×3 row vector.

(a) Show the data dependencies and corresponding variables for the matrix multiplication problem.

(b) How many time units are necessary to process this matrix multiplication problem, as given by transformation $\mathbf{T}$?

(c) What can you say about sequential or parallel execution of original indices i, j, and k when this transformation is used?

Solution.

(a)

$$
\mathbf{D} = \begin{bmatrix} 1 & 0 & 0 \\ 0 & 1 & 0 \\ 0 & 0 & 1 \\ b & a & c \end{bmatrix}
$$

(b) Time is the product of the two rows of $\mathbf{\Pi}$

$$
\left[(101) \left[\begin{pmatrix} 3 \\ 3 \\ 3 \end{pmatrix} - \begin{pmatrix} 1 \\ 1 \\ 1 \end{pmatrix} \right] + 1 \right] \times \left[(010) \left[\begin{pmatrix} 3 \\ 3 \\ 3 \end{pmatrix} - \begin{pmatrix} 1 \\ 1 \\ 1 \end{pmatrix} \right] + 1 \right]
$$

$$= 5 \times 3 = 15$$

(c) The fact that $\mathbf{\Pi}$ has two rows indicates that the computations called by the first row are done first, followed by the computations called by the second row. The first row of $\mathbf{\Pi}$ shows some limited parallelism in the (i, k) plane (along a line $i + k = constant$), and the second row indicates that computations along coordinate j are done sequentially.

3.3.A.

for $I = 1, 8$
  for $J = 1, 9$
    for $K = 1, 10$
    $A(J, K) = A(J + 1, K) + A(J, K + 1) + A(J - 1, K) + A(J, K - 1)$
    end K
  end J
end I

This program is to be transformed into a parallel version by the transformation

$$\mathbf{T} = \begin{pmatrix} 2 & 1 & 1 \\ 0 & -1 & 0 \\ 0 & 0 & 1 \end{pmatrix}$$

where $\mathbf{\Pi} = (2\ 1\ 1)$.

(a) Write the parallel form of this program that results from applying transformation $\mathbf{T}$. Indicate which of the new indices are executed in parallel and which are executed serially.

(b) Calculate the time difference between the execution of points $(I, J, K) = (1, 2, 3)$ and $(I, J, K) = (5, 3, 1)$.

Solution.

  (a)

$$\begin{bmatrix} I \\ J \\ K \end{bmatrix} = \mathbf{T}^{-1} \begin{bmatrix} \hat{I} \\ \hat{J} \\ \hat{K} \end{bmatrix}$$

$$\mathbf{T}^{-1} = \begin{pmatrix} 1/2 & 1/2 & -1/2 \\ 0 & -1 & 0 \\ 0 & 0 & 1 \end{pmatrix}$$

for $\hat{I} = 4$, 35 serially
   DOACROSS $\hat{J} = -9, -1$ in parallel
      DOACROSS $\hat{K} = 1$, 10 in parallel
        $A(1/2\hat{I} + 1/2\hat{J} - 1/2\hat{K}, -\hat{J}, \hat{K}) =$
          $A(1/2\hat{I} + 1/2\hat{J} - 1/2\hat{K} - 1, -\hat{J} + 1, \hat{K}) + \cdots$
      end $\hat{K}$
   end $\hat{J}$
end $\hat{I}$

$\quad$ *(b)* $t = 14 - 7 = 7$

3.4.A. For the loop

$\quad$ For $I = 1$ to 6
$\quad$ S_1: $A(I) = 2 * A(I - 1)$
$\quad$ S_2: $B(I) = 3 * B(I - 1)$
$\quad$ S_3: $C(I) = C(I - 1) + A(I) * B(I)$
$\quad$ end

show the time-space diagram for statements S_i^j with $1 < i < 6$ and $1 < j < 3$ when pipelining and DOACROSS transformations are used.

Solution. See Figure 3.17.

3.5.A. Vectorize the following loop by using one of the techniques presented in this chapter.

$\quad$ DO $I = 1, N$
$\quad$ S_1 : $A(I) = B(I) + C(I)$
$\quad$ S_2 : $A(I + 1) = A(I) + 2 * D(I)$
$\quad$ END DO

Solution. There is a dependence cycle between the two statements: data dependence and output dependence. The data dependence cycle can be broken by adding a temporary array using node splitting.

$\quad$ DO $I = 1, N$
$\quad$ S_1 : $\text{ATEMP}(I) = B(I) + C(I)$
$\quad$ S_2 : $A(I + 1) = \text{ATEMP}(I) + 2 * D(I)$
$\quad$ S_1' : $A(I) = \text{ATEMP}(I)$
$\quad$ END DO

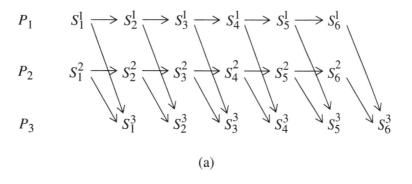

(a)

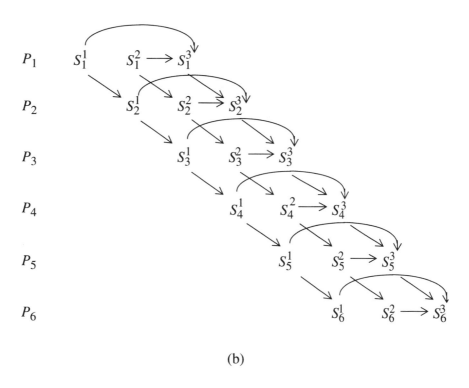

(b)

Figure 3.17 Time-space diagram for (a) pipelining and
(b) DOACROSS.

The data dependence graph for the modified loop has no cycles and can now be vectorized:

$$S_1 : \text{ATEMP}(1 : N) = B(1 : N) + C(1 : N)$$
$$S_2 : A(2 : N + 1) = \text{ATEMP}(1 : N) + 2 * D(1 : N)$$
$$S_1' : A(1 : N) = \text{ATEMP}(1 : N)$$

3.6.A. Consider the algorithm

```
for i = 1, 5
   for j = 1, 11
      for k = 1, 21
         x(i, j, k) = x(i − 1, j, k) + y(i, j − 1, k − 1)
         y(i, j, k) = y(i, j, k − 1) * y(i − 1, j, k − 1)
      end k
   end j
end i
```

(a) For this algorithm, find the data dependence matrix **D**.

(b) Find the optimal time transformation for this algorithm and calculate the parallel processing time.

(c) What is the speedup factor achieved?

Solution.

(a)

$$\mathbf{D} = \begin{matrix} & \mathbf{d_1} & \mathbf{d_2} & \mathbf{d_3} & \mathbf{d_4} \\ & \begin{bmatrix} 1 & 0 & 0 & 1 \\ 0 & 0 & 1 & 0 \\ 0 & 1 & 1 & 1 \end{bmatrix} \\ & x & y & y & y \end{matrix}$$

(b) The optimal time transformation is $\mathbf{\Pi} = [1 \ 0 \ 1]$.

$$\mathbf{\Pi D} = [1 \ 1 \ 1 \ 2]; \quad \mathbf{\Pi d}_i > 0$$

Time calculation:

$$t_{\Pi} = 1 + \frac{\max \mathbf{\Pi}(\mathbf{I}_2 - \mathbf{I}_1)}{\min \mathbf{\Pi d}_i}$$

$$= 1 + \frac{[1 \ 0 \ 1][(5 \ X \ 21)^t - (1 \ X \ 1)^t]}{\min[1 \ 1 \ 1 \ 2]}$$

$$= 1 + \frac{[1 \ 0 \ 1][4 \ 0 \ 20]^t}{1} = 1 + \frac{4 + 0 + 20}{1} = 25$$

(c) Speedup factor:

$$\frac{(5 - 1 + 1)(11 - 1 + 1)(21 - 1 + 1) \times 2}{25} \approx 92.4$$

3.7.A.

DO 2 $I_1 = 0, 9$
    DO 2 $I_2 = 0, 9$
        DO 2 $I_3 = 0, 9$
$S_1 : A(I_1, I_2 + 1, I_3) = B(I_1, I_2, I_3 + 2) * C(I_1, I_2) + U * V$
$S_2 : B(I_1 + 1, I_2, I_3) = A(I_1, I_2, I_3 + 6) * D(I_2, I_3)$
2   CONTINUE

(a) Find the data dependence matrix for this loop.

(b) Can this program be executed serially with respect to I_1 and I_2 and in parallel with respect to I_3? Why or why not? What is the speedup factor?

(c) Can this program be executed serially with respect to I_1 and in parallel with respect to I_2 and I_3? Why or why not? Find the speedup factor.

(d) Find a transformation matrix $\mathbf{T}$ that will transform the index set so this program can be executed in parallel. What is the speedup factor?

(e) Explain parts (b) and (c) of this problem using the method of transformation of index sets.

(f) What is the fastest processing time for this program? Explain.

Solution.

(a)

$$\mathbf{D} = \begin{bmatrix} 1 & 0 \\ 0 & 1 \\ -2 & -6 \end{bmatrix} \begin{matrix} I_1 \\ I_2 \\ I_3 \end{matrix}$$

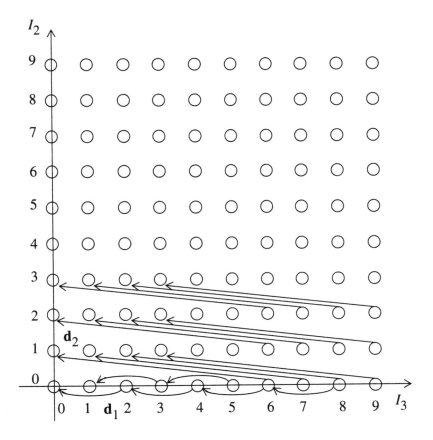

Figure 3.18 Dependencies for Problem 3.7.A.

The projection of these dependencies on the (I_2, I_3) plane is shown in Figure 3.18.

   (b) I_1 serially provides ordering for dependence $\mathbf{d}_1$; I_2 serially provides ordering for dependence $\mathbf{d}_2$. Thus, I_3 can be executed in parallel and the speedup factor is

$$S = \frac{1000}{100} = 10$$

   (c) If we look only at the dependence matrix the answer is no, because of $\mathbf{d}_2$. However, because the low limits on indices I_1, I_2, I_3, the answer is yes. This can be seen in Figure 3.18. The speedup factor is found by observing that the parallel time is 10 iterations along I_1 times 2 steps for all computations in the (I_2, I_3) plane.

$$S = \frac{1000}{10 \times 2} = 50$$

(d) One possible **T** that satisfies $\mathbf{\Pi d}_i > 0$ is

$$\mathbf{T} = \begin{bmatrix} 1 & 1 & 0 \\ 0 & 1 & 0 \\ 0 & 0 & 1 \end{bmatrix}$$

The speedup factor achieved by this transformation is

$$S = \frac{1000}{19}$$

(e) The transformation for part *(b)* has

$$\mathbf{\Pi} = \begin{pmatrix} 1 & 0 & 0 \\ 0 & 1 & 0 \end{pmatrix}$$

By checking condition $\mathbf{\Pi d}_i > 0$, one can see that this $\mathbf{\Pi}$ is valid, which is consistent with the result in part *(b)* of this problem. The transformation for part *(c)* leads to

$$\mathbf{\Pi} = (1 \ 0 \ 0)$$

This $\mathbf{\Pi}$ violates condition $\mathbf{\Pi d}_i > 0$; thus we need

$$\mathbf{\Pi} = \begin{pmatrix} 1 & 0 & 0 \\ 0 & 1 & 1 \end{pmatrix}$$

Notice that the parallelism analysis via transformation does not take into account the limits of indices. Also notice that the sequential execution of a program corresponds to

$$\mathbf{\Pi} = \begin{bmatrix} 1 & 0 & 0 \\ 0 & 1 & 0 \\ 0 & 0 & 1 \end{bmatrix}$$

3.8.A. An algorithm with three nested loops I, J, and K has the following data dependence matrix:

$$\mathbf{D} = \begin{bmatrix} 1 & 0 & 0 & 1 & 0 \\ 0 & 1 & 0 & -1 & 2 \\ 1 & -1 & 1 & 1 & 0 \end{bmatrix} \begin{matrix} I \\ J \\ K \end{matrix}$$

(a) Is it possible to execute loops I, J, and K in parallel? Explain.

(b) Can this algorithm be executed with loop I serially and loops J and K in parallel? Explain.

(c) Is it possible to execute the following four index points simultaneously? Explain.

$$(I \quad J \quad K)$$

$$(1 \quad 1 \quad 1)$$
$$(1 \quad 2 \quad 2)$$
$$(0 \quad 3 \quad 1)$$
$$(2 \quad 0 \quad 2)$$

Solution.

(a) Try to find a $\mathbf{\Pi}$ satisfying $\mathbf{\Pi d}_i > 0$. One of the many possible $\mathbf{\Pi}$ is $\mathbf{\Pi} = [2\ 2\ 1]$.

$$\mathbf{\Pi D} = [3\ 1\ 1\ 1\ 4]$$

All $\mathbf{\Pi d}_j > 0$. Since there exists a $\mathbf{\Pi}$, loops I, J, and K can be done in parallel, at least partially if not completely. Let us take three loop instances, (2 1 1), (1 2 1), and (1 1 3), to illustrate this point.

$$\mathbf{\Pi}(2\ 1\ 1)^t = \mathbf{\Pi}(1\ 2\ 1)^t = \mathbf{\Pi}(1\ 1\ 3)^t = 7$$

(b) Yes, this algorithm can be executed serially with respect to I and in parallel with respect to J and K. This can be done easily by fixing $I = a$ where a ranges from 0 to 9 and executing all instances (a, j, k) such that $2a + 2j + k = $ constant for each $I = a$.

(c) No, these four loop instances cannot be done in parallel.

$$\mathbf{d} = (1\ 2\ 2)^t - (0\ 3\ 1)^t = (1\ -1\ 1)^t$$

Since **d** is in **D**, these four loop instances cannot be done in parallel. Another way to prove this is to show that there is no valid hyperplane **Π** that contains all four index points.

3.9.A. For the loop in the relaxation example (Section 2.2.3), knowing that all points on each plane $2i + j + k = constant$ can be computed in parallel, calculate the overall speedup factor achieved by this parallel scheme over sequential processing.

Solution. The solution to this problem is straightforward. $\mathbf{\Pi} = [2\ 1\ 1]$, from the relation $2i + j + k = constant$. We need to find the data dependence matrix **D** and then apply the equation for parallel time calculation.

$$\mathbf{\Pi} = [\,2\ 1\ 1\,]$$

$$t_1 = l \times m \times n$$

$$\mathbf{D} = \begin{bmatrix} 1 & 1 & 0 & 0 \\ -1 & 0 & 1 & 0 \\ 0 & -1 & 0 & 1 \end{bmatrix}$$

$$\mathbf{\Pi D} = [\,1\ 1\ 1\ 1\,]$$

$$t_p = \frac{\mathbf{\Pi}\left(\begin{bmatrix} l \\ m \\ n \end{bmatrix} - \begin{bmatrix} 1 \\ 1 \\ 1 \end{bmatrix}\right)}{\min(\mathbf{\Pi D})} + 1$$

$$= 2l + m + n - 3$$

$$\text{speedup} = \frac{l \times m \times n}{2l + m + n - 3}$$

3.1.B. For the loop

DO 10 $I = 1, 100$
DO 10 $J = 1, 5$
DO 10 $K = 2, 9$

$S_1:$ $A(I, J - 1, K) = A(I - 1, J - 2, K) + B(I, J, K - 1)$
$S_2:$ $B(I + 1, J, K - 1) = A(I + 1, J - 2, K + 1) * C(I + 1, J, K)$
$S_3:$ $C(I, J, K) = C(I - 2, J, K) +$
$\qquad\qquad + A(I - 3, J, K + 1) * C(I - 3, J + 1, K - 2)$

10 CONTINUE

find the data dependence vectors and identify a transformation **T**. Calculate the speedup factor achieved with this transformation.

3.2.B. Some programs contain array subscript expressions of the form

$$\text{DO } I = L, U$$
$$S_1: \quad A(c * I + j) = \ldots$$
$$S_2: \quad \ldots \qquad = A(c * I + k)$$
$$\text{END DO}$$

where c, d, j, and k are integer constants. Find a condition for detecting the existence of a dependence between the two statements.

3.3.B. Select some criteria and provide a taxonomy of program transformations which, in addition to being input-output equivalent, perform semantic and syntactic changes. Comment on the properties of these transformations.

3.4.B.

$$\text{DO } 10 \ I = 1, 20$$
$$\text{DO } 10 \ J = 1, 10$$
$$\text{DO } 10 \ K = 1, 5$$
$$S_1: A(I, J, K) = A(I - 1, J + 1, K) + B(I, J, K) + C(I, J, K - 1)$$
$$S_2: B(I + 2, J + 1, K + 2) = A(I, J + 1, K) * C(I, J, K)$$
$$S_3: C(I, J, K) = C(I, J - 1, K) + A(I, J, K - 2) * C(I - 1, J, K)$$
$$\text{10 CONTINUE}$$

(a) Find the data dependence vectors.

(b) Can the loop be executed serially with respect to I and in parallel with respect to J and K? Explain. If it is possible, what is the speedup factor?

(c) What is the shortest execution time (maximum parallelism) for this loop? What is the speedup factor in this case?

3.5.B. Consider the sequential algorithm

$$\text{for } i = 1, 10$$
$$\quad \text{for } j = 1, 20$$
$$\quad\quad \text{for } k = 1, 30$$
$$\quad\quad\quad A(i, j, k) = A(i, j - 1, k - 2) + B(i - 1, j, k)$$
$$\quad\quad\quad B(i, j, k) = B(i, j - 1, k + 1)$$
$$\quad\quad \text{end } k$$
$$\quad \text{end } j$$
$$\text{end } i$$

This sequential algorithm is to be transformed into parallel forms using the transformation method.

(a) Write the parallel form that results when the transformation is

$$\mathbf{T} = \begin{bmatrix} \mathbf{\Pi} \\ \mathbf{S} \end{bmatrix} = \left[\begin{array}{ccc} 1 & 2 & 1 \\ \hline 0 & 0 & 1 \\ 1 & 0 & 0 \end{array} \right]$$

where $\mathbf{\Pi}$ is the first row.

(b) Write the parallel form that results when the transformation is

$$\mathbf{T} = \begin{bmatrix} \mathbf{\Pi} \\ \mathbf{S} \end{bmatrix} = \left[\begin{array}{ccc} 1 & 2 & 1 \\ 0 & 0 & 1 \\ \hline 1 & 0 & 0 \end{array} \right]$$

where $\mathbf{\Pi}$ is the first two rows.

3.6.B. For the nested loop

$$\text{for } I = 1, 5$$
$$\quad \text{for } J = 1, 5$$
$$\quad\quad \text{for } K = 1, 5$$
$$\quad\quad A(J, K) = A(J + 1, K) + A(J, K + 1) + A(J - 1, K) + A(J, K - 1)$$
$$\quad\quad \text{end } K$$
$$\quad \text{end } J$$
$$\text{end } I$$

is it possible to calculate in parallel the values of A at the following points ?

$$
\begin{array}{ccc}
(I & J & K) \\
(5 & 3 & 1) \\
(1 & 1 & 1) \\
(3 & 4 & 5)
\end{array}
$$

3.7.B. For the program with a dependence matrix

$$
\mathbf{D} = \begin{bmatrix} 2 & 4 \\ 6 & 3 \\ 0 & 2 \end{bmatrix} \begin{matrix} I_1 \\ I_2 \\ I_3 \end{matrix}
$$

how many independent processes can be formed? Demonstrate and generalize the result for m dependencies and n indices.

3.8.B. The following algorithm describes a recurrence relation:

$$
\begin{aligned}
A(j_1, j_2) = A(j_1 - 5, j_2 - 1) * \; & (A(j_1 - 1, j_2) + A(j_1 - 2, j_2) + \\
& +A(j_1 - 3, j_2) + A(j_1 - 4, j_2))
\end{aligned}
$$

$$
0 \le j_1 \le 19, \quad 0 \le j_2 \le 19
$$

(a) For this algorithm, find the data dependence matrix and the optimal time transformation, and calculate the parallel time.

(b) Modify the structure of the algorithm such that it will result in a faster processing time. What is the speedup factor obtained?

3.9.B. Consider the algorithm described by the program

```
      for j₁ = 0 to N − 1
            for j₂ = 0 to N − 1
                  for j₃ = 0 to N − 1
(j₄ = 0)          if j₃ = 0 then C(j₁, j₂) = C(j₁ − 2, j₂ − 1) * C(j₁ − 1, j₂)
(j₄ = 1)                A(j₁, j₂, j₃) = C(j₁ − 1, j₂ − 1) * A(j₁ − 1, j₂, j₃ − 1)
                  end j₃
            end j₂
      end j₁
```

which has the index set

$$\mathbf{J}^4 = \{(j_1, j_2, j_3, j_4) : 0 \le j_i \le N - 1, \quad i = 1, 2, 3, \quad 0 \le j_4 \le 1\}$$

Use coordinate j_4 to distinguish between the two computations of the inner loop body. Find an equivalent form for this algorithm for which a linear transformation exists. Calculate the processing time.

3.10.B. For the program in Problem 2.13.B, find a valid Π transformation. Explain your solution.

3.11.B. For the following algorithm:

for $i = 1, 10$
  for $j = 1, 10$
    for $k = 1, 10$
      $a(i, j, k) = a(i - 1, j + 1, k) + a(i, j, k - 2) * a(i, j - 1, k)$
    end k
  end j
end i

(a) Can this algorithm be executed serially with respect to i and j and in parallel with respect to k? What is the speedup factor?

(b) Can this algorithm be executed serially with respect to i and in parallel to j and k? What is the speedup factor?

3.12.B. For the program in Problem 3.7.A, which loops can be interchanged?

3.13.B. Apply a DOACROSS trasformation to the program shown in Example 3.14.

3.14.B. For the Cholesky algorithm presented in Problem 2.5.A, find a time transformation that provides a parallel execution time $t = 3(n - 1) + 1$.

3.15.B.

for $i = 1$ to 5
   for $j = 1$ to 6
      for $k = 1$ to 7
      $x(i, j, k) = x(i - 1, j, k - 1) + y(i, j, k - 1)$
      $y(i, j, k) = 2 * y(i - 1, j - 1, k)$
      end k
   end j
end i

This program is to be transformed into a parallel form with DOACROSS loops by the transformation

$$\mathbf{T} = \left[\begin{array}{ccc} 1 & 1 & 1 \\ \hline 0 & 1 & 0 \\ 0 & 0 & 1 \end{array} \right]$$

Write the new parallel form in terms of the transformed indices. Pay attention to the limits of the new indices. What is the speedup achieved by this transformed algorithm over the sequential form?

Chapter 4

ARRAY PROCESSORS

An *array processor* is a synchronous parallel computer that consists of multiple processing elements (PEs) under the supervision of a single control unit (CU). The CU fetches and decodes instructions from the program memory, then broadcasts control signals to all processors in the array such that the processors perform the same operation at the same time.

Depending upon the PEs' mode of operation and the controls received, array processors may be classified as traditional single-instruction multiple-data (SIMD) processors, systolic processors, or associative processors. *Traditional SIMD processors* are simply extensions of the von Neumann model in which the data processing unit is replicated. These processors closely follow the von Neumann mode of operation and, historically, were the first array processors built. *Systolic processors* combine the idea of using numerous simple data-processing units with pipelining. Instead of storing data in local memories, like the traditional SIMD model, systolic arrays move data rhythmically from processor to processor until all operations are performed. *Associative processors* also depart from the von Neumann concept in the sense that data accessing is content-dependent, not address-dependent. Many operations are executed locally inside memory.

Today the possibility of building integrated circuit technology opens the way for array processors with tens of thousands, even hundreds of

thousands, of PEs. Two examples of large systems achieving supercomputer performance are presented in this chapter: the Connection
Machine and the Hughes 3-D Computer.

4.1   SINGLE-INSTRUCTION MULTIPLE-DATA (SIMD) COMPUTERS

An SIMD computer consists of an array of processing elements, memory
elements (M), a control unit, and an interconnection network (IN).
Such computers are attached to a host machine, which from the user's
point of view is a front-end system. The role of the host computer is
to perform compilation, load programs, perform I/O operations, and
execute other operating system functions.

We will examine three distinct organizations of SIMD computers:
local-memory, shared-memory, and three-dimensional wafer-scale.

4.1.1   Local-Memory SIMD Model

Specific to the model shown in Figure 4.1 is the fact that each PE
has its own memory unit. The control unit fetches instructions from
the CU's memory. It executes the instructions if they are control-
type instructions or if they have scalar operands. If they are vector
instructions, the CU broadcasts the instructions to the PE array. The
CU can also broadcast data words as they may be needed for vector
scalar operations.

In the case in which the PEs need to fetch data from their own
memories, the CU broadcasts the addresses to the PEs. The instruction
issued by the CU normally supplies the same address to all processors.
However, in order to increase the addressing capability of processors,
an index register may be used to modify the memory address supplied
by the controller. The programmer may set the index register in each
processor. Flexible addressing schemes are possible. Data communication is realized by moving data from one processor to another via
an interconnection network. Each processor, or group of processors,
has communication ports and data buffers. The interconnection network performs several mapping functions, depending on the network

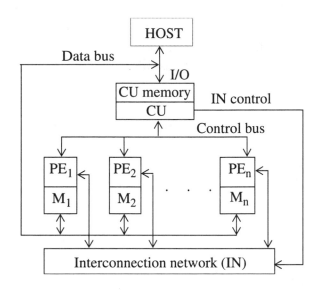

Figure 4.1 Local-memory SIMD computer.

topology and the control received from the CU.

The processors are equipped with status registers that store flags resulting from arithmetic or logic tests. In some instances, the CU checks the status of the PEs' condition flags. Most often, the condition flags are ORed together for all the PEs. A typical operation might be a jump that results from an accumulator being set to zero in the previous operation.

The granularity and the number of PEs, the size of the local memory, and the type of interconnection network vary from one implementation to another. One of the earliest parallel computers ever built used this model. This was the Illiac IV system, at the University of Illinois in the late 1960s. The experience gained with this computer has significantly influenced the development of parallel processing and especially the development of array processors. Illiac IV had 64 processors, organized in an 8×8 array. Each processor was connected to its four neighbors; a processor consisted of an ALU and several registers.

The Connection Machine (CM), built at Thinking Machines Corporation in 1985, is an example of a supercomputer that basically fits this model. In the CM, the number of processors was increased dramatically to 64K, while their granularity was decreased to the point where processors perform bit-serial operations. The local memory for each processor is 64K bits of bit-addressable memory. Because of the large number of processors in the CM, it is not possible to achieve interconnections for each individual PE. Instead, 16 PEs are grouped into a node that is served by a router, and the 4K nodes are connected in a 12-cube network.

Next, it is shown how a problem such as matrix multiplication can be mapped and executed on a local-memory SIMD model.

Example 4.1. Consider the matrix multiplication problem in Section 2.2.2. Let **A** and **B** be two $n \times n$ matrices, to be multiplied on a SIMD computer with n processors:

$$\mathbf{C} = \mathbf{AB} \quad \text{or} \quad c_{ij} = \sum_{k=1}^{n} a_{ik} b_{kj}$$

Considering that computations along index j are performed in parallel, a parallel program can be written as shown in Program 4.1.

Program 4.1.

```
for i = 1 to n
    in parallel for all j,   1 ≤ j ≤ n
        c(i, j) = 0
        for k = 1 to n
            c(i, j) = c(i, j) + a(i, k) * b(k, j)
        end loop k
end loop i
```

Assume that the CU has several index registers and that it can broadcast their contents to PEs. Indices are used by PEs to form operand addresses. The registers in each PE are denoted by $RA, RB,$

M_1	M_2	M_3	M_4
a_{11}	a_{12}	a_{13}	a_{14}
a_{21}	a_{22}	a_{23}	a_{24}
a_{31}	a_{32}	a_{33}	a_{34}
a_{41}	a_{42}	a_{43}	a_{44}
b_{11}	b_{12}	b_{13}	b_{14}
b_{21}	b_{22}	b_{23}	b_{24}
b_{31}	b_{32}	b_{33}	b_{34}
b_{41}	b_{42}	b_{43}	b_{44}
c_{11}	c_{12}	c_{13}	c_{14}
c_{21}	c_{22}	c_{23}	c_{24}
c_{31}	c_{32}	c_{33}	c_{34}
c_{41}	c_{42}	c_{43}	c_{44}

Figure 4.2 Storage format.

and RC. Consider the particular case in which $n = 4$:

$$
\begin{array}{c}
k \longrightarrow \\
i \downarrow
\end{array}
\begin{bmatrix}
a_{11} & a_{12} & a_{13} & a_{14} \\
a_{21} & a_{22} & a_{23} & a_{24} \\
a_{31} & a_{32} & a_{33} & a_{34} \\
a_{41} & a_{42} & a_{43} & a_{44}
\end{bmatrix}
\times
\begin{array}{c}
j \longrightarrow \\
k \downarrow
\end{array}
\begin{bmatrix}
b_{11} & b_{12} & b_{13} & b_{14} \\
b_{21} & b_{22} & b_{23} & b_{24} \\
b_{31} & b_{32} & b_{33} & b_{34} \\
b_{41} & b_{42} & b_{43} & b_{44}
\end{bmatrix}
$$

$$
=
\begin{array}{c}
j \longrightarrow \\
i \downarrow
\end{array}
\begin{bmatrix}
c_{11} & c_{12} & c_{13} & c_{14} \\
c_{21} & c_{22} & c_{23} & c_{24} \\
c_{31} & c_{32} & c_{33} & c_{34} \\
c_{41} & c_{43} & c_{43} & c_{44}
\end{bmatrix}
$$
$$P_1 \quad P_2 \quad P_3 \quad P_4$$

The storage format for each memory is shown in Figure 4.2. The matrix multiplication shown above can now be rewritten for an SIMD machine as Program 4.2.

Program 4.2.

for $i = 1$ to n
  in parallel for all j, $1 \leq j \leq n$
    $RC(j) = 0$ /* processors clear RC registers */
    for $k = 1$ to n
      fetch $a(i, k)$ /* by control unit */
      broadcast $a(i, k)$ /* by control unit */
      $RA(j) = a(i, k)$ /* processors store broadcast data */
      $RB(j) = b(k, j)$ /* processors fetch local operands */
      $RA(j) = A(j) * RB(j)$ /* processors multiply */
      $RC(j) = RA(j) + RC(j)$ /* processors update RC registers */
    end loop k
    $c(i, j) = RC(j)$ /* processors store RC registers */
end loop i.

The complexity of this program is $O(n^2)$ because there are two nested loops i and k, and only loop j is done in parallel. There are several possible ways in which data may be stored in memory. Each way requires a slightly modified program, possibly leading to different performance. The complexity may be reduced further if more processors are available. If the number of processors is smaller than n, then it is necessary to *partition* the algorithm. One simple way of partitioning the algorithm is to allocate more than one column of the matrix to memory modules.

The nature of SIMD programming makes it easy to execute instructions broadcast from the controller to array processors (one-to-many), but it is more difficult for the controller to collect data or status information from array processors (many-to-one). Collecting data from processors should be avoided as much as possible.

Another difficulty is dealing with subsets of processors instead of the entire set. In many situations some processors need to be *masked off* so they will not participate in the next instruction execution. The turning off of processors can be achieved based on local information stored within each processor, such as flags that have resulted from previous operations, or the controller may deliberately turn off some processors by specifically addressing them. SIMD programs should avoid condi-

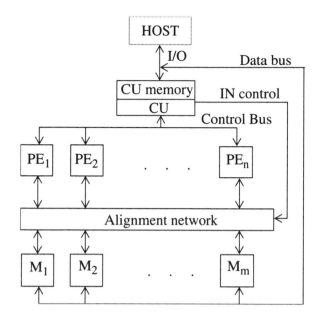

Figure 4.3 Shared-memory SIMD computer.

tional branches as much as possible, because it is inherently difficult for array processors to handle split instruction streams.

An important and rather difficult design problem is fanning out control signals and clocks to all processing elements. This problem is exacerbated when the number of PEs becomes large. It tends to limit the clock rate, and often restricts the growth of the system.

4.1.2   Shared-Memory SIMD Model

In the shared-memory model shown in Figure 4.3, the memories are separated from the processing elements through an interconnection network. Any processor can access any memory, and the network is such that it allows parallel access to shared memories. An advantage of this model is that more processor-to-memory mapping functions are obtained, which means that more algorithms can be more easily mapped into the hardware. This is achieved, of course, at the cost of more data switching, which translates into increased memory-access time.

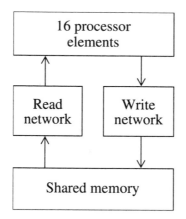

Figure 4.4 Cyclic pipeline used in a BSP array processor.

The CU performs functions similar to those it performed in the previous model. However, since memory access is more frequent, network control is more complex.

Pipelined Operation

Pipelining is a powerful idea that can significantly improve SIMD computer performance. As with any control unit, pipelining may be used to overlap phases of intruction execution and data communication. In addition to this rather straightforward pipelining operation, a cyclic pipeline may be formed among processors, memories, and the interconnection network. Such an operation was first used in the Burroughs Scientific Processor (BSP).

The array unit shown in Figure 4.4 consists of 16 large granularity processing elements, 8M words of memory that are partitioned into 17 modules, and two interconnection networks (one for writing to memories and one for reading from memories). These four components of the array unit form a cyclic pipeline.

The operations or tasks performed by this pipeline are as follows:

1. Read operands from parallel memories;

2. Transfer operands from memories to processing elements using read network;

3. Execute instruction using processors;

4. Transfer results to memories using write network; and

5. Store results in parallel memories.

Each array instruction is broken down into these five stages by the controller unit. Stages of successive vector instructions are overlapped. Thus, in addition to the parallelism achieved by simultaneous operation of processing elements, more parallelism is provided through pipelining. Because of this five-stage cyclic pipeline, the BSP can efficiently compile vector instructions with one to five operands. (See Problem 4.11.B.)

4.1.3   Three-Dimensional SIMD Model

Recent progress made in wafer-scale integration (WSI) technology opens, for the first time, the possibility of building three-dimensional computers. Figure 4.5 shows a model of a system consisting of a stack of wafers. There are several types of wafers, such as an ALU, registers, memory, interconnection networks, and possibly many others, placed one on top of another. The electrical connections between wafers are made via vertical buses; one bus links a column of modules, and there are $N \times N$ such columns. Thus, a novel feature of this model is the way in which the system is partitioned. Instead of packaging an ALU, registers, memory, and IN logic together as a distinct processor module, as in the conventional approach to building parallel computers, in the three-dimensional WSI model these basic building blocks are distributed over a stack of wafers. With this three-dimensional partitioning of the system, the complexity of each of the processors in the array is determined by the depth of the three-dimensional stack.

Because of the regularity of array processors and their rather simple method of programming, they are the first candidates among parallel computers to benefit from three-dimensional wafer-scale integration technology. So far, the only computer using this technologically driven SIMD model is the 3-D Computer, built at Hughes Research Laboratories, where this technology was developed. Each wafer contains 128 × 128 hardware cells. These cells perform serial arithmetic. Data communication is achieved by allowing data to move north, south, east, and

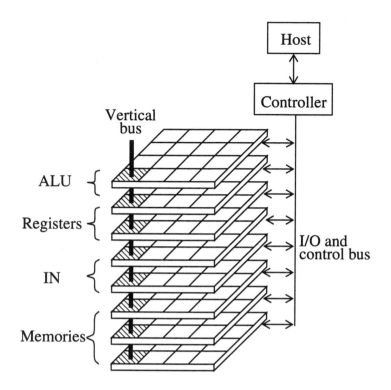

Figure 4.5 Three-dimensional SIMD model.

west locally in most of the wafers, and by providing interconnection wafers with row and column broadcasts.

In the operation of such a model, as with any SIMD computer, the controller broadcasts instructions to each wafer type; thus, several wafers may be active at the same time. However, massive parallelism is achieved by simultaneous operation of all cells in each active wafer.

Note that this SIMD model may achieve processor-processor communication (as in the local-memory SIMD model) as well as processor-memory communication (as in the shared-memory SIMD model). Among the INs that are practical for this model are nearest-neighbor, common buses, and crossbars. This model features large-number, small-granularity processors.

4.2 INTERCONNECTION NETWORKS FOR SIMD COMPUTERS

An important part of a SIMD computer is the interconnection network used to exchange information among PEs or between PEs and memory modules. Often the communication networks can be described by a set of interconnection functions. These functions map the set of N inputs into a set of N outputs. The inputs and outputs are processors or memories.

A network performing all possible mappings is called a *generalized connection* network. There are N^N such mappings. If we limit the mappings only to *bijections* (one-to-one and onto mappings), the number of mappings is reduced to $N!$.

The number of processors in a modern machine can easily reach the hundreds of thousands, or in some cases even more. To interconnect these processors is a nontrivial task. In SIMD computers, processors must send data to other processors simultaneously. Ideally, one wants each processor connected to any other processor, as shown in Figure 4.6(a). This fully connected network requires $N(N-1)$ links or $O(N^2)$ links. Clearly, this becomes prohibitively expensive when N is large.

An obvious way to implement a generalized connection is by using the crossbar switch, as shown in Figure 4.6(b). Such a network has been used in the BSP computer and in several other parallel computers in which the number of processors were small.

4.2.1 Permutation Functions

In this section, several permutation functions are described. Permutations are simple bijection functions in which each input is mapped into one and only one output. They play an important role in the design of interconnection networks. By combining several bijections, complex connections may be achieved.

When a routing function f is executed in an SIMD interconnection network, the data from PE_i is sent to $PE_{f(i)}$. This data routing occurs simultaneously for all active PE_i in the set. An inactive PE may receive data from another PE when a routing function is executed, but it

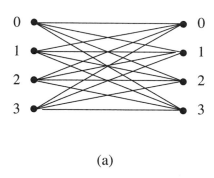
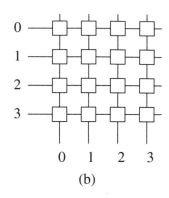

(a)   (b)

Figure 4.6 Fully connected networks: (a) dedicated links;
(b) crossbar switch.

cannot transmit data. It is necessary to assign an address to each PE
in the array. Several addressing schemes may be used. In one scheme,
processors are addressed by m-bit address fields, where $N = 2^m$. In
other cases, when processors are displayed in a two-dimensional array,
it is advantageous to address the PEs by their cartesian coordinates.

Let x be an address of a PE expressed by the m-bit address field:

$$x = (b_m, \; b_{m-1}, ..., \; b_1) \tag{4.1}$$

The network interconnections can be described as permutations on binary representations of inputs. The permutations that have been used
are discussed below.

Exchange

The exchange permutation is defined as

$$E_k(x) = (b_m, ...\bar{b}_k, ...b_1) \quad 1 \le k \le m \tag{4.2}$$

The exchange IN for the case $m = 3$ is shown in Figure 4.7. An intuitively appealing representation of these permutations is achieved by
considering that processors are the vertices of a cube; then the exchanges are the links between these vertices. $E_1(x) = b_3 b_2 \bar{b}_1$ corresponds to horizontal links, $E_2(x) = b_3 \bar{b}_2 b_1$ corresponds to oblique links,
and $E_3(x) = \bar{b}_3 b_2 b_1$ corresponds to vertical links.

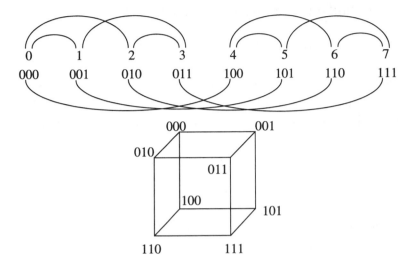

Figure 4.7 Exchange interconnection.

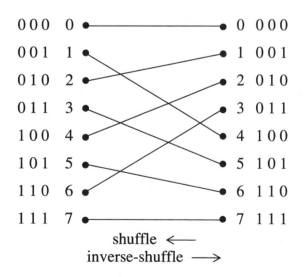

Figure 4.8 Perfect-shuffle interconnection.

Perfect-Shuffle

The perfect-shuffle permutation is defined as

$$S(x) = (b_{m-1}, b_{m-2}, ..., b_1, b_m) \qquad (4.3)$$

The perfect-shuffle interconnection for the case $m = 3$ is shown in Figure 4.8. The kth subshuffle S_k and the kth supershuffle S^k can also be used on the least and most significant k bits, respectively:

$$S_k(x) = (b_m, ..., b_{k+1}, b_{k-1}, ..., b_1, b_k)$$

$$S^k(x) = (b_{m-1}, ..., b_{m-k+1}, b_m, b_{m-k}, ..., b_1)$$

Suppose, for example, that $m = 6$ and $k = 3$. The subshuffle and supershuffle in this case are:

$$S_3(x) = (b_6\ b_5\ b_4\ b_2\ b_1\ b_3)$$

$$S^3(x) = (b_5\ b_4\ b_6\ b_3\ b_2\ b_1)$$

Butterfly

The butterfly permutation is defined as

$$B(x) = (b_1, b_{m-1}, ..., b_2, b_m) \qquad (4.4)$$

The butterfly interconnection for the case $m = 3$ is shown in Figure 4.9. The kth subbutterfly and k^{th} superbutterfly can also be defined as

$$B_k(x) = (b_m, ..., b_{k+1}, b_1, b_{k-1}, ..., b_k)$$

$$B^k(x) = (b_{m-k+1}, ..., b_{m-k+2}, b_m, b_{m-k}, ..., b_1)$$

Bit-Reversal

The bit-reversal permutation is defined as

$$R(x) = (b_1, b_2, ..., b_m) \qquad (4.5)$$

The bit-reversal interconnection for the case $m = 3$ is shown in Figure 4.10.

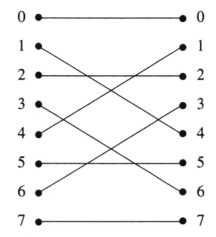

Figure 4.9 Butterfly interconnection.

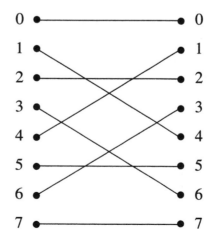

Figure 4.10 Bit-reversal interconnection.

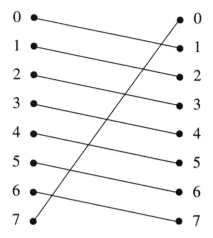

Figure 4.11 Shift interconnection.

Shift
The shift permutation is defined as

$$SH(x) = |x + 1|_N \tag{4.6}$$

where $| \ |_N$ means modulo N. The shift interconnection for the case $m = 3$ is shown in Figure 4.11.

It is easy to determine relations between different permutations. Notice for example that for $m = 3$,

$$R_3 = B_3$$

For some interconnections, such as the Illiac network, it is preferable to use directly the index of each processing element PE_x, for $0 \le x \le N - 1$. The connections from PE_x are defined by the destination processor element. In the discussion that follows, $r = \sqrt{N}$.

Illiac Network
A popular interconnection used in the Illiac IV computer, called the Illiac network, is defined as

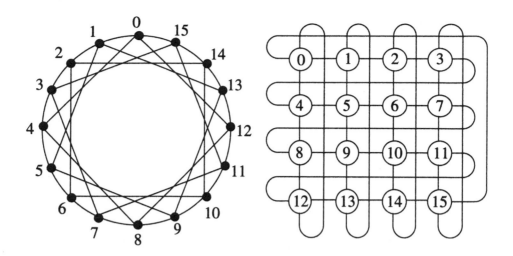

Figure 4.12 Two representations of the Illiac network.

$$\left. \begin{array}{l} R_{+1}(x) = (x + 1) \mod N \\ R_{-1}(x) = (x - 1) \mod N \\ R_{+r}(x) = (x + r) \mod N \\ R_{+r}(x) = (x - r) \mod N \end{array} \right\} \quad (4.7)$$

For the case in which $N = 16$ and $r = 4$, the Illiac network is shown in Figure 4.12. The Illiac network is a partially connected network. When $N = 16$, four PEs can be reached in one step, seven PEs can be reached in two steps, and eleven PEs can be reached in three steps. In general, it takes $I \leq \sqrt{N} - 1$ steps to reach any processor.

Barrel-Shifter
The barrel-shifter, or plus-minus $2I$, interconnection is defined as

$$\left. \begin{array}{l} B_{+i}(x) = (x + 2^i) \mod N \\ B_{-i}(x) = (x - 2^i) \mod N \end{array} \right\} \quad (4.8)$$

where $0 \leq x \leq N - 1, 0 \leq i \leq \log N - 1, n = \log N$, and $r = \sqrt{N}$.

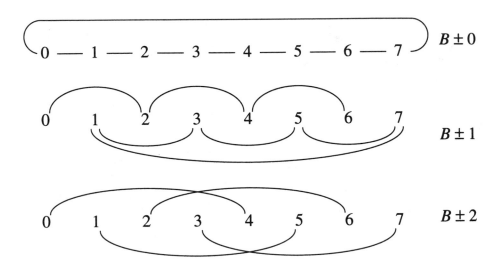

Figure 4.13 Barrel-shifter interconnection for $N = 8$.

for $i = 0$
$$B_{+0} = R_{+1}$$
$$B_{+0} = R_{-1}$$
$$B_{+n/2} = R_{+r}$$
$$B_{-n/2} = R_{-r}$$

The conclusion is that the functions of the Illiac network are only a subset of the barrel-shifting functions. Displacements ± 1, ± 2, ± 4, ..., $\pm 2^{n/2}$, ..., $\pm 2^{n-1}$ are achieved by the barrel-shifter. The barrel-shifter interconnection for $N = 8$ is shown in Figure 4.13; the one for $N = 16$ is shown in Figure 4.14.

4.2.2   Single-Stage Networks

In practice, two types of interconnection networks are used in SIMD computers: *single-stage* and *multistage* networks.

Figure 4.15(a) shows the concept behind single-stage, or recirculating, networks. The inputs are connected to outputs via the connection network. The outputs of a cycle become the inputs of the next cy-

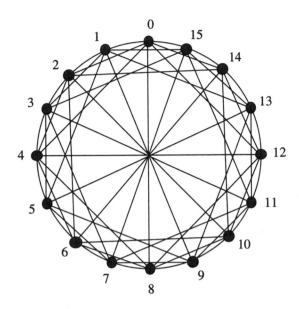

Figure 4.14 Barrel-shifter interconnection for $N = 16$.

cle, and the process repeats. Thus, in reality, the network has only N terminals, as shown in Figure 4.15(b).

Single-stage networks perform only a limited number of functions in each cycle, but more complex functions can be achieved by using the network iteratively. The design tradeoff is that the cost is decreased at the expense of increasing the operation time. Single-stage networks can be described mathematically by the set of bijection functions that the network can perform in one cycle.

$$NET = \{F_1, F_2, ..., F_k\}$$

The number of functions performed simultaneously depends on the hardware complexity. Usually communication hardware is shared between several functions. Also, it is important to realize that at any given time, some processors may be masked off and therefore may not participate in data transfer. Let I be the identity permutation $I(x) = x$. Examples of single-stage networks are discussed below.

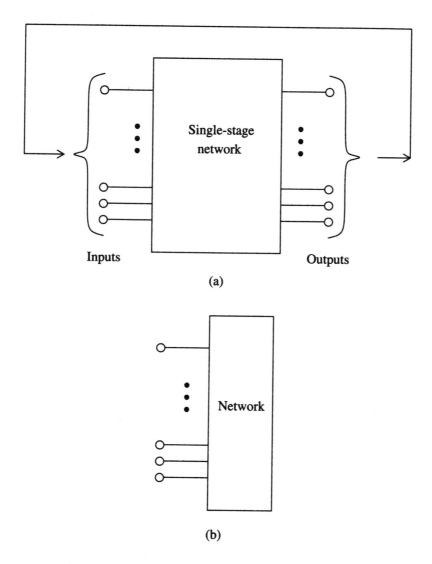

Figure 4.15 Single-stage networks: (a) conceptual view of single-stage
network; (b) actual connection of single-stage network.

Ring Network

$$RING = \{I, SH\}$$

consists of identity and circular shift permutations.

Nearest-Neighbor

$$NN = \{SH^{-1}, I, SH\}$$

consists of bidirectional rings. The inverse of a permutation function F is such that $FF^{-1} = I$. For example, $SH^{-1}SH = I$.

Shuffle-Exchange

$$SE = \{S^{-1}, E_1^{-1}, I, E_1, S\}$$

This is a popular network because a large number of applications map naturally into it.

Perfect-Shuffle Nearest-Neighbor

$$SNN = \{S^{-1}, SH^{-1}, I, SH, S\}$$

consists of bidirectional shuffles and shifts.

4.2.3 Multistage Networks

Multistage networks are normally used when a rich connection is required and the number of processors is large. As shown in Figure 4.16, these networks consist of a series of switching stages, with two consecutive stages connected by a permutation network. They can be described by three parameters: switching box, network topology, and control structure.

The *switching box* building block is typically a two-input–two-output connection device. More than two inputs or outputs may be used. Several switching boxes are arranged in a column that constitutes one stage of the network. A two-function switching box is capable of either straight or exchange connections. A four-function switching box

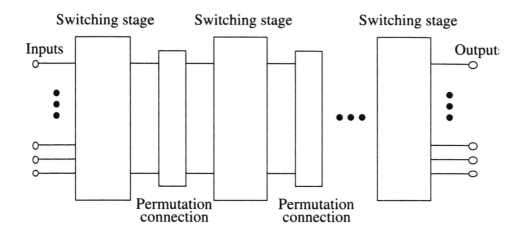

Figure 4.16 Multistage network.

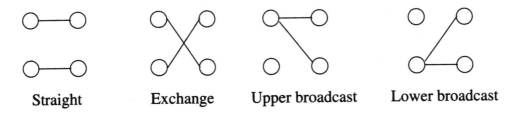

Figure 4.17 Two-input–two-output switching boxes.

can perform straight, exchange, lower-broadcast, and upper-broadcast connections, as illustrated in Figure 4.17.

The *network topology* is defined by the interconnection pattern that is used to connect the outputs of one stage to the inputs of the next stage. The network topology is usually a permutation function, such as cube, perfect-shuffle, butterfly, and so on.

The *control structure* determines the operation of switching boxes. Two types of control strategies are possible: individual stage control and individual box control. Individual stage control uses the same control signals to set the states of all boxes in a stage; individual box control uses separate control signals for each box. Obviously, in the

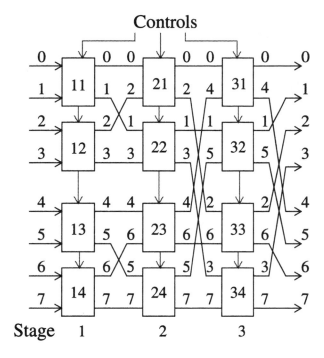

Figure 4.18 Multistage cube network.

second case, more flexibility is gained at the cost of increased hardware complexity.

Next, two multistage networks are described.

Multistage Cube Network

This multistage network, connecting N inputs to N outputs, consists of $\log N$ stages of $N/2$ switching boxes. The multistage cube network for $N = 8$ is shown in Figure 4.18. The network topology is such that stage i implements the E_i exchange (cube) routing function. This means that the switch boxes at stage i connect lines differing in the ith bit position. The control scheme implements individual stage control; that is, all the boxes in a column perform similar functions. Only two out of four possible functions are implemented; these are $f_i = 1$, for exchange, and $f_i = 0$, for straight connections for each column i. This network has been implemented in the Staran computer.

Omega Network

The Omega network, studied by D. Lawrie [Lawrie 1975], has $\log N$ identical stages of $N/2$ switching boxes. Between two adjacent stages, there is a perfect-shuffle connection, as shown in Figure 4.19. The switch boxes in each stage are under independent control. Each box is a four-function switch. Thus, more interconnections are possible on this network. For example, the Omega network can perform connections 0 to 5 and 1 to 7 simultaneously, but the multistage cube network cannot. In general, the Omega network can perform connections of the one-to-many type, whereas the cube network cannot. For bijection interconnections, the two networks are functionally equivalent through some relabeling technique. The Cedar multiprocessor is an example of a parallel machine using the Omega network.

By varying the design parameters—functions and size of switching boxes, network topology, and network control—one can design many interconnection networks with different characteristics.

4.3   SIMD SUPERCOMPUTERS

4.3.1   The Connection Machine

The Connection Machine, model CM-2, which was produced by Thinking Machines in 1987, is an example of a fine-grain SIMD computer. From the beginning it was designed to achieve supercomputer performance. Supercomputers are those computers which achieve the highest performance for their time. With its peak performance of 40 Gflops, the CM-2 is one of the top supercomputers of the early 1990s. As we have indicated in Chapter 1, future Connection Machines have the potential to lead the race to achieve Tflop performance.

In 1991, a new model, the CM-5, became available. It is expected that Connection Machine models will reach Tflop performance by the mid-1990s.

System Organization

The architectural design of the CM-2 was dominated by two main goals: (1) massive parallelism, achieved through a large number of small-grain processors, and (2) programmable interconnections.

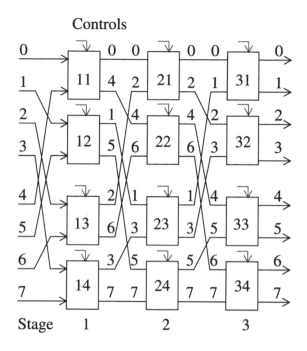

Figure 4.19 Omega network.

The first goal derives from the need to cope with large-size problems. The desire for massive parallelism implied that the processors would be as small and as simple as possible. Each processor has some memory associated with it. The second design goal, programmable connections, derives from the desire to provide fast communication for problems in which the communication requirements are not necessarily regular and can change rapidly. The cells are connected together into data dependent patterns (active data structures). The CM has the ability to change the pattern of connections, and thus to configure its topology to match the connection requirements of various problems. A connection between two processors is achieved by storing pointers in the memories associated with the cells. This is an important feature of the machine; in fact, its name, Connection Machine, is related to this property.

The CM-2 is a large, fine-grain, parallel computer system. A system block diagram is shown in Figure 4.20. At the heart of the system are

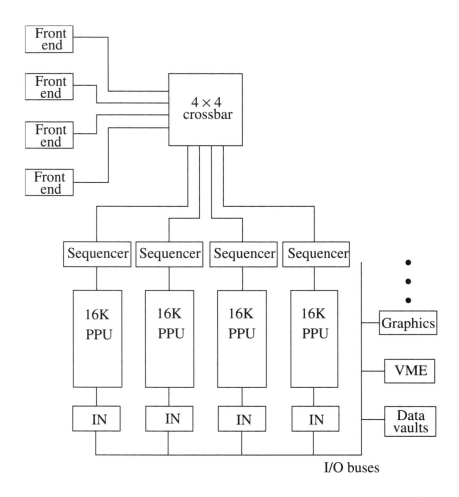

Figure 4.20 Connection Machine system organization.

the 64K processors, organized in four 16K partitions. Each partition
is controlled by a sequencer. The four sequencers are connected to as
many as four front-end computer systems through a 4 × 4 cross-point
switch. The front-end systems act as host machines and provide the
execution environments for system software. The sequencer acts as a
controller for the parallel processing unit (PPU). The commands from
the front-end computer are decoded by the sequencer and transformed
into nanoinstruction signals that are broadcast to the entire array of

processors. The data I/O system is designed for interfacing the processing units with mass-storage units (called data vaults), VME interface, graphics, and other components.

Systems Architecture

The CM-2 processors are grouped into nodes of 16 processors. Each node is constructed using four types of chips:

- A custom chip incorporating 16 processors and interconnection network interface;

- Memory chips;

- A custom floating-point interface chip; and

- A floating-point execution chip.

Each of the four PPUs of 16K processors is structured as a set of 4K nodes. The node organization is shown in Figure 4.21. The memory and floating-point chips are shared between two nodes. The memory is organized such that each processor has 256K bits of bit-addressable memory.

The CM-2 processors perform instructions one bit at a time. Figure 4.22 shows the organization of a processor. The ALU consists of logic implementing a three-input, two-output logic circuit. On each bit cycle a processor reads two bits from its off-chip memory and writes back one bit. It can also read any of its four flags and write any flag bit. The bit-serial ALU computes two functions of three input bits. Using 16 control bits, the circuit provides 2 result bits, one of which is stored back into memory and the other one into a flag.

The floating-point interface chip provides memory address control for indirect addressing, and provides 32-bit operands to the floating-point execution chip. The floating-point chips significantly enhance the processing power of the CM-2.

Data Communication

Interprocessor communication in the CM-2 is accomplished by special-purpose hardware. Through message-passing, all processors can simultaneously read/write data from/to the local memories of other processors. The flexibility of CM communication derives from the fact that several distinct communication mechanisms are possible:

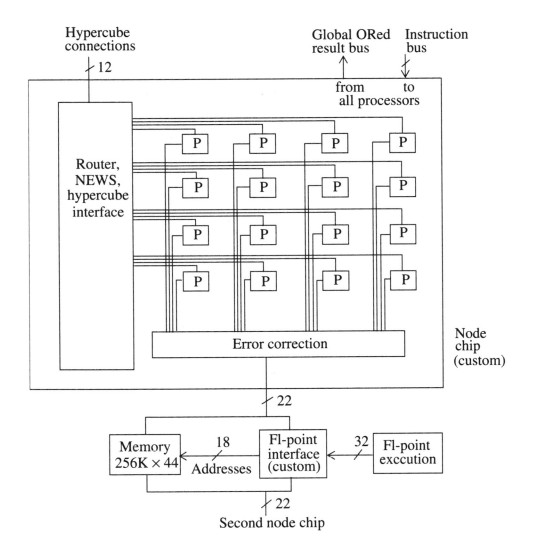

Figure 4.21 CM-2 node organization.

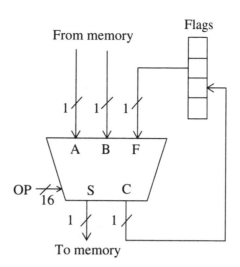

Figure 4.22 CM-2 bit-serial data processor.

- *Broadcast communication* allows instruction or data to be broad-cast from the front-end computer, through the sequencers, to all the data processors.

- *Hypercube communication* provides a boolean n-cube connection among the 4096 processor chips; that is, each 16-processor chip is a vertex of a 12-cube network. The router in each chip uses the hypercube connection for data transmission. Communication is message-based, with routing decisions, buffering, and the com-bining of messages all directed to the same address.

- *Nearest-neighbor communication* is provided among the proces-sors in each chip, as well as among the chips. The 16 processors within each chip are arranged in a two-dimensional array. In the CM-2, the nearest-neighbor communication between chips is sup-ported by the 12-cube network. Nearest-neighbor communication assures simple and fast data routing for a wide range of problems, especially numeric.

Programming the CM-2.

When solving large problems on the CM-2, the programmer deals with virtual processors that are mapped into real processors. This is achieved by dividing the storage of a physical processor into smaller portions so that many virtual processors share one physical processor.

The CM-2 can be programmed in Fortran, C*, *Lisp, and CM assembly language. The first three are extensions of the high-level languages, which contain parallel constructs to support CM-2 data structures. An effort was made to utilize existing languages and software environments as much as possible.

The CM programs execute on a front-end computer. This computer issues instructions to the sequencer, which in turn translates these instructions into single-cycle nanoinstructions that drive the array processor hardware.

4.3.2   The Hughes 3-D Computer

System Organization

The 3-D Computer, developed recently at Hughes Research Laboratories, represents a significant technological achievement because it is the first system built with three-dimensional wafer-scale integration technology. The functional blocks of the individual array processing elements, such as the arithmetic logic unit, registers, comparator, memory, and other logic, are distributed across a number of vertically aligned wafers. Each wafer in the stack contains an entire 128×128 array constituting one particular functional block. The stack of wafers is approximately 1 inch high and 4 inches in diameter. This massively parallel cellular configuration is particularly well suited to on-board processing, as in image-based aerospace applications.

Figure 4.23 is a block diagram of a complete 3-D system. The 3-D processor is connected to a controller that is capable of providing control signals and data. The controller is connected through a standard VME bus to a host computer and a frame grabber. The host has software for transforming an application program into microinstructions that are readily executable by the controller. The role of the frame grabber is to continuously provide row-image data to the 3-D processor. Of course,

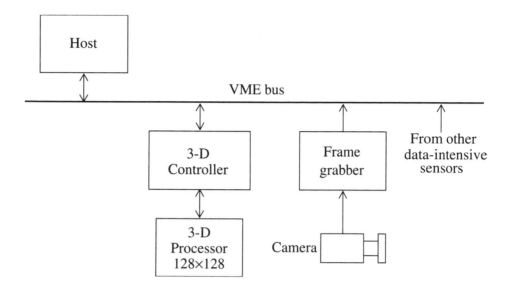

Figure 4.23 Organization of a complete 3-D system.

other input devices for other data-intensive applications may be used instead of the frame grabber.

The system operation starts with the VME master (host computer) setting controls in the 3-D controller. This puts the controller interface into a proper state for receiving information. The host sends program instructions into the controller program memory. The address space in which these instructions are stored is provided by the host. After an application program, written in microinstruction format, is loaded into the controller, the controller operates independently of the host and executes the microinstruction program.

3-D Processor

The 3-D processor consists of a number of wafers (the current system has 15) that are connected vertically. Each wafer has $N \times N$ computing elements; presently N is 128, and it is likely that N will reach 1,024. The wafers are penetrated by a set of $N \times N$ bus lines made up of termo-migrated feedthroughs and aluminum microbridges. The $N \times N$ buses connect the respective vertically aligned processing units. The

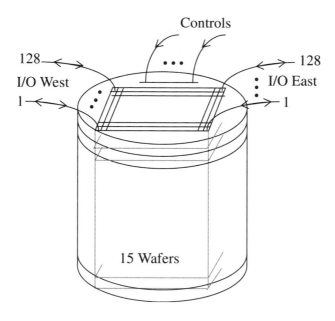

Figure 4.24 View of 3-D Computer.

schematic of a 3-D stack is shown in Figure 4.24. In this architecture, data flows in parallel from the elements of one wafer to the corresponding elements of another. All data transfers are bit-serial. Since the functional elements are linked together vertically by a bus, data can pass between *any* two wafers in the stack, not just between adjacent wafers. The architecture is *word-parallel* and *bit-serial;* in other words, while the individual processors in the array employ serial arithmetic, they all operate simultaneously, in word-parallel fashion. Thus the circuitry of the individual computing elements can be extremely simple, achieving the high density necessary for its anticipated applications. The massive parallelism at the processor level more than compensates for the loss of speed incurred by using serial arithmetic.

There are five wafer types, as described here.

- *Memory.* This type of wafer has the capacity to store one word of data (16 bits) per cell, to communicate the content of a cell to its four nearest neighbors, and to perform some simple logical operations on the data. The nearest-neighbor communication channels enable this wafer type to shift data into the array from the controller and vice versa. This is one of the wafer types that facilitate I/O data communication between the controller and the processor. Several memory wafers are employed in the system.

- *Accumulator.* This wafer type is used to perform arithmetic and logic operations between a data word stored in the accumulator and another word arriving bit-serially over the feedthrough data bus. The incoming word may be from one of the memory wafers or from other wafers. The operations are performed bit-serially.

- *Counter.* This is a special-purpose wafer that speeds up applications that involve frequent occurrences of a single-bit piece of data. The accumulator cell could be used to handle single-bit occurrences, but a full 16-bit clock cycle would be wasted. The counter cell requires a single clock cycle. The motivation for including a counter wafer was provided by the need to perform histogram distributions of image data.

- *Replicator.* This wafer type is used to perform row or column broadcasts of data values that originate either from the controller or from the northwesternmost feedthrough data bus of the array. It serves as a bus interconnection network in the system.

- *Comparator.* This wafer type contains cells that can compare words arriving bit-serially over the feedthrough data buses, with the words stored locally. A comparator wafer speeds up operations that could be performed more slowly by the accumulator.

Two wafer types are necessary to form a minimum configuration for a three-dimensional computer: memory and accumulator wafers. A complex system may be achieved by using a larger number of wafers. Moreover, new special-purpose wafers can be designed and assembled into the stack, allowing the realization of application-specific processors. The complexity of each memory or accumulator cell is approximately 150 to 200 gates.

I/O operations are performed over two bidirectional N-line buses. Data moves rhythmically in either an eastward or a westward direction, in or out of the stack. Inside the 3-D stack, data can also move north or south.

Control signals, provided by the controller, are used to move and process data inside the 3-D stack. Several wafers may be active simultaneously. For example, under software control, data may be shifted in one direction in one memory wafer and in a different direction in another memory wafer, while the accumulator performs some arithmetic functions.

3-D Controller

This section presents the structure of a controller designed to handle the 3-D stack. The role of the controller is to: (1) interface the 3-D Computer with the host machine, (2) provide control signals to the 3-D stack, and (3) perform I/O data transfers with the stack.

The design of controllers for high-performance array processors is a nontrivial task. A basic design rule is that the controller should not in any way restrict the performance of the array processor. Usually this means that controllers are microprogrammed to provide speed and programming flexibility and have special logic for achieving high I/O throughput.

The controller block diagram is shown in Figure 4.25. This section contains a brief description of the role and structure of each module in the block diagram.

Control Buffer Logic. The control buffer logic is an interface for the control signals exchanged between the controller and the VME bus. All signals are buffered by driver chips. The VME controls available for the controller hardware are called *host control* (HC) signals. The control signals derived from the microinstructions are called *local control* (LC) signals; some of them are used by the control buffer logic.

Address Logic. The role of address logic is twofold:

1. To provide addresses to program memory when application programs are loaded from the host into program memory; and

2. To provide addresses for the operation of data memory.

The addresses provided to the data memory use the data memory address bus (DAB); the addresses provided to the program memory use the microinstruction address bus (MIAB). The address logic receives addresses from the VME bus and some LC and HC signals. The address logic contains buffer logic to buffer the VME addresses, decoding logic, and multiplexing logic to select between addresses provided by the VME bus and addresses provided by the microinstruction sequencer for addressing the program memory.

The address logic is responsible for providing the remapping function for correct addressing of data memory. The problem occurs because this memory is accessed by the frame grabber, the host, and the I/O logic, and the data format may differ from one to another.

Data Logic. The role of the data logic is to provide an interface between the VME data bus and the controller data bus. It contains buffers and miscellaneous gates. Through this module, input data is loaded into the data memory and application program microinstructions are loaded into the program memory. Output data from the data memory is transferred to the host. Thus data logic supports data movement in both directions.

Data Memory. The data memory is a temporary data buffer between the 3-D processor and the outside world. Input data is normally provided by the frame grabber. A large-size data memory is desired. The data memory is loaded at some address supplied by the address logic over the data address bus. The data memory also serves as temporary storage for 3-D partial results.

I/O Interface. The role of the I/O interface is to extract data from data memory in either byte or word format, to perform a parallel-to-serial conversion, and to clock the data into the 3-D stack. In the opposite direction, the I/O interface reads data from the stack, performs serial-to-parallel conversions, and places data in the data memory. There are 128 pairs of I/O lines. The controls for the I/O interface are provided by LC signals generated in the control and timing logic. The I/O logic contains conversion registers, gates, and drivers. Because of the large number of I/O lines, optimization of this logic must be taken seriously.

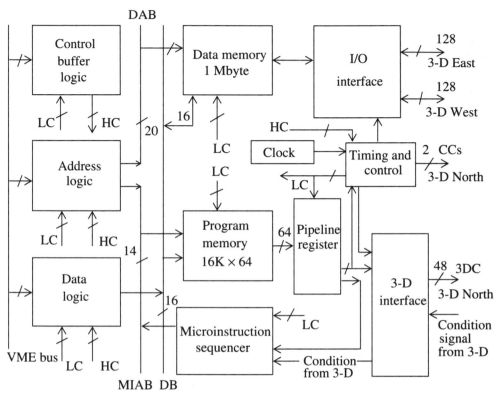

Figure 4.25 Controller block diagram.

Key: HC (host controls)
      LC (local controls)
      DAB (data address bus)
      MIAB (microinstruction address bus)
      DB (data bus)

Program Memory. The program memory holds microinstructions that drive the 3-D processor and provide local controls. The program memory can be addressed either by the address logic or by the microinstruction sequencer. When the program memory is loaded, microinstructions coming from the host pass through the data logic to the memory. Microinstructions are loaded at addresses supplied by the address logic. During the loading operation the microinstruction controller idles. After an application program is loaded into the program memory, the microinstruction controller takes over and supplies addresses to the program memory.

Microinstruction Sequencer. The role of the sequencer is to provide addresses to the program memory during normal program execution. This sequencer is implemented with an advanced, highly integrated device in order to ease software development and gates.

3-D Interface. The role of the 3-D interface module is to transform the bits of microinstructions into electrical signals for 3-D control lines. This logic contains latches and a counter. The latches hold 3-D configuration signals and the counter is used for the bit-serial execution of instructions. The number of clock cycles for a current operation is supplied by the microinstruction. During counter clocking, the microinstruction sequencer is stopped.

Control and Timing Logic. The control and timing logic module provides the main control signals for the rest of the controller's logic. Seen from the point of view of this module, the controller is a state machine whose inputs are the bits of microinstructions. Depending upon the current state and on these inputs, the control and timing logic module provides local controls and gated clocks for all other modules. This unit is implemented with counters and miscellaneous gates.

4.4 SYSTOLIC ARRAY PROCESSORS

4.4.1 Principles of Systolic Processing

VLSI technology has made possible the integration of circuits with hundreds of thousands of components into a single silicon chip. As we have already seen, this high level of integration opens the way for massive parallel computations. Systolic processing originated with the work of H. T. Kung and C. Leiserson at Carnegie-Mellon University [Kung and Leiserson 1980]. It came at a time when a solution for the application of VLSI technology to signal processing was being sought. Systolic processing, which is essentially pipelined array processing, constitutes a feasible solution for massive parallel computations. Its principles are compatible with VLSI technology characteristics. The processing elements are simple cells that usually contain one or two registers, an adder, and a multiplier. In order to achieve the best utilization of the silicon area, the types of cells should be as few as possible. Also, the interconnection pattern should be simple and regular, with only local connections of processing elements and without long wires that would need more area or more energy to drive them. Since the speed of operation of these arrays is usually very high, any long connection might introduce delays. Thus VLSI structures are characterized by a high degree of modularity, absence of long data paths, localized connectivity for data transfer, limited capabilities of processing elements, absence of central control, and simple timing mechanisms.

The VLSI chips that conform to these rules are characterized by simple geometries (arrays) of cells, with the cells rhythmically acting on one or more data streams that move smoothly across the chip. Because it is feasible to implement them with today's technology, systolic arrays receive considerable attention. Since systolic arrays are highly regular, only algorithms with repetitive computations perform well on them. Algorithms with nested loops fall into this category. The algorithms used in signal processing and other number-crunching applications are especially suitable to systolic arrays. High performance is achieved if algorithms are properly mapped into systolic arrays.

Figure 4.26 illustrates the basic operation mode of systolic processing systems. A systolic array operates under the supervision of a controller. The controller provides control signals and input data, and it collects the results. It is also the interface with the host computer, where programs are compiled. Input data streams enter the systolic array, where they are processed; then they leave the array. Only boundary cells communicate with the outside world. The performance of such systems is highly dependent on I/O characteristics. Systolic processing is recommended for those algorithms that are computation-intensive; in other words, once data is fetched from memory, it is desirable to perform as many operations as possible before it is sent back to memory. The I/O channel is likely to be the bottleneck of the systolic system.

The general idea in applying systolic processing to a problem is to transform the problem to meet the VLSI circuit requirements, rather

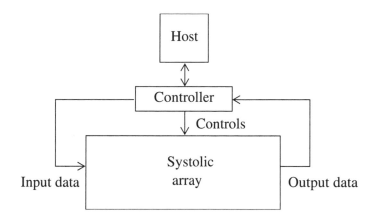

Figure 4.26 Basic principle of systolic processing.

than the other way around. This shifts much of the design complexity from the chip layout designer to the algorithm designer. This approach also minimizes overall design efforts, because the layout design is much more time- and labor-intensive than are the algorithm manipulations needed to "systolicize" algorithms.

The challenge is to design algorithms that are computation and I/O balanced; that is, the processing and data transfer rates in a systolic array should be comparable with the I/O bandwidth.

The overall computation time includes actual processing time and interconnection time. In a systolic array, because of the pipelining principle, the processing time must be comparable with the communication time. The allocation of computations to an array of mesh-connected processors constitutes the mapping problem. The mapping problem is complicated even more by the necessity to partition algorithms when the size of the actual array is smaller than that required by the algorithm. Systolic solutions exist for most of the data and signal processing algorithms. Some typical topologies of systolic arrays are shown in Figure 4.27. We will give two examples: one algorithm leading to a one-dimensional array, and the other leading to a two-dimensional array.

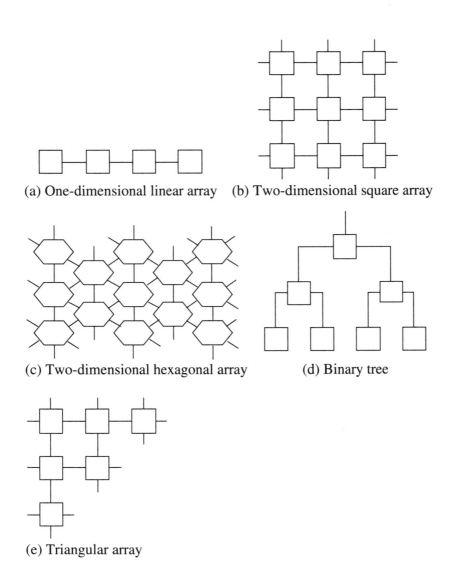

Figure 4.27 Typical systolic arrays.

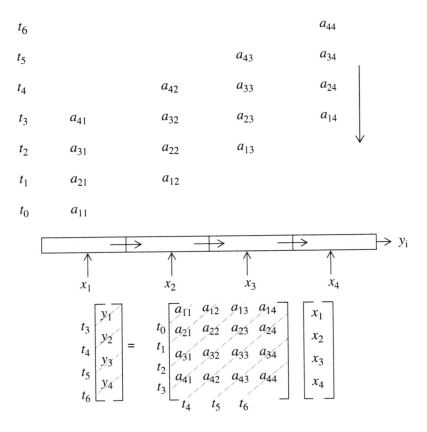

Figure 4.28 Linear array for matrix-vector multiplication.

Example 4.2. Matrix-Vector Multiplication: The array is shown in Figure 4.28. One of the most important aspects of systolic processing is timing; that is, operand pairs meet at the right time in the right cell. In this example, notice how matrix A is input to the array, such that partial products move from left to right inside the array, finally resulting in the correct y_i.

Example 4.3. Band Matrix-Matrix Multiplication: The array is shown in Figure 4.29. In this example, a two-dimensional array is necessary. Matrices A and B enter the systolic array such that respective elements that need to be multiplied meet in the same cell to produce a partial product. These partial products move upward, and are updated in the next cell. Finally, the result is available at the upper edges of the array.

4.4.2   Warp and *i*Warp

Two systolic computers called Warp have been designed and built, as a result of joint efforts between Carnegie-Mellon University and Intel Corporation, under the direction of H. T. Kung. The project proved the feasibility of the systolic processing concept, and software tools were developed for automatic mapping of application programs into the hardware. The first Warp machine, built in the mid-1980s, is a one-dimensional systolic array; the *i*Warp, built in 1989–1990, is a two-dimensional systolic array. The designers of the Warp machines have opted for fewer, more complex cells instead of numerous fine-grained cells. The main reason for this decision was the desire to produce versatile machines, capable of supporting a broad range of applications. With today's technology, the design of processor chips is still an expensive and time-consuming process.

Warp: One-Dimensional Array

The Warp consists of a linear systolic array of 10 or more identical cells. As shown in Figure 4.30, the Warp machine has three components: the Warp processor array, the interface unit (IU), and the host. The Warp array is the systolic processor, intended for computation-intensive routines. The IU is the controller and provides I/O interface with the host, generates data addresses, and control signals for the systolic array. The host executes parts of the application program that are not mapped onto the systolic array, such as initialization subroutines and sequential code. The host supplies the data to, and receives the results from, the array.

Since Warp architecture was one of the first implementations of systolic arrays and was designed with off-the-shelf components, it departs in some ways from the systolic processing principles stated at the beginning of Section 4.4, which are more applicable to VLSI implementations. Most remarkable, Warp architecture has large granularity and independently operating processing cells.

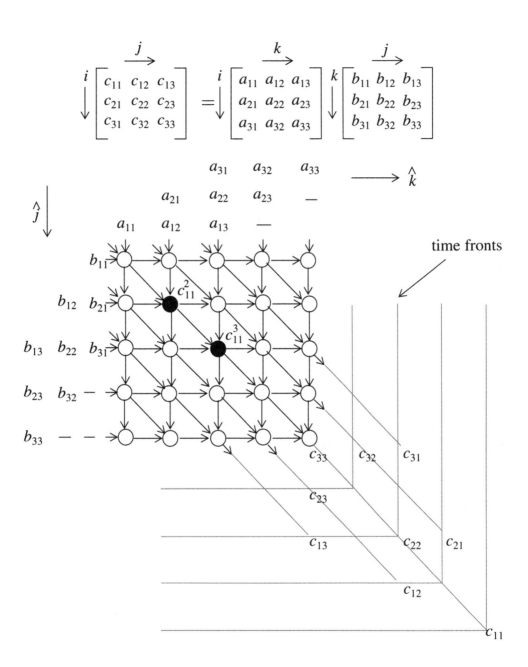

Figure 4.29 A two-dimensional systolic array for matrix multiplication.

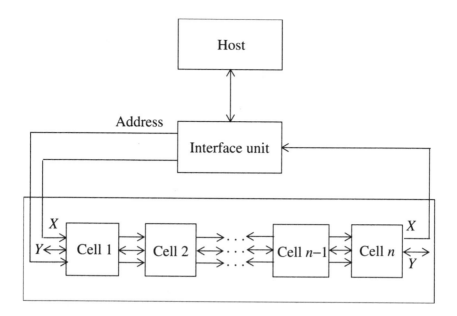

Figure 4.30 Warp systolic array [Annaratone et al., 1987].

Cell Structure

Each Warp cell is a microprogrammable processor with its own program memory and microsequencer. The cells are far more complex than in the original systolic array concept. In the Warp, the designers wanted to have the flexibility to reconfigure the array for a large number of applications. The structure of a Warp cell is shown in Figure 4.31. Warp cells are implemented with commercially available parts (as opposed to specialized VLSI chips). The following are the major modules constituting a Warp cell:

The *ALU* and the *MPY* are floating-point five-stage pipelined units used, respectively, for performing arithmetic and multiplication operations. The data paths and all registers are 32 bits wide. Since pipelined arithmetic is used, the Warp is capable of two levels of pipelining: at the cell level and at the array level. This enhances system throughput.

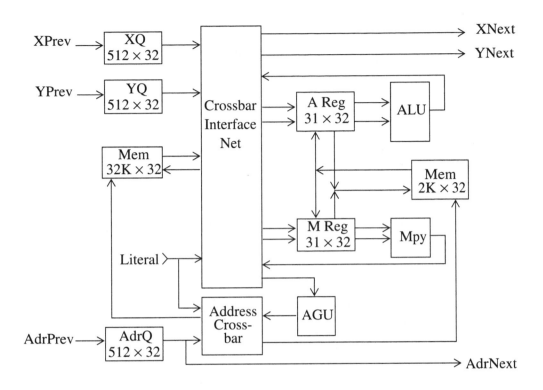

Figure 4.31 Structure of a Warp cell [Annaratone et al., 1987].

The *A* and *M registers* are general register files for the ALU and the MPY. Each register file contains 32 registers. *M* registers can also compute functions such as square roots by using the lookup table contained in the register file.

The *X Queue*, the *Y Queue* and the *Address Queue* contain 512 words each. Their role is to provide programmable delays to ensure the availability of data at the proper time. Addresses are precomputed and stored in the host. Address patterns move along the address bus. The address generation unit (AGU) has a self-contained ALU and 64 registers for address modification. Addresses are required to access the memories that provide operands to the floating point operations.

Data RAM is a 32K-word memory that buffers data, implements lookup tables, and stores intermediate results. Its purpose is to reduce

I/O requests and to allow algorithm partitioning and multiplexing. Because of this memory, the Warp can implement algorithms designed for two-dimensional systolic arrays on its one-dimensional array structure. Memory can perform read and write operations simultaneously during every cycle, using addresses selected from the address queue, the crossbar, or data RAM itself.

Intercell communication is supported by the six I/O ports, two ports for X and Y, and one port for the address in each side. Data flows through the array on X and Y channels, and the addresses and control signals generated by the interface unit propagate through the address channel. The direction of the Y channel is statically reconfigurable. The latching of data into queues is controlled by the sender; that is, the sender provides a signal to the receiver's queue to latch the input data.

The *crossbar switch* was selected as an interconnection network among the cell's data modules. This switch has six input (read) ports and eight output (write) ports. The crossbar can be reconfigured every cycle, under the control of microinstructions, to allow a read port to access any of the write ports.

A compiler and a language were developed at CMU to help program the Warp machine. The compiler combines a novel program model, based on *skewed* computation. It is capable of optimization. Programming is done in a language called W2. The compiler transforms W2 into microcode, which is executed in the processing cells.

iWarp: Two-Dimensional Array

Since many applications map naturally into two-dimensional arrays, it was necessary to extend the design of one-dimensional cells. The iWarp consists of identical cells interconnected in a two-dimensional mesh, with possible wraparound connections. Each cell has its own local memory outside of the systolic chip. This configuration allows a larger local memory and the possibility of integrating more specialized logic in each chip. A systolic processor chip has two main components: a computation element capable of 20 Mflops, and a communication element capable of 320 Mbytes/sec. The operations of the two units overlap; computations take place while communications are in progress.

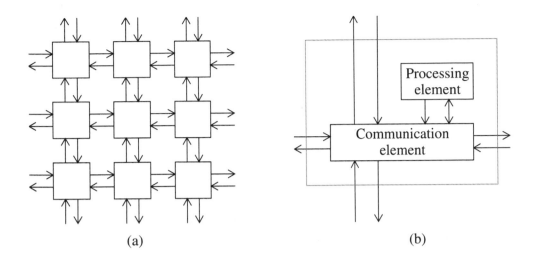

Figure 4.32 (a) iWarp interconnections; (b) iWarp cell.

The connections between the chips and the organization of a chip is shown in Figure 4.32.

The communication element has four input ports and four output ports; each port has a transfer rate of 40 Mbytes/sec.

An important innovation in the iWarp is the time multiplexing of physical buses. Many logical buses are allowed to coexist in the system. Logical buses are statically allocated over the physical buses. A scheduler allocates bus cycles to active logical buses. Advanced communication methods are implemented directly in hardware inside the communication element. The iWarp, with 32×32 processing cells, has a peak performance of 20 Gflops.

4.5 ASSOCIATIVE PROCESSING

Associative processing is a special case of array processing. An associative processor is built around an *associative memory* (AM), or *content-addressable memory* (CAM). A memory is content-addressable when each memory cell has sufficient logic to determine whether or not it holds data that match some pattern that is broadcast from the central control unit. Thus a cell is addressed on the basis of its content rather than on the basis of its memory location. This is the basic difference between CAM and ordinary memory operation. CAMs are sometimes called *intelligent memories* or *distributed logic memories,* because memory functions are achieved with some local processing. An associative processor is a CAM with additional control logic.

The major benefits of associative processing are speed of operation and a more natural way to solve some computational problems. Because of CAM's ability to perform in parallel read, write, search, comparisons, and other primitive operations, it is possible to reduce the execution time of some problems by a factor of n, where n is the number of words in the memory. A significant advantage of associative processors is that operations are performed locally, where data are stored, thus eliminating the so-called von Neumann bottleneck between processors and memory. Associative processors have been used in many important applications, such as radar signal tracking and processing, image processing, real-time artificial intelligence, and others. A disadvantage of associative processing, which is diminishing, is increased hardware cost per bit of storage, which results from the additional processing logic it requires.

4.5.1 The Structure of an Associative Memory

An AM consists of an actual memory, a control unit, and additional logic (such as tags and data-gathering logic). It is shown in Figure 4.33. The memory is organized into n words, with m bits per word. Each of these $n \times m$ memory bits has a flip-flop, comparison logic, and read-write logic. The ith word is denoted as

$$w_i = (b_{i1}, b_{i2}, ..., b_{im})$$

and the jth bit-slice (a vertical column) is denoted as

$$b_j = (b_{1j}, b_{2j}, ..., b_{nj})$$

Information and commands are broadcast from the control unit to every cell of the memory. Each bit cell B_{ij} can be written, read out, or compared with external signals. The control unit consists of actual

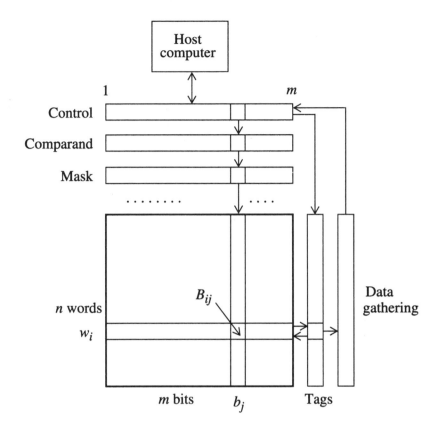

Figure 4.33 Structure of an associative memory.

control logic, comparand, and masking registers. The *comparand register* $C = (C_1, C_2, ..., C_m)$ is used to hold key operands being searched for or being compared with. The *masking register* $M = (M_1, M_2, ..., M_m)$ is used to enable or disable the bit slices involved in a comparison at a given instance. Each memory word has associated with it at least one tag bit T_i. The collection of tag bits is usually referred to as the *response store*. It is often necessary to use the tag bits from previous operations. Through some data-gathering logic, the control unit can read the status of a tag bit, which in fact represents the results of associative processing.

AM Instructions

The basic instructions performed by a typical AM are discussed below. The hardware that is necessary to perform these instructions is shown in Figure 4.34.

Set. This is a command that can be used by the central control unit to set all tag bits to 1. The *set* signal can be seen in Figure 4.34.

Search. When the central control unit issues a search command marked by an active S signal, any word whose content does not match the comparand will generate a signal that causes its tag bit to be reset. After a search instruction, only those words whose content equals the comparand will be left with their tag bits set. The mask signals M_i are active only for the bits in the field of interest. The comparand bit C_i indicates whether or not we expect a logical 1 or 0 in that bit position. The search signal S, together with M_i and C_i, enables the AND gates at the output of the flip-flop. The logic circuit is such that a mismatch signal is generated to reset the tag bit when the control unit is looking for a logical 1 and the storage bit is 0, or when the control unit is looking for a 0 and the storage bit is 1. If several bits in one word disagree with those broadcast by the controller, the effect is the same as for a single bit. Thus, if the comparand and the memory word disagree, the tag bit of that word is reset, and comparison is performed only for the bits masked on.

Read. The read operation in CAM consists of sending out the contents of words that are responders (have their tag bits T_i set). This operation is enabled by the R signal. In the case in which there are several responders, the output is determined by performing a logical OR on corresponding bits. As we will see, it is always possible to keep only one responder if we wish to read only one word at a time.

Write. The write operation in CAM consists of writing in parallel to all words that are responders. This operation is enabled by the W signal. Writing a word to memory consists of copying the contents of the comparand into each word that is a responder. The write operation does not change the bits for which the mask register is zero, and the write operation does not affect the tag bits in any way.

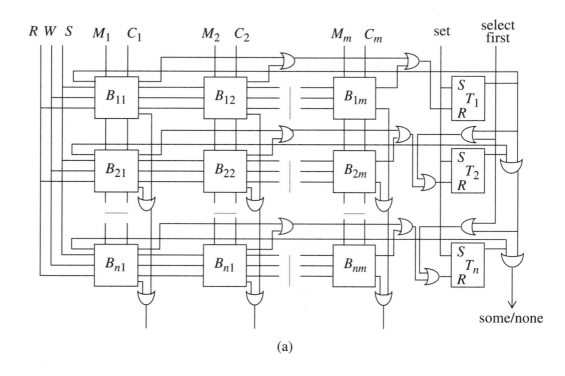

(a)

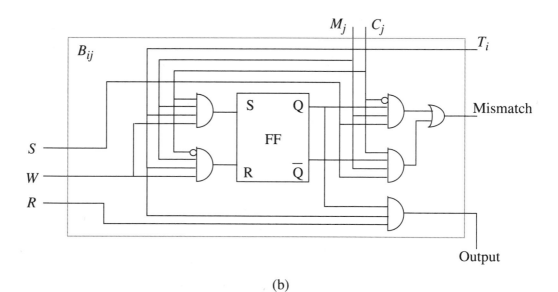

(b)

Figure 4.34 Internal structure of an associative processor: (a) the
array; (b) logic circuit for storage of a bit.

Select First Responder. There are times when more than one memory word responds to the same search. Further, there are times when we want to single out just one of these responders and deal with it alone. To provide this capability, the memory words are organized such that each word has a predecessor and a successor. In this sense, there is always an "earliest" or "first" responder, the one nearest the beginning of the string. The signal *select first responder* turns off the tag bits of all cells following the first cell with the tag bit set on.

Report. The *some/none* line in Figure 4.34 is an output of the circuit reporting to the central control unit that some, or none, of the words have their tag bits set; that is, telling the central control unit whether or not there are any responders to the previous search. Once the first responder has been selected or processed, it may be reset (via some additional circuitry). Then, by repeating the original search, followed by the first-responder operation, we can single out each responder. This way, all the responders to a search may be processed one at a time.

4.5.2   Algorithms

This section shows how computations can be implemented on an associative processor. The algorithms can be implemented basically by using the primitive operations discussed in the previous section. The circuit presented in the previous section was intended to illustrate the power of associative processors for search-intensive operations. More circuitry is required to implement a complete CPU capable of arithmetic operations.

Exact Match
This algorithm compares all words with the content of the comparand register. The bits where the mask register holds 0 do not compare. A search instruction is used. The algorithm begins with all words in the "undecided" state; that is, with their tags set to 1. Bits are examined one by one, and at the end, those words left in the "undecided" state are exact matches with the comparand, and those words whose tags are reset are mismatches.

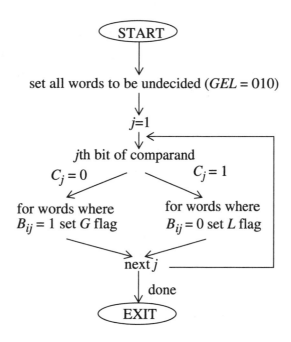

Figure 4.35 Flow chart for compare-magnitude algorithm.

Compare Magnitude with Comparand

This algorithm is used to sort words in memory into three classes: greater than, equal to, and less than. The algorithm uses three flag bits: G, E, and L. Consider an example in which the values of the comparand and three positive numbers are:

$$0\ 1\ 0\ 0\ 1\ 1\ 0 \quad C$$

$$
\begin{array}{ll}
1\ 0\ 1\ 1\ 0\ 1\ 0 & G \text{ set} \\
0\ 1\ 0\ 0\ 1\ 1\ 0 & E \text{ set} \\
0\ 0\ 0\ 1\ 1\ 1\ 0 & L \text{ set}
\end{array}
$$

The flags get set accordingly. These flags may actually be some bits in each word that are reserved as flags, or may be tags if tags are available. The algorithm is shown in Figure 4.35. Note that in order to carry out this algorithm, two more tags and additional hardware are needed.

Maximum

This algorithm finds the largest number among all the words stored
in the AM. It operates on all words in parallel by scanning bits from
left to right (i.e., from the most significant to the least significant bit).
The algorithm uses the report instruction. As we go through the bits,
we ask if any candidates have a 1 in the current position. If they do,
discard all words that do not have a 1 in that position. At any instant,
all remaining candidates are equal in terms of the extent to which they
have been examined. Note that special hardware is needed to find the
maximum.

Calculate the Mean

To calculate the mean of a set of numbers, we add them all up and
then divide by the number of elements. The sum of a set of positive
numbers is calculated by adding together the numbers of responders in
each column (number of 1s), weighted by the appropriate powers of 2.
Then the sum is placed in a central register and divided by the number
of elements.

Arithmetic Algorithms

Arithmetic operations are essential in any numeric application. In order
for associative processors to be considered general computing devices,
they must be able to perform arithmetic operations. So far, in this section, we have discussed one-dimensional, or linear, associative processors. The basic arithmetic operations easily implementable on these devices include one's and two's complements, add constant, and add fields
in parallel for all words in the associative memory. Subtraction, multiplication, and division between memory words and comparands can
also be implemented. As we will see in the next section, more general
parallel arithmetic operations may be achieved with two-dimensional
associative arrays.

   The addition of the comparand to each word in the memory may be
performed simultaneously for all the words. The arithmetic operation
is done in the memory, without moving the words out of the memory.
The addition is performed bit-serially, starting from the least significant
bit and proceeding toward the most significant bit. The carry needs to
be propagated. Hardware modifications are necessary to store a carry
flag bit for every cell.

4.5.3   Associative Array Processors

The associative processor we presented earlier was based on a linear, or one-dimensional, associative memory. This organization has severe limitations for handling applications from relational databases, artificial intelligence, and other domains. In these applications, it is not sufficient to retrieve or process the contents of independent words; it is also necessary to express relationships between words.

Consider for example the sentence "John loves Mary." This may be represented by the relationship $A\ R\ B$, in which concept A represents "John," concept B is "Mary," and relation R is "loves." Such representations require pointers between words that are difficult to handle on one-dimensional associative memories. Yet the idea of applying associative processing to search problems is intuitively appealing.

By combining the concepts of associative processing with cellular-array processing, we can construct two-dimensional associative arrays that are capable of handling complex pattern search problems. One such architecture, proposed by Moldovan [Moldovan 1983a], constituted the starting point of the SNAP (Semantic Network Array Processor) machine constructed at the University of Southern California for artificial intelligence applications. The SNAP will be discussed in Chapter 8 in the context of knowledge-processing applications.

Next, we present some ideas for structuring an associative-array processor that may be developed further for specific applications.

Array Organization

Figure 4.36 shows the organization of an associative-array processor. The cells are connected as a two-dimensional grid, but other interconnections are possible. The associative property of this array is provided by the content-addressable memory available in each processing cell. Cells may also be addressed by their cartesian location. In addition to the CAM, each cell contains memory control logic and communication logic. The array is operated by an outside controller that also provides an interface with a host computer.

A Pattern-Search Example

This example shows how complex search operations, such as pattern searches, may be done using associative array processors.

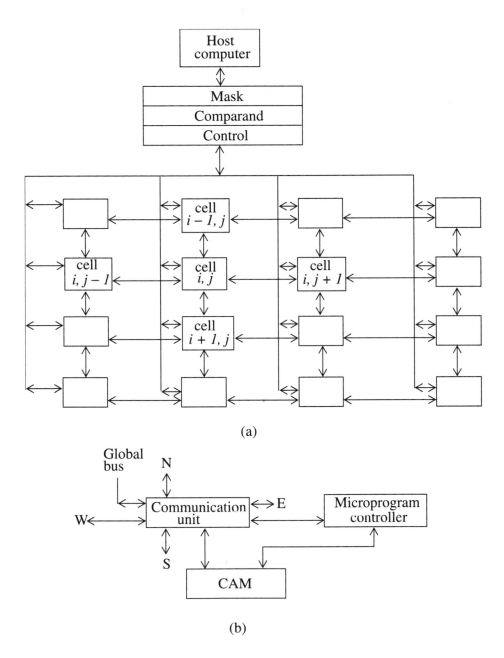

(a)

(b)

Figure 4.36 (a) Associative-array processor; (b) cell structure.

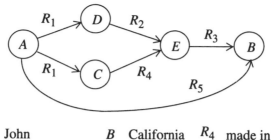

A	John	B	California	R_4	made in
D	Mary	R_1	loves	R_5	born in
E	Los Angeles	R_2	lives		
C	movies	R_3	is in		

Figure 4.37 A network representing sentences.

In Figure 4.37 a simple network representation of sentences is shown:

> John loves Mary.
> John loves movies.
> Mary lives in Los Angeles.
> Movies are made in Los Angeles.
> Los Angeles is in California.
> John was born in California.

There are several ways in which a network such as the one shown in Figure 4.37 may be mapped on the associative array. One possibility is to dedicate a cell to a node and to store in the cell's CAM all relations and pointers related to that node. Such a mapping is shown in Figure 4.38.

Suppose now that we want to search the database stored on the associative array for a pattern

$$A \xrightarrow{R_1} X_1 \xrightarrow{R_2} X_2 \xrightarrow{R_3} B$$

This pattern links John and California through relations R_1, R_2 and R_3; however, the intermediate concepts are considered unknown. In Chapter 8, we will consider more complex search operations that

11 (A)		12 (D)	
$A \ R_1 \ D$;	11 001 12	$D \ R_2 \ E$;	12 010 22
$A \ R_1 \ C$;	11 001 21		
$A \ R_5 \ B$;	11 101 31		
21 (C)		22 (E)	
$C \ R_4 \ E$;	21 100 22	$E \ R_3 \ B$;	22 011 31
31 (B)			

Figure 4.38 Mapping network from Figure 4.37 into cell's CAM.

link two or more concepts without knowing their interrelationships a priori.

The pattern search problem stated above can easily be solved on the associative-array processor as follows:

1. Set marker (or tag) **#1** in the processing cell containing node A.

2. From the nodes marked with marker **#1**, send a message to nodes connected to node A via relation R_1, and mark such nodes with marker **#2**.

3. From the nodes marked with marker **#2**, send a message to nodes connected to these nodes via relation R_2, and mark such nodes with marker **#3**.

4. From nodes marked with marker **#3**, send a message to nodes connected to these nodes via relation R_3, and mark such nodes with marker **#4**.

5. Set marker **#5** in node B.

6. Perform logical AND between marker **#4** and marker **#5**, and set marker **#6** if true.

Now the retrieval part follows. If there are any cells with marker #6 set, it means that there is such a pattern on the database, as is our case. By retrieving the contents of cells marked with markers #2 and #3, we find X_1 and X_2, respectively.

In this example, we have assumed that cells are capable of forming, sending, and processing messages. This implies that processing cells may be quite complex. Since cells need extensive logic to operate, it is advantageous to store several network nodes inside a cell so that they can share communication and processing logic.

4.6   BIBLIOGRAPHICAL NOTES AND FURTHER READING

The principles of array processors are described in [Stone 1980] and [Hockney and Jesshope 1981], to mention only a few. [Hockney and Jesshope 1981] covers example architectures, parallel languages, and algorithms for SIMD computers. Interconnection networks for array processors are described in [Almasi and Gottlieb 1989] and [Lipovski and Malek 1987]. Systolic processing research was pioneered in [Kung 1979] and [Kung and Leiserson 1980]. The Warp systolic computer, designed at CMU under the leadership of H. T. Kung, is described in [Annaratone, Arnould, Gross, Kung, Lam, Menzilcioglu, and Webb 1987]. The Connection Machine, designed at Thinking Machines Corporation is based on the design ideas of [Hillis 1985]. The description of the CM-2 follows the [Connection Machine Model CM-2 Technical Summary 1989]. The 3-D Computer, designed at Hughes Research Laboratories, is described in [Little and Grinberg 1988]. The material on associative processors follows the work of [Foster 1976]. An example of an associative linear array processor is described in [Finnila and Love 1977]. Two-dimensional associative arrays and applications are described in [Moldovan 1983a] and [Moldovan and Tung 1985].

4.7   PROBLEMS

4.1.A. An SIMD computer has 128 processors, denoted as $PE_0 - PE_{127}$. The interprocessor communication network consists of perfect-shuffle (PS), butterfly (B), and shift (SH). In what processor will data from processor PE_{99} be placed after the sequence of permutations $(PS)^2 \cdot SH \cdot (B)^2$?

Solution. The decimal number 99 in binary representation is

$$PE_{99} = PE_{(1100011)}$$

$$PS(1100011) = (1000111)$$
$$PS(1000111) = (0001111)$$
$$SH(0001111) = (0010000)$$
$$B(0010000) = (0010000)$$
$$B(0010000) = (0010000)$$

Therefore, $(PS)^2 \cdot SH \cdot (B)^2(PE_{99}) = PE_{16}$.

4.2.A.

```
for I = 0,7
    for J = 0,3
        X(I + 1, J) = X(I, 2J)X(I, J + 4) − 1
    end J
    for J = 4,7
        X(I + 1, J) = X(I, 2J − 7)X(I, J − 4) + 2
    end J
end I
```

This algorithm is mapped into the array processor shown in Figure 4.39. The mapping is such that $X(I,0), ..., X(I,7)$ are assigned respectively to $PE_0, ..., PE_7$, for all $0 \leq I \leq 7$.

(a) Show the interconnections between the processing elements necessary to execute this program; assume that the interconnections form a single-stage network as shown in Figure 4.39.

(b) Do you recognize what these connections are? Explain.

(c) Briefly explain how the program is executed on this simple array processor. Indicate what control signals are necessary during each iteration (I, J) for enabling or disabling communication ports and masking processors ON and OFF.

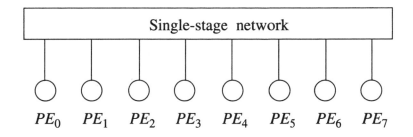

Figure 4.39 Array processor for Problem 4.2.A.

Solution. Two dependence matrices are obtained, one for each J loop:

(a)

$$\mathbf{D}_1 = \begin{pmatrix} 1 & 1 \\ -J & -4 \end{pmatrix} \begin{matrix} I \\ J \end{matrix}$$

$$\mathbf{D}_2 = \begin{pmatrix} 1 & 1 \\ 7-J & 4 \end{pmatrix} \begin{matrix} I \\ J \end{matrix}$$

These dependencies represent the following transfers:

$$PE_0 \leftarrow PE_0, PE_4$$

$$PE_1 \leftarrow PE_2, PE_5$$

$$PE_2 \leftarrow PE_4, PE_6$$

$$PE_3 \leftarrow PE_6, PE_7$$

$$PE_4 \leftarrow PE_1, PE_0$$

$$PE_5 \leftarrow PE_3, PE_1$$

$$PE_6 \leftarrow PE_5, PE_2$$

$$PE_7 \leftarrow PE_7, PE_3$$

The interconnection network is shown in Figure 4.40.

(b) The interconnection network is a combination of

1. inverse perfect-shuffle: $b_1 b_3 b_2 \leftarrow b_3 b_2 b_1$

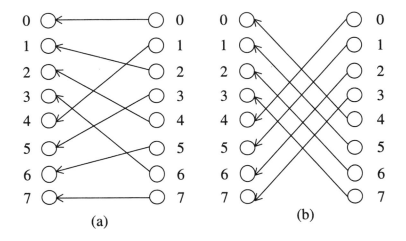

Figure 4.40 Interconnection network for Problem 4.2.A.

2. exchange $E_3 : \bar{b}_3 b_2 b_1 \leftarrow b_3 b_2 b_1$ or
   barrel-shifter

$$BS_{+2}(j) = (j + 2^i) \mod N$$
$$= (j + 2^2) \mod 8$$

(c) By performing the I loop serially, all J iterations can be done in parallel. Thus for each I step:

Masking
NO	Enable inverse perfect-shuffle connection and transmit.
NO	Enable exchange connection and transmit.
NO	Multiply operands and store result in accumulator.
ON	Processors 0–3: Acc $-$ 1 $\rightarrow$ Acc.
ON	Processors 4–7: Acc $+$ 2 $\rightarrow$ Acc.
	Repeat.

Each step requires one control signal. Masking is required to distinguish PE_{0-3} from PE_{4-7}.

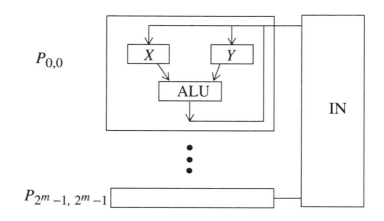

Figure 4.41 The SIMD computer for Problem 4.3.A.

4.3.A. Consider a matrix $\mathbf{A}$ of order $2^m \times 2^m$ whose elements are a_{ij}. We want to compute a new matrix B whose elements b_{ij} are

$$b_{ij} = a_{ij} * a_{i,j+1} * a_{j,i} * a_{j+1,i}$$

The elements a_{ij} outside the array are zero, i.e., $a_{0,2^m} = a_{2^m,0} = 0$. This is to be done on an SIMD computer, as shown in Figure 4.41, with $2^m \times 2^m$ processors. The interconnection network is a single-stage network consisting of a perfect-shuffle S and an exchange E_1.

$$IN = \{S, E_1\}$$

Each processor has an ALU and two accumulator registers X and Y. Write the sequence of operations that have to be provided by the control unit to compute matrix B. Specify the operations in terms of

E_1 exchange
S shuffle
MUL multiplication $(X \leftarrow X \cdot Y)$

Solution.

$$A = \begin{bmatrix} a_{00} & a_{01} & \cdots & a_{0,2^m-1} \\ a_{10} & a_{10} & & a_{1,2^m-1} \\ \vdots & \vdots & & \vdots \\ a_{2^m-1,0} & a_{2^m-1,1} & \cdots & a_{2^m-1,2^m-1} \end{bmatrix}$$

The matrix A can be stored such that each element a_{ij} is stored in the register Y of P_{ij}.

$$a_{00} \;\; \rightarrow \;\; P_{00}$$
$$\vdots \qquad \vdots$$
$$a_{2^m-1,2^m-1} \;\; \rightarrow \;\; P_{2^m-1,2^m-1}$$

Then the sequence of operations can be specified as follows:

$$\begin{array}{lll} SH^{-1} & Y_{i,j+1} \rightarrow X_{ij} & ; \quad a_{i,j+1} \rightarrow X_{ij} \\ MUL & X_{ij} * Y_{ij} \rightarrow X_{ij} & ; \quad a_{i,j+1} * a_{ij} \rightarrow X_{i,j} \end{array}$$

$$m \text{ times} \left\{ \begin{array}{c} S \\ S \\ \vdots \\ S \end{array} \right\} Y_{ji} \rightarrow Y_{ij} \qquad ; \quad a_{ji} \rightarrow Y_{ij}$$

$$\begin{array}{lll} MUL & X_{ij} * Y_{ij} \rightarrow X_{ij} & ; \quad (a_{ij} * a_{i,j+1}) * a_{ji} \rightarrow X_{ij} \\ SH^{-1} & Y_{i,j+1} \rightarrow Y_{i,j} & ; \quad a_{j+1,i} \rightarrow Y_{ij} \\ MUL & X_{ij} * Y_{ij} \rightarrow X_{ij} & ; \quad (a_{ij} * a_{i,j+1} * a_{ji}) * a_{j+1,i} \rightarrow Y_{ij} \end{array}$$

The result is $b_{ij} = Y_{ij}$.

4.4.A. Multistage networks versus single-stage networks.

(a) Show that the Omega multistage network can be implemented using a single-stage shuffle-exchange network.

(b) Show that the n-cube multistage network can be implemented using a single-stage cube network.

Solution.

(a) The Omega network from Figure 4.19 is implemented with a perfect-shuffle connection between stages and four-function switches in each stage. A four-function switch can be realized with a maskable exchange E_1. Thus, each stage of the Omega network corresponds to one cycle on the single-stage shuffle-exchange.

(b) The first stage of the Multistage cube network in Figure 4.18 is an exchange E_1, the second stage is an exchange E_2, and the third stage is an exchange E_3. The exchanges are provided by the single-stage cube network. The result can be generalized to an arbitrarily selected n.

4.1.B. Following the matrix multiplication example from Example 4.1, show how the dynamic programming program in Section 2.3.2 may be processed on a shared-memory SIMD computer. Map the input and output data to memories and write a SIMD program. Be specific as to how the interconnection network selected by you is controlled.

4.2.B. Consider a SIMD machine with 256 PEs using a perfect-shuffle interconnection network. If the shuffle is performed 10 times, where will the data item originally stored in PE_{123} be transferred?

4.3.B. Propose a systolic array for solving the following recurrence equation:

$$x_k + a_1 x_{k-1} + a_2 x_{k-2} = b$$

4.4.B. Devise a procedure to perform a search for the maximum (minimum) element in an array of N elements using an SIMD computer with a shuffle-exchange interconnection network. How many iterations (shuffles) are required to find the maximum element? How many iterations are necessary to order the elements (sorting) from maximum to minimum?

4.5.B.

Process 1
```
        for I := 1 to N step 1 do
        begin
            A(I) := B(I) + 1;
```

$$B(I+1) := C(I)$$
end

Process 2

for $I := 1$ to N step 1 do
    for $J := 1$ to N step 1 do
       $A(I,J) := A(I-1) + A(I, J-1)$

(a) Analyze the parallelism in these programs. What is the minimum computation time in each case? How many processors are needed to achieve this in each case?

(b) Consider that these two programs are to be executed on an SIMD computer with N PEs. Explain briefly the key issues in each case. Write high-level language SIMD programs. What are the processing times for *Process 1* and *Process 2?*

4.6.B. For an associative processor with primitive instructions—compare, read, write, and first responder—write a program to sort a table of five numbers.

4.7.B. Consider the loop

for $I = 1$ to N
    $P(I) = A(I) \times B(I)$
    $S(I) = P(I) + S(I-1)$
end I

Determine the evaluation time of this loop in each of the following computer systems. Briefly explain your answers.

(a) An SIMD system with n PEs and a ring interconnection network.

(b) An SIMD system with $(\frac{N}{2} - 1)$ PEs and a shuffle-exchange interconnection network.

Addition and multiplication require one and two time units, respectively. Memory access time is ignored, and data transfer time from one PE to another PE is assumed to take one time unit.

4.8.B. For a linear associative processor, propose an algorithm to perform subtraction of two fields $A \leftarrow A - B$, where for example A represents bits $1-10$ of a word and B represents bits $21-30$ of the same word. Specify the additional hardware required and how it works.

4.9.B. Modify the matrix multiplication Program 4.2 for the general case in which the number of processors is not necessarily equal to the size of the matrix n.

4.10.B. For one-dimensional associative memory, propose an algorithm and related hardware for adding a constant, stored in the comparand register, to each word in memory.

4.11.B. Show how the statement

DO $I = 1, N$
    DO $J = 1, N$
      $X(I, J) = (X(I - 1, J) + X(I, J - 1) + X(I, J + 1) +$
          $X(I + 1, J)) / 4$
    END DO
END DO

can be compiled and executed on the BSP five-element cyclic pipeline shown in Figure 4.4.

4.12.B. For the pattern search example from Section 4.5.3, design the processing cells:
    (a) Specify a set of instructions required to be implemented by processing cells.
    (b) Show the structure of CAM at flip-flop level, including tags.

4.13.B. Explain how an image of 256×256 pixels may be mapped into CM-2 memory. Give three alternatives and indicate which one is preferable in order to achieve the fastest data communication.

4.14.B. Demonstrate that the bitonic sorting presented in Section 2.3.5 and illustrated by the multistage network shown in Figure 2.27 can be implemented by a single-stage shuffle-exchange network.

Chapter 5

MAPPING ALGORITHMS INTO ARRAY PROCESSORS

The *mapping problem* is defined as finding an optimal assignment of computations to processors to minimize the execution time. The execution time of an algorithm on an array processor has two components: the *computation time* (t_c) and the *data routing time* (t_r). Traditionally, the design of parallel algorithms has focused exclusively on the minimization of computation steps. The assumption was that the data routing time between processors, and between processors and memories, is negligible by comparison to the computation time. While this assumption was true in the early days when the number and capabilities of processors were small, today, because of many technological improvements, processors operate at clock speeds of tens of megahertz, and the data routing component cannot be neglected any longer. As the number of processors increases, along with an increase in their computing power, the communication time tends to become the dominant performance factor. When the data transfers required by the data dependencies match the interconnection network, the communication time is reduced; otherwise, the system has to spend more time on data routing.

The mapping problem is complicated by the fact that normally the size of a problem is larger than the number of processing elements available in a machine. In such cases, algorithm partitioning and time multiplexing of hardware resources must take place. Consider, for example, two concurrent processes that interact with each other during execution. In the case in which the two processes are mapped to different processors, their execution proceeds in parallel until data communication is required. At that point, data is sent from one processor to another, after which the execution continues. In the other case, in which the processes are mapped to the same processor, they are executed sequentially. The time lost through decreased parallelism may be gained in interprocessor communication. This suggests that an analysis of the tradeoff between processing time and communication time may be in order as part of the mapping problem solution.

The data transfer required by an algorithm is called the *logical transfer*. Computations are assigned to processors (or processors' memories) prior to the execution of an algorithm. After this mapping, the actual data transfer performed is called the *physical transfer*. The relation between logical transfers and physical transfers is discussed.

5.1   MAPPING OF ALGORITHMS INTO SYSTOLIC ARRAYS

The relations among data dependencies in algorithms with nested loops and several systolic arrays' design parameters are presented in this section. These relations are established via the algorithm transformation introduced in Chapter 3. The idea is to transform an algorithm into a "systolicized" form that exactly fits a systolic array.

5.1.1   Systolic Array Model

It is useful to incorporate the global features, such as the interconnections and the number of processors, of systolic arrays into a mathematical model. Let Z be the set of integers.

Definition 5.1 A systolic array is a tuple $(\mathbf{J}^{n-1}, \mathbf{P})$, where $\mathbf{J}^{n-1} \subseteq \mathbf{Z}^{n-1}$ is the index set of the array, and $\mathbf{P} \in \mathbf{Z}^{(n-1) \times r}$ is a matrix of interconnection primitives.

Although we consider for the sake of generality that systolic arrays are $(n-1)$-dimensional, practical arrays have a two-dimensional layout. The position of each processing cell in the array is described by its

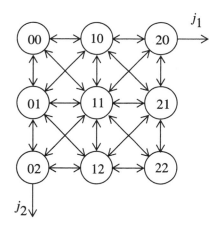

Figure 5.1 A square array with eight-neighbor connections.

cartesian coordinates. The interconnections between cells are described by the different vectors between the coordinates of adjacent cells. The matrix of interconnection primitives is

$$\mathbf{P} = [\; \mathbf{p}_1 \; \mathbf{p}_2 \; \cdots \; \mathbf{p}_r \;] \qquad (5.1)$$

where $\mathbf{p}_j$ is a column vector indicating a unique direction of a communication link. Consider, for example, the array shown in Figure 5.1; its model can be described as $(\mathbf{J}^2, \mathbf{P})$ where

$$
\begin{aligned}
\mathbf{J}^2 &= (j_1, j_2) \text{ for } 0 \le j_1 \le 2, \; 0 \le j_2 \le 2 \\
\mathbf{P} &= \begin{bmatrix} 0 & 1 & -1 & -1 & 1 & 0 & 0 & 1 & -1 \\ 0 & 1 & -1 & 1 & -1 & 1 & -1 & 0 & 0 \end{bmatrix} \begin{matrix} j_1 \\ j_2 \end{matrix}
\end{aligned}
\qquad (5.2)
$$

This array has eight-neighbor bidirectional connections and also has a connection within each cell, meaning that data may be temporarily stored in a register. Triangular systolic arrays have been proposed for matrix inversion, Cholesky decomposition, dynamic programming, and other types of algorithms. These arrays can be modeled in the same way. For example, the array shown in Figure 5.2 is described by $(\mathbf{J}^2, \mathbf{P})$ where

$$\mathbf{J}^2 = \{(j_1, \; j_2) : j_1 \le 3, \; 0 \le j_2 \le j_1\}$$

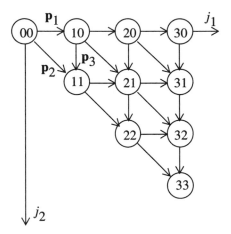

Figure 5.2 A triangular systolic array.

$$\mathbf{P} = [\mathbf{p}_1 \mathbf{p}_2 \mathbf{p}_3] = \begin{bmatrix} 1 & 1 & 0 \\ 0 & 1 & 1 \end{bmatrix} \begin{matrix} j_1 \\ j_2 \end{matrix}$$

The structural details of the cells and the timing are related to the algorithm, but are not part of this model. Also, for simplicity, we assume that all cells are identical.

5.1.2   Space Transformations

In Chapter 3, an algorithm transformation that transforms an algorithm A into an algorithm $\hat{A}$ was defined as

$$\mathbf{T} = \begin{bmatrix} \mathbf{\Pi} \\ \mathbf{S} \end{bmatrix}$$

where mappings $\mathbf{\Pi}$ and $\mathbf{S}$ are functions, where $\mathbf{\Pi} : \mathbf{J}^n \to \hat{\mathbf{J}}^1$ and $\mathbf{S} : \mathbf{J}^n \to \hat{\mathbf{J}}^{n-1}$. In this chapter, we consider only linear transformations $\mathbf{T}$. Thus, algorithm dependencies $\mathbf{D}$ are transformed into $\hat{\mathbf{D}} = \mathbf{TD}$. Notice that for simplicity, $\mathbf{\Pi}$ is reduced to the first row of matrix $\mathbf{T}$ that corresponds to $k = 1$. Thus, the timing of the new algorithm is given only by the first transformed coordinate. The mapping $\mathbf{\Pi}$

is selected such that the transformed data dependence matrix $\hat{\mathbf{D}}$ has positive entries in the first row. This ensures a valid execution ordering, and can be written as

$$\hat{d}_{1i} = \mathbf{\Pi d}_i > 0 \quad \text{for any } \mathbf{d}_i \in \mathbf{D} \tag{5.3}$$

The question now is how to select the space transformation $\mathbf{S}$ such that the transformed algorithm fits into a systolic array. This may be done by constraining the modified data dependencies to match the systolic array interconnections. For each dependence $\mathbf{d}_i$, the product $\mathbf{Sd}_i$ represents an $((n-1) \times 1)$–column vector. Now consider that the index point where dependence vector $\mathbf{d}_i$ originates is mapped by transformation $\mathbf{S}$ into a cell of the systolic array and the terminal point of the dependence vector is mapped into another processing cell. The result is that the product $\mathbf{Sd}_i$ corresponds to the interconnection between the two cells. But, from Definition 5.1, the interconnections are described by matrix $\mathbf{P}$. It follows that

$$\mathbf{SD} = \mathbf{P} \tag{5.4}$$

relates algorithm dependencies to the systolic array interconnections. Two distinct possibilities exist:

Case 1. Given an algorithm with a dependence matrix $\mathbf{D}$ and a transformation $\mathbf{S}$, find $\mathbf{P}$. This is a systolic array design problem and its solution follows directly from Equation (5.4).

Case 2. Given an algorithm with a dependence matrix $\mathbf{D}$ and a systolic array with interconnections $\mathbf{P}$, find a transformation $\mathbf{S}$ that maps the algorithm into the array. This is a mapping problem.

In the second case, the number of interconnections, namely the number of columns of matrix $\mathbf{P}$, may not coincide with the number of dependencies, and Equation (5.4) cannot be applied directly. Let us introduce a new matrix $\mathbf{K}$, called the *utilization matrix*. This matrix multiplies $\mathbf{P}$ and maintains proper dimensionality. Thus, a more general form of Equation (5.4) is

$$\mathbf{SD} = \mathbf{PK} \tag{5.5}$$

An element $k_{ji} = 1$ in matrix $\mathbf{K}$ means that the ith dependence utilizes (or is mapped into) communication channel j; when $k_{ji} = 0$, the

ith dependence does not map into channel j. Naturally, the utilization matrix is very sparse (i.e., contains many zero elements). Several conditions may be imposed on the elements of $\mathbf{K}$.

1. Since $\mathbf{K}$ indicates how interconnections are used, the elements k_{ji} are positive integers:

$$0 \leq k_{ji} \tag{5.6}$$

   Numbers larger than 1 may be possible, and indicate repetitive use of an interconnection by a dependence.

2. A dependence may map into several interconnections. For example, if an algorithm requires diagonal connections and the systolic array has only vertical and horizontal connections, then the dependence may be satisfied by using a combination of the two types of connections. Thus, an additional constraint for $\mathbf{K}$ is that the number of time units spent by a dependence along its corresponding connections cannot exceed the time allocated by the transformation to that dependence. This may be expressed as

$$1 \leq \Sigma_j k_{ji} \leq \mathbf{\Pi d}_i \tag{5.7}$$

Equation (5.5) can also be used in situations when one starts with an algorithm (thus $\mathbf{D}$ is known) and looks for both systolic array interconnection $\mathbf{P}$ and transformation $\mathbf{S}$. By starting with some rather large $\mathbf{P}$, such as the one in Equation (5.2), it is possible to find a transformation that utilizes only a small number of interconnections.

Most often, many transformations $\mathbf{S}$ can be found, each of which leads to a different array. This flexibility appears to complicate matters but, in fact, it gives the designer the option of choosing from a large number of arrays with different characteristics. As we will see, tradeoffs between time and space characteristics are possible.

Example 5.1. Consider again the algorithm in Chapter 3:

$$\text{for } j_0 = 1 \text{ to } N$$
$$\quad \text{for } j_1 = 1 \text{ to } N$$
$$\quad\quad \text{for } j_2 = 1 \text{ to } N$$
$$S_1: \quad a(j_0, j_1, j_2) = a(j_0 - 1, j_1 + 1, j_2) * b(j_0 - 1, j_1, j_2 + 1)$$
$$S_2: \quad b(j_0, j_1, j_2) = b(j_0 - 1, j_1 - 1, j_2 + 2) + b(j_0, j_1 - 3, j_2 + 2)$$
$$\quad\quad \text{end } j_2$$
$$\quad \text{end } j_1$$
$$\text{end } j_0$$

It is desired to map this algorithm into a systolic array with $\mathbf{P}$ as in Equation (5.2), using the transformation technique we have just outlined. We search for a transformation

$$\begin{bmatrix} \mathbf{\Pi} \\ \mathbf{S} \end{bmatrix} = \begin{bmatrix} t_{11} & t_{12} & t_{13} \\ t_{21} & t_{22} & t_{23} \\ t_{31} & t_{32} & t_{33} \end{bmatrix}$$

In Chapter 3 it was determined that a valid $\mathbf{\Pi}$ for this algorithm is

$$\mathbf{\Pi} = (\, 1 \ 0 \ -1\,)$$

and

$$\mathbf{\Pi D} = [\, 1 \ 2 \ 3 \ 2\,]$$

The next step is to find transformation $\mathbf{S}$. A computer program written to generate all possible $\mathbf{K}$ matrices and then solve for $\mathbf{S}$ in Equation (5.5) found 12 $\mathbf{S}$ matrices that satisfy Equations (5.6) and (5.7). These $\mathbf{S}$ matrices, together with $\mathbf{\Pi}$ selected, form 12 distinct, valid transformations:

$$\mathbf{T}_1 = \begin{bmatrix} 1 & 0 & -1 \\ 1 & 1 & 1 \\ 2 & 2 & 3 \end{bmatrix} \quad \mathbf{T}_2 = \begin{bmatrix} 1 & 0 & -1 \\ 1 & 2 & 2 \\ 2 & 2 & 3 \end{bmatrix} \quad \mathbf{T}_3 = \begin{bmatrix} 1 & 0 & -1 \\ 1 & 1 & 1 \\ 1 & 1 & 2 \end{bmatrix}$$

$$\mathbf{T}_4 = \begin{bmatrix} 1 & 0 & -1 \\ 2 & 2 & 2 \\ 1 & 0 & 0 \end{bmatrix} \quad \mathbf{T}_5 = \begin{bmatrix} 1 & 0 & -1 \\ 2 & 2 & 2 \\ 1 & 0 & 0 \end{bmatrix} \quad \mathbf{T}_6 = \begin{bmatrix} 1 & 0 & -1 \\ 2 & 2 & 3 \\ 1 & 0 & 0 \end{bmatrix}$$

$$\mathbf{T}_7 = \begin{bmatrix} 1 & 0 & -1 \\ 1 & 1 & 1 \\ 1 & 0 & 0 \end{bmatrix} \quad \mathbf{T}_8 = \begin{bmatrix} 1 & 0 & -1 \\ 2 & 2 & 2 \\ 1 & 0 & 0 \end{bmatrix} \quad \mathbf{T}_9 = \begin{bmatrix} 1 & 0 & -1 \\ 1 & 0 & 0 \\ 2 & 1 & 1 \end{bmatrix}$$

$$\mathbf{T}_{10} = \begin{bmatrix} 1 & 0 & -1 \\ 2 & 2 & 2 \\ 3 & 2 & 2 \end{bmatrix} \quad \mathbf{T}_{11} = \begin{bmatrix} 1 & 0 & -1 \\ 1 & 0 & 0 \\ 2 & 1 & 1 \end{bmatrix} \quad \mathbf{T}_{12} = \begin{bmatrix} 1 & 0 & -1 \\ 1 & 0 & 0 \\ 3 & 2 & 2 \end{bmatrix}$$

For example, one possible utilization for matrix $\mathbf{K}$ is

$$\mathbf{K} = \begin{bmatrix} 0 & 0 & 0 & 0 \\ 0 & 0 & 0 & 0 \\ 0 & 0 & 0 & 0 \\ 0 & 0 & 0 & 0 \\ 0 & 0 & 0 & 0 \\ 1 & 1 & 1 & 0 \\ 0 & 0 & 0 & 0 \\ 0 & 0 & 0 & 1 \\ 0 & 0 & 0 & 0 \end{bmatrix}$$

This utilization matrix leads to transformation $\mathbf{T}_7$ because it satisfies the equation $\mathbf{S}_7\mathbf{D} = \mathbf{PK}$. In the discussion that follows it is assumed that

$$\mathbf{T} = \mathbf{T}_7 = \begin{bmatrix} \Pi \\ \mathbf{S}_7 \end{bmatrix}$$

5.1.3 Design Parameters

Once a transformation is selected, the new parallel algorithm and systolic array follow immediately. The original index set $\mathbf{J}$ is transformed into a new index set $\hat{\mathbf{J}}$ such that to every point $\mathbf{j} \in \mathbf{J}$ there corresponds a new index point $\hat{\mathbf{j}} = (\hat{j}_0, \hat{j}_1, \hat{j}_2) \in \hat{\mathbf{J}}$.

$$\hat{\mathbf{j}} = \mathbf{Tj} \tag{5.8}$$

In Figure 5.3, the original index set and the transformed index set of this algorithm are shown. Because of the way in which the transformation was selected, the first coordinate $\hat{j}_0$ indicates the time at which the computation indexed by the corresponding $\mathbf{j}$ is computed, and the pair $(\hat{j}_1, \hat{j}_2)$ indicates the processor at which that computation is performed. For instance, we want to know at what time and in what processor a computation indexed by $(3, 4, 1)$ is performed. The transformed coordinates are $(\hat{j}_0, \hat{j}_1, \hat{j}_2)^t = \mathbf{T}(3, 4, 1)^t = (2, 8, 3)^t$, meaning that the computation time is 2 and the processor cell is $(8, 3)$. Notice that the transformed coordinates are offset by some initial values.

Next, let us construct the entire array in which $\mathbf{T}$ maps the algorithm. The interprocessor communications result from the transformed data dependencies

$$
\hat{\mathbf{D}} = \mathbf{TD} = \begin{bmatrix} 1 & 0 & -1 \\ 1 & 1 & 1 \\ 1 & 0 & 0 \end{bmatrix} \begin{bmatrix} 1 & 1 & 1 & 0 \\ -1 & 0 & 1 & 3 \\ 0 & -1 & -2 & -2 \end{bmatrix} = \begin{bmatrix} 1 & 2 & 3 & 2 \\ 0 & 0 & 0 & 1 \\ 1 & 1 & 1 & 0 \end{bmatrix}
$$
$$
\qquad\qquad\qquad\qquad\qquad\;\; a \quad b \quad b \quad b \qquad\qquad\; a \quad b \quad b \quad b
$$

The first row of the transformed dependencies is $\mathbf{\Pi D} = [1, 2, 3, 2]$. Each element indicates the number of time units allowed for its respective variable to travel from the processor in which it is generated to the processor in which it is used. Only two interconnection primitives are required, namely $(0, 1)^t$ and $(1, 0)^t$. The systolic array is shown in Figure 5.4. This corresponds to the fact that the utilization matrix $\mathbf{K}$ is very sparse; in general, the simpler the $\mathbf{K}$ matrix is (the fewer nonzero elements), the simpler the systolic array will be. Notice that in this example we started with a rather complex systolic array model as a tentative solution, but via the transformation technique presented here it was found that actually a much simpler array was needed. The process of finding transformations, and thus systolic solutions, and of comparing their merits can be automated.

All the cells in the array in Figure 5.4 are identical. The structure of a cell depends on the algorithm computations and the transformation used. While the algorithm operations influence the structure of the arithmetic logic unit, the transformed data dependencies dictate the timing and the data communication. The structure of the cell is shown in Figure 5.5. It consists of an adder, a multiplier, and delay elements. Notice that variable a, which has dependence $\mathbf{d}_1$, moves from one cell to the next via a vertical channel with direction $(0\ 1)^t$, and that it has one time unit delay in each cell (in the multiplier). Variable b is

Time			processor			Time			processor			Time			processor		
j_0	j_1	j_2	$\hat{j}_0$	$\hat{j}_1$	$\hat{j}_2$	j_0	j_1	j_2	$\hat{j}_0$	$\hat{j}_1$	$\hat{j}_2$	j_0	j_1	j_2	$\hat{j}_0$	$\hat{j}_1$	$\hat{j}_2$
1	1	1	0	3	1	2	5	1	1	8	2	4	4	1	3	9	4
1	1	2	-1	4	1	2	5	2	0	9	2	4	4	2	2	10	4
1	1	3	-2	5	1	2	5	3	-1	10	2	4	4	3	1	11	4
1	1	4	-3	6	1	2	5	4	-2	11	2	4	4	4	0	12	4
1	1	5	-4	7	1	2	5	5	-3	12	2	4	4	5	-1	13	4
1	2	1	0	4	1	3	1	1	2	5	3	4	5	1	3	10	4
1	2	2	-1	5	1	3	1	2	1	6	3	4	5	2	2	11	4
1	2	3	-2	6	1	3	1	3	0	7	3	4	5	3	1	12	4
1	2	4	-3	7	1	3	1	4	-1	8	3	4	5	4	0	13	4
1	2	5	-4	8	1	3	1	5	-2	9	3	4	5	5	-1	14	4
1	3	1	0	5	1	3	2	1	2	6	3	5	1	1	4	7	5
1	3	2	-1	6	1	3	2	2	1	7	3	5	1	2	3	8	5
1	3	3	-2	7	1	3	2	3	0	8	3	5	1	3	2	9	5
1	3	4	-3	8	1	3	2	4	-1	9	3	5	1	4	1	10	5
1	3	5	-4	9	1	3	2	5	-2	10	3	5	1	5	0	11	5
1	4	1	0	6	1	3	3	1	2	7	3	5	2	1	4	8	5
1	4	2	-1	7	1	3	3	2	1	8	3	5	2	2	3	9	5
1	4	3	-2	8	1	3	3	3	0	9	3	5	2	3	2	10	5
1	4	4	-3	9	1	3	3	4	-1	10	3	5	2	4	1	11	5
1	4	5	-4	10	1	3	3	5	-2	11	3	5	2	5	0	12	5
1	5	1	0	7	1	3	4	1	2	8	3	5	3	1	4	9	5
1	5	2	-1	8	1	3	4	2	1	9	3	5	3	2	3	10	5
1	5	3	-2	9	1	3	4	3	0	10	3	5	3	3	2	11	5
1	5	4	-3	10	1	3	4	4	-1	11	3	5	3	4	1	12	5
1	5	5	-4	11	1	3	4	5	-2	12	3	5	3	5	0	13	5
2	1	1	1	4	2	3	5	1	2	9	3	5	4	1	4	10	5
2	1	2	0	5	2	3	5	2	1	10	3	5	4	2	3	11	5
2	1	3	-1	6	2	3	5	3	0	11	3	5	4	3	2	12	5
2	1	4	-2	7	2	3	5	4	-1	12	3	5	4	4	1	13	5
2	1	5	-3	8	2	3	5	5	-2	13	3	5	4	5	0	14	5
2	2	1	1	5	2	4	1	1	3	6	4	5	5	1	4	11	5
2	2	2	0	6	2	4	1	2	2	7	4	5	5	2	3	12	5
2	2	3	-1	7	2	4	1	3	1	8	4	5	5	3	2	13	5
2	2	4	-2	8	2	4	1	4	0	9	4	5	5	4	1	14	5
2	2	5	-3	9	2	4	1	5	-1	10	4	5	5	5	0	15	5
2	3	1	1	6	2	4	2	1	3	7	4						
2	3	2	0	7	2	4	2	2	2	8	4						
2	3	3	-1	8	2	4	2	3	1	9	4						
2	3	4	-2	9	2	4	2	4	0	10	4						
2	3	5	-3	10	2	4	2	5	-1	11	4						
2	4	1	1	7	2	4	3	1	3	8	4						
2	4	2	0	8	2	4	3	2	2	9	4						
2	4	3	-1	9	2	4	3	3	1	10	4						
2	4	4	-2	10	2	4	3	4	0	11	4						
2	4	5	-3	11	2	4	3	5	-1	12	4						

$$\begin{bmatrix} \hat{j}_0 \\ \hat{j}_1 \\ \hat{j}_2 \end{bmatrix} = \begin{bmatrix} 1 & 0 & -1 \\ 1 & 1 & 1 \\ 1 & 0 & 0 \end{bmatrix} \begin{bmatrix} j_0 \\ j_1 \\ j_2 \end{bmatrix}$$

Figure 5.3 Mapping of the index set into a systolic array
(nonpartitioned case).

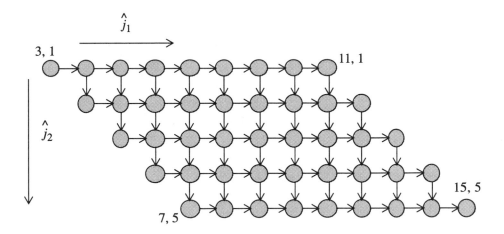

Figure 5.4 Systolic array [Moldovan and Fortes 1986].

used for three operands, each of which has its own direction and timing according to the dependence obtained from the algorithm. For example, variable b, which is the second multiplication operand, has dependence $\mathbf{d}_2$, to which a vertical channel $(0\ 1)^t$ corresponds, and a delay of two time units between the moment when the variable is generated and the moment when it is used; this means that a one-unit delay must be inserted in front of the multiplier for this operand. The operands for the adder are traced in the same way.

It is important to remark here that tradeoffs are possible between the time and space characteristics of the systolic array. Simply selecting another transformation results in a different parallel execution time, different array dimensions, different delays inside processing cells, and different interprocessing connections.

So far, we have assumed arbitrarily large arrays. Next, the case of fixed-size arrays is considered. As we will see, the mapping in this case is done by the same transformation if an additional constraint is satisfied.

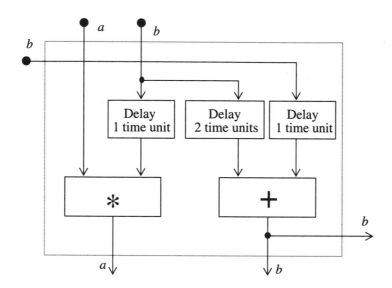

Figure 5.5 Cell structure [Moldovan and Fortes 1986].

5.2 ALGORITHM PARTITIONING FOR FIXED-SIZE SYSTOLIC ARRAYS

5.2.1 The Partitioning Problem

Algorithm partitioning is essential when the size of a computational problem is larger than that of the systolic array intended for that problem.

The sizes of systolic arrays are constrained by technological factors. Physical limitations are imposed by the number of I/O pins. While the level of chip integration is expected to continue to rise, the number of pins will be limited to several hundred; this makes systolic arrays I/O-bounded. A natural solution to the I/O problem, as well as one that overcomes the limited size of the array, is to divide the computational problem into smaller pieces.

For several reasons, the partitioning of algorithms for systolic arrays is not a simple problem. First, partitioning may introduce undesired side-effects that degrade the numerical stability of algorithms. Second, a poor allocation of computations to processors may lower the speedup factor. This is caused by the amount of overhead operations resulting from communications between partitions. Also related to this problem is the amount of external storage, and the communication links, introduced by partitioning. In this section it is shown that algorithm partitioning can be achieved with algorithm transformations. An approach to the partitioning problem is to divide the algorithm index set into bands and to map these bands into the processor space.

Statement of the Problem

In this section we consider the class of algorithms with nested loops for which computations are almost identical over the entire index space. The size of a computational problem may be expressed in a number of ways: for example, the number of points in the index set, the number of data inputs, the number of rows in a matrix, or others. The size of a systolic array is expressed by the number of processors.

The *partitioning problem* can be formulated as follows: Divide the computational problem into smaller subproblems and map these subproblems into the systolic array while pursuing the following goals:

- The accuracy of computation should not be affected by the partitioning process.

- The computation time of a partitioned algorithm is proportional only to the product of the number of partitions and the time taken to process one partition; in other words, no additional delays caused by the partitioning process are allowed.

- Partitioning does not require any increase in the complexity of systolic processors.

- The amount of overhead in external hardware and external communication caused by partitioning is as small as possible.

These goals indicate that partitioning should be performed such that its side-effects are minimized.

The approach presented here for the partitioning problem is to divide the index space into bands that fit into the fixed-size systolic array. The partitioning of the index space is done by hyperplanes, so that when the index space is mapped into a systolic array only near-neighbor processor communications are necessary for index points inside the bands, and communication between bands is done by external first-in-first-out (FIFO) queue registers.

5.2.2   Examples of Algorithm Partitioning

We will introduce the partitioning technique through two examples, followed by the presentation of the general case.

Example 5.2. The following program describes an algorithm for the computation of a matrix-vector product $\mathbf{y} = \mathbf{Ax}$, where $\mathbf{A}$ is a 10×10 matrix:

$$
\begin{aligned}
&\text{for } j_0 = 0 \text{ to } 9 \\
&\quad \text{for } j_1 = 0 \text{ to } 9 \\
&\quad\quad y(j_0, j_1) = y(j_0, j_1 - 1) + a(j_0, j_1) * x(j_1) \\
&\quad \text{end } j_1 \\
&\text{end } j_0
\end{aligned}
$$

The input variables are vector $\mathbf{x}$ and matrix $\mathbf{A}$, and the output variable is vector $\mathbf{y}$. The dependence matrix is

$$
\mathbf{D} = \begin{bmatrix} 0 \\ 1 \end{bmatrix}
$$

As indicated in Chapter 4, this algorithm maps into a linear systolic array. Now consider the case in which the systolic array consists of only three cells. A partitioning that quickly comes to mind is to divide matrix $\mathbf{A}$ into four bands, of which the first three contain three columns each, and the last only one column, as shown in Figure 5.6. The operation starts with band 0 meeting the first three elements of vector $\mathbf{x}$. The partial results are sent to the FIFO register in the order in which they are produced. Then the next band enters the array, together with the next three elements of vector $\mathbf{x}$ and partial results from the output of the FIFO queue, and so on.

This operation can easily be described by using an algorithm transformation. A valid transformation is

$$
\mathbf{T} = \begin{bmatrix} 1 & 1 \\ 0 & 1 \end{bmatrix}
$$

The first row of this transformation is the time hyperplane $\mathbf{\Pi}$, explained in Chapter 3. The second row of the transformation is regarded here as a partitioning hyperplane, denoted as $\mathbf{\Pi}_p$. The partitioning hyperplane $\mathbf{\Pi}_p$ divides the index set of the algorithm into bands such that each band requires only three processors. The band boundaries—that is, the beginning of each band—must satisfy the equation $\mathbf{\Pi}_p\mathbf{j} \bmod 3 = 0$. For example, (2 3) is on a boundary and $(0\ 1)(2\ 3)^t \bmod 3 = 0$. Thus, the size of the band is correlated to the number of processors.

The sequencing inside the band is achieved by the time hyperplane. Each band is swept by lines with the equation $\mathbf{\Pi}\mathbf{j} = constant$. All index points along each line are executed simultaneously; notice that there are, at most, three such points on each line inside one band. The rule that assigns computations to processors is: A computation indexed by $\mathbf{j}$ is executed by the processor numbered $\mathbf{\Pi}_p\mathbf{j} \bmod 3$. The time hyperplane $\mathbf{\Pi}$ and the partitioning hyperplane $\mathbf{\Pi}_p$ together form a transformation

$$\mathbf{T} = \left[\begin{array}{c} \mathbf{\Pi} \\ \mathbf{\Pi}_p \end{array} \right]$$

that partitions and maps the original algorithm into an array with only three processors. A necessary condition for a transformation to be valid is that $\mathbf{\Pi}$ and $\mathbf{\Pi}_p$ be linearly independent.

A partitioning hyperplane must be selected with respect to data dependencies such that the dependencies cross the hyperplane only in one direction. The reason for this is that all computations on one side of the plane must be able to finish before computations on the other side of the plane begin. Remember that similar considerations were made for the time hyperplane. Thus, this simple observation is represented mathematically as

$$\mathbf{\Pi}_p\mathbf{d}_i > 0 \tag{5.9}$$

This condition is for the case in which there is only one hyperplane. In general, when the index space is n-dimensional, the transformation matrix is of order $n \times n$. The partitioning of an index space of order n

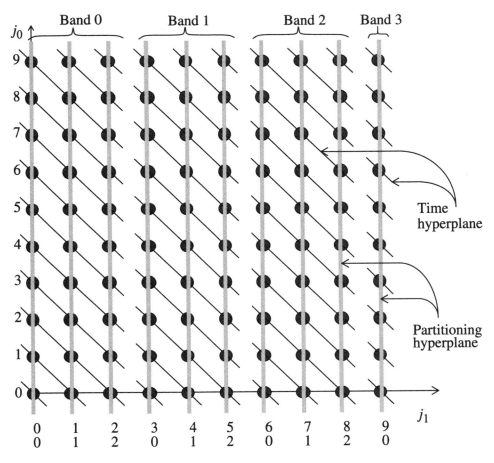

Partitioned index set for $\mathbf{y} = \mathbf{A}\mathbf{x}$ by $\mathbf{T} = \begin{bmatrix} 1 & 1 \\ 0 & 1 \end{bmatrix}$

(a)

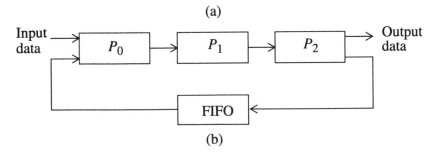

(b)

Figure 5.6 Partitioning of matrix-vector multiplication.

requires $n - 1$ independent hyperplanes; thus, $\mathbf{T}$ can be written as

$$
\mathbf{T} = \begin{bmatrix} \mathbf{\Pi} \\ \mathbf{\Pi}_{p1} \\ \mathbf{\Pi}_{p2} \\ . \\ . \\ . \\ \mathbf{\Pi}_{p(n-1)} \end{bmatrix}
$$

In this case, a sufficient but not necessary condition equivalent to Equation (5.9) is that

$$
\mathbf{\Pi}_{pj}\mathbf{d}_i > 0 \quad \text{for} \quad 1 \le j \le n - 1 \tag{5.10}
$$

These represent additional constraints imposed on a partitioning transformation, and are, in fact, the conditions that make the difference between a nonpartition and a partition case.

The reader can now easily verify that this partitioning scheme uses only near-neighbor communications for all computations inside the same band. Communication between computations in adjacent bands is performed via the external FIFO queue register. The data is sent out by processor P_2 and is input by processor P_0. Both these peripheral processors have I/O capabilities; this partitioning scheme does not require any extra pins. Notice that external data communication is performed in an orderly manner, and no complicated outside control or memory management is necessary. The maximum number of locations inside the FIFO is 10; in general, this number is related to the size of the problem. Data leaving processor P_2 has at least three time units to reach P_0; this is the same amount of time as if data traveled inside the array.

The partitioning of matrix-vector multiplication is rather obvious without transformation. However, in other more complex algorithms, it is not easy to visualize the solution. This is where the transformation technique helps.

Example 5.3. In this example, we consider the partitioning of the algorithm in Example 5.1, which has a three-dimensional index space. The problem addressed now is how to map this algorithm into a rectangular systolic array of size $m \times m$ where $m = 3$. In the previous section, an algorithm transformation $\mathbf{T}$ was found for this algorithm. This transformation can be used for partitioning the algorithm if we enhance its interpretation. Consider that the second and third row of $\mathbf{T}$ are some partitioning hyperplanes. We define them:

$$\mathbf{\Pi}_{p1} = (1 \ 1 \ 1)$$

$$\mathbf{\Pi}_{p2} = (1 \ 0 \ 0)$$

Each of these two hyperplanes satisfies the condition in Equation (5.10). They partition the index space into bands, as shown in Figure 5.7. The timing hyperplanes sweep all index points in each band before another band is processed. The band boundary must satisfy the equations

$$\begin{aligned} \mathbf{\Pi}_{p1}\mathbf{j} \ \bmod \ 3 &= 0 \\ \mathbf{\Pi}_{p2}\mathbf{j} \ \bmod \ 3 &= 0 \end{aligned} \qquad (5.11)$$

All index points inside one band are processed before another band is considered. Inside each band, the index points are swept by a family of parallel time hyperplanes $\mathbf{\Pi} = [1 \ 0 \ -1]$. Conditions in Equation (5.11) assume that at any given moment no more than $m \times m$ index points are processed. For each index point $\mathbf{j} \in \mathbf{J}$ we want to determine the band to which it belongs and in what processor it is mapped. Figure 5.8 depicts the index set of the original algorithm and the allocation of the indices to bands and to processors. Based on this printout, we constructed the array shown in Figure 5.9, which illustrates how the nonpartitioned virtual array is partitioned into bands. Notice how the bands from Figure 5.8 were allocated to the systolic array. In order to distinguish between different bands, let us assign two coordinates (b_1, b_2) to each band. Coordinate b_1 indicates the band number along the direction of $\mathbf{\Pi}_{p1}$, and b_2 indicates the band number along the direction $\mathbf{\Pi}_{p2}$. Thus an index point $\mathbf{j}$ will be assigned to a band

$$b_1 = \lfloor \frac{\mathbf{\Pi}_{p1}}{3}\mathbf{j} \rfloor$$

$$b_2 = \lfloor \frac{\mathbf{\Pi}_{p2}}{3}\mathbf{j} \rfloor \qquad (5.12)$$

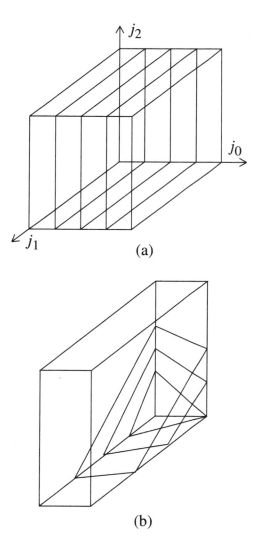

Figure 5.7 Partitioned index space: (a) the partitioning of the index set by hyperplane $\mathbf{\Pi}_{p_2} = (1\ 0\ 0)$; (b) the partitioning of one slice from (a) by hyperplane $\mathbf{\Pi}_{p_1} = (1\ 1\ 1)$. The space between planes forms a band [Moldovan and Fortes 1986].

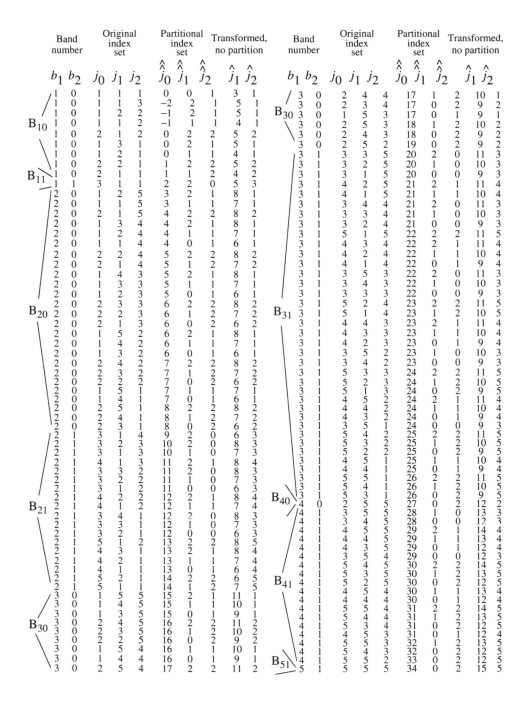

Figure 5.8 Partitioning and mapping the index set into a 3 × 3 systolic array.

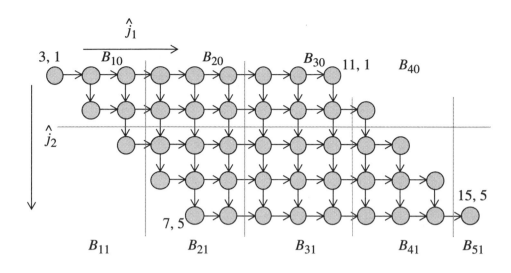

Figure 5.9 Mapping of partitioning bands into the array [Moldovan and Fortes 1986].

The allocation of computations to processors is done according to the following formulas:

$$\hat{\hat{j}}_1 = \mathbf{\Pi}_{p1}\mathbf{j} \quad \text{mod} \quad 3$$

$$\hat{\hat{j}}_2 = \mathbf{\Pi}_{p2}\mathbf{j} \quad \text{mod} \quad 3 \tag{5.13}$$

where $\hat{\hat{j}}_1$ and $\hat{\hat{j}}_2$ are the processor coordinates in the partitioning case. For example, index point $(3, 4, 1)$ is allocated to processor $(2, 0)$ in band $(2, 1)$.

It remains now to determine the exact processing time for each index point $\mathbf{j}$. The processing time for the partitioning case depends on the order in which the bands are executed. Many execution orderings are possible. In our example, we choose to execute the bands in the order $B_{10}, B_{11}, B_{20}, \ldots$. The time coordinate $\hat{j}_0$ in Figure 5.8 was determined by first executing all points inside one band according to the ordering imposed by $\mathbf{\Pi}$, then moving to the next band. For example, index point $(1, 2, 5)$ is processed at time $\hat{j}_0 = -4$ for the nonpartitioned case, but because of partitioning, its processing starts only after the previ-

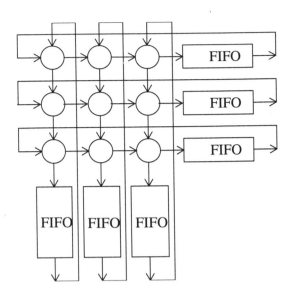

Figure 5.10 3×3 array with FIFO queue registers for partitioning [Moldovan and Fortes 1986].

ous band has finished; thus, $\hat{\hat{j}}_0 = 3$. The dependencies are mapped by the transformation such that only local communications are required inside each band. The communications between computations in adjacent bands are performed via external FIFO queue registers, which temporarily store variables, as shown in Figure 5.10.

5.2.3   Partitioning Methodology

In this section, the transformation technique is summarized as a procedure for partitioning and mapping algorithms into fixed-size systolic arrays. Assume we have an algorithm A, described by index set $\mathbf{J}^n$ and dependence matrix $\mathbf{D}$, and a systolic structure of size $\mathbf{M}$ $= m_1 \times m_2 \times \cdots m_{n-1}$ that is characterized by a set of interconnection primitives $\mathbf{P} = [\mathbf{p}_j]$. The procedure consists of the following steps:

Step 1. Find a transformation $\mathbf{\Pi}$, such that $\mathbf{\Pi d}_i > 0$, that minimizes

$$t = 1 + \lceil \frac{\max \mathbf{\Pi}(\mathbf{j}^2 - \mathbf{j}^1)}{\min \mathbf{\Pi d}_i} \rceil$$

$$\mathbf{j}_1, \mathbf{j}_2 \in \mathbf{J}^n, \text{ and } \mathbf{d}_i \in \mathbf{D}$$

From this step, the first row of the transformed dependencies $\mathbf{\Pi D}$ follows.

Step 2. Generate all possible $\mathbf{K}$ matrices, $\mathbf{K} = [k_{ji}], \mathbf{K} \in Z^{t \times m}$, that satisfy the conditions

1. $0 \leq k_{ji}$

2. $0 < \Sigma_j k_{ji} \leq \mathbf{\Pi d}_i$

Step 3. Find all possible transformations $\mathbf{S} \in \mathbf{Z}^{(n-1) \times n}$ that satisfy the conditions:

1. The diophantine equation $\mathbf{SD} = \mathbf{PK}$ can be solved for $\mathbf{S}$;

2. The matrix transformation

$$\mathbf{T} = \begin{bmatrix} \mathbf{\Pi} \\ \mathbf{S} \end{bmatrix}$$

is nonsingular; and

3. Each row of $\mathbf{S}$ defined as $\mathbf{\Pi}_{pj}$ with $1 \leq j \leq n - 1$ is such that

$$\mathbf{\Pi}_{pj} \mathbf{d}_i > 0$$

for all rows of $\mathbf{S}$ and all dependence vectors.

As a result of this step, one may obtain some valid transformations $\mathbf{T}$. If no $\mathbf{S}$ can be found that satisfies all the above conditions, then either compromise the fast execution time by selecting another $\mathbf{\Pi}$ in Step 1, or compromise the locality of data communication by selecting another set of primitives $\mathbf{P}$. For each valid transformation $\mathbf{T}$, the partitioning hyperplanes $\mathbf{\Pi}_{pj}$ are given by the rows of matrix $\mathbf{S}$:

$$\mathbf{S} = \begin{bmatrix} \mathbf{\Pi}_{p1} \\ \mathbf{\Pi}_{p2} \\ \vdots \\ \mathbf{\Pi}_{p(n-1)} \end{bmatrix}$$

Step 4. The mapping of indices to processors is as follows: Each index point $\mathbf{j}$ is processed in a processor whose jth coordinate is

$$\hat{\hat{j}}_j = \mathbf{\Pi}_{pj}\mathbf{j} \bmod m_j$$

Step 5. A policy for scheduling the bands is selected. Any ordering containing the partitioning ordering is an acceptable execution ordering (see Problem 5.9.A). A possible policy would be to order the execution of bands in a lexicographical manner (i.e., for fixed $\mathbf{\Pi}_{p1}, ..., \mathbf{\Pi}_{p(n-2)}$, execute all bands given by $\mathbf{\Pi}_{p(n-1)}$, then change $\mathbf{\Pi}_{p(n-2)}$ and execute all $\mathbf{\Pi}_{p(n-1)}$ again, etc.).

Some of the main advantages of the partitioning technique are its general applicability and the fact that the algorithms are partitioned with a minimum of side-effects. The partitioning is done such that the algorithm accuracy is not affected; no extra time or increase in processor complexity is required by partitioning. The amount of external hardware required by partitioning in order to circulate data outside the array is reduced by the regularity of data communication. An important feature of this mapping procedure is the possibility of making tradeoffs between the time performance and the space complexity of the systolic array.

5.3 MAPPING OF ALGORITHMS INTO SIMD PROCESSORS

5.3.1 Remapping Transformations

In this section, we consider the mapping of nested loop algorithms into SIMD computers with eight-neighbor and broadcast interconnections, as shown in Figure 5.11. The mapping technique discussed here is basically an extension of the technique for systolic arrays. Recall that some of the differences between systolic arrays and SIMD computers are that the former are pipelined arrays, whereas the latter usually are not; and that systolic array processors have low granularity with only limited storage, whereas SIMD processors have local memories. However, there are similarities between them that make the mapping

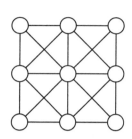 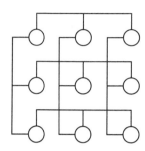

Figure 5.11 Eight-neighbor and broadcast interconnections.

technique applicable to both. For systolic arrays, interconnections between adjacent processors are required. This requirement is compatible with the SIMD interconnections considered here. Also, both systolic and SIMD computers work synchronously.

The mapping of nested loop algorithms into SIMD computers consists of two phases. With minor modifications, the first phase is basically the same as the mapping of algorithms to systolic arrays. The second phase consists of a remapping transformation to reduce communication time.

One difference between systolic and SIMD mappings is the condition for finding the time transformation $\mathbf{\Pi}$. Since data broadcasts are possible in SIMD arrays, the number of time units required to move data from source to destination may include zero, instead of being strictly positive as in systolic arrays. Thus

$$\mathbf{\Pi}\mathbf{d}_i \geq 0 \qquad (5.14)$$

Suppose, following the procedure used for systolic arrays, a transformation $\mathbf{T}$ was found. Then one could ask, "Can a remapping transformation $\mathbf{T}_r$ be found such that the computation complexity time achieved by using $\mathbf{T}$ is retained, while the communication time is reduced?" The communication time can be reduced simply by keeping results in local memories and using them later. This translates into forcing the transformed dependencies to require zero communication.

This problem can be solved by reexamining the transformed data dependence matrix. Transformation $\mathbf{T}$ maps $\mathbf{J}^n$ into $\hat{\mathbf{J}}^n$. After the algorithm is transformed, $\hat{j}_0$ is the time index and $\hat{j}_1, ..., \hat{j}_{n-1}$ are the space indices. Let $\hat{\mathbf{D}}$, the dependence matrix of the transformed algorithm, be $[\hat{\mathbf{d}}_1, \hat{\mathbf{d}}_2, ..., \hat{\mathbf{d}}_m]$. Each $\hat{\mathbf{d}}_i$ is an $(n \times 1)$–column vector that specifies the behavior of variable v_i. Then $\hat{d}_{ji}$, the jth component of $\hat{\mathbf{d}}_i, 1 \leq j \leq n-1$, means that variable v_i moves along the $\hat{j}_j$ direction $\hat{d}_{ji}$ units between two computation steps. If $\hat{d}_{ji}$ is zero, then the variable v_i does not move in the $\hat{j}_j$ direction during computation.

The remapping transformation $\mathbf{T}_r$ is found by transforming the data dependence matrix $\hat{\mathbf{D}}$. If one can find a $\mathbf{T}_r$ such that $\hat{d}_{ji}$ of $\hat{\mathbf{D}}$ becomes zero $(j \neq 1)$, then when the algorithm is executed, variable v_i does not have to move in the $\hat{j}_j$ direction because it stays in the same processing element. In this case, the communication time encountered in the execution of the algorithm is reduced, as far as v_i is concerned. This argument suggests that a good $\mathbf{T}_r$ should transform as many nonzero $\hat{d}_{ji}$ into zeros as possible.

Next, some expressions are derived for the computation and communication time. These will be used to perform mapping tradeoffs. Given a transformation $\mathbf{T} = [\mathbf{\Pi}\ \mathbf{S}]^t$, and $\hat{\mathbf{D}} = [\hat{\mathbf{d}}_1, \hat{\mathbf{d}}_2, ..., \hat{\mathbf{d}}_m] = \mathbf{TD}$, the number of computation steps of A under $\mathbf{T}$ is given by Equation (5.10). Let us denote this number by M^T. If each computation step takes t_{cu} time units, then the total computation time t_c is

$$t_c = M^T t_{cu} \tag{5.15}$$

For variable v_i, the number of data routing steps between two consecutive computations under $\mathbf{T}$ is $\sum_{1 \leq j \leq n-1} |\hat{d}_{ji}| = R_i$. (If $\hat{d}_{0i} = 0$, then $R_i = 0$, since data are broadcast before computations begin.) The routing cost of an algorithm between two computation steps under $\mathbf{T}$ is

$$R^T = \max_{1 \leq i \leq m} R_i \tag{5.16}$$

Suppose each step of data routing takes t_{ru} units of time. Then the total data routing time (communication time) t_r is

$$t_r = (M^T - 1)R^T t_{ru} \tag{5.17}$$

In order to reduce the communication time of the algorithm, we seek a remapping transformation $\mathbf{T}_r$, which reduces t_r while keeping t_c unchanged (since t_c has already been minimized by transformation $\mathbf{T}$).

Example 5.4. The data dependence matrix for matrix multiplication, LU decomposition, and many other algorithms is

$$\mathbf{D} = \begin{bmatrix} 1 & 0 & 0 \\ 0 & 1 & 0 \\ 0 & 0 & 1 \end{bmatrix}$$

The first phase of the mapping provides several possible transformations, such as

$$\mathbf{T} = \begin{bmatrix} 1 & 0 & 0 \\ -1 & 1 & 0 \\ -1 & 0 & 1 \end{bmatrix} \quad \mathbf{T} = \begin{bmatrix} 1 & 1 & 1 \\ -1 & 1 & 0 \\ -1 & 0 & 1 \end{bmatrix} \quad \mathbf{T} = \begin{bmatrix} 1 & 1 & 1 \\ -1 & 1 & 0 \\ 0 & 0 & 1 \end{bmatrix}$$

Consider

$$\mathbf{T} = \begin{bmatrix} 1 & 0 & 0 \\ -1 & 1 & 0 \\ -1 & 0 & 1 \end{bmatrix}$$

In this case, $\hat{\mathbf{D}}$ is the same as $\mathbf{T}$, because $\mathbf{D}$ is the identity matrix. Notice that two entries of the first row of $\hat{\mathbf{D}}$ are zeros. A zero entry in the first row means that the corresponding variable is broadcast, which is not allowed in systolic arrays. Here, since we are mapping algorithms to an SIMD machine, we can choose a zero entry to save communication time. The number of computation steps is

$$M^T = [1 \ 0 \ 0]([n \ n \ n]^t - [1 \ 1 \ 1]^t) + 1 = n$$

and the computation time is $t_c = M^T t_{cu} = n t_{cu}$. The routing cost between two computations is $R^T = |-1| + |-1| = 2$. Therefore the communication time is

$$\begin{aligned} t_r &= (M^T - 1)R^T t_{ru} \\ &= (n - 1)2 t_{ru} \end{aligned}$$

We now seek a remapping transformation $\mathbf{T}_r$ to reduce the communication cost. Algorithms for finding $\mathbf{T}_r$ can be easily designed; the goal is to zero as many elements as possible in the new data dependence matrix. One possible $\mathbf{T}_r$ is

$$\mathbf{T}_r = \begin{bmatrix} 1 & 0 & 0 \\ 1 & 1 & 0 \\ 1 & 0 & 1 \end{bmatrix}$$

So

$$\mathbf{D}' = \mathbf{T}_r\hat{\mathbf{D}} = \begin{bmatrix} 1 & 0 & 0 \\ 1 & 1 & 0 \\ 1 & 0 & 1 \end{bmatrix} \begin{bmatrix} 1 & 0 & 0 \\ -1 & 1 & 0 \\ -1 & 0 & 1 \end{bmatrix} = \begin{bmatrix} 1 & 0 & 0 \\ 0 & 1 & 0 \\ 0 & 0 & 1 \end{bmatrix}$$

The communication cost under this remapping is zero! This is because the variable corresponding to the first data dependence does not leave the processing cell, and the second and third variables are broadcast. Therefore, this $\mathbf{T}_r$ is the optimal remapping transformation.

5.3.2   Design Tradeoffs Using Transformations

Tradeoff Between Computation and Communication Time
The parallel computation time t_c of a transformed algorithm is given by Equation (5.15) and the communication time t_r is given by Equation (5.17). The total execution time t is

$$t = t_c + t_r = M^T t_{cu} + (M^T - 1)R^T t_{ru} \qquad (5.18)$$

From the mapping technique described in the previous section, it is known that M^T is a function of time transformation $\mathbf{\Pi}$ and R^T is calculated from $\hat{\mathbf{D}}$, which in turn depends on $\mathbf{S}$.

Therefore, given an algorithm, the execution time is determined by the selected transformation. Consider an algorithm A with the dependence matrix $\mathbf{D}$. Assume $\mathbf{T}_1$ and $\mathbf{T}_2$ are two viable transformations. The following proposition provides a criterion for selecting between two viable transformations $\mathbf{T}_1$ and $\mathbf{T}_2$ when the goal is to minimize the overall processing time.

Proposition 5.1. The criteria for selecting between $\mathbf{T}_1$ or $\mathbf{T}_2$ are:

1. When $M^{T_1} < M^{T_2}$ and $R^{T_1} < R^{T_2}$, select $\mathbf{T}_1$.

2. When $M^{T_1} < M^{T_2}$ and $R^{T_1} > R^{T_2}$, select $\mathbf{T}_2$ if

$$\frac{M^{T_1}R^{T_1} - M^{T_2}R^{T_2}}{M^{T_2} - M^{T_1}} > \frac{t_{cu}}{t_{ru}} \tag{5.19}$$

Otherwise select $\mathbf{T}_1$.

Proof: This proposition is easily proved by simply comparing the parallel processing times given by the two transformations:

$$t_1 = M^{T_1}t_{cu} + (M^{T_1} - 1)R^{T_1}t_{ru}$$

$$t_2 = M^{T_2}t_{cu} + (M^{T_2} - 1)R^{T_2}t_{ru}$$

Normally $M^T \gg 1$. The Inequality (5.19) results from condition $t_2 < t_1$ and is useful for solving the tradeoff between computation time and communication time. The ratio t_{cu}/t_{ru} is known from hardware constraints, and if the Inequality (5.19) is used to test any two transformations, the better one may be selected.

Example 5.5. Consider an algorithm whose $\mathbf{D}$ is the identity matrix, and an array processor that has $t_{cu} = t_{ru}$. Suppose $\mathbf{T}_1$ and $\mathbf{T}_2$ are

$$\mathbf{T}_1 = \begin{bmatrix} 1 & 0 & 1 \\ 3 & 8 & 2 \\ 1 & 3 & 3 \end{bmatrix} \quad \mathbf{T}_2 = \begin{bmatrix} 2 & 1 & 1 \\ 2 & 3 & 1 \\ 1 & 2 & 0 \end{bmatrix}$$

Since $\mathbf{D}$ is the identity, the new data dependence matrices are $\hat{\mathbf{D}}_1 = \mathbf{T}_1$ and $\hat{\mathbf{D}}_2 = \mathbf{T}_2$. Assuming that all three coordinates of the algorithms range from 1 to n,

$$M^{T_2} = 4n - 3, \ R^{T_2} = 5$$

and

$$M^{T_1} = 2n - 1, \ R^{T_1} = 11$$

From the Inequality (5.19),

$$\frac{11(2n - 1) - 5(4n - 3)}{(4n - 3) - (2n - 1)} > \frac{t_{cu}}{t_{ru}}$$

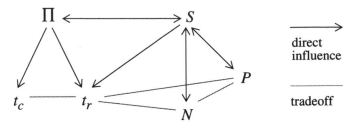

Figure 5.12 Tradeoffs provided by an algorithm transformation.

$$\frac{2n+4}{2n-2} > 1$$

This inequality is true. Thus, according to Proposition 5.1, transformation $\mathbf{T}_2$ is selected over transformation $\mathbf{T}_1$.

Tradeoff Among Number of Processors, Communication Time, and Interconnection Links

The number of processors required to execute a transformed algorithm results directly from the index set $\hat{\mathbf{J}}^n$. As we have mentioned, a computation indexed by $\mathbf{j}$ is executed at time $\hat{j}_0$ in processor $p = (\hat{j}_1, ..., \hat{j}_{n-1})$. The number of processors N is the number of distinct points p in the set $\hat{\mathbf{J}}^n$. The important fact is that the number of processors is directly related to the space transformation $\mathbf{S}$, which is part of $\mathbf{T}$. Thus, all other design parameters influenced by $\mathbf{S}$, or influencing $\mathbf{S}$, such as communication time, number of communication links, and so on, can be traded against the number of processors. The tradeoffs are shown in Figure 5.12.

The communication time t_r depends on $\mathbf{S}$, as can be seen from Equation (5.17). Because of this dependence, a tradeoff is possible between the number of processors and the communication time. Moreover, the number of distinct interconnection links is the number of columns in matrix $\mathbf{P}$. From the relation in Equation (5.5) it is clear that $\mathbf{P}$ is related to the space transformation $\mathbf{S}$. Thus, the number of communication links is related to the algorithm through dependence matrix $\mathbf{D}$ and $\mathbf{S}$. The larger the size of $\mathbf{P}$ (the more connections), the more solutions for $\mathbf{S}$ exist.

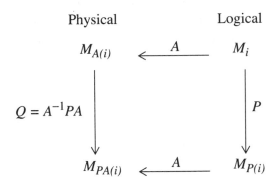

Figure 5.13 Relation between logical memory transfer and physical memory transfer.

5.3.3 Relation Between Logical Transfers and Physical Transfers

Consider an algorithm that requires a data transfer described by permutation P between logical memories M_i. Assume that the realization of P on a given interconnection network requires $R(P)$ routing steps, and that the realization of another permutation Q on the same network requires $R(Q)$ routing steps. When $R(Q) < R(P)$ it is more advantageous to seek a bijection function A that maps P onto Q, such that permutation Q is actually performed instead of P. Permutation Q has the meaning of a physical transfer between physical memory modules M. In Figure 5.13, the relation between logical and physical transfers is shown. The problem of *mapping logical to physical permutations* can be posed as follows:

Given a logical permutation P and a physical permutation Q, find the bijection A such that

$$PA = AQ \qquad (5.20)$$

This relation indicates that the diagram in Figure 5.13 commutes. Since A is a bijection, Equation (5.20) is equivalent to

$$Q = A^{-1}PA \qquad (5.21)$$

In reality, only P is known from the algorithm, and we want to find A such that Q will match the computer interconnection network as closely as possible. The idea of *locality* is introduced here as a measure of routing steps.

Definition 5.2 Locality is a measure of the distance in the processor's space between the source and the destination of an interaction as it is mapped to a network. An interaction has low locality if the number of cycles of the interconnection network necessary to implement it is large.

Note that the meaning of the word interaction in this definition is similar to the meaning of data routing function. The next example illustrates the relationship between logical and physical transfers. Here the logical transfers require two permutations, P and S. It is shown that the locality is increased if we map logical data into physical memory using bijection A. Assume that P and S are permutations, and A is the mapping function

$$P = \begin{pmatrix} 0 & 1 & 2 & 3 \\ 3 & 0 & 2 & 1 \end{pmatrix} = (0\ 3\ 1)(2)$$

$$S = \begin{pmatrix} 0 & 1 & 2 & 3 \\ 2 & 1 & 3 & 0 \end{pmatrix} = (0\ 2\ 3)(1)$$

$$A = \begin{pmatrix} 0 & 1 & 2 & 3 \\ 1 & 3 & 0 & 2 \end{pmatrix} = (0\ 1\ 3\ 2)$$

$$A^{-1} = \begin{pmatrix} 0 & 1 & 2 & 3 \\ 2 & 0 & 3 & 1 \end{pmatrix}$$

Then

$$A^{-1}PA = \begin{pmatrix} 0 & 1 & 2 & 3 \\ 0 & 2 & 3 & 1 \end{pmatrix}$$

and

$$A^{-1}SA = \begin{pmatrix} 0 & 1 & 2 & 3 \\ 2 & 0 & 1 & 3 \end{pmatrix}$$

The logical and physical transfers are shown in Figure 5.14(a). Now consider that the interconnection network available is one-dimensional with bidirectional connections, as shown in Figure 5.14(b). Assume that the network control is such that transmissions can be done in only one direction at a time. It can be seen that $A^{-1}PA$ and $A^{-1}SA$ have higher locality on such a linearly connected network than do P and S. Three routing steps are required by $A^{-1}PA$; $A^{-1}SA$ also requires three, as opposed to the five steps needed for either P or S. Thus, fewer routing steps are required after using mapping A.

Depending on the structure of the algorithm, sometimes a single mapping is not sufficient to minimize the number of routing steps. In this case several mappings are necessary, and it is important to decide when to perform these mappings so that the total number of routing steps is minimized. Consider an algorithm consisting of m consecutive permutations P followed by a sequence of n identical permutations S. Suppose A is the optimal mapping for transfer P; that is, $R(A^{-1}PA)$ is minimized. This mapping A may not be optimal for permutation S. Suppose we find that B is the optimal mapping for transfer S. This implies that the actual permutations between physical memories consist of a sequence of m $A^{-1}PA$ permutations followed by a sequence of n $B^{-1}SB$ permutations. However, another small correction is necessary. When the transfer $A^{-1}PA$ is performed, the relation between logical memory and physical memory is A; in the case of transfer $B^{-1}SB$, that relation is B. Consequently, the alignment of data will not be correct when $B^{-1}SB$ is performed after $A^{-1}PA$. The solution is to perform a single permutation $A^{-1}B$ between the last $A^{-1}PA$ permutation and the first $B^{-1}QB$ permutation. Figure 5.15 illustrates this idea. In general, whenever the mapping function is changed, one must take into consideration the alignment of data so that the relation between logical memory and physical memory remains correct.

Next, consider the execution of an algorithm with a sequence of routing functions $P_0, P_1, ..., P_{m-1}$. Before such an algorithm is executed, map data to processors using function A. For each transfer P_i, the

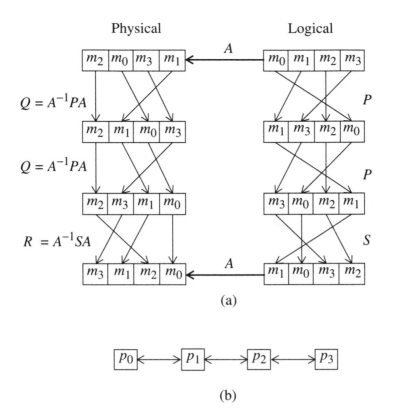

(a)

(b)

Figure 5.14 (a) Example of logical and physical transfer;
(b) interconnection network.

actual transfer to be performed in physical memory is $A^{-1}P_iA$. If the total number of routing steps is less than it would be if the mapping A were used, it is worth performing such a mapping prior to the execution of the algorithm. If a single mapping is not good enough for reducing the routing steps, perhaps several mappings are better. Based on this, the mapping problem can now be defined formally.

Let R be the distance function for measuring the number of routing steps of a data transfer on a network, and let W be a set of permutation transfers required for executing an algorithm $W = \{P_1, P_2, ..., P_r\}$.

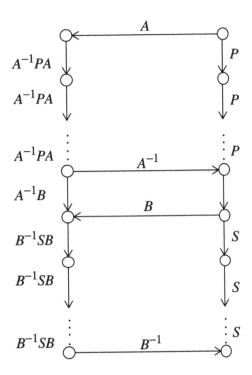

Figure 5.15 Relation between logical and physical transfers using two mapping functions.

Definition 5.3 The mapping problem is to find bijections A_i, for $1 \leq i \leq r$, such that the performance index

$$ J = \sum_{i=1}^{r} R(A_i^{-1} P_i A_i) + \sum_{i}^{r-1} R(A_i^{-1} A_{i+1}) $$

is minimized.

Here an algorithm is considered to be a sequence of permutations, but one should keep in mind that there are computations between two consecutive permutations. (The transfers that are not permutations will not be considered here.) The focus is on permutation-type transfers because other types of transfers can always be achieved by performing several permutations and masking off processors.

From the mapping-problem point of view, the structure of algorithms can be classified as follows:

- *Type 1.* Algorithms that have a single type of permutation—in other words, data transfers—are described by the sequence

$$P, P, P, ..., P$$

  Later it is shown that for a mesh-connected network, an optimal mapping for this type of algorithm can always be found.

- *Type 2.* Algorithms that have sequences of identical permutations

$$P, P, ..., P, Q, Q, ..., Q, ..., T, T, ..., T.$$

  This mapping problem can be solved using the same techniques as for Type 1.

- *Type 3.* Algorithms that have a totally random sequence of permutations

$$P, Q, R, T, ..., S$$

  The mapping of these algorithms is most difficult. The optimal mapping for one permutation may not be adequate for the others.

Properties of $A^{-1}PA$–Type Permutations

In the previous section it was shown that the permutation $A^{-1}PA$ plays a key role in reducing the number of routing steps. Some properties of $A^{-1}PA$–type permutations are derived here that will eventually allow us to find the mapping A.

Definition 5.4 *Cycle characteristics.* Two permutations P and Q are said to have the same cycle characteristics if

1. P and Q are permutations of the same number of elements;

2. P and Q have the same number of disjoint cycles; and

3. There is a one-to-one correspondence between the cycle lengths of P and Q (i.e., if P has a cycle of length m, then Q must also contain a cycle of length m).

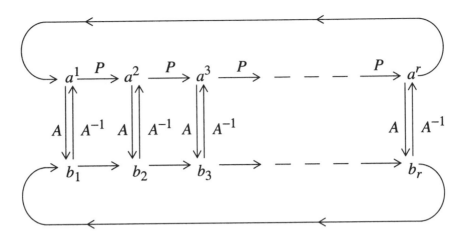

Figure 5.16 Relation among P, A, A^{-1}.

Theorem 5.1 Let P and A be two different permutations of N elements. Then permutations P and $A^{-1}PA$ have the same cycle characteristics.

Proof: Assume that permutation P can be decomposed into s disjoint cycles with lengths $l_1, l_2, ..., l_s$. Assume that the cycle containing element 0 has length r. Let us denote these r elements in the permutation sequence as $a^1, a^2, a^3, ..., a^r$, and assume that element 0 is a^r. Without loss of generality, P can be expressed as follows:

$$P = \begin{pmatrix} 0 & 2 & 5 & \cdots & 16 & \cdots & m & \cdots & N-1 \\ a^1 & a^2 & a^3 & \cdots & a^k & \cdots & 0 & \cdots & g \end{pmatrix}$$

Note that $2 = a^1$, $5 = a^2$, $16 = a^{k-1}$, $m = a^{r-1}$. Now assume that permutation A maps a^i to $b_i, 1 \leq i \leq r$. Since A is an arbitrary permutation, b_i can be any element between 0 and $N-1$. Consider only the cycle containing $a^1, a^2, ..., a^r$. The relation among P, A, and A^{-1} is shown in Figure 5.16.

Starting from b_1, permutation $A^{-1}PA$ maps b_1 to b_2 through the sequence a^1 (by A^{-1}), a^2 (by P), then b_2 (by A). Further, b_2 will be mapped to b_3. After $r - 1$ iterations, b_1 will be mapped to b_r. At this time, if $A^{-1}PA$ is applied once more, b_r will be mapped to b_1. Also, since $a^1, a^2, ..., a^r$ are r different elements, b_i is different from b_j if i is not equal to j. Therefore $b_1, b_2, ..., b_r$ is a cycle of r elements. It follows that for any cycle in permutation P, there is a corresponding cycle of the same length in permutation $A^{-1}PA$. Consequently, P and $A^{-1}PA$ have the same cycle characteristics. **Q.E.D.**

Example 5.6. Consider a permutation P of 16 elements and another arbitrary permutation A with cycle characteristics different from those of P.

$$P = \begin{pmatrix} 0 & 1 & 2 & 3 & 4 & 5 & 6 & 7 & 8 & 9 & 10 & 11 & 12 & 13 & 14 & 15 \\ 13 & 11 & 5 & 4 & 1 & 6 & 0 & 2 & 10 & 8 & 12 & 15 & 9 & 7 & 3 & 14 \end{pmatrix}$$
$$= (0\ 13\ 7\ 2\ 5\ 6)(1\ 11\ 15\ 14\ 3\ 4)(8\ 10\ 12\ 9)$$
$$A = \begin{pmatrix} 0 & 1 & 2 & 3 & 4 & 5 & 6 & 7 & 8 & 9 & 10 & 11 & 12 & 13 & 14 & 15 \\ 2 & 5 & 13 & 11 & 15 & 8 & 7 & 0 & 1 & 4 & 14 & 6 & 3 & 9 & 12 & 10 \end{pmatrix}$$
$$A^{-1} = \begin{pmatrix} 0 & 1 & 2 & 3 & 4 & 5 & 6 & 7 & 8 & 9 & 10 & 11 & 12 & 13 & 14 & 15 \\ 7 & 8 & 0 & 12 & 9 & 1 & 11 & 6 & 5 & 13 & 15 & 3 & 14 & 2 & 10 & 4 \end{pmatrix}$$

and the permutation $A^{-1}PA$ is

$$A^{-1}PA = \begin{pmatrix} 0 & 1 & 2 & 3 & 4 & 5 & 6 & 7 & 8 & 9 & 10 & 11 & 12 & 13 & 14 & 15 \\ 13 & 14 & 9 & 4 & 1 & 6 & 10 & 2 & 7 & 0 & 12 & 15 & 11 & 8 & 3 & 5 \end{pmatrix}$$
$$= (0\ 13\ 8\ 7\ 2\ 9)(1\ 14\ 3\ 4)(5\ 6\ 10\ 12\ 11\ 15)$$

Note that P and $A^{-1}PA$ have the same cycle characteristics.

Theorem 5.2 Let P and T be two different permutations of N elements. There exists a permutation A, such that $T = A^{-1}PA$, if and only if P and T have the same cycle characteristics.

Proof: From Theorem 5.1, if $T = A^{-1}PA$, then P and T have the same cycle characteristics. Now assume P and T have the same cycle characteristics and consider one arbitrary cycle of length m. The elements of this cycle in P are $p^1, p^2, ..., p^m$, and the elements in T are $t^1, t^2, ..., t^m$. (If there are several cycles of the same length, pick one arbitrarily.) Let A be the permutation that maps p^i to $t^i, 1 \leq i \leq m$. The relation between P and T is shown in Figure 5.17.

From Figure 5.17, it is clear that $A^{-1}PA(t^i) = t^{i+1}, 1 \leq i \leq m$, and $t^{m+1} = t^1$. Therefore, for this cycle, $A^{-1}PA$ equals T. Since P and

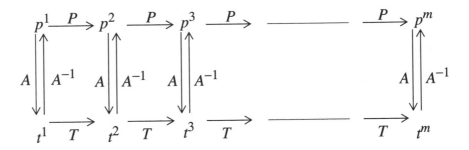

Figure 5.17 Relation between the two permutations P and T.

T have the same cycle characteristics, one can build similar mappings between the elements of two cycles of P and T that have the same length. All these mappings form the permutation A, which is one-to-one and onto. **Q.E.D.**

This theorem is helpful for mapping algorithm permutations into interconnection networks. A permutation with low locality can be transformed into a permutation with high locality if the cycle characteristics are retained. According to Theorem 5.2, such a mapping exists.

5.4 MAPPING OF ALGORITHMS INTO MESH-CONNECTED NETWORKS

5.4.1 Mapping Techniques

In this section, some methods are presented for mapping algorithms to *mesh-connected networks* (MCN). The procedure is first to extract the permutations from the algorithm, then to map these permutations to the MCN using the techniques described below. Different permutations have different characteristics; therefore, their mappings might be different. The mappings presented here are classified as either *cyclic mappings* or *linear mappings,* depending on how bijection A was determined.

Cyclic Mapping

Definition 5.5 A is a cyclic mapping if for any permutation P:

1. $A^{-1}PA$ and P have the same cycle characteristics; and

2. In each cycle of $A^{-1}PA$, the elements are shifted circularly by one step.

If mapping A is used, the permutation $A^{-1}PA$ has higher locality on the MCN than does permutation P. The procedure for finding the cyclic mapping A is as follows:

Cyclic Mapping Procedure.

1. Decompose P into disjoint cycles. Assume P has m cycles $p_1, p_2, ..., p_m$, with lengths $l_1, l_2, ..., l_m$.

2. Form the mapping A^{-1} as follows:

$$A^{-1} = \begin{pmatrix} c_1 & c_2 & \cdots & c_i & \cdots & c_m \\ p_1 & p_2 & \cdots & p_i & \cdots & p_m \end{pmatrix}$$

where c_i is a sequence of l_i members that form a rectangle on an MCN.

3. From A^{-1} find A. A is the cyclic mapping we want to find.

When A is set as above, the transformed permutation $A^{-1}PA$ will have higher locality than P. In addition, every cycle of $A^{-1}PA$ is a circular-shift permutation, which is a good property when the target interconnection is an MCN.

Example 5.7. Consider a permutation P, defined as

$$P = \begin{pmatrix} 0 & 1 & 2 & 3 & 4 & 5 & 6 & 7 & 8 & 9 & 10 & 11 & 12 & 13 & 14 & 15 \\ 13 & 11 & 0 & 4 & 15 & 6 & 1 & 2 & 10 & 8 & 12 & 5 & 9 & 7 & 3 & 14 \end{pmatrix}$$

First, decompose P into disjoint cycles:

$$P = (0\ 13\ 7\ 2)(5\ 6\ 1\ 11)(15\ 14\ 3\ 4)(8\ 10\ 12\ 9)$$

A^{-1} is formed as follows:

$$A^{-1} = \begin{pmatrix} 0 & 1 & 2 & 3 \mid & 4 & 5 & 6 & 7 \mid & 8 & 9 & 10 & 11 \mid & 12 & 13 & 14 & 15 \\ 0 & 13 & 7 & 2 \mid & 5 & 6 & 1 & 11 \mid & 15 & 14 & 3 & 4 \mid & 8 & 10 & 12 & 9 \end{pmatrix}$$

and

$$A = \begin{pmatrix} 0 & 1 & 2 & 3 & 4 & 5 & 6 & 7 & 8 & 9 & 10 & 11 & 12 & 13 & 14 & 15 \\ 0 & 6 & 3 & 10 & 11 & 4 & 5 & 2 & 12 & 15 & 13 & 7 & 14 & 1 & 9 & 8 \end{pmatrix}$$

The resulting $A^{-1}PA$ is

$$A^{-1}PA = \begin{pmatrix} 0 & 1 & 2 & 3 \mid & 4 & 5 & 6 & 7 \mid & 8 & 9 & 10 & 11 \mid & 12 & 13 & 14 & 15 \\ 1 & 2 & 3 & 0 \mid & 5 & 6 & 7 & 4 \mid & 9 & 10 & 11 & 8 \mid & 13 & 14 & 15 & 12 \end{pmatrix}$$

$$= (0\ 1\ 2\ 3)(4\ 5\ 6\ 7)(8\ 9\ 10\ 11)(12\ 13\ 14\ 15)$$

as expected.

Through cyclic mapping, a high locality is achieved. For the purpose of the MCN, cycle lengths that are even numbers are desirable. When P has this property, it is always possible to implement P on an MCN and to achieve high locality. When P contains cycles with odd cycle-length numbers, cyclic mapping does not perform well. In such situations another type of mapping, called linear mapping, achieves better results.

Linear Mapping

Again, decompose P into disjoint cycles. Assume P has m cycles $p_1, p_2, ..., p_m$, with lengths $l_1, l_2, ..., l_m$. Denote the elements of the ith cycle as $a_i^1, a_i^2, ..., a_i^{l_i}, 1 < i < m$.

Definition 5.6 A is a linear mapping if it is a mapping formed as follows:

$$A = \begin{pmatrix} p_1 & p_2 ... & p_i ... & p_m \\ s_1 & s_2 ... & s_i ... & s_m \end{pmatrix}$$

where s_i is a sequence of numbers of the form

$$L_i, \ L_i + 2, \ L_i + 4, ... L_i + l_i - 1, ... L_i + 5, \ L_i + 3, \ L_i + 1$$

and where $L_i = l_1 + l_2 + ... + l_{i-1}$ (if $i = 1, L_1 = 0$).

Example 5.8. Consider a permutation P of 16 elements, defined as

$$P = (0\ 13\ 7\ 2\ 5\ 6)(1\ 11\ 15\ 14\ 3\ 4)(8\ 10\ 12\ 9)$$

Construct the linear mapping A according to the definition above:

$$A = \begin{pmatrix} 0 & 13 & 7 & 2 & 5 & 6 & | & 1 & 11 & 15 & 14 & 3 & 4 & | & 8 & 10 & 12 & 9 \\ 0 & 2 & 4 & 5 & 3 & 1 & | & 6 & 8 & 10 & 11 & 9 & 7 & | & 12 & 14 & 15 & 13 \end{pmatrix}$$

$$A^{-1} = \begin{pmatrix} 0 & 1 & 2 & 3 & 4 & 5 & 6 & 7 & 8 & 9 & 10 & 11 & 12 & 13 & 14 & 15 \\ 0 & 6 & 13 & 5 & 7 & 2 & 1 & 4 & 11 & 3 & 15 & 14 & 8 & 9 & 10 & 12 \end{pmatrix}$$

$$A^{-1}PA = \begin{pmatrix} 0 & 1 & 2 & 3 & 4 & 5 & 6 & 7 & 8 & 9 & 10 & 11 & 12 & 13 & 14 & 15 \\ 2 & 0 & 4 & 1 & 5 & 3 & 8 & 6 & 10 & 7 & 11 & 9 & 14 & 12 & 15 & 13 \end{pmatrix}$$

The resulting $A^{-1}PA$ permutation takes no more than four routing steps on the linearly connected network and on the mesh-connected network.

Applications of Cyclic Mapping

In parallel processing algorithms, some permutations are frequently used. In the discussion that follows, the mapping of some of these permutations into MCNs is considered. Assume that the permutations are on N elements, $N = 2^n \times 2^n$, and n is an integer. Also assume an MCN composed of $2^n \times 2^n$ processing elements.

Case 1. Permutation P consists of $N/2$ cycles, each of length 2. For this type of permutation, cyclic mapping is optimal. If the elements of P are denoted as $a_1^1, a_1^2, a_2^1, a_2^2, ..., a_{N/2}^1, a_{N/2}^2$, then the mapping is simply

$$A^{-1} = \begin{pmatrix} 0 & 1 & 2 & 3... & N-4 & N-3 & N-2 & N-1 \\ a_1^1 & a_1^2 & a_2^1 & a_2^2... & a_{N/2-1}^1 & a_{N/2-1}^2 & a_{N/2}^1 & a_{N/2}^2 \end{pmatrix}$$

Permutations of this type include the exchange, butterfly, and bit-reversal permutations. Some of the cycles in butterfly and bit-reversal permutations degenerate to length 1. After mapping to the MCN, the actual permutations performed in physical memory, namely $A^{-1}PA$, are all the same. The resulting $A^{-1}PA$ permutation has high locality. The number of routing steps needed is 2, independent of the size N.

Case 2. Permutation P has cycles with an even number of elements. The cyclic mapping is such that each cycle P_i is mapped into a sequence r_i of $2l_i$ numbers, which are obtained by counting clockwise the processors of an $l_i \times 2$ rectangle in the MCN. The mapping is

$$A^{-1} = \begin{pmatrix} r_1 & r_2... & r_i... & r_m \\ p_1 & p_2... & p_i... & p_m \end{pmatrix}$$

Permutations of this type include some of the cyclic-shift permutations; for example, $x \to x + N/4 \bmod N$, plus 2^i permutations, and minus 2^i permutations. In this case, the permutation can be achieved on an MCN in just one routing step.

Example 5.9. Consider the mapping of a barrel-shifter permutation $B_{+2}(x) = (x + 2^2) \bmod 16$ into a 4×4 MCN.

$$\begin{aligned} B_{+2} &= \begin{pmatrix} 0 & 1 & 2 & 3 & 4 & 5 & 6 & 7 & 8 & 9 & 10 & 11 & 12 & 13 & 14 & 15 \\ 4 & 5 & 6 & 7 & 8 & 9 & 10 & 11 & 12 & 13 & 14 & 15 & 0 & 1 & 2 & 3 \end{pmatrix} \\ &= (0,\ 4,\ 8,\ 12)(1,\ 5,\ 9,\ 13)(2,\ 6,\ 10,\ 14)(3,\ 7,\ 11,\ 15) \end{aligned}$$

A^{-1} is formed as

$$A^{-1} = \begin{pmatrix} 0 & 1 & 5 & 4 & | & 2 & 3 & 7 & 6 & | & 8 & 9 & 13 & 12 & | & 10 & 11 & 15 & 14 \\ 0 & 4 & 8 & 12 & | & 1 & 5 & 9 & 13 & | & 2 & 6 & 10 & 14 & | & 3 & 7 & 11 & 15 \end{pmatrix}$$

It follows that $A^{-1}BA$ is

$$\begin{aligned} A^{-1}BA &= \begin{pmatrix} 0 & 1 & 2 & 3 & 4 & 5 & 6 & 7 & 8 & 9 & 10 & 11 & 12 & 13 & 14 & 15 \\ 1 & 5 & 3 & 7 & 0 & 4 & 2 & 6 & 9 & 13 & 11 & 15 & 8 & 12 & 10 & 14 \end{pmatrix} \\ &= (0,\ 1,\ 5,\ 4)(2,\ 3,\ 7,\ 6)(8,\ 9,\ 13,\ 12)(10,\ 11,\ 15,\ 14) \end{aligned}$$

Figure 5.18 illustrates the improvement achieved by mapping A.

5.4.2 Mapping of Algorithms with the Perfect-Shuffle Permutation

The perfect-shuffle permutation is considered as a special case because it is frequently used and its cycle characteristics do not fall within

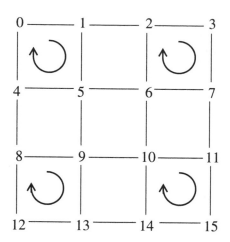

Figure 5.18 Mapping of a barrel-shifter permutation into an MCN.

either of the two cases discussed above. First, the cycle characteristics of the perfect-shuffle permutation are analyzed for different N, and then optimal mappings for several different cases are identified. Cycle characteristics constitute important information, which is absolutely necessary for finding the mapping function A.

Cycle Characteristics of the Perfect-Shuffle Permutation
Let S_n be the perfect-shuffle permutation of $N = 2^n$ elements:

$$S_n(x) = \begin{cases} 2x & 0 \le x < N/2 \\ 2x + 1 - N & N/2 \le x < N \end{cases}$$

Decompose S_n into disjoint cycles, and let C_i be the number of cycles of length i in this decomposition. The analysis of C_i is important for the mapping of S_n into an MCN. However, no single formula can describe C_i's for all different N. The following two theorems indicate how to find C_i recursively.

Theorem 5.3 [Lin and Moldovan 1986] Let S be the perfect-shuffle permutation of $N = 2^n$ elements, and C_i be the number of cycles of length i in S. Permutation S contains cycles of length m if and only if $m|n$ (m divides n); i.e., $C_m > 0$ iff $m|n$.

Corollary: If n is a prime number, then S has only two kinds of cycles: cycles of length 1 and of length n. Moreover, the numbers of cycles are $C_1 = 2$ and $C_n = (2^n - 2)/n$.

The case in which n is not a prime number is considered in the next theorem. However, first it is necessary to introduce the notion of the cycle spectrum for the perfect-shuffle permutation.

Definition 5.7 *Cycle spectrum ψ_N.* The cycle spectrum of a perfect shuffle of $N = 2^n$ elements is a p-tuple number $\psi_N = (C_{l_1}, C_{l_2}, ..., C_{l_p})$, where C_{l_i} is the number of cycles of length l_i in the decomposition of the perfect-shuffle permutation.

For example, if n is prime, then $\psi_N = (C_1, C_n) = (2, (2^n - 2)/n)$.

Theorem 5.4 [Lin and Moldovan 1986] Let n be a number that is not prime. The cycle spectrum of a perfect shuffle of 2^n numbers can be found from the following two rules:

1. n is even. Case 1: $n = 2p$, p odd. In this case, 2^p of the 2^n numbers form the same cycle-characteristics set as the perfect shuffle of 2^p elements. The other $2^n - 2^p$ numbers form cycles of lengths 2 and n, with $C_2 = 1$ and $C_n = (2^n - 2^p - 2)/n$. Case 2: $n = 2p$, p even. 2^p of the 2^n numbers form the same cycle-characteristics set as the perfect shuffle of 2^p numbers. The rest of the numbers form cycles of length n, with $C_n = (2^n - 2^p)/n$.

2. n is odd. Assume $n = p_1 p_2 ... p_r$, where p_i are prime with $2 < p_1 < p_2 < ... < p_r$. Then $\psi_N = (C_1, C_{p_1}, C_{p_2}, ..., C_{p_r}, C_n)$, where

$$C_1 = 2$$

$$C_{p_i} = (2^{p_i} - 2)/p_i, \ i = 1, 2, ..., r$$

$$C_n = (2^n - 2 - \Sigma p_i C_{p_i})/n$$

In the next example, the cycle spectra for several cases are shown.

Example 5.10. Find the cycle spectrum of a perfect shuffle of N elements. $N = 2^n$.

1. $n = 2$:
$$S_2 = \begin{pmatrix} 0 & 1 & 2 & 3 \\ 0 & 2 & 1 & 3 \end{pmatrix} = (0)(1\ 2)(3)$$
$\psi_2 = (C_1, C_2) = (2, 1)$.

2. $n = 3$: Since 3 is prime, from the corollary of Theorem 5.3, $C_1 = 2, C_3 = (2^3 - 2)/3 = 2$. Therefore, $\psi_3 = (2, 2)$.

3. $n = 4$: Since $4 = 2 \times 2$, from Theorem 5.4, $C_1 = 2, C_2 = 1$. In addition, $C_4 = (2^4 - 2^2)/4 = 3$. Therefore, $\psi_4 = (2, 1, 3)$.

4. $n = 5$: Since 5 is prime, $C_1 = 2, C_5 = (2^5 - 2)/5 = 6$. $\psi_5 = (2, 6)$.

5. $n = 6$: $6 = 3 \times 2$. By Theorem 5.4, S_6's cycle spectrum contains that of S_3: $C_1 = 2, C_3 = 2$. In addition, $C_2 = 1, C_6 = (2^6 - 2^3 - 2)/6 = 9$. Therefore, $\psi_6 = (2, 1, 2, 9)$.

6. $n = 7$: Since 7 is prime, $C_1 = 2, C_7 = (2^7 - 2)/7 = 18$. Therefore, $\psi_7 = (2, 18)$.

7. $n = 8$: Since $8 = 4 \times 2$, from Theorem 5.4, $C_1 = 2, C_2 = 1, C_4 = 3$, and $C_8 = (2^8 - 2^4)/8 = 30$. $\psi_8 = (2, 1, 3, 30)$.

By the same argument, the cycle spectrum of S_n for n greater than 8 can be found recursively.

Mapping a Perfect Shuffle into a Mesh-Connected Network

After the above analysis of cycle characteristics of perfect shuffle, the mapping of a perfect shuffle into an MCN can now be discussed. Again, let $N = 2^n$ with n even. The mesh network is $N^{1/2} \times N^{1/2}$. From Theorem 5.3 is known that the cycle lengths of S_n must be n or factors of n. Therefore, if $N^{1/2}$ is a multiple of n, by using cyclic mapping the perfect shuffle can be achieved in a single step. The algorithm for the mapping of parallel algorithms whose data routing function is only a perfect shuffle is described in the following theorem:

Theorem 5.5 [Lin and Moldovan 1986] Let $N = 2^n$. The perfect shuffle can be achieved on the MCN in one step if $n = 2^m$, $m > 1$; otherwise, four steps are sufficient.

Proof: When $n = 2^m$, and $m > 1$, $N^{1/2}/n = 2^{2^{m-1}}/2^m = 2^{2^{m-1}-m}$, which is an integer if $m > 1$. In this case, $N^{1/2}$ is a multiple of the cycle length, and cyclic mapping is applicable. Therefore, only one step is required for the perfect-shuffle routing. Otherwise, treat the mesh-connected network as a linear network. Using linear mapping, four steps are sufficient to perform the perfect-shuffle routing. **Q.E.D.**

Example 5.11. Consider the perfect-shuffle permutation of 16 elements,

$$P = (0)(1\ 2\ 4\ 8)(3\ 6\ 12\ 9)(5\ 10)(7\ 14\ 13\ 11)(15)$$

A valid cyclic mapping is

$$A^{-1} = \begin{pmatrix} 0 & 1 & 5 & 4 \mid 2 & 3 & 7 & 6 \mid 8 & 9 & 13 & 12 \mid 10 & 11 \mid 14 \mid 15 \\ 1 & 2 & 4 & 8 \mid 3 & 6 & 12 & 9 \mid 7 & 14 & 13 & 11 \mid 5 & 10 \mid 0 \mid 15 \end{pmatrix}$$

The effective permutation using A is

$$A^{-1}PA = (0\ 1\ 5\ 4)(2\ 3\ 7\ 6)(8\ 9\ 13\ 12)(10\ 11)(14)(15)$$

Figure 5.19 illustrates the communication pattern of $A^{-1}PA$ on an MCN.

The mapping of Type 1 and Type 2 algorithms into an MCN can be done effectively using cyclic and linear mapping. These types of algorithms include polynomial functions, FFT, and others. For Type 3 algorithms, the permutations change frequently and randomly, and the overhead of adjustment cost may become very large.

5.5 BIBLIOGRAPHICAL NOTES AND FURTHER READING

The technique for mapping nested loop algorithms into systolic arrays based on matrix transformation was first presented in [Moldovan 1983b]. Extensions of this method for algorithm partitioning are due to [Fortes 1983] and [Moldovan and Fortes 1986]. Other approaches for mapping algorithms into systolic arrays were proposed in [Li and Wah 1985], [Quinton 1984], [Cappelo and Steiglitz 1983], and many

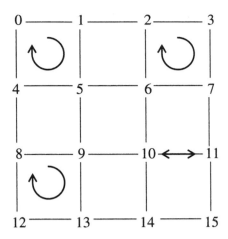

Figure 5.19 Cyclic mapping of perfect shuffle.

others. [Kung and Stevenson 1977] studied the relation between logical transfers and physical transfers in an effort to map algorithms into fixed interconnection networks. Kung and Stevenson developed the linear mapping technique. [Lin and Moldovan 1986] described cyclic mapping for mapping of algorithms into mesh-connected arrays and described the mapping of algorithms with perfect-shuffle permutations. The properties of array processors with multiple broadcast buses were presented in [Raghavendra and Kumar 1984], and the mapping of algorithms into mesh arrays with reconfigurable buses was described in [Miller and Stout 1989]. The mapping of algorithms into arrays, trees, and hypercubes is presented in [Leighton 1992].

5.6   PROBLEMS

5.1.A. Consider the algorithm

for $I = 1$ to 5
    for $J = 2$ to 6
        for $K = 3$ to 7
$$A(I, J, K) = A(I - 1, J + 1, K) * B(I - 1, J, K + 1)$$
$$B(I, J, K) = B(I - 1, J - 1, K + 2) + B(I, J - 3, K + 2)$$

end K

end J

end I

This algorithm is mapped into a systolic array by the transformation

$$\mathbf{T} = \begin{bmatrix} 1 & 0 & -1 \\ 2 & 2 & 3 \\ 2 & 1 & 1 \end{bmatrix}$$

(a) List all indices that are computed in parallel with index

$$(I, J, K) = (3, 4, 5)$$

(b) How many time steps are required to process the parallel algorithm obtained with this transformation?

(c) Show the global structure of the systolic array (interconnections between cells only).

(d) Indicate what indices are processed in what cells of this array at the time when index (3,4,5) is processed.

Solution.

(a) The index point (3,4,5) is computed at time

$$t = [1 \ 0 \ -1][3 \ 4 \ 5]^T = -2$$

The problem is to find all the index points in the algorithm's index set that satisfy the equation

$$-2 = [1 \ 0 \ -1][I \ J \ K]^T$$

The index points are

$$\begin{array}{lllll}
(1\ 2\ 3) & (2\ 2\ 4) & (3\ 2\ 5) & (4\ 2\ 6) & (5\ 2\ 7) \\
(1\ 3\ 3) & (2\ 3\ 4) & (3\ 3\ 5) & (4\ 3\ 6) & (5\ 3\ 7) \\
(1\ 4\ 3) & (2\ 4\ 4) & (3\ 4\ 5) & (4\ 4\ 6) & (5\ 4\ 7) \\
(1\ 5\ 3) & (2\ 5\ 4) & (3\ 5\ 5) & (4\ 5\ 6) & (5\ 5\ 7) \\
(1\ 6\ 3) & (2\ 6\ 4) & (3\ 6\ 5) & (4\ 6\ 6) & (5\ 6\ 7)
\end{array}$$

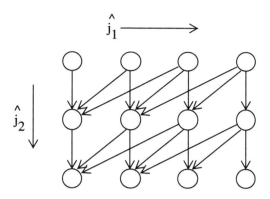

Figure 5.20 Array for Problem 5.1.A.

(b) Indices $(1, X, 7)$ are executed at $t = -6$. Indices $(5, X, 3)$ are executed at $t = 2$. Total execution time $= 2 - (-6) + 1 = 9$.

(c)

$$\hat{\mathbf{D}} = \mathbf{TD} = \begin{bmatrix} 1 & 0 & -1 \\ 2 & 2 & 3 \\ 2 & 1 & 1 \end{bmatrix} \begin{bmatrix} 1 & 1 & 1 & 0 \\ -1 & 0 & 1 & 3 \\ 0 & -1 & -2 & -2 \end{bmatrix} = \begin{bmatrix} 1 & 2 & 3 & 2 \\ 0 & -1 & -2 & 0 \\ 1 & 1 & 1 & 1 \end{bmatrix}$$

The array is shown in Figure 5.20.

(d) The problem is to find all (I, J, K) that satisfy the constraints

$$\begin{cases} I - K = [1, 0, -1][3, 4, 5]^T = -2 \\ 5 \geq I \geq 1 \\ 6 \geq J \geq 2 \\ 7 \geq K \geq 3 \end{cases}$$

Then for each such (I, J, K), the processing cells have coordinates $(2I + 2J + 3K, \ 2I + J + K)$. The results are summarized in Table 5.1.

Index	Processor	Index	Processor	Index	Processor
(1 2 3)	(15 7)	(2 5 4)	(26 13)	(4 3 6)	(32 17)
(1 3 3)	(17 8)	(2 6 4)	(28 14)	(4 4 6)	(34 18)
(1 4 3)	(19 9)	(3 2 5)	(25 13)	(4 5 6)	(36 19)
(1 5 3)	(21 10)	(3 3 5)	(27 14)	(4 6 6)	(38 20)
(1 6 3)	(23 11)	(3 4 5)	(29 15)	(5 2 7)	(35 19)
(2 2 4)	(20 10)	(3 5 5)	(31 16)	(5 3 7)	(37 20)
(2 3 4)	(22 11)	(3 6 5)	(33 17)	(5 4 7)	(39 21)
(2 4 4)	(24 12)	(4 2 6)	(30 16)	(5 5 7)	(41 22)
				(5 6 7)	(43 23)

Table 5.1: Mapping of indices to processors for Problem 5.1.A.

5.2.A. Consider the following two algorithms:

Matrix Multiplication

for $i = 1$ to n
  for $j = 1$ to n
    for $k = 1$ to n
    $c(i, j) = c(i, j) + a(i, k) * b(k, j)$
    end k
  end j
end i

LU Decomposition

for $k = 0$ until $n - 1$ do
  begin
  $u_{kk} = 1/a_{kk}$
  for $j = k + 1$ until $n - 1$ do
    $u_{kj} = a_{kj}$
  for $i = k + 1$ until $n - 1$ do
    $l_{ik} = a_{ik} u_{kk}$
  for $i = k + 1$ until $n - 1$ do
    begin
      for $j = k + 1$ until $n - 1$ do
      $a_{ij} = a_{ij} - l_{ik} u_{kj}$
    end
  end

For these two algorithms, derive five valid transformations that map the algorithms into systolic arrays and/or array processors with broadcasts. Draw the interconnections corresponding to each transformation; indicate the number of cells and the execution time in each case.

Solution. The transformations are shown in Figure 5.21 and the corresponding arrays in Figures 5.22 and 5.23.

Figure number	Figure 5.23(a)	Figure 5.23(b)	Figure 5.23(c)	Figure 5.24(a)	Figure 5.24(b)
Transformation matrix	$\begin{smallmatrix}1&1&1\\0&1&0\\0&0&1\end{smallmatrix}$	$\begin{smallmatrix}1&1&1\\-1&1&0\\-1&0&1\end{smallmatrix}$	$\begin{smallmatrix}1&1&1\\1&1&0\\1&0&1\end{smallmatrix}$	$\begin{smallmatrix}1&1&1\\-1&1&0\\0&0&1\end{smallmatrix}$	$\begin{smallmatrix}1&0&0\\-1&1&0\\-1&0&1\end{smallmatrix}$
Number of cells for full matrix	n^2	$(2n-1)^2$	$(2n-1)^2$	$n(2n-1)$	$(2n-1)^2$
Number of cells for band matrix (bandwidth=w)	n^2	w^2	n^2	wn	w^2
Executing time — Processing time	$3n-2$	$3n-2$	$3n-2$	$3n-2$	$n-1$
Executing time — I/O time	-------	$2n$	0	$2n$	$2n$
Executing time — Total	-------	$5n-2$	$3n-2$	$5n-2$	$3n-1$
Feature of architecture	The results stay in each cell.	The number of cells is reduced to w^2 for band matrix.	I/O time is zero. The number of cells is not reduced for band matrix.	Data communication is only vertical and horizontal.	Processing time is fast, because broadcasting is used.

(a)

Number of cells for full matrix	n^2	n^2	$(2n-1)^2$	n^2	n^2
Number of cells for band matrix (bandwidth=w)	n^2	w^2	$(2n-1)^2$	wn	w^2
Executing time — Processing time	$3n-4$	$3n-4$	$3n-4$	$3n-4$	n
Executing time — I/O time	-------	$2n$	0	$2n$	n
Executing time — Total	-------	$5n-4$	$3n-4$	$5n-4$	$2n$

(b)

Figure 5.21 (a) Transformations for matrix multiplication; (b) The number of cells and the timing for LU decomposition. (The transformations and architectural features are the same as for matrix multiplication.)

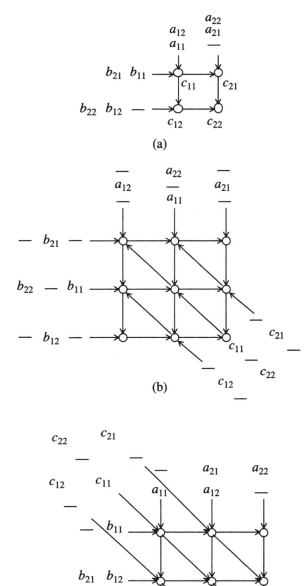

Figure 5.22 Systolic architectures for matrix multiplication and LU decomposition.

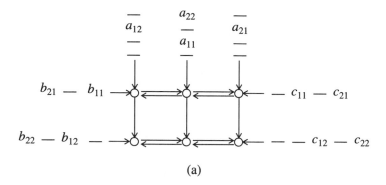

(a)

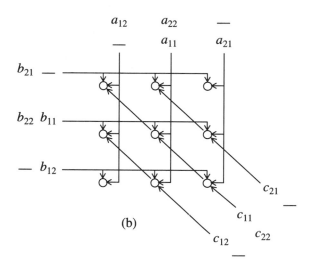

(b)

Figure 5.23 Systolic architectures for matrix multiplication and LU decomposition.

Original index set I J	Transformed index set w/o partitioning $\hat{I}$ $\hat{J}$	Partitioned index set $\hat{I}$ $\hat{J}$	Band number b

Table 5.2: Table for Problem 5.3.A.

5.3.A. Consider the following algorithm:

```
for I = 1, 4
    for J = 1, 4
        a(I, J) = a(I, J − 1) + a(I − 1, J)
    end J
end I
```

In order to map this algorithm into a systolic array of size 2, use the partitioning transformation

$$\mathbf{T} = \begin{bmatrix} 1 & 1 \\ 1 & 0 \end{bmatrix}$$

Complete Table 5.2 by hand.

Solution.

$$\begin{bmatrix} \hat{I} \\ \hat{J} \end{bmatrix} = \mathbf{T} \begin{bmatrix} I \\ J \end{bmatrix} \qquad \mathbf{T} = \begin{bmatrix} 1 & 1 \\ 1 & 0 \end{bmatrix}$$

$$\hat{J} = (\Pi_p \begin{bmatrix} I \\ J \end{bmatrix}) \ \text{mod} \ 2 \qquad b = \lfloor \frac{1}{2}(\Pi_p \begin{bmatrix} I \\ J \end{bmatrix}) \rfloor$$

I	J	$\hat{I}$	$\hat{J}$	$\hat{\hat{I}}$	$\hat{\hat{J}}$	b
1	1	2	1	1	1	0
1	2	3	1	2	1	0
1	3	4	1	3	1	0
1	4	5	1	4	1	0
2	1	3	2	5	0	1
2	2	4	2	6	0	1
2	3	5	2	7	0	1
2	4	6	2	8	0	1
3	1	4	3	6	1	1
3	2	5	3	7	1	1
3	3	6	3	8	1	1
3	4	7	3	9	1	1
4	1	5	4	10	0	2
4	2	6	4	11	0	2
4	3	7	4	12	0	2
4	4	8	4	13	0	2

Table 5.3: Solution to Problem 5.3.A.

5.4.A. An algorithm with three nested loops has the dependence matrix

$$\mathbf{D} = \begin{bmatrix} 1 & 0 & 1 \\ 0 & 1 & 0 \\ -1 & 1 & 0 \end{bmatrix}$$

This algorithm is to be mapped into a systolic array using the transformation

$$\mathbf{T} = \begin{bmatrix} 2 & 0 & 1 \\ 1 & 0 & 0 \\ 0 & 2 & -1 \end{bmatrix}$$

Can this algorithm be mapped into an array of the type shown in Figure 5.24?

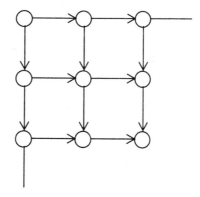

Figure 5.24 Array for Problem 5.4.A.

Solution.

$$\hat{\mathbf{D}} = \mathbf{TD} = \begin{bmatrix} 2 & 0 & 1 \\ 1 & 0 & 0 \\ 0 & 2 & -1 \end{bmatrix} \begin{bmatrix} 1 & 0 & 1 \\ 0 & 1 & 0 \\ -1 & 1 & 0 \end{bmatrix} = \begin{bmatrix} 1 & 1 & 2 \\ 1 & 0 & 1 \\ 1 & 1 & 0 \end{bmatrix}$$

The answer is no because the first dependence requires a diagonal connection (1 1) unavailable in the array. Also, data routing is not possible because this dependence must be transferred within one time unit.

5.5.A.

```
for i = 1 to 5
    for j = 1 to 11
        for k = 1 to 21
            x(i, j, k) = x(i − 1, j, k) + y(i, j − 1, k − 1)
            y(i, j, k) = x(i, j, k − 1) * y(i − 1, j, k − 1)
        end
    end
end
```

This algorithm is to be mapped into a systolic array by the transformation

$$\mathbf{T} = \begin{bmatrix} 1 & 1 & 1 \\ 0 & 1 & 0 \\ 1 & 1 & 0 \end{bmatrix}$$

(a) Show the interprocessor connections as they are derived from the transformed data dependencies.

(b) Show the internal organization of each cell (at register level) and explain the movement of variables in the array.

(c) At what time is a computation indexed by $(i, j, k) = (3, 10, 2)$ performed?

(d) What is the speedup factor achieved with this array over a uniprocessor?

(e) Can this transformation be used to partition the algorithm? Why or why not?

Solution.

(a)

$$\mathbf{D} = \begin{bmatrix} 1 & 0 & 0 & 1 \\ 0 & 0 & 1 & 0 \\ 0 & 1 & 1 & 1 \end{bmatrix}$$

$$\hat{\mathbf{D}} = \mathbf{TD} = \begin{bmatrix} 1 & 1 & 1 \\ 0 & 1 & 0 \\ 1 & 1 & 0 \end{bmatrix} \begin{bmatrix} 1 & 0 & 0 & 1 \\ 0 & 0 & 1 & 0 \\ 0 & 1 & 1 & 1 \end{bmatrix} = \begin{bmatrix} 1 & 1 & 2 & 2 \\ 0 & 0 & 1 & 0 \\ 1 & 0 & 1 & 1 \end{bmatrix} \begin{matrix} \hat{i} \\ \hat{j} \\ \hat{k} \end{matrix}$$

The interconnections between PEs are shown in Figure 5.25(a).

(b) See Figure 5.25(b).

(c)

$$\begin{pmatrix} \hat{i} \\ \hat{j} \\ \hat{k} \end{pmatrix} = \mathbf{T} \begin{pmatrix} 3 \\ 10 \\ 2 \end{pmatrix} = \begin{pmatrix} 15 \\ 10 \\ 13 \end{pmatrix}$$

Index $(3, 10, 2)$ is processed at time 15 in processor $(10, 13)$.

(d) The parallel time is

$$\begin{aligned} t &= 1 + \max \mathbf{\Pi j} - \min \mathbf{\Pi j} \\ &= 1 + 5 + 11 + 21 - 1 - 1 - 1 \end{aligned}$$

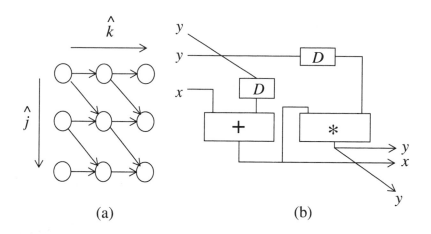

Figure 5.25 (a) Interprocessor connections and (b) cell structure for Problem 5.5.A.

$$S = \begin{array}{l} = \quad 35 \\[4pt] = \dfrac{5 \times 11 \times 21 \times 2}{35} = 66 \end{array}$$

(e) No, because the second transformed dependence has zeros along $\hat{j}$ and $\hat{k}$, meaning accumulation of variables in cells.

5.6.A. Consider the permutation $P = (0\ 2\ 5\ 3\ 7\ 6\ 4\ 1)$.

For this permutation,

(a) Find a cycle mapping A_c and show $A_c^{-1}\ PA_c$.

(b) Find a linear mapping A_l and show $A_l^{-1}\ PA_l$.

(c) Assuming that a computer with a shuffle-exchange 1 interconnection is available, which mapping, if any, would you choose when permutation P needs to be executed on this computer? (Use the criterion of minimum routing steps for your selection).

Solution.

(a)

$$A_c^{-1} = \begin{pmatrix} 0 & 1 & 2 & 3 & 4 & 5 & 6 & 7 \\ 0 & 2 & 5 & 3 & 7 & 6 & 4 & 1 \end{pmatrix}$$

Transition	Steps needed	Routing path
$0 \rightarrow 1$	1	E(0,1)
$1 \rightarrow 2$	1	S(1,2)
$2 \rightarrow 3$	1	E(2,3)
$3 \rightarrow 4$	2	E(2,3),S(2,4)
$4 \rightarrow 5$	1	E(4,5)
$5 \rightarrow 6$	2	S(5,3),S(3,6)
$6 \rightarrow 7$	1	E(6,7)
$7 \rightarrow 0$	5	E(7,6),S(6,5),E(5,4),S(4,1),E(1,0)

Table 5.4: Routing for Problem 5.6.A using cyclic mapping.

$$A_c = \begin{pmatrix} 0 & 1 & 2 & 3 & 4 & 5 & 6 & 7 \\ 0 & 7 & 1 & 3 & 6 & 2 & 5 & 4 \end{pmatrix}$$

$$A_c^{-1}PA_c = \begin{pmatrix} 0 & 1 & 2 & 3 & 4 & 5 & 6 & 7 \\ 1 & 2 & 3 & 4 & 5 & 6 & 7 & 0 \end{pmatrix}$$

(b)

$$A_l = \begin{pmatrix} 0 & 2 & 5 & 3 & 7 & 6 & 4 & 1 \\ 0 & 2 & 4 & 6 & 7 & 5 & 3 & 1 \end{pmatrix}$$

$$A_l^{-1} = \begin{pmatrix} 0 & 1 & 2 & 3 & 4 & 5 & 6 & 7 \\ 0 & 1 & 2 & 4 & 5 & 6 & 3 & 7 \end{pmatrix}$$

$$A_l^{-1}PA_l = \begin{pmatrix} 0 & 1 & 2 & 3 & 4 & 5 & 6 & 7 \\ 2 & 0 & 4 & 1 & 6 & 3 & 7 & 5 \end{pmatrix}$$

(c) Examine the routing steps needed for both cyclic and linear mapping of permutation P, and determine which one is better based on the maximum and average number of routing steps.

The routing for cyclic mapping is shown in Table 5.4. The average number of routing steps is $\frac{14}{8}$. The maximum number of steps is 5. E(0,1) means exchange data in PE0 and PE1. S(1,2) means send the data from PE1 to PE2 by perfect shuffle.

The average time for linear mapping is $\frac{14}{8}$, and the maximum number of steps is 3, as shown in Table 5.5. Therefore, linear mapping is chosen because even its worst case is better than cyclic mapping.

Transition	Steps needed	Routing path
$0 \rightarrow 2$	2	$E(0,1), S(1,2)$
$1 \rightarrow 0$	1	$E(1,0)$
$2 \rightarrow 4$	1	$S(2,4)$
$3 \rightarrow 1$	3	$E(3,2), S(2,4), S(4,1)$
$4 \rightarrow 6$	3	$E(4,5), S(5,3), S(3,6)$
$5 \rightarrow 3$	1	$S(5,3)$
$6 \rightarrow 7$	1	$E(6,7)$
$7 \rightarrow 5$	2	$E(7,6), S(6,5)$

Table 5.5: Routing for Problem 5.6.A using linear mapping.

5.7.A. Consider the permutation

$$P = (0,3,1,4)(7,2,5,6)$$

(a) Find a cyclic mapping A_c and show $A_c^{-1} P A_c$.
(b) Find a linear mapping A_l and show $A_l^{-1} P A_l$.
(c) Assume a parallel computer with the interconnection network described by Table 5.6. Indicate the routing steps necessary to execute P, $A_c^{-1} P A_c$, and $A_l^{-1} P A_l$ on this interconnection. Which mapping minimizes the number of routing steps?

Solution.
(a) Cyclic mapping:

$$A_c^{-1} = \begin{pmatrix} 0 & 1 & 2 & 3 & 4 & 5 & 6 & 7 \\ 0 & 3 & 1 & 4 & 7 & 2 & 5 & 6 \end{pmatrix}$$

$$A_c = \begin{pmatrix} 0 & 1 & 2 & 3 & 4 & 5 & 6 & 7 \\ 0 & 2 & 5 & 1 & 3 & 6 & 7 & 4 \end{pmatrix}$$

$$A_c^{-1} P A_c = \begin{pmatrix} 0 & 1 & 2 & 3 & 4 & 5 & 6 & 7 \\ 1 & 2 & 3 & 0 & 5 & 6 & 7 & 4 \end{pmatrix}$$

$$= (0\ 1\ 2\ 3)(4\ 5\ 6\ 7)$$

		0	1	2	3	4	5	6	7
	0	0	0	1	0	0	0	0	0
	1	0	0	0	1	0	0	0	0
	2	0	0	0	0	1	0	0	0
$S =$	3	0	0	0	0	0	1	0	0
	4	0	0	0	0	0	0	1	0
	5	0	0	0	0	0	0	0	1
	6	0	1	0	0	0	0	0	0
	7	1	0	0	0	0	0	0	0

Table 5.6: Interconnection Network for Problem 5.7.A.

(b) Linear mapping:

$$A_l^{-1} = \begin{pmatrix} 0 & 3 & 1 & 4 & 7 & 2 & 5 & 6 \\ 0 & 2 & 3 & 1 & 4 & 6 & 7 & 5 \end{pmatrix}$$

$$A_l = \begin{pmatrix} 0 & 1 & 2 & 3 & 4 & 5 & 6 & 7 \\ 0 & 4 & 3 & 1 & 7 & 6 & 2 & 5 \end{pmatrix}$$

$$A_c^{-1}PA_c = \begin{pmatrix} 0 & 1 & 2 & 3 & 4 & 5 & 6 & 7 \\ 2 & 0 & 3 & 1 & 6 & 4 & 7 & 5 \end{pmatrix}$$

$$= (0\ 2\ 3\ 1)(4\ 6\ 7\ 5)$$

(c) $S = (0\ 2\ 4\ 6\ 1\ 3\ 5\ 7\ 0)$.
From Table 5.7, cyclic mapping is better in this case.

5.8.A. The matrix multiplication computation is mapped by a transformation **T** into the systolic array in Figure 4.29 (reproduced for convenience in Figure 5.26). Find this transformation **T**; explain your solution.

Solution. Choose

$$\mathbf{T} = \left[\begin{array}{ccc} t_{11} & t_{12} & t_{13} \\ \hline t_{21} & t_{22} & t_{23} \\ t_{31} & t_{32} & t_{33} \end{array} \right]$$

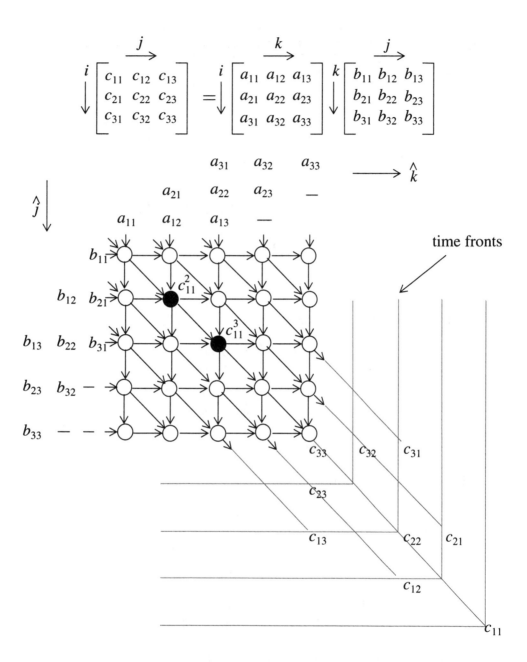

Figure 5.26 A two-dimensional systolic array for matrix
multiplication.

Cyclic		P		Linear	
Transition	Steps needed	Transition	Steps needed	Transition	Steps needed
$0 \rightarrow 1$	4	$0 \rightarrow 3$	5	$0 \rightarrow 2$	1
$1 \rightarrow 2$	5	$1 \rightarrow 4$	6	$1 \rightarrow 0$	4
$2 \rightarrow 3$	4	$2 \rightarrow 5$	5	$2 \rightarrow 3$	4
$3 \rightarrow 0$	3	$3 \rightarrow 1$	7	$3 \rightarrow 1$	7
$4 \rightarrow 5$	4	$4 \rightarrow 0$	6	$4 \rightarrow 6$	1
$5 \rightarrow 6$	5	$5 \rightarrow 6$	5	$5 \rightarrow 4$	4
$6 \rightarrow 7$	4	$6 \rightarrow 7$	4	$6 \rightarrow 7$	4
$7 \rightarrow 4$	3	$7 \rightarrow 2$	2	$7 \rightarrow 5$	7
	max:5		max:7		max:7

Table 5.7: Solution to Problem 5.7.A.

$$= \left[\begin{array}{c} \Pi \\ -- \\ S \end{array} \right]$$

D for matrix multiplication is

$$\mathbf{D} = \mathbf{I} = \begin{bmatrix} 1 & 0 & 0 \\ 0 & 1 & 0 \\ 0 & 0 & 1 \end{bmatrix} \begin{array}{c} i \\ j \\ k \end{array}$$
$$\phantom{\mathbf{D} = \mathbf{I} = } \begin{array}{ccc} b & a & c \end{array}$$

$$\mathbf{SD} = \mathbf{P}$$

P is known from Figure 5.26:

$$\mathbf{P} = \begin{bmatrix} 0 & 1 & 1 \\ 1 & 0 & 1 \end{bmatrix} \begin{array}{c} \hat{j} \\ \hat{k} \end{array}$$
$$\phantom{\mathbf{P} = } \begin{array}{ccc} b & a & c \end{array}$$

$$\begin{bmatrix} t_{21} & t_{22} & t_{23} \\ t_{31} & t_{32} & t_{33} \end{bmatrix} \mathbf{I} = \begin{bmatrix} 0 & 1 & 1 \\ 1 & 0 & 1 \end{bmatrix}$$

(a) c_{11} is actually c_{11}^3; $i = 1, j = 1, k = 3$;

(b) c_{12} is actually c_{12}^3; $i = 1, j = 2, k = 3$;

(c) c_{21} is actually c_{21}^3; $i = 2, j = 1, k = 3$.

From Figure 5.26,
$$t_{c_{12}^3} - t_{c_{11}^3} = 1$$

From this and *(a)* and *(b)*, it follows that
$$(t_{11} + 2t_{12} + 3t_{13}) - (t_{11} + t_{12} + 3t_{13}) = 1 \Rightarrow t_{12} = 1$$
$$t_{c_{21}^3} - t_{c_{11}^3} = 1$$

From this and *(a)* and *(c)*, it follows that
$$(2t_{11} + t_{12} + 3t_{13}) - (t_{11} + t_{12} + 3t_{13}) = 1 \Rightarrow t_{11} = 1$$
$$t_{c_{11}^3} - t_{c_{11}^2} = 1$$

From this it follows that
$$(t_{11} + t_{12} + 3t_{13}) - (t_{11} + t_{12} + 2t_{13}) = 1 \Rightarrow t_{13} = 1$$

$$\mathbf{T} = \left[\begin{array}{ccc} 1 & 1 & 1 \\ - & - & - \\ 0 & 1 & 1 \\ 1 & 0 & 1 \end{array} \right]$$

5.9.A. Regarding the partitioning methodology in Section 5.2.3, consider a partitioning ordering, denoted as $>_p$, such that for any algorithm A, and $\mathbf{\Pi}$, and any $\mathbf{S}_p = \{\mathbf{\Pi}_{p1}, \mathbf{\Pi}_{p2}, ..., \mathbf{\Pi}_{p(n-1)}\}$, two points $\mathbf{j}^1, \mathbf{j}^2 \in \mathbf{J}^n$ are related such that $\mathbf{j}^2 >_p \mathbf{j}^1$ if and only if either Equation (5.22) or Equation (5.23) holds:

$$\mathbf{\Pi}(\mathbf{j}^2) > \mathbf{\Pi}(\mathbf{j}^1) \text{ and } \mathbf{\Pi}_{pk}(\mathbf{j}^1)/m_k = \mathbf{\Pi}_{pk}(\mathbf{j}^2)/m_k \qquad (5.22)$$

$$\mathbf{\Pi}_{pk}(\mathbf{j}^2)/m_k > \mathbf{\Pi}_{pk}(\mathbf{j}^1)/m_k \text{ for } k \in \{1, ..., n-1\} \qquad (5.23)$$

The meaning of Equation (5.22) is that $\mathbf{j}^1$ and $\mathbf{j}^2$ belong to the same partitioning band, and computations are sequenced by time hyperplanes $\mathbf{\Pi}$; Equation (5.23) indicates that $\mathbf{j}^1$ and $\mathbf{j}^2$ belong to different bands and have a precedence relation that is independent of the time hyperplanes $\mathbf{\Pi}$ to which they belong.

Demonstrate that the partitioning ordering $>_p$ is an execution ordering; in other words, that the dependencies of the algorithm are not violated by the partitioning scheme.

Solution.

By the definition of execution ordering, it is enough to prove that $\mathbf{d}_i >_p 0$ for all $\mathbf{d}_i \in \mathbf{D}$. Let $\mathbf{d}_i = \mathbf{j}^2 - \mathbf{j}^1$. Two cases must be considered:

Case 1. $\mathbf{j}^1$ and $\mathbf{j}^2$ belong to the same band, implying that

$$\lfloor \boldsymbol{\Pi}_{pk}(\mathbf{j}^1)/m_k \rfloor = \lfloor \boldsymbol{\Pi}_{pk}(\mathbf{j}^2)/m_k \rfloor \quad k = 1, ..., v$$

From Equation (5.3), $\boldsymbol{\Pi}(\mathbf{d}_i) = \boldsymbol{\Pi}(\mathbf{j}^2) - \boldsymbol{\Pi}(\mathbf{j}^1) > 0$. Then $\boldsymbol{\Pi}(\mathbf{j}^2) > \boldsymbol{\Pi}(\mathbf{j}^1)$ and by the definition of $>_p$, $\mathbf{j}^2 >_p \mathbf{j}^1$. Hence $\mathbf{d}_i >_p 0$.

Case 2. $\mathbf{j}^1$ and $\mathbf{j}^2$ belong to distinct bands; thus,

$$\lfloor \boldsymbol{\Pi}_{pk}(\mathbf{j}^1)/m_k \rfloor \neq \lfloor \boldsymbol{\Pi}_{pk}(\mathbf{j}^2)/m_k \rfloor \quad k = 1, ..., v$$

Then, using Equation (5.23), $\boldsymbol{\Pi}_{pk}(\mathbf{j}^2)/m_k > \boldsymbol{\Pi}_{pk}(\mathbf{j}^1)/m_k$. Hence, by the definition of $>_p$, $\mathbf{j}^2 >_p \mathbf{j}^1$, i.e., $\mathbf{d}_i >_p 0$.

5.1.B.

for$I = 1$ to 3
   for$J = 2$ to 4
      for$K = 3$ to 6
         $A(I, J, K) = A(I - 1, J - 1, K - 1) + B(I - 1, J - 1, K + 1)$
         $B(I, J, K) = B(I, J, K - 3) + A(I - 1, J + 1, K)$
      end K
   end J
end I

This algorithm is mapped into a systolic array by the transformation

$$\mathbf{T} = \begin{bmatrix} 2 & 1 & 1 \\ 1 & 0 & 0 \\ 0 & 1 & 0 \end{bmatrix}$$

(a) How many time steps are required to process the parallel algorithm obtained with this transformation?

(b) Show the global structure of the systolic array (interconnections between cells only). Show the entire array.

(c) Indicate what indices are processed in what cells of this array at the time when index (2,4,5) is processed.

5.2.B. The following program performs a multiplication of 3×3 matrices:

$$
\begin{aligned}
&\text{for } i = 1 \text{ to } 3 \\
&\quad \text{for } j = 1 \text{ to } 3 \\
&\qquad \text{for } k = 1 \text{ to } 3 \\
&\qquad\quad c_{ij}^k = c_{ij}^{k-1} + a_{ik}b_{kj} \\
&\qquad \text{end } k \\
&\quad \text{end } j \\
&\text{end } i
\end{aligned}
$$

This problem is to be mapped into a systolic array processor by the following transformation:

$$
\mathbf{T} = \begin{bmatrix} \mathbf{\Pi} \\ \mathbf{S} \end{bmatrix} = \begin{bmatrix} 1 & 0 & 0 \\ 0 & 1 & 0 \\ -- & -- & -- \\ 0 & 0 & 1 \end{bmatrix}
$$

Here $\mathbf{\Pi}$ is 2×3 matrix, and $\mathbf{S}$ is a 1×3 row vector.

(a) Show the architecture into which this transformation maps the matrix multiplication problem. Mark on your figure the processors in which c_{11}, c_{12}, and c_{22} are computed.

(b) How many time units are necessary to process this matrix multiplication problem as given by transformation $\mathbf{T}$?

(c) What can you say about sequential or parallel execution of the original indices i, j, and k?

5.3.B.

$$
\begin{aligned}
&\text{for } I = 1 \text{ to } 4 \\
&\quad \text{for } J = 2 \text{ to } 3 \\
&\qquad \text{for } K = 3 \text{ to } 4
\end{aligned}
$$

$$X(I, J, K) = Y(I, J - 1, K + 2) - X(I - 1, J + 2, K - 2)$$
$$Y(I, J, K) = X(I, J - 1, K + 1) * Y(I - 1, J - 1, K + 3)$$
     end K
   end J
end I

This algorithm is to be mapped into a systolic array by the transformation

$$T = \begin{bmatrix} 3 & 1 & 0 \\ 1 & 1 & 1 \\ 1 & 0 & 0 \end{bmatrix}$$

(a) Find the data dependence matrix.

(b) How many time steps are required to process the parallel algorithm?

(c) Show the systolic array including all processors, all interconnections between processors, and the structure of one processor at register level.

(d) Can this algorithm be partitioned and mapped into an array of size 2 × 2 using the above transformation? Explain. If possible, partition the index set into bands.

5.4.B. An algorithm is mapped into a systolic array of size $\mathbf{M} = m_1 \times m_2 \times \cdots \times m_{n-1}$, following the procedure given in Section 5.2.3. Show that the total number of bands resulting from partitioning the index set is

$$r = \prod_{k=1}^{n-1} (1 + \lceil \frac{\max \Pi_{pk}(\mathbf{j}^2 - \mathbf{j}^1)}{m_k} \rceil) \text{ for } \mathbf{j}^1, \mathbf{j}^2 \in J^n$$

5.5.B.

     for $i = 1, 4$
       for $j = 1, 4$
         for $k = 1, 3$
           $x(i, j, k) = x(i - 1, j, k) * y(i - 1, j, k + 1)$
           $y(i, j, k) = (x(i - 3, j + 1, k) + y(i - 1, j, k - 1))/2$
         end k

end j

end i

This program is to be mapped into a systolic array by the transformation

$$\mathbf{T} = \begin{bmatrix} 2 & 1 & 1 \\ 0 & -1 & 0 \\ 0 & 1 & 1 \end{bmatrix}$$

where the first row is the time transformation $\mathbf{\Pi}$ and the second and third rows represent the space transformation $\mathbf{S}$.

(a) Show the entire array with the interconnections between cells.

(b) Show the internal structure of the cell using register-level representation.

5.6.B. An algorithm consists of logical transfers P and S, where

$$P = \begin{pmatrix} 0 & 1 & 2 & 3 & 4 & 5 & 6 & 7 \\ 3 & 7 & 5 & 4 & 0 & 2 & 1 & 6 \end{pmatrix}$$

$$S = \begin{pmatrix} 0 & 1 & 2 & 3 & 4 & 5 & 6 & 7 \\ 2 & 4 & 6 & 7 & 0 & 3 & 1 & 5 \end{pmatrix}$$

(a) Find a cyclic mapping A only for permutation P.

(b) The diagram shown in Figure 5.27 indicates that the algorithm consists of logical transfer P followed by logical transfer S. The physical transfers are $A^{-1}PA$ and $A^{-1}SA$. Fill in the memory locations m_0 through m_7 in all the appropriate locations in the diagram, and show the connections from one stage to another. In other words, show how m_0 through m_7 are switched by each transfer.

(c) Suppose that the target architecture is an eight-node hypercube multiprocessor. Is it advantageous to use mapping permutation A to assign a logical memory to a processor and then to perform $A^{-1}PA$ followed by $A^{-1}SA$, or is it better not to use mapping A and just to perform P followed by S on the hypercube? Assume that in each cycle the hypercube is capable of performing either Exchange 1, Exchange 2, or Exchange 3 in only one direction. Justify your answer by indicating the number of cycles taken by each permutation on the hypercube.

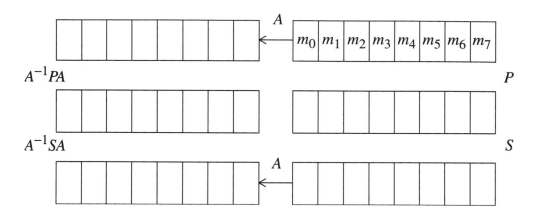

Figure 5.27 Transformation for Problem 5.6.B.

5.7.B. Consider the permutation

$$P = (1\ 15\ 12\ 11\ 2\ 5)(7\ 6\ 3\ 13\ 10\ 9)(0\ 4\ 8\ 14)$$

(a) Find a cyclic mapping A_1 for this permutation.

(b) Find a linear mapping A_2 for this permutation.

(c) Assuming that the available computer has a shift interconnection network $(SH(X) = |X + 1|_{16})$, compare the locality of the three permutations

$$P,\ A_1^{-1}PA_1,\ A_2^{-1}PA_2$$

when performed on this computer.

5.8.B. Map the polynomial function $f(x) = \sum_0^{15} a_i x^i$ into a 4×4 MCN such that the number of routing steps is minimized.

5.9.B. Find a mapping of a butterfly interconnection network of 16 elements into a 4×4 MCN such that the number of routing steps is 1.

5.10.B. For a bit-reversal permutation of three bits defined as

$$R(b_3b_2b_1) = (b_1b_2b_3)$$

find the cyclic mapping A_c and compute the mapping $A^{-1}RA$.

Is it advantageous to use this cyclic mapping to allocate an algorithm with a bit-reversal permutation to an array processor with a ring interconnection (shift and inverse shift)? Explain your answer.

5.11.B. Using the transformation method, design a systolic array for multiplying two n-bit integers

$$X = x_1 x_2 ... x_n$$

$$Y = y_1 y_2 ... y_n$$

5.12.B. Map the permutation P into an MCN.

$$P = \begin{pmatrix} 0 & 1 & 2 & 3 & 4 & 5 & 6 & 7 & 8 & 9 & 10 & 11 & 12 & 13 & 14 & 15 \\ 13 & 11 & 5 & 4 & 1 & 6 & 0 & 2 & 10 & 8 & 12 & 15 & 9 & 7 & 3 & 14 \end{pmatrix}$$

$$P = (0\ 13\ 7\ 2\ 5\ 6)(1\ 11\ 15\ 14\ 3\ 4)(8\ 10\ 12\ 9)$$

Chapter 6

MULTIPROCESSOR SYSTEMS

Multiprocessing is the simultaneous execution of tasks on a parallel asynchronous computer system. A parallel asynchronous computer is a system whose active nodes are either processors or simple computers that cooperate closely but independently. These are multiple-instruction multiple-data stream (MIMD) computers. There are two basic multiprocessor models: shared-memory and message-passing systems. The shared-memory model provides a globally shared physical address space, which is highly desirable from the programmer's point of view. However, simultaneous access to shared memory by many processors complicates the design of such systems. In contrast, message-passing systems are easier to design but are more difficult to program.

MIMD computers are suitable for a much larger class of computations than SIMD computers because they are inherently more flexible. This flexibility is achieved at the cost of a considerably more difficult mode of operation.

6.1 MULTIPROCESSOR ORGANIZATION AND OPERATING PRINCIPLES

A multiprocessor system is a single computer incorporating a number of independent processors that work together to solve a given problem. Figure 6.1 shows the relations among algorithm granularity, degree of hardware coupling, and communication mode, and the difference between distributed and parallel processing. Distributed processing oc-

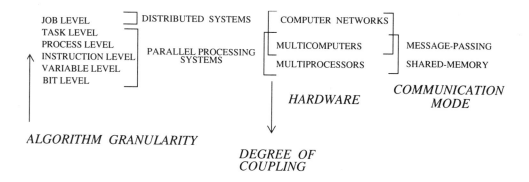

Figure 6.1 Relation between algorithm granularity and
multiprocessing systems.

curs when hardware resources cooperate loosely to process jobs. Examples of distributed systems are computer networks and some multiple computers. When hardware resources cooperate closely to process tasks simultaneously, this is referred to as parallel processing.

There is an important difference between multiprocessors and multiple computers. A multiple computer consists of several computers—each with its own processor(s), memory, I/O, and operating system—whereas a multiprocessor system has only one operating system and its processors share memory and I/O resources.

As the number of processors increases, the interconnection network plays a larger and larger role in overall performance. Some of the most difficult problems in multiprocessing are software-related. The lack of parallel languages that explicitly express parallelism puts a considerable burden on compiler designs. Operating systems for large multiprocessors are also difficult to design. In spite of all these difficulties, a number of multiprocessors are already available commercially, and their number and performance continue to grow. Multiprocessors can be classified as shared-memory systems or message-passing systems.

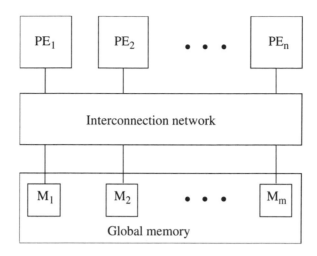

Figure 6.2 Shared-memory systems.

6.1.1   Shared-Memory Systems

Multiprocessor architectures with shared memory are tightly coupled systems in which there is complete connectivity between processors and memory modules. A simplified block diagram of shared-memory systems is shown in Figure 6.2. It consists of a set of n processor elements, not necessarily identical, a set of m memory modules, and an interconnection network. The primary memory may be centralized ($m = 1$) or partitioned into several modules. The common memory must be accessed by all processors in the system.

Data exchange between processors and memories is frequent and intense. The interconnection network is a potential bottleneck for these systems. While memory contention (memory access conflict) has always been a performance factor in uniprocessor systems, it becomes more important in parallel shared-memory systems simply because of the need of many processors to simultaneously access the same memory locations. To decrease the communication traffic in the network and the chance of memory contention, several alternative solutions exist. A local memory (LM), directly accessed by the processor, may be placed near the processor, thus reducing the number of memory

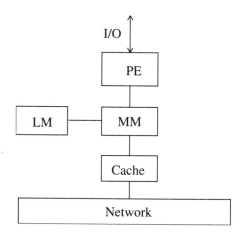

Figure 6.3 Processing element with local memory and cache.

requests through the interconnection network. Also, a cache memory may be provided in order to increase the memory bandwidth, as shown in Figure 6.3. A memory mapping (MM) unit is required to decide which memory requests are local and which are global.

In a multiprocessing system, it is desirable that processors have the following characteristics: Processors should be provided with a large set of registers so that the effect of interrupts is decreased; processors should have a large physical address space; and processors should have efficient means of handling synchronization and interrupts.

In a shared-memory system, a single common operating system controls and coordinates the interactions between processors and processes. Each of the cooperating processors can execute significant computations individually. Coordination between processors is facilitated by an interprocessor communication mechanism, such that some processors can directly interrupt other processors. Synchronization between cooperating processors is needed. In highly efficient systems, the operating system distributes the load as uniformly as possible across all processors. The I/O units and other system resources are usually shared among the processors. However, some resources may be dedicated to specific processors. The major limitation of a shared-memory system

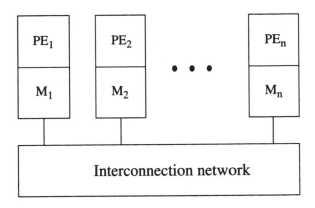

Figure 6.4 Message-passing systems.

is the possibility of primary memory access conflicts. This restriction tends to put an upper bound on the number of processors that can be effectively incorporated in the system and supported by a single operating system. Shared-memory systems are efficient for small to medium-sized multiprocessors. Examples of shared-memory systems are the Cedar multiprocessor, developed at the University of Illinois; the Ultracomputer, developed at New York University; and commercial systems such as the Alliant, the Encore Sequent, the Cray Y-MP, and others.

6.1.2 Message-Passing Systems

A typical message-passing system consists of several computer modules and an interconnection network, as shown in Figure 6.4. Each computer module has a processor, a memory, and an I/O interface. Data communication is carried out through messages, not through shared variables as in the previous case. The length of messages varies, but usually each message consists of a number of fixed-size packets. Intercomputer communication follows a predetermined communication protocol. The intercomputer links are high-speed serial or parallel links. Thus the active node in a message-passing system is a computer, and the degree of coupling is not as great as that of shared-variable systems.

The message-passing model can be further subdivided based on whether or not the interconnection topology is visible to the user. As will be seen, in hypercube systems, the topology is visible and the programmer can sometimes specify the data routing explicitly. There are *direct links* between nodes. By mapping algorithms to the particular interconnection geometry, one can obtain a very high performance. When the network topology consists only of *indirect links* between processors (messages pass through intermediate switching modules), the topology is hidden from the programmer and routine placement becomes a characteristic of the network and not of the application program.

Shared-memory models can perform message-passing primitives easily, but the reverse is not true. This is because data structures are shared among processors in the former model. Properties such as simplicity and scalability make message-passing multiprocessors prime candidates for very large systems, which will undoubtedly be built in the future.

Message-passing systems are more efficient for problems that can be partitioned into larger tasks that do not interact very frequently. The performance of message-passing systems is more difficult to determine because their performance becomes directly dependent on the communication patterns specified in the algorithms. The hypercubes described in Section 6.6 are examples of message-passing systems.

6.1.3   Primary Issues in Multiprocessing Systems

The main reasons for using multiprocessors are to exploit their inherent parallelism and to speed up computations for a broad range of problems.

Identification of Parallelism

One of the first difficulties encountered when using multiprocessors is the problem of how to express parallelism. There are two possibilities: Either the programming language used has the capability of explicitly expressing parallelism, in which case the user handles the parallelism, or the language has implicit parallelism, in which case parallelizing compilers must be used. Often the languages used today for programming multiprocessors are only minor variations on those used for uniprocessors. Parallelism is detected by compilers based on dependence analysis. Automatic parallelization of sequential programs for multiprocessors has been only partially successful. In addition to determining parallelism between loop iterations (as in vector processing), it is also necessary to detect dependencies between subroutines. This is why considerable effort is being made to develop languages with concurrent constructs in which a parallel code is structured in closed form, with implicit synchronization at the end of each parallel block. A parallel program for multiprocessors consists of two or more interacting processes.

Partitioning

After parallelism identification, it is necessary first to partition the computational task into processes and to identify the objects that they share. A process is a sequential program that is executed in one processor; it is executed concurrently with other processes running on other processors. The basic mechanism provided for creating parallelism is the *spawn operation,* which is used to support parallel loop and parallel block constructs. Spawn is essentially an n-way fork of control in which n identical processes are created. The "parent" process usually waits for termination of its spawned "children," which occurs automatically at the end of the parallel code block. Thus the parent process and the subsequent program statements are synchronized with the completion of the spawned parallel processes. The programmer may use primitive operations such as *fork* and *join* to create and terminate processes. The *"fork loop"* statement initiates a new process at address *loop*. *"join n"* causes n independent processes to merge into a single one.

As an example, consider the execution of a matrix multiplication algorithm on a multiprocessor. The parallel algorithm may be written as follows:

```
for j = 1, n
    fork loop;           /spawn n independent processes,
end j                         each with a different value of j/
loop: for i = 1, n
         c(i, j) = 0;
         for k = 1, n
```

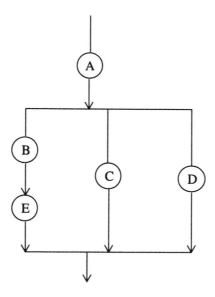

Figure 6.5 A example of an execution graph.

$$c(i, j) = c(i, j) + a(i, k) * b(k, j);$$
$$\quad \text{end } k;$$
$$\quad \text{end } i;$$
$$\text{join } n;$$

The *"fork loop"* instruction is visited n times, each time with a different value of j. As a result, n processes are formed, each with a different j value. In this example, a process is the nested loop i, k, which computes a column of matrix **C**. Once processes have been spawned, the operating system schedules them on available processors according to some scheduling policy.

The parallel execution of code can also be controlled by *parbegin/parend* constructs. The statements between parbegin and parend are executed concurrently. However, sequential execution within parbegin/parend may be specified by *begin/end* constructs. Consider, for example, the computation graph shown in Figure 6.5. The control for this can be written as

```
            A
         parbegin
            C
            D
          begin
            B
            E
           end
         parend
```

Parbegin/parend constructs are less powerful than fork/join constructs because they can handle only nested execution graphs (a parbegin/parend pair within another pair). In contrast, the construct *join n, label* waits until all n processes terminate and then moves control to *label*. Thus fork/join is a more powerful operation, but the programmer has the responsibility of ensuring proper control flow (see Problem 6.4.A).

Memory Allocation

The creation of new processes requires allocation of memory space. As in SIMD systems, the allocation of data to memory has an impact on how well logical transfers match physical transfers, and thus an impact on the routing time. Memory allocation is influenced by the memory organization and by the interconnection network.

Memory Access

The way in which memory is accessed becomes particulary important in large shared-memory multiprocessors where processors compete to access the same memory locations. It is desirable that memory access be fast and accurate. A fast memory access has been the goal of every computer system, but for large multiprocessors it becomes even more important because of many factors that may introduce delays in accessing memories. Another problem specific to multiprocessors is that of maintaining memory consistency in systems where different processors attempt to read and write from and to the same memory locations.

Scheduling

After processes are formed, they need to be assigned to processors for execution. Scheduling can be performed at compile time or at run time. The main goal is to assign processes to processors such that communication time and overhead are minimized. Scheduling is multiprocessor-dependent; it is especially a function of interconnection network and processor characteristics.

Synchronization

Once processes are assigned to hardware resources and start their execution, it is necessary to maintain the correct execution order by imposing the satisfaction of data dependencies. This is achieved through hardware and software synchronization. Some processes are functional in nature, meaning that once the inputs are available, these processes can run to completion without interacting with other processes. The outputs of these processes are pure functions of their inputs. The processes in the matrix multiplication example were independent processes. There is no need for synchronization during the execution of such processes. However, usually processes interact with other processes during their execution, and therefore synchronization is necessary.

System Balancing

The problem of balancing a system involves selecting the main components of the system such that the system as a whole achieves high performance. For example, the processor speed needs to match the interconnection network bandwidth and the memory speed. The main objective is overall high throughput; this is achieved by avoiding potential bottlenecks.

6.2   MULTIPROCESSOR INTERCONNECTION NETWORKS AND MEMORIES

6.2.1   Interconnection Organizations

As a result of increasing the number of functional modules in a multiprocessor, the interconnection network becomes increasingly complex.

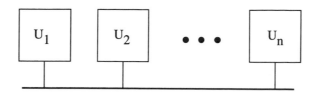

Figure 6.6 Single bus.

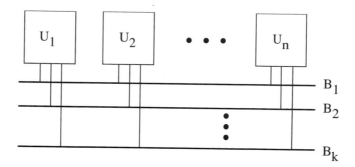

Figure 6.7 Multiple buses.

Examples of multiprocessor interconnection networks are time-shared or common buses, crossbar switches, multiport memories, hypercubes, meshes, and multistage interconnection networks.

Common Bus

This simple interconnection shown in Figure 6.6 is useful both for message-passing systems, in which each unit U is a computer, as well as for shared-memory systems, in which some units are processors, some are shared memories, and some are I/O units. The bus can be totally passive, with transfer operations controlled completely by the bus interfaces of the sending and receiving units. It is also possible to use a centralized bus arbiter. The main advantages of this interconnection are its simplicity and its extendability, i.e., the possibility of adding or removing functional units easily. Its main disadvantages are its poor reliability and the fact that it can be used for only a limited number

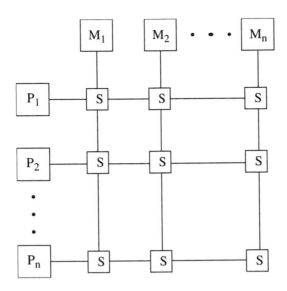

Figure 6.8 Crossbar switch.

of processors because of the bottleneck caused by the bus itself. To obtain more reliability and parallelism, one can use multiple buses, as shown in Figure 6.7. However, these benefits are gained at the cost of increased complexity.

Crossbar Switch
The crossbar switch shown in Figure 6.8, mostly used for shared-memory systems, provides nonblocking simultaneous memory accesses and communications among functional units. To provide a maximum of simultaneous transfers, each crosspoint S must be capable of switching parallel transmissions and resolving possible conflicts among requesting units. This interconnection is used only for a small number of processors because the number of switches is $O(N^2)$, where N is the number of processors. It has been used in the C.mmp (16 processors) and other systems.

Multiport Memories
The availability of multiport memories makes possible the construction of interconnection networks in which processors communicate via

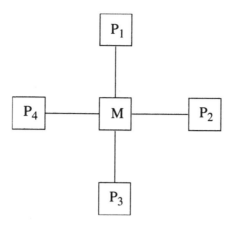

Figure 6.9 Interprocessor communication using a four-port memory.

memories instead of buses. As shown in Figure 6.9, four processors can simultaneously access a four-port memory chip. The only restriction is writing to the same memory location, which is prevented through some built-in priority mechanism. Complex interconnection networks may be built using multiport memories. The advantage of this interconnection scheme over buses is that communication protocol is reduced because transferred data can be temporarily stored in the memory.

Multistage Interconnection Networks

Multistage interconnection networks, as shown in Figure 6.10, are feasible interconnections for large multiprocessor systems. Multistage interconnections allow processor-to-processor and processor-to-memory communications in a more general way than the other organizations. Feng and Wu [Feng and Wu 1979] have classified these interconnections into the following four categories:

1. *Strictly nonblocking.* A network is called strictly nonblocking if it can connect any idle input to any idle output regardless of what other connections are currently in process. This means that it is possible to make connections in any arbitrary order. For example, a crossbar interconnection is strictly nonblocking. Since large crossbars are prohibitively expensive, there were many efforts in

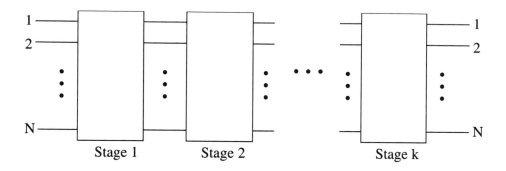

Figure 6.10 A multistage network.

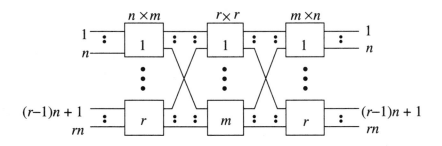

Figure 6.11 A three-stage Clos network.

the 1950s and 1960s to construct crossbars with smaller switch boxes. Clos networks, discussed below, are examples of efficient network implementations. A three-stage Clos network is shown in Figure 6.11. Each stage consists of a number of smaller crossbar switches. The number of inputs is $N = rn$, where r is the number of crossbar switches in the first and last columns, and n is the number of inputs to each crossbar. Clos has shown that the network has fewer than N^2 crosspoints for $N \geq 24$, and in general it requires $O(Ne^{\sqrt{logN}})$ crosspoints. For $m \geq 2n - 1$ the three-stage Clos network is strictly nonblocking.

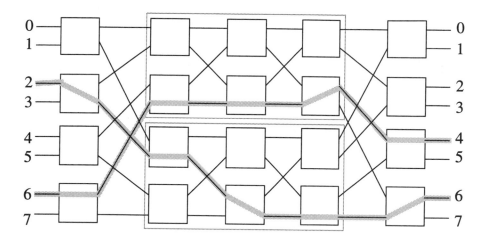

Figure 6.12 Benes network: connections $2 \rightarrow 6$ and $6 \rightarrow 4$ are shown.

2. *Wide-sense nonblocking.* A network is called wide-sense nonblocking if it can handle all possible connections without blocking, but can do so only if specific routing rules are used to make its connections. Clos has shown that for $m \geq 3n/2$ the network shown in Figure 6.11 is a wide-sense nonblocking network. Obviously, these networks have fewer nodes than strictly nonblocking networks.

3. *Rearrangeable nonblocking.* A network is called rearrangeable nonblocking if it can perform all possible connections between inputs and outputs by rearranging its existing connections. All desired connections must be specified before routing computation begins. The Clos network shown in Figure 6.11 is rearrangeable if $m \geq n$. An example of a rearrangeable network leading to the minimum number of crosspoints was proposed by Benes [Benes 1965]. Figure 6.12 shows a Benes binary network with eight inputs and eight outputs. In general, when the number of inputs is $N = 2^n$, the number of stages is $2n - 1$ and the number of switching boxes is $N(2n - 1)/2$.

4. *Blocking interconnection.* A network is said to be blocking if it can perform many, but not all, possible connections between ter-

minals. Examples are the Banyan network, the Omega network, the Data Manipulator, and others.

6.2.2   Network Characteristics

Some important characteristics of a multistage interconnection network are its operation mode, switching technique, routing technique, and interconnection network topology.

Operation Modes

There are two basic modes of network operation: *synchronous* and *asynchronous*. In the synchronous mode, the network is centrally supervised. The connection paths are established simultaneously and remain set until the control disconnects them. In the asynchronous mode, connection paths are set up or disconnected on an individual basis. The asynchronous mode of operation is more appropriate for multiprocessor systems.

Switching Techniques

There are three basic switching techniques: *circuit switching, packet switching*, and *wormhole switching*. Circuit switching sets up the switches and ports and establishes a dedicated path between an input-output pair. This technique is efficient for larger transmissions. Packet switching refers to a technique in which messages between any two terminals are broken into several shorter, fixed-length packets, which are routed independently to their destination using store-and-forward procedures. In wormhole switching a message is also broken into smaller parts (called flits), as in packet switching; however, the difference is that here all flits follow the same route. Thus wormhole routing is a combination of circuit switching and store-and-forward switching. The advantage of wormhole routing over store-and-forward is that the overhead for setting switches is decreased because the leading flit sets the switches for the rest of the message.

Compared with circuit switching, packet switching is efficient for shorter and more frequent transmissions. The blocking problem that occurs in interconnection networks can be alleviated by using packet switching. The increased flexibility offered by packet switching is achieved at the cost of increased hardware in the switch, i.e., buffers and other logic. Of course it is possible to use both circuit switching and packet switching.

Routing Techniques

The routing technique is the method of establishing communication paths and resolving conflicts. Three basic routing techniques have been considered: *centralized, distributed,* and *adaptive.* In the centralized routing scheme, a central control makes all the logic decisions needed to set up communication paths. This scheme is more feasible for small to medium-scale systems. In the distributed scheme, logical decisions are made locally, based on current conditions. In the adaptive scheme, information about the network is collected globally, but routing decisions are made locally.

Interconnection Network Topology

The network topology is the way in which the switches are interconnected. The topology is perhaps the most important factor determining network performance.

6.2.3   NYU Enhanced Omega Network

The NYU Ultracomputer is a shared-memory multiprocessor using an enhanced Omega network. As indicated by Gottlieb, one of the designers of the Ultracomputer [Gottlieb 1987], the following design goals were set for the interconnection network, which connects a large number of processors and memories:

1. Bandwidth proportional to the number of processors N;

2. Latency, defined as memory access time, logarithmic in N;

3. $O(N \ log \ N)$ identical switches;

4. Routing decisions local to each switch; and

5. Concurrent access by multiple processors to the same memory cell without causing any performance penalty.

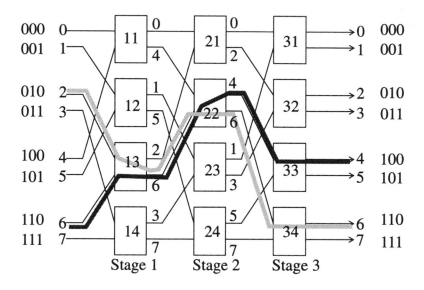

Figure 6.13 Omega network: connections $2 \to 6$ and $6 \to 4$ are shown.

A network designed to meet these objectives is an enhanced Omega network. For convenience, the topology of the Omega network, presented above in Chapter 4, is shown in Figure 6.13. Suppose that the modules connected to the left are processors, and the modules connected to the right are memories. A unique path connects each processor-memory pair. Suppose that the processors are numbered $PE_{(p_1, \cdots, p_d)}$ and memories are numbered $M_{(m_1, \cdots, m_d)}$, where d is the number of bits required to represent N units (i.e., $d = log\ N$).

The *routing algorithm* is as follows: At the input of each stage j, the switch checks the jth bit of the destination address, starting with the first stage, looking at the most significant bit. If the bit is 0, the switch selects the upper port of the switch; if the bit is 1, the switch selects the lower port of the switch.

In Figure 6.13, the routings of connections $2 \to 6$ and $6 \to 4$ are shown. Notice that these two connections overlap, unlike those in the Benes network shown in Figure 6.12.

An important factor that contributes to this network's high efficiency is that messages are pipelined. Network pipelining is possible only for packet-switching networks. In order to support pipelining, a queue must be associated with each switch.

An effort was made to keep the number of address bits in each message to a mimimum. There is no need to store both destination and return addresses entirely ($2d$ bits). If a combination of origin and destination addresses is used, only d bits are necessary. When a message first enters the network, its origin is determined by the input ports, so only the destination address is needed. Switches at the jth stage route messages based on memory address bit m_j, then replace this bit with the PE number bit p_j.

The *bit-replacing algorithm* is as follows: If a message came from an upper input port, replace the destination bit used at that stage with 0; if it came from a lower port, replace that bit with 1. The reader may check this algorithm with the connections shown in Figure 6.13. Thus, when a message reaches its destination, the return address is already available.

Combining Loads and Stores

One of the side-effects of shared-memory systems is the occurrence of congestion points or "hot spots" around memory locations frequently addressed. The entire system performance may be seriously degraded by these hot spots. One clever way of ameliorating the congestion around hot spots is to implement *combining* networks. The idea is to combine concurrent loads and stores directed at the same memory location whenever they meet at a switch. Usually, a load is a transfer from memory to a processor, and a store is a transfer from a processor to memory. The following possibilities have been considered in the NYU enhanced Omega network:

- *Load-load.* When two or more identical load requests meet at a switch, forward only one to memory. When data are available, replicate them and send them to the processors.

- *Load-store.* When a load and a store meet at a switch, stop the load by returning the store value, and forward only the store to memory.

- *Store-store.* When two (or more) stores meet at a switch, forward only one to memory.

When designing combining networks, one must consider tradeoffs between advantages such as reduced communication traffic and lower network latency, and disadvantages such as increased design complexity and cost.

Network Switches

Network switches contribute significantly to the system performance. As shown in Figure 6.14, a switch is a 2×2 bidirectional routing device that transmits a message from its input ports to the appropriate output port on the oposite side. Each of the four terminals has bidirectional ports. A queue is attached to each output port. A message entering a switch with empty queues leaves the switch at the next cycle. The switch has the capability of combining memory requests. Each request consists of several components: function indicator (e.g., load or store), address, and data. The address itself consists of a combination of the PE port number and the M port number, and the internal address within the specified M. When a request enters a combining queue, a search takes place over the requests already stored in the queue. If the function indicator, M port number, or internal address does not match, then no combining is possible, and the new request is placed at the end of the queue. If there is an address match between two requests, the addresses are placed in the wait buffer to await the return of the old request from memory. The new request is deleted from the queue.

6.2.4   Multiprocessor Memories

Memory Design Issues

One of the most difficult design issues for multiprocessors is the design of a memory system. The problem is particularly challenging in shared-memory multiprocessors because of the fact that memories are shared among processors. In message-passing systems, memories are disjointed and the memory design process is similar to that used for uniprocessors.

Our discussion will focus on shared-memory systems. In these systems, processors not only exchange data through memories, but also

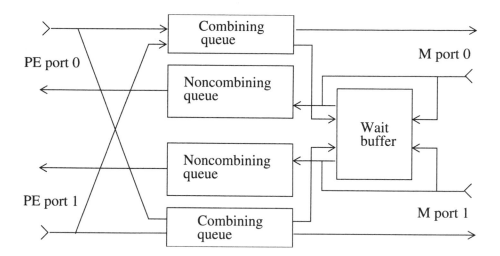

Figure 6.14 Block diagram of a network switch in the NYU
Ultracomputer.

become synchronized through the shared address space. The global
shared memory is partitioned into a number of independent memory
modules, mainly to allow processors simultaneous access to more than
one module. Cache memories have been used in uniprocessors to increase the memory bandwidth. In multiprocessors, there is an even
larger need for cache use in order to overcome interconnection network
delays. Some of the main design problems are:

1. *Memory contention.* Several processors may attempt to access
   the same memory space at the same time.

2. *Efficiency of processor-memory access.* The presence of an interconnection network between processors and memory, in addition
   to the large size of memory space, introduces delays in memory
   access. Latency time is defined as the network propagation time
   when a processor requests a memory access. The larger the multiprocessor system, the larger the delay through the interconnection
   network.

3. *Memory consistency or coherence.* Copies of a shared memory

block may exist in different caches at the same time. These copies must be consistent, because if they are not, a cache incoherence problem occurs.

When two or more processors simultaneously attempt to access the same memory module, and the network does not perform the combine operation, a memory interference occurs. Memory interferences degrade system performance. Clever memory organization can alleviate this problem. A technique called *memory interleaving* is used to distribute memory addresses among the memory modules. In one such scheme, consecutive addresses are located within a module. This technique allows for easy memory expansion. Another technique is to assign consecutive addresses to consecutive memory modules. This approach is advantageous when a program or data segment is shared by several processors. Memory interleaving provides better reliability. It is advantageous when the address space for active processes is shared intensively. When there is little sharing, interleaving may cause undesirable effects. A technique called *home memory* is sometimes used to provide preferential access for a processor to its dedicated memory module. The home memory for a processor contains the entire set of active files belonging to a process currently running on that processor. The processor can access its home memory without encountering any competition from other processors.

Analogous to techniques that reduce the effective memory access time in uniprocessor systems is the use of a *memory hierarchy* in the parallel system. This hierarchy usually consists of a cache associated with each processing element, local memory, and a large shared memory. The inclusion of the caches reduces the effective memory access time.

Multicache Systems

While caches are highly desirable in multiprocessor systems, they introduce the cache coherence problem, which is a major obstacle in building very large shared-memory systems. Below, we describe some hardware and software techniques for handling this problem. Multiple copies of a main memory block may exist in several private caches. Modification of any copy of this shared block by a processor in its cache will change these shared data into an absolute value in the main memory, or in every other cache. Thus data inconsistency may exist. Before we present some solutions to the cache coherence problem, let us understand the sources of data inconsistencies.

Consider a multicache system, as shown in Figure 6.15, with n caches, C_i for $i = 1, \ldots, n$, and a main memory shared by all processor elements PE_i. Let X be the physical address of a main memory block, and y_i the cache address of this block in cache C_i. The coherence problem occurs when:

1. Block X is stored in C_i at y_i and in C_j at y_j. An inconsistency between y_i and y_j may occur because:

   - A process P that migrates from processor PE_i to PE_j modifies block y_i in one way and block y_j in a different way.

   - A process running on PE_i modifies y_i, and another process running on PE_j modifies y_j differently.

2. Block X is not able to keep up with the caches. For example, a copy of X is in y_i, but when y_i is modified X is not updated. If block X is needed in PE_j, then as a result of the miss, X is copied into C_j, but this is not the latest X.

Solutions to the cache coherence problem may be provided through hardware or software means or by some combination of the two.

Hardware-based solutions maintain cache consistency by allowing multiple readers and a single writer at a given time. Achieved only through hardware means, these solutions become expensive for large systems. The two policies used are *write-invalidate* and *write-update*. Under the write-invalidate policy, consistency is achieved by invalidating cache copies of a block at the moment when one of the copies has been updated. This implies that all copies are aware when one of them is changed. While this is easily achieved in a simple bus architecture by simply broadcasting cache changes, in larger systems with multistage interconnection networks it is difficult to keep track of all cache updates. The write-update policy maintains consistency by updating all cache copies of a block immediately after one has been modified.

As with the previous policy, this policy also requires consistency commands between caches, which can be prohibitively expensive for large systems.

A straightforward technique, easily achieved in bus-based multiprocessors, is the *snoopy cache* protocol. The caches "snoop" at the bus for all consistency commands provided by any unit connected to the bus. Unfortunately, this simple way of achieving cache consistency cannot be used in multiprocessors with general interconnection networks. By simply observing that consistency commands need not be sent to all caches, but only to caches that have copies of the same memory block, some improvements can be made. Cache coherence protocols that keep track of which caches hold what copies of blocks are referred to as *directory schemes*. The information stored in the directory depends on the coherence policy used.

Software-based solutions to the cache coherence problem have been suggested to avoid complex hardware techniques. A simple way of bypassing the coherence problem is to mark variables as cacheable and noncacheable at compile time. However, this trivial solution is too conservative, and often useless, because most of the shared variables are read-write variables. More elaborate techniques, known as safe-to-cache, allow read-write variables to be cacheable only some of the time. The compiler designer now faces the new, challenging problem of deciding when to call a variable cacheable and when not to.

So far, software-based techniques have not yet been implemented in commercial systems, although considerable work is in progress because of the importance of the problem.

6.3   MAPPING ALGORITHMS INTO MULTIPROCESSORS

Some of the basic problems to be solved when mapping a program into a multiprocessor are:

1. Identifying parallelism in the program;

2. Partitioning the program into sequential tasks; and

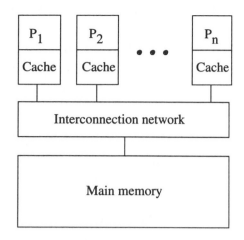

Figure 6.15 Multicache system.

3. Scheduling the tasks on processors.

The parallelism in a program depends on the nature of the problem and the algorithm used by the programmer. The parallelism analysis is usually independent of the target machine. On the other hand, partitioning and scheduling are designed to minimize the parallel execution of a program on a target machine, and depend on parameters such as number of processors, processor performance, communication overhead, scheduling overhead, and others.

6.3.1   Parallelism Detection

The problem of implementing parallel languages on multiprocessors has fallen behind hardware development. Automatic parallelization of sequential programs is still the most attractive approach from an industry viewpoint.

Programming Languages for Multiprocessors
Vivek Sarkar [Sarkar 1989] has classified languages for multiprocessors using the criteria of implicit versus explicit parallelism, partition, and schedule.

1. *Implicit versus explicit parallelism.* Some languages have explicit constructs for concurrence, such as fork/join, parbegin/parend, DOALL, and so on. In others, the parallelism is implicit, and parallelism detection is performed based on dependence analysis. Languages with explicit parallelism include Concurrent Pascal, Ada, Occam, and others.

2. *Implicit versus explicit partition.* This issue is relevant only for languages with explicit parallelism. The partition of a parallel program specifies the sequential units of computation in the program, and hence the granularity of execution. In implicit partitioning, the language parallelism is expressed in terms of general constructs; in explicit partitioning, processes and tasks are well identified by the language. For example, Ada and Occam have explicit partitioning capability, whereas Concurrent Pascal does not.

3. *Implicit versus explicit schedule.* For languages with explicit parallelism and explicit partitioning, the schedule may be either implicit, when tasks are not assigned to processors, or explicit, when tasks are assigned a priori to processors. The explicit schedule of a parallel program specifies the mapping of computations into processors. For example, scheduling is explicit in Occam but not in Ada.

4. *Shared-memory versus message-passing.* Because of the different ways of implementing communication used by the two models, languages for shared-memory models do not perform well for a message-passing model. However, a message-passing model may be implemented on a shared-memory multiprocessor.

Parallel programming languages should have the capability to define tasks executable in parallel, start and stop their execution, and control the interconnection between tasks. The declaration of parallel tasks, as well as the starting and stopping of their execution, is achieved with fork/join, parbegin/parend, and similar constructs. The interactions between tasks are usually controlled with synchronization primitives, which will be discussed later.

Dependencies

The way to detect parallelism is, again, to study data dependencies between processes. While the material from Chapter 2 regarding dependencies at the variable level is directly applicable here, often in multiprocessors it is necessary to detect dependencies at the process and task levels. This change in granularity reflects the nature of MIMD computing.

Some simple conditions for parallelism may be derived as follows: Consider two tasks T_1 and T_2. The input variables of a task (variables fetched from memory) are denoted by I and the output variables (variables stored) are denoted by O. Then, for two tasks to be parallel, it is sufficient that

$$I_2 \cap O_1 = \emptyset$$
$$I_1 \cap O_2 = \emptyset$$
$$O_1 \cap O_2 = \emptyset$$

These conditions are equivalent to data dependence, antidependence, and output dependence conditions defined in Chapter 2. As an example, consider some tasks for evaluating matrix expressions:

$$T_1: \mathbf{X} \leftarrow (\mathbf{A+B})$$
$$T_2: \mathbf{Y} \leftarrow \mathbf{CD}^{-1}$$
$$T_3: \mathbf{Z} \leftarrow (\mathbf{X+Y})$$

$I_1 = \mathbf{A}, \mathbf{B}, I_2 = \mathbf{C}, \mathbf{D}, O_1 = \mathbf{X}, O_2 = \mathbf{Y}$. Since $I_1 \cap O_2 = \emptyset$, $I_2 \cap O_1 = \emptyset$, and $O_1 \cap O_2 = \emptyset$, tasks T_1 and T_2 can be executed in parallel. Task T_3 cannot be executed in parallel with either T_1 or T_2 because $I_3 \cap O_2 \neq \emptyset$ or $I_3 \cap O_1 \neq \emptyset$. A parallel program is

```
begin
        parbegin
                    X ← (A+B);
                    Y ← CD⁻¹;
        parend
        Z ← X+Y;
end
```

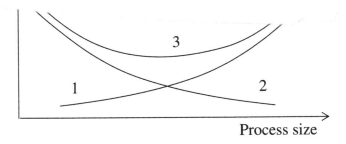

Process size

1. Ideal execution time
2. Overhead time
3. Actual execution time

Figure 6.16 Execution time is affected by parallelism and overhead.

6.3.2 Partitioning

Partitioning is necessary to ensure that the granularity of the parallel program is coarse enough for the target multiprocessor, without losing too much parallelism. While parallelism detection is multiprocessor-independent, partitioning and scheduling are highly dependent on the architecture. The partition of a program specifies the sequential units of computation in the program. Let us refer to these units as processes. Some properties of interest to us are:

1. The process sequential execution time, which is a measure of the process size;

2. The process inputs and outputs, which impact communication overhead; and

3. The process precedence constraints, which specify the synchronization requirements.

The execution time of a parallel program is heavily influenced by the partition. Figure 6.16 illustrates the way in which the process size affects the execution time. The execution time is the sum of the ideal execution time plus the overhead time. The ideal execution time, in the absence of overhead, increases with the process size due to the loss of parallelism, while the overhead time decreases with the process size. The actual execution time is determined by adding the two curves. Partitioning should be designed such that it provides a process size for which the effective execution time is minimized.

It is important to realize that continuous variation of process size is an oversimplification of the partitioning process. Real programs are discrete structures, and it may not be possible to partition a program into processes of equal size. Moreover, the overhead incurred by a process depends on the partition. Thus, finding the optimum partition for a real program is rather difficult.

The starting point for partitioning and scheduling is the construction of a graphical representation of the programs. This is an abstraction that provides performance characteristics and ignores the remaining aspects, such as semantics. Directed acyclic graphs (or dags), flow graphs, and data-flow graphs are commonly used to represent programs. In dags, an internal node represents an expression or a statement. Edges express data dependencies. A basic-block dag is similar to an expression dag, but represents an entire basic block. In the data-flow graph of a program, the nodes represent computations and the edges represent control flow. A path in the flow graph represents a possible execution sequence in the program. The main difference between a flow graph and a dag is that a flow graph expresses sequential execution. The graphical representation contains information on program structure, parallelism, execution frequencies, and costs for communication and execution time.

A *partitioning technique* proposed by Sarkar [Sarkar 1989] is to start with an initial fine-granularity partition and then iteratively to merge processes selected by heuristics until the coarsest partition is reached, as illustrated in Figure 6.17. For each iteration, compute a cost function and then select the partitioning that minimizes the cost function. The partitioning cost function is a combination of two terms: the *critical path term* and the *overhead term*. The overhead term decreases monotonically with the number of iterations because a move to a coarser granularity cannot increase the total overhead.

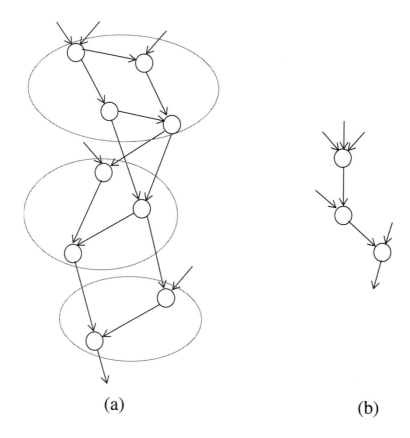

(a)   (b)

Figure 6.17 Partitioning a computational graph: (a) Fine grain;
(b) coarse grain.

Compilers for Multiprocessors

Compilers are essential components of general-purpose multiprocessors.
Less ambitious compilers perform only modest parallelism detection
and partitioning functions, whereas more sophisticated compilers handle even scheduling problems. The possibilities for performing automatic partitioning and scheduling are:

1. Run-time partitioning and run-time scheduling;

2. Compile-time partitioning and run-time scheduling; and

3. Compile-time partitioning and compile-time scheduling.

The first approach is practical only for simpler applications. There is considerable overhead when partitioning and scheduling are done at run time, which affects performance. The second approach, compile-time partitioning and run-time scheduling, is the most common model of program execution in current multiprocessor systems. The scheduling of tasks on processors is performed automatically at run time, but the programmer or the compiler must explicitly partition the program into tasks and control their synchronization and communication. The third approach, in which both partitioning and scheduling are done by the compiler, requires the most advanced compiler technology. The advantage of this approach is the elimination of overhead at run time. However, the scheduling may be far from optimum, especially in cases when it is difficult to estimate the program execution time a priori. If the compiler is able to provide a good time estimate, a global scheduling strategy is beneficial, since a better match of dependencies to the interconnection network may be possible.

There are compilers, such as Paraphrase and Bulldog, that use program restructuring techniques to transform a sequential program into a parallel form suitable for multiprocessors.

The *Paraphrase compiler,* developed at the University of Illinois in the early 1980s by a group led by David Kuck [Kuck, Kuhn, Padua, Leasure, and Wolfe 1981], is a source-to-source restructuring tool that utilizes a complex data dependence test and transforms Fortran programs from their original sequential form into a form suitable for execution in a high-speed multiprocessor. Paraphrase has two phases. The first phase, called the front-end pass, performs machine-independent transformations and restructures the program into an intermediate form that expresses the maximum parallelism of the programs. Techniques such as those outlined in Chapter 3 are used in this phase. The second phase, called the back-end pass, maps the intermediate form into a specific architecture, such as simple execution of array instructions, multiple execution of scalar instructions, and multiple execution of array instructions selected by the user.

Paraphrase has been successful in extracting parallelism from Fortran programs for execution on vector machines such as the Cray X/MP.

This parallelism is typically present at the innermost level because global parallelism (between subroutines, say) is difficult to extract from a sequential language. Vector machines use parallelism in innermost DO loops only. In multiprocessors, there is a need to recognize parallelism at all levels, small-grain as well as large-grain. Moreover, there is a need to make tradeoffs between levels. (Paraphase is the compiler used by the Cedar multiprocessor.)

The *Bulldog compiler,* developed at Yale University by John Ellis [Ellis 1986], is another example of a system that aims at automatic parallelism, written for scientific computations. Unlike Paraphrase, it is designed to detect parallelism not usually derived from loops or vectorization. Bulldog takes advantage of the fact that most of the time, in scientific computation, a conditional branch proceeds in the same direction. Sequences of code blocks are linked together in a trace if there is a higher probability that they will be executed from beginning to end without interruption. The jump predictions either are programmer-specified or result from experiments on sample data. Bulldog does not perform the tedious, but exact, dependence analysis used in Paraphrase; instead, it relies on the formation of traces. This makes Bulldog more useful for highly unstructured programs (those with many conditionals). A problem, however, is that traces can be formed only for blocks inside loops, and in Fortran most of the loops are not very large. In order to increase the size of traces, the compiler unrolls the bodies of the loops.

6.3.3   Scheduling

Scheduling is defined as a function that assigns processes to processors. The goals of the scheduling, or allocation, function are to spread the load to all processors as evenly as possible in order to obtain processor efficiency and to minimize data communication, which will lead to shorter overall processing time. The processor allocation problem is almost nonexistent in multiprogrammed uniprocessor systems. However, an analogy can be made between the processor allocation problem and the memory allocation problem in the case of uniprocessors. Allocation policies can be classified as *static* and *dynamic*.

Static allocation. Under the static allocation policy, tasks are assigned to processors before run time either by the programmer or by the compiler. In some parallel languages, the programmer can specify the processor on which a task is to be performed, the communication channel used, and so on. There is no run-time overhead, and allocation overhead is incurred only once even when the programs are run many times with different data. The disadvantage of static allocation, however, is the impossibility of guessing the run-time profile of each task.

Dynamic allocation. Under the dynamic allocation policy, tasks are assigned to processors at run time. This scheme offers better utilization of processors, but at the price of additional allocation time. Dynamic allocation can be distributed or centralized. In distributed allocation, there is a pool of tasks and any free processor can take tasks from the pool. A task may be distributed over several processors. In centralized allocation, a task is allocated to a processor by a central control. With the centralized allocation scheme, a bottleneck may develop when the number of processors becomes large.

A major factor affecting allocation in a multiprocessor system is the type of processor mix used to implement the multiprocessor system. Consideration must be given to homogeneous versus heterogeneous processor system types. In a homogeneous system, each processor is treated identically and has identical capabilities. A heterogeneous system has different processor types for different specialized functions. Homogeneous allocation can be implemented using an extension of single-processor scheduling techniques. A task requiring execution is assigned to the next available processor. This considerably simplifies the allocation algorithms and reduces allocation overhead time.

Scheduling also includes information regarding the time when a process will start to be executed on a processor. From this point of view, scheduling policies can be divided into *preemptive* and *nonpreemptive*. In a preemptive environment, tasks may be halted before completion by another task that requires service. This method requires that a task be interruptible, which is not always possible. In general, preemptive techniques can generate more efficient schedules than those that are nonpreemptive. However, a penalty is also paid in the preemptive case. This penalty lies in the overhead of task switching, which includes discontinuous processing and the additional memory required to save the processor state. This overhead is negligible if such switching occurs infrequently.

One form of task scheduling used in a multiprocessor environment is *periodic scheduling*. This method assumes that tasks are simultaneously available for execution. The objective is to minimize the number of processors used to execute a particular job while ensuring that individual jobs begin and end exactly at their specified time intervals. In general, this is a very complex method and often a straightforward optimal scheduling does not exist.

Another scheduling method is the use of *deadlines,* or scheduled completion times established for individual processes. If there is some slack, or spare, time associated with the completion time of individual tasks, and this slack time is bounded, it is called a *hard deadline* or a *hard real-time schedule*. If the slack time is based on a statistical distribution of terminations, we say it is a *soft deadline* or a *soft real-time schedule*.

Deadline-driven schedules can be managed by using critical-path or longest-path scheduling techniques. However, these methods are often difficult to implement in multiprocessor systems. In order to work, the methods described above assume that task execution time is known before initiation. Also, no branching (of unequal-length paths) can be done, since this affects task completion time.

Next, some of the most prominent scheduling approaches are described.

Self-service. With this approach, idle processors help themselves from a central queue that keeps processes. It is an effective approach because the load is shared evenly among all processors. However, it has some disadvantages. The process queue might become a bottleneck, especially in large systems when several processors seek work simultaneously. Also, sometimes it is desired to run related processes concurrently, on separate processors (so-called gang scheduling), and this is difficult to achieve under the self-service implementation. This scheduling policy has been implemented on multiprocessors such as the NYU Ultracomputer, the Sequent Balance, and the Encore Multimax.

Local queues. This approach consists of providing a process queue to each processor, and mapping a set of processes to these local queues.

The processors execute processes from their local queues just as uniprocessors execute their loads. The distributive nature of this approach makes it more suitable for message-passing multiprocessors than for shared-memory multiprocessors.

Precedence graph. This approach consists of forming a program dependence graph in which the nodes are processes and the arcs are their dependence relations. An estimate of process execution time may also be provided. Once such a graph has been constructed, it becomes easy to map it onto a multiprocessor. This scheme achieves good performance, but considerable work is necessary to form the dependence graph. An example follows.

Suppose that a program has the dependence graph shown in Figure 6.18. The connectivity matrix for this graph is shown in Figure 6.19. For simplicity, it is assumed that all processes, marked by the nodes of the graph, have the same execution time. We wish to find the permissible execution time intervals for each process; that is, the time during which a process may be scheduled such that no unnecessary delays are introduced. For this we need to determine first the earliest possible execution time for each process, and then the latest possible execution time. The following procedure may be used:

Step 1. Find the earliest processing time. This may be determined through a sequence of steps that identify nodes that could be started at the same, earliest time. First, the nodes whose columns contain only zeroes are identified. Now eliminate the columns and the rows corresponding to these nodes. This process is repeated until the entire connectivity matrix disappears. The following sets of nodes are obtained:

$$\{1\}, \{2, 3\}, \{4, 5, 6, 7\}, \{8, 9, 11\}, \{10\}, \{12\}$$

It is interesting to notice that the same result is obtained by drawing wave fronts on the dependence graph starting from the top down. As shown in Figure 6.20(a), six time steps are required, and each wave front indicates the earliest permissible execution time for processes on that wave front.

Step 2. Find the latest processing time. This is determined in a similar way. The difference is that we first locate the nodes that have rows containing only zeros, instead of columns as before. Then these

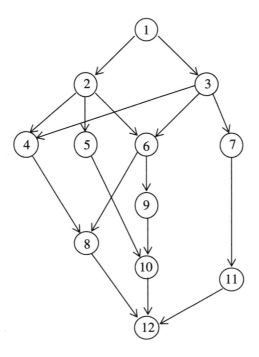

Figure 6.18 Dependence graph.

```
        1  2  3  4  5  6  7  8  9  10 11 12
   1    0  1  1  0  0  0  0  0  0  0  0  0
   2    0  0  0  1  1  1  0  0  0  0  0  0
   3    0  0  0  1  0  1  1  0  0  0  0  0
   4    0  0  0  0  0  0  0  1  0  0  0  0
   5    0  0  0  0  0  0  0  0  0  1  0  0
   6    0  0  0  0  0  0  0  1  1  0  0  0
   7    0  0  0  0  0  0  0  0  0  0  1  0
   8    0  0  0  0  0  0  0  0  0  0  0  1
   9    0  0  0  0  0  0  0  0  0  1  0  0
  10    0  0  0  0  0  0  0  0  0  0  0  1
  11    0  0  0  0  0  0  0  0  0  0  0  1
  12    0  0  0  0  0  0  0  0  0  0  0  0
```

Figure 6.19 Connectivity matrix.

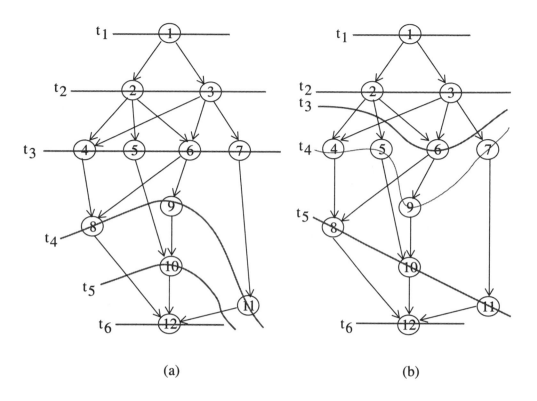

(a)   (b)

Figure 6.20 (a) Earliest possible execution time; (b) latest possible
execution time.

rows and their respective columns are eliminated from the connectivity
matrix. The process then repeats. The following sets of nodes are
obtained:

$$\{12\}, \{8, 10, 11\}, \{4, 5, 7, 9\}, \{6\}, \{2, 3\}, \{1\}$$

As shown in Figure 6.20(b), these sets of nodes are also found if
we draw wave fronts starting from the bottom up, such that the dependence relations are satisfied in the opposite direction. The time
instances indicate the latest time at which each node may be processed
without introducing any unnecessary delays.

Step 3. Find the permissible execution time. The time interval
during which each task may be scheduled without delaying the overall

Task	Earliest time	Latest time	Permissible time
1	t_1	t_1	t_1
2	t_2	t_2	t_2
3	t_2	t_2	t_2
4	t_3	t_4	t_3, t_4
5	t_3	t_4	t_3, t_4
6	t_3	t_3	t_3
7	t_3	t_4	t_3, t_4
8	t_4	t_5	t_4, t_5
9	t_4	t_4	t_4
10	t_5	t_5	t_5
11	t_4	t_5	t_4, t_5
12	t_6	t_6	t_6

Table 6.1: Permissible task execution time.

execution starts at the earliest permissible time found in the previous steps, as shown in Table 6.1.

6.4 OPERATING SYSTEMS FOR MULTIPROCESSORS

6.4.1 Operating System Functions

An operating system (OS) is a system of programs that communicate with each other and with the external world, and that are designed to coordinate the computer modules. Operating system design for multiprocessors lags far behind hardware development. However, as parallel machines become more accessible to users, considerable progress is being made in this area. From the standpoint of complexity, operating systems for multiprocessors may be classified as follows:

1. Operating systems that provide only simple functions, such as access to the hardware. Programs are cross-compiled on large

machines, then downloaded for execution. These OS make possible the use of target machines, but the user's environment is rudimentary. Some of the early multiprocessors, such as Cosmic Cube and Butterfly, had such operating systems.

2. Operating systems that are simple modifications of uniprocessor OS for use in multiprocessor environments. VMS and UNIX have been modified to run on some multiprocessors. Usually, these systems have single bus interconnections and run in a master/slave configuration.

3. Operating systems designed specifically for a multiprocessor. Examples of these are the Hydra OS, for the C.mmp multiprocessor, and Medusa, designed for the Cm* multiprocessor, both from Carnegie-Mellon University.

4. General-purpose OS designed to run on a variety of multiprocessors. The MACH OS, also developed at Carnegie-Mellon University, is the most representative example.

Operating systems perform functions such as system initialization, program partitioning and scheduling, interprocess communication and synchronization, system managing and monitoring, and others.

System Initialization
This part of the OS is ROM-based, and is intended to prepare the system for operation. One of the first functions performed is hardware and software diagnostics. The main multiprocessor modules are tested, using predetermined procedures, and they must respond satisfactorily before actual processing starts. Another initialization aspect is system-setting. The interconnection network, processing elements, and memories must be put into an initial state. Once the multiprocessor has been set for operation, programs are either downloaded into the system or developed directly on the multiprocessor.

Scheduling
In a uniprocessor, one of the OS's roles is to determine when processes are being executed. Processes requiring intensive I/O interaction tend

to run first, followed by computation-intensive processes. In a multiprocessor, the OS must provide an answer to an additional question: *where* are the processes going to run? It is required that the OS be able to schedule processes across the entire machine, unless this scheduling has been specified by the user or at the compile time. The allocation of processes to processors may be done by the OS either once at the beginning (committed), regardless of future events, or by rescheduling the processes based on the priorities of processes running at a given moment.

System Managing and Monitoring

In addition to process handling, the OS performs many other functions, which can be regarded as managing and monitoring of resources.

One important task in this group is *memory management*. Part of memory management is to handle the coherence problem; that is, to avoid inconsistencies that may occur in memory.

Another managerial function is to control the operation of the interconnection network. In some systems this includes procedures for forming messages, and for setting communication ports, links, and switches. Keeping track of routing tables and fault detections may also be functions of the OS.

The OS is usually responsible for servicing interrupts and I/O activities. Its monitoring functions include maintaining statistics related to errors or to performance.

6.4.2 Synchronization

Either two processes are independent, in which case they neither compete nor cooperate with each other, or they interact with each other. Interaction among parallel processes takes the forms of cooperation and competition. This leads to the need for *coordination* or *synchronization* in order to enable:

1. Cooperation of processes to facilitate sequence control that assures correct results; and

2. Competition of processes for shared resources by providing access control for these resources.

A simple example of cooperation is the producer-consumer relation. For instance, a producer accumulates, from an input device, a buffer of data to be consumed by a processor. A major problem with cooperating processes is *mutual exclusion.* This means the necessity of enforcing strict sequential use of a resource by competing or cooperating processes until the task is finished.

Most of the synchronization constructs or primitives used for multiprocessors still come from work on operating systems for uniprocessors. In a uniprocessor system, concurrency occurs among CPU, I/O, and memory modules. There, synchronization exists among large operations, unlike the interactions of smaller but more numerous processes in multiprocessors. In uniprocessors, access control is more critical than sequence control. Access control is typically implemented with a mutual exclusion mechanism. In this section, several synchronization techniques are presented for both access control and sequence control. However, before we discuss these techniques, we need to remember the main issues of the mutual exclusion problem.

Mutual Exclusion

A *critical region* is a section of code in a concurrent system that is controlled so that only one process at a time can enter. It is analogous to a railway track that only one train can traverse at a time. Entrance to, and exit from, these regions are controlled by a *semaphore.* "UP," or 1, indicates that the region is occupied. The procedure is that before entering the critical section, a process must examine the flag. Several problems are possible:

1. What happens if two processes simultaneously attempt to examine the flag?

2. How does a process wait if the semaphore is set to 1?

3. How is the waiting process restarted when the semaphore is reset to 0?

The first problem is the most difficult one. Some arbitration procedure is required. One possibility is to use an indivisible operation and a semaphore. The semaphore (flag) is examined and manipulated as part of

```
LOOP:   [if flag = 0 then flag = 1
            else] go to loop;
[ ] indicates indivisibility.
```

Any process wishing to enter a critical region performs this test. It loops on this piece of code until it finds the flag set to 0. A process finding the flag set loops until the flag is 0; this is called *busy wait*.

To avoid the overhead of busy wait, a process can be suspended if a critical region is occupied and a new process (which has nothing to do with the critical section) can be allowed to run on the processor. This new process is selected from the ready-to-run (RTR) queue. The suspended process is put in a separate queue to await the availability of the critical region. A new process state, called WAIT, is created by this queue where processes wait.

The semaphore is a logical construct that is used to control entry to and exit from a critical region without busy waiting. It includes the appropriate queues and procedures for suspending a process.

Interprocess synchronization can be done using critical sections. The common data can be manipulated as part of the critical section. For example, a pointer to a full data buffer can be passed from producer process to consumer process. This procedure solves the exclusionary problem. Semaphores can also be used to synchronize the producer and consumer with respect to the events "all buffers empty" or "all buffers full". A mechanism is required within the critical region which can schedule process interaction in a more structured way; for example, a process may need to jump outside the critical region depending on a condition variable. When this happens, the semaphore protecting the critical region must be signaled to allow the entry of another process.

In uniprocessor multiprogramming, synchronization takes place whenever a shared resource must be accessed by only one process at a time. In an asynchronous parallel processing system, synchronization is required to coordinate the execution of tasks to assure the correctness of the result. Basically, synchronization is imposed by data and control dependencies. Thus we can distinguish between two different synchronization mechanisms: *control-level synchronization*, usually done by processor interrupts and start or reset commands, in order to enforce control dependencies, and *data-level synchronization*, used whenever one or more variables inside a task are shared.

Let us consider an example of shared-variable synchronization. Initially assume that $X = A = 0$, and define two processes as follows:

Process 1	Process 2
$A = 10$	loop: if $X = 0$ go to loop
$X = 5$	$C = 2 * A$

Assuming that in serial execution Process 2 follows Process 1, at termination we should have $C = 20$. The shared variables are X and A, and X is a control dependence. A violation occurs when the store of A in Process 1 is delayed (for instance because of network traffic) and the read of A in Process 2 gets the old value $A = 0$ instead of $A = 10$. Therefore, the technique is to delay Process 2 until the store of A in Process 1 has taken place. Multiprocessors may include special hardware to perform synchronization.

Test-and-Set

The test-and-set method is used for coordination or synchronization as well as for creation of new processes. Basically, test-and-set enforces mutual exclusion by executing an instruction as an uninterruptable operation.

```
Test-and-set (a)
     {temp ← a; a ← 1; return a;}
     Access to shared variable
     Reset (a)
     {a ← 0;}
```

The synchronization flag a is also called *lock*. While the value of a is 0, the first process that gets the 0 is allowed to access the shared variable. Synchronization at this level implies some form of busy waiting, which ties up a processor in an idle loop and increases memory traffic. The type of lock that relies on busy waiting is called *spin-lock*. To avoid looping or waiting for a flag to change, interrupts may be used. A lock that relies on interrupts is called *suspend-lock* or *sleep-lock*.

Compare-and-Swap

Compare-and-swap is a synchronization primitive that locks a shared variable, updates it, and and then unlocks it. The semantic is

> Compare-and-swap ($r\_$old, $r\_$new, addr)
>   {temp$\leftarrow m$(addr); if temp $= r\_$old
>   then{m(addr) $\leftarrow r\_$new; $z \leftarrow 1$;}
>   else{$r\_$old $\leftarrow m$(addr); $z \leftarrow 0$;}
>   }

The shared variable $m(addr)$ is the content of a memory location called $addr$, and $r\_$old and $r\_$new are two registers used, respectively, to store the current value and the new value of the shared variable. The success of compare-and-swap is indicated by a flag z. Compare-and-swap is more powerful than test-and-set because after the new value of a shared variable is available, in one uninterrupted operation this synchronization primitive refetches the shared variable, checks whether its value has been changed, and if not, performs an update.

Fetch-and-Add

A simple yet effective interprocessor synchronization called fetch-and-add was proposed in [Gottlieb, Grishman, Kruskal, McAalifte, Randolf, and Smir 1983] and implemented in the New York University Ultracomputer. It is a synchronization primitive designed for multiprocessors. While it is based on the idea used in test-and-set, its operation is different. In reponse to n simultaneous accesses, test-and-set yields at most one go-ahead, whereas fetch-and-add hands out n different numbers. So the effect of n simultaneous accesses is the same as if they had occured in some (unspecified) ordering. In other words, instead of lining up processes as in the case of test-and-set, in fetch-and-add each process is given a unique number and each goes further.

The format of this operation is fetch-and-add (x, e) where x is an integer variable and e is an integer expression. The indivisible operation is defined to return the old value of x and to replace x by the sum $x + e$. The semantic is

> fetch-and-add (x, e)
>   {$temp \leftarrow x, x \leftarrow temp + e$

return $temp$}

The fetch-and-add must satisfy the *serialization* principle: if x is a shared variable and many fetch-and-add operations simultaneously address x, the effect of these operations is exactly what it would be if they occurred in some unspecified serial order. Consider that x is a shared variable and PE_i and PE_j execute simultaneously.

PE_i: $temp_i \leftarrow$ Fetch-and-add (x, e_i)
PE_j: $temp_j \leftarrow$ Fetch-and-add (x, e_j)
   then either

$$temp_i \leftarrow x \qquad \text{or} \qquad temp_i \leftarrow x + e_j$$
$$temp_j \leftarrow x + e_j \qquad\qquad temp_j \leftarrow x$$

In either case the value of x at the end becomes $x + e_i + e_j$. Fetch-and-add can be generalized to any operation fetch-and-operation (x, e). This can be implemented either in the switching network or in the memory. ALUs are necessary. If fetch-and-operations are available, other synchronization functions such as test-and-set may be performed. For example, fetch-and-operation $(x, true)$ is equivalent to

test-and-set(x)
     {$temp \leftarrow x$
     $x \leftarrow true$
   return $temp$ }

Fetch-and-add is efficient for forking processes with identical code that operate on different indices. For example, an algorithm may have the form

doall $I = 1$ to 15
     loop body
   end do

Suppose that there are no dependencies between loop iterations. Processes may be spawned by each processor performing a fetch-and-add on index I prior to working on a specific loop iteration. Each processor will return a specific value of I that can be used in the loop. This may be implemented as

```
i ← fetch-and-add(I, 1)
  while i ≤ 15 do
  {loop body
    i ← fetch-and-add(I, 1);
  }
```

Counter Method

The *counter method* synchronization is used for a larger number of processes. Let's consider four processes, P_1, P_2, P_3, and P_4, which access a shared variable. A counter is associated with the shared variable. Each process P_n may access the shared-variable location only when the counter contains the same number as the key assigned to that process.

Barriers

Semaphores are used primarily for *access control*, to resolve competition among parallel processors. Barrier synchronization is used for *sequence control;* that is, to ensure data dependencies among cooperating processes. All the processes that synchronize at the barrier must reach the barrier before any of them can continue. A barrier synchronization primitive has a queue for temporarily holding processes and a counter for keeping track of the number of processes in the queue. Initially, the counter is reset to zero. The barrier is implemented as

```
barrier(N)
{count := count + 1;
    if (count < N) then
        {stop process and place in barrier queue;}
    else
        {resume all processes on barrier queue;
          reset count;}
}
```

For a barrier synchronizing N processes, the first $N - 1$ processes arriving at the barrier are stopped and placed in the queue until the Nth process arrives, after which the processes are allowed to proceed.

Data-level synchronization can also be implemented through the *message-passing* method. Instead of using a shared variable, processes send and receive messages. Synchronization is accomplished because a message can be received only after it has been sent, and some actions are triggered in another process only after the message is received.

6.4.3 The MACH Operating System

MACH is a state-of-the-art operating system developed at Carnegie-Mellon University [Accetta et al. 1986]. It is essentially an extension of UNIX for multiprocessors. MACH supports several languages and runs with small adaptations on the Sequent Balance, the Encore Multimax, the BBN Butterfly, and other machines. It consists of a kernel and a nonkernel for user-level services. The basic services provided by the MACH kernel are:

- Interprocess communication;

- Task management, including the creation, destruction, and control of threads of execution;

- Virtual memory management, including paging and the sharing of memory between tasks;

- Resource management, including the assignment of physical resources to tasks for performance or monitoring purposes; and

- Controlled access to physical devices.

Most traditional operating system functions, such as synchronization, semaphores, file servers, and so on, are performed outside of the MACH kernel in user-level server programs. This arrangement has the advantage of increased modularity and protection among unrelated operating system functions. It provides a natural separation of functions in a multiprocessor system. Individual components of MACH can run on different processors.

Execution Control Primitives
MACH provides two execution control abstractions:

- *Task* refers to all resources associated with a process; for example, address space, file descriptors, port-access, and so on. A task does not perform computations itself, but serves as a framework for threads. Each task is associated with an address map that describes the regions of memory that a process uses.

- *Thread* refers to a control unit for a process, containing the minimal process state associated with a computation program counter, a stack pointer, hardware register information, and more. Thus, a UNIX process is a MACH task with a single thread.

A task plus a thread is equivalent to what we have been calling a process. A MACH task may have several threads, and multiple threads may be active at the same time. Each thread may access all of the task's resources, including shared memory. A thread has a program counter and some other controls, and can perform computations on a task's data. An example of a simple thread is a procedure call. One thread can temporarily halt another thread's operation by sending a suspend message to that thread's port.

The MACH designers have selected the approach of having multiple threads within a task because it produces less overhead than creating processes. Moreover, the communication between threads within a task is easier than communication between processes. This approach also has the capability of changing the granularity from fine-grain to coarse-grain, which is essential in general-purpose multiprocessors.

Tasks are created by other tasks; thus there are parent tasks and child tasks. A child task inherits from its parent task the same address space, resources, and port rights. Once a task is created it may evolve independent of the parent task. The memory space inherited from its parent task may be modified such that by overlapping memory space with other tasks it may exchange data with them. Tasks are created without any threads. Threads may be created later and destroyed via kernel calls on task ports. A thread may be assigned for execution to an available processor and, after termination, return the processor to the processor pool.

Each task may be associated with some resources. As in the case of memory, several tasks may share the same resources. A task indicates the use of a resource by locking it, but the rest of the resources are not locked.

Communication Mechanism

Interprocess communication in the MACH system is based on two elements: the *port* and the *message*. A port is a kernel-protected queue where messages may be queued or dequeued. A message contains a fixed-length header and data objects used in communication between threads. The length of the message varies. MACH supports message-passing as well as shared-memory techniques.

Ports cannot be accessed directly by user programs, but are referenced by the kernel. Attached to a port object are a set of access rights, including the ability to remove a message from a port and the ability to add a message to a port.

Tasks communicate through ports created by themselves as necessary. When a task creates a port it has the access rights of that port. Through messages, it may then transfer that port's access rights to other tasks.

6.4.4 Multiprocessor Operating System Organization

This section describes four basic organizations that have been used in the design of multiprocessor operating systems. These are *master/slave, separate executive* for each processor, *symmetric* (or anonymous) treatment of each processor, and *floating control* between individual processors. For many current multiprocessors, the master/slave organization is used. This type is the easiest to implement and can often be produced by making simple extensions to a uniprocessor OS. Unfortunately, this type of OS also tends to be inefficient in its control and utilization of system resources. All components of the OS are heavily dependent on the master component. This tends to cause bottlenecks and, in the worst case, can lead to complete system failure due to a failure in the master. This organization is very poor from the standpoint of graceful degradation, and is very susceptible to catastrophic failure. While it is not clear which of the other organizations is best, they all appear to offer better performance characteristics; however, they are more complex and more costly to implement.

Master/Slave Organization

In general, a master/slave operating system has the following character-istics: The operating system is permanently assigned to one particular processor and always operates in that processor. If a slave processor re-quires service, that service can only be provided by the executive. The slave must interrupt the executive and request service. It must then wait until the program currently being executed is interrupted and the executive is dispatched to the slave processor. The executive routines need not be reentrant, because only one processor accesses them. Since one processor has overall control, there is no conflict or lockout problem for the control tables used by the executive. The system is subject to catastrophic failure in the case of a failure in the master CPU, or at least severe degradation in the case of a failure in a slave processor.

The overall system is comparatively inflexible, since functions are permanently assigned to various processors. The processing load dis-tribution between processors is not evenly balanced. Idle time on par-ticular processors is a function of the current task and the mapping of the required functions to functions performed in each processor.

The main advantage of this organization is that very simple software and hardware structures are required. Interprocessor communication and synchronization can be very simple and well defined.

This operating system is most effective for special applications in which the workload is well defined and relatively static (unchanging as a function of time). This type of system is best designed with a particular application in mind; then the design can be directed toward this application. It is a poor choice for a general-purpose system that executes a dynamically changing workload.

Separate Executive

A very different operating system organization is implemented when each processor has its own identical copy of the operating system. The characteristics of this system are quite different from the master/slave organization. In this configuration, each processor can service its own needs. Therefore, no service requests or service from a single executive are required. This eliminates a major bottleneck problem of the first scheme. Because some supervisor code must be shared, parts must now be reentrant. An alternative to this is to replicate this code in each local processor memory that requires it. Because each processor now has its own set of control tables, this virtually eliminates the contention and deadlock problems associated with OS control and status tables.

Because each processor now has its own executive, the system is much less sensitive to catastrophic failure. A failure of one or more processors will cause a proportional loss of system capability, but will not bring down the entire multiprocessor system. However, in this configuration the restarting of an individual failed processor can be quite difficult.

In effect, each processor executive must have its own set of I/O hardware and operating system primitives. This is advantageous in terms of increased flexibility and performance, but a penalty is paid in increased complexity and hardware. For this reason, any reconfiguration of the I/O hardware (or software) may require manual intervention, as opposed to automatic switching.

In this configuration the OS code may be replicated in each of the processors, or a single copy, placed in one CPU local memory, may be accessed by all the processors. The former method has the disadvantage of requiring vast amounts of redundant code and much extra memory. The latter method causes one processor (the one with direct access to the executive) to operate much faster than other processors (those that must request and receive access to the kernel). This causes uneven load balancing and is very inefficient.

Symmetric (or Anonymous) Treatment

This is the most difficult method of operation, both from a design viewpoint and from an operating viewpoint. However, the benefits of this configuration may well be worth the effort. This mode is characterized by a master that floats from one processor to another. However, several processors may be simultaneously executing supervisor service routines.

Because each processor is treated symmetrically in this configuration, better load balancing can be achieved over all types of resources. In the ideal case, each processor possesses identical software, which allows any available processor to perform the next required task. Conflicts in service requests can be resolved by a set of priorities that can be fixed or under dynamic control. The priorities in use also depend on which processor the executive is currently residing in. Supervisory code must be reentrant because several processors may be executing the same routines simultaneously. Table access conflicts and lockout delays can occur; however, these will always be present when multiple executives are run simultaneously. These tables are necessary for interprocessor communication.

The principal advantages of this operating system configuration are that it provides better graceful degradation capability; it provides greater flexibility to run in reduced-capacity mode with fewer processors; and true redundancy is provided in case of single-processor failure. This method makes the most efficient use of available system resources. In addition, this configuration is the best suited to general-purpose processing, in which the tasks to be performed may not be known a priori.

Distributed Operating System

This organization differs from the one described above in the type of functions performed in each processor. In the previous section, each processor ran an identical copy of the entire executive. Each OS was self-contained and did not depend on the other processors. In a distributed configuration, the various OS utilities and functions are distributed among the various processors. Each processor is dedicated to a particular utility or function. Together they implement all OS functions.

For this organization, the OS is divided into several disjoint utilities, with no guarantee that a given processor contains a copy of the code for any particular utility. A given processor is allowed to execute code only if that code is in the processor's local memory. This avoids the need for global memory access, reentrant code, and most interprocessor synchronization.

Since no processor is guaranteed to be capable of executing any particular piece of utility code, it may be necessary for a program's flow to switch processors when a utility function is invoked or a system call is made. Trap or subroutine call instructions cannot be used because they are incapable of crossing processor boundaries. In this system a message/mailbox mechanism can be implemented to provide interprocessor communication.

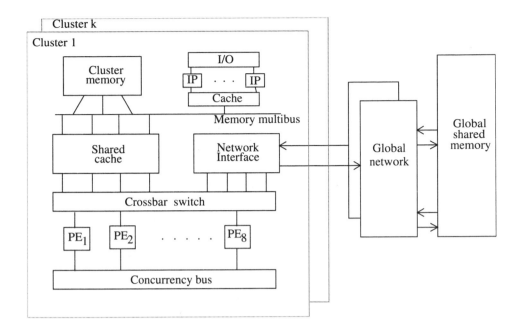

Figure 6.21 Architecture of Cedar multiprocessor.

6.5 THE CEDAR MULTIPROCESSOR

The Cedar system is a multiprocessor developed at the University of Illinois [Kuck, Davidson, Lawrie, and Sameh 1986]. The Cedar combines vector processing, multiprocessor architecture, a hierarchical memory system, high-speed interconnection networks, restructuring compiler technology, and algorithm design. The architecture and software of this system are described below.

6.5.1 Architecture

The hierarchical architecture of the Cedar multiprocessor is shown in Figure 6.21. At the lowest level of the hierarchy are processing elements. The next level is a cluster consisting of eight PEs, a memory, and an interconnection network. At the highest level, there are several clusters interconnected through a global network and sharing a global memory.

A Cedar cluster is a modified Alliant FX/8 multiprocessor. The
PEs are custom-made pipelined processors implementing the Motorola
68020 microprocessor instruction set, enhanced with some high-level
vector instructions. Parallel loop iterations are assigned to different
processors. The concurrency control bus shared by the eight PEs provides hardware synchronization among processors. Special instructions
that use this bus allow PEs to perform self-scheduling by dynamically
assigning loop iterations to available processors at run time, and provide a fast mechanism for enforcing data dependencies between loop
iterations.

The eight PEs share a 128-Kbyte cache through an 8×8 crossbar
switch. The cache is interleaved and uses write-back update policy.
The four additional ports of the crossbar are used to connect to a
network interface for off-cluster communication. In addition to the
cache memory, each cluster has up to 32 Mbytes of local memory in
order to reduce traffic to the global memory.

Each cluster may be equipped with a number of interactive processors (IPs) used to execute the OS programs and to perform I/O and
other user tasks. The IPs connect through a cache to a multibus that
allows access to cluster memory.

The global interconnection network connecting clusters to the global
shared memory consists of two unidirectional Omega networks. The
networks are multistage, pipelined, and packet-switched. They use 8×8
crossbar switches as building blocks, with 80-bit-wide data paths.

The global shared memory consists of several interleaved modules.
A synchronization processor is present in each memory module which
implements a set of indivisible synchronization operations. The synchronization processors implement critical sections for mutual exclusion
as requested by the cluster processors.

6.5.2   Software

The Cedar system supports three levels of parallelism: vector, loop,
and task parallelism. The finest level is provided at processor level
through vector instructions. Medium-grain parallelism is the parallelism at cluster level, provided by cluster processors cooperating in
loop executions. Task-level parallelism allows parts of a program to

execute asynchronously across Cedar clusters. To exploit the parallel processing capabilities of the Cedar architecture, a multitasking operating system, parallel languages, and a restructuring compiler have been developed.

The Cedar operating system, Xylem, is a modification of Alliant's Concentrix operating system, extended for multitasking and virtual memory management of Cedar's memory hierarchy. Both are UNIX extensions. A Xylem process consists of one or more cluster tasks. Each cluster task executes on a single Cedar cluster. Multiple cluster tasks execute asynchronously across the Cedar system. Xylem provides system calls for starting and stopping tasks, and for waiting for tasks to finish. System calls are also provided for coarse-grained intertask synchronization. In addition to multitasking, Xylem supports multiprogramming.

The Xylem virtual memory provides convenient access to the Cedar physical memory hierarchy. Each cluster task of a Xylem process has its own virtual address space, made up of fixed-size pages. Each page has attributes that indicate accessibility (share or private) and locality (global or cluster). Xylem implements run-time mechanisms for dynamic memory allocation. Cache coherence is software-based, using a directory scheme.

Cedar Fortran is the main language used, although other languages such as C, Lisp, and Prolog are also available. Cedar Fortran allows the declaration of variables and arrays at global or cluster level. There are routines for spawning new cluster tasks. There are also constructs to express DOALL and DOACROSS parallelisms. For synchronization purposes, the language includes special subroutines.

One of the goals of the Cedar design team was to implement an efficient multiprocessor by balancing the system. Part of this effort went into compiler optimizations for vectorization, parallelization, and memory allocation. The parallel language is being restructured by the Paraphrase compiler through an iterative process. Most of the restructuring techniques discussed in Chapter 3 have been implemented in the Paraphrase compiler.

6.6   HYPERCUBE COMPUTERS

The hypercube represents a class of message-passing architectures using cube (or exchange) interconnection topology. Hypercube computers were some of the first and most successful commercial multiprocessors. Each node is connected through bidirectional, asynchronous point-to-point communication channels to n other nodes. The first hypercube system was built at Caltech in the early 1980s as an experimental parallel computer for scientific numeric computations. A 64-node "cosmic cube" was designed and investigated; the success of this project stimulated the design of commercial hypercubes at several companies, including Intel, NCUBE, AMETEK, and others.

6.6.1   Hypercube Topology

A hypercube multiprocessor consists of 2^n processors, consecutively numbered with binary integers using a string of n bits. Each processor is connected to every other processor whose binary number differs from its own by exactly one bit. As described in Chapter 4, this connection scheme places the processors at the vertices of an n-dimensional cube. Hypercube interconnection networks for n varying from 1 to 4 are shown in Figure 6.22. The hypercube has the property that it can be defined inductively. A hypercube of order 0 has a simple node, and the hypercube of order $n + 1$ is constructed by taking two hypercubes of order n and connecting their respective nodes. This interconnection has several properties of great importance for parallel processing, such as these:

1. As the number of processors increases, the number of connection wires and related hardware (such as ports) increases only logarithmically, so that systems with a very large number of processors become feasible.

2. A hypercube is a superset of other interconnection networks such as rings, MCNs, trees, and others, because these can be embedded into a hypercube by ignoring some hypercube connections.

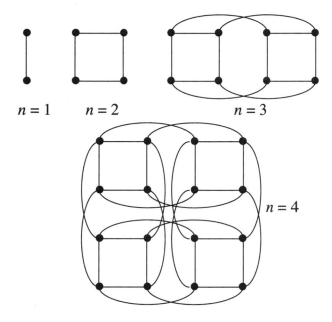

Figure 6.22 Hypercube interconnection.

3. Hypercubes are scalable, a property that results directly from the fact that hypercube interconnections can be defined recursively.

4. Hypercubes have simple routing schemes. A message-routing policy may be to send a message to the neighbor whose binary tag agrees with the tag of the final destination in the next bit position, with the bits scanned in some order. The path length for sending a message between any two nodes is exactly the number of bits in which their tag bits differ. The maximum is of course n, and the average is $n/2$. Numerous possible paths connecting any two nodes exist; this redundancy can be used to enhance the communication bandwidth and the fault tolerance of the hypercube network.

Hypercube nodes are usually identical. However, they do not have to be identical as long as their message-routing protocols are the same.

In some heterogeneous systems, some nodes may have special I/O or processing capabilities.

6.6.2   Design Issues

Generally, a hypercube node consists of a processor, local memory, communication ports for other nodes, and I/O ports. The fact that the system memory is distributed over all the nodes, and is physically mixed with processors, constitutes a desirable feature, important to the progress toward constructing very large scale systems. Below, we discuss some hardware and software design issues, then show how they have been resolved in practical systems.

Latency

The message communication latency may be defined as the interval between the time when the beginning of a message leaves the source node and the time when the end of the message reaches the destination.

In hypercubes, the processor and memory reside in the same node, so processor-memory communication is not a problem as it was in shared-memory multiprocessors. However, processes running on separate processors need to communicate with each other via messages. It is believed that for many applications interprocess communication is less frequent than memory access. This implies that network traffic is reduced, as compared to that of shared-memory multiprocessors, and also that some larger latency may be tolerated. Because of this, the scaling of systems to a large number of nodes is more feasible than for shared-memory multiprocessors.

Node Granularity

The node size, or granularity, is influenced mainly by the amount of memory per node and the processor complexity. Earlier hypercube systems used many chips mounted on a board to implement one node. The trend has been toward reducing the number of chips per node while increasing processor computing power and memory size. The goal is to achieve one node per chip, including processor, memory, and message routing functions. Only then may some packaging and cooling constraints be overcome to build systems with hundreds of thousands of nodes.

Routing Protocol

A message exchange between nodes consists of a sequence of packets pipelined through the network. The packet at the head of the message sets the route followed by the rest of the packets. In most hypercube computers, message routing is software-controlled. An important design goal is to free the processor from time-consuming routing processing by implementing this function in specialized hardware.

Wormhole routing has been proposed in [Dally and Seitz 1987] and has been implemented in the AMETEK 2010 multiprocessor and recently in the Intel Touchstone Delta supercomputer. Wormhole routing differs from store-and-forward packet switching. Packets are handled by special switches rather than by node software. When the packet at the head of the message finds a channel occupied, the packets in the sequence are blocked where they are until the head proceeds. The packet at the head of the message, usually consisting of only a few bits, sets up the switches such that the rest of the packets can follow without wasting more time. This routing technique reduces the amount of node storage as well as the software necessary for handling messages.

I/O

The early hypercube systems were intended for computation-intensive applications with modest I/O requirements. As hypercubes become more general-purpose, the need for I/O bandwidth increases.

The NCUBE/ten system, which has up to 1,024 nodes, has provided eight I/O boards, each board handling the I/O requirements of a 128-node subcube.

Mapping Algorithms to a Hypercube

Although hypercubes are general-purpose MIMD computers, given their processor uniformity and network regularity, they are most suitable for highly regular computational problems. To execute a program on the hypercube, the user first compiles or assembles the code on a host machine and then loads the resulting object code onto node processors. Here a process is a sequential program that sends and receives messages. A single node may contain several processes. The parallelism is obtained by concurrent execution of processes in different nodes. Also, the processes assigned to the same node can be processed in a multiprogrammed manner. The process allocation may be static or dynamic.

The distribution of processes to processors is a tradeoff between load balancing and message locality.

In the Intel hypercube, for example, the host and nodes operate asynchronously, and coordination is achieved only by the exchange of messages containing program data or control information. First, the process must "open" or establish a communication channel between the two processes involved. One process then executes a "send" to transmit a message, while the other executes a "receive" to read the message. While the channel remains open, a process may send and receive multiple messages from other processes.

The operating systems are usually UNIX extensions and are partitioned into layers, with kernels residing in each node. The node kernel supervises process execution and sends, receives, and queues messages. The kernel performs the construction and the interpretation of message headers from the descriptor information. Messages being sent are queued in the sending process instead of being copied into the kernel message buffer, unless the message is local to the node. The inner kernel schedules user processes.

6.6.3   From Hypercubes to Touchstones

Hypercube computers have been contemplated since the appearance of microprocessors in the 1970s. The first hypercube multiprocessor was built and used at Caltech in 1983. Since then, interest in this type of parallel computer has grown so fast that today there are several companies offering a wide range of hypercubes. In this short but rapid evolution, we can distinguish two generations of hypercubes. Recently, Intel Corporation, which has manufactured two generations of hypercubes, has taken the lead in message-passing supercomputers with a new architecture that is not hypercube-connected. The new series, called Touchstone, uses powerful mesh-connected microprocessors.

First Generation of Hypercubes
The machines in the first generation include the Caltech Cosmic Cube, the Intel iPCS 1, the AMETEK System 14, the NCUBE/ten, and the Floating Point Systems T Series. We will focus on the NCUBE/ten because it is one of the most powerful.

The NCUBE/ten is described in [Hayes, Mudge, Stout, Colley, and Palmer 1986]. It has up to 1,024 nodes; each node consists of a processor chip and several memory chips. The processor is a powerful custom-made 32-bit processor, capable of executing a VAX-like instruction set, and the node memory is 128 Kbytes. To support I/O activities, the NCUBE/ten is equiped with eight front-end host processor boards, each board directly connected to a set of 128 nodes. Thus each node has eleven bidirectional channels: ten for other nodes and one for the I/O board. The internode channels operate at 10 MHz, achieving a 1 Mbyte/sec transfer rate in each direction. The NCUBE/ten achieves a peak performance of 500 Mflops.

The operating system is an extension of UNIX. It has a layer running on the I/O front-end boards, called Axis, and another layer running on hypercube nodes, called VERTEX. The messages have fields for source, destination, length, and type. They may be as long as 64 Kbytes. A message is broken into packets of 512 bytes.

Second Generation of Hypercubes

In 1988, some more powerful message-passing systems were introduced. This is regarded as the beginning of the second generation. Representative machines of this generation are the Intel iPSC/2 and the AMETEK 2010 series.

The main characteristics of this generation are: (1) 32-bit processors with integrated floating-point accelerators; (2) large node memory, facilitated by the availability of megabit-chip RAM technology; and (3) message routing that is performed in hardware and becomes invisible to programmer. The elimination of software overhead for message passing, coupled with the technological improvements in CPU and memory, has improved the node performance by one or two orders of magnitude. Moreover, because the message communication speed has been improved, second-generation machines are better balanced. In the first generation the ratio of CPU speed to message communication was about 1:10, which indicates that message communication was the bottleneck. Improvements have been made in the I/O system as disk interfaces with file systems have been introduced.

An interesting aspect of the second generation is the fact that a departure from the hypercube topology has occurred. In the AMETEK

2010 series, the network topology is mesh-connection rather than hypercube. As the number of processors increases and message routing is improved, better alternatives to hypercube topology are sought. For now, mesh connection is one such alternative.

The first and second generations did not aggressively push VLSI chip technology, and most systems were built with off-the-shelf components. It may be possible to build larger, more powerful systems by taking advantage of submicron VLSI technology that may allow one to build an entire node on a chip.

Intel Touchstone Delta

Intel Touchstone is a family of supercomputers characterized by their mesh-connection topology, their wormhole message routing, and their use of the most powerful microprocessors. Touchstone Gamma, the first of the series, was produced in 1990; it has 128 processors, collectively delivering a peak performance of approximately 10 Gflops. The next in the series, the Delta, was produced in 1991; it has 512 processors, delivering 30 Gflops. The Sigma, produced in 1992, has 2,048 processors. This series is expected to provide Tflop performance by the mid-1990s.

The organization of the Delta computer is shown in Figure 6.23. There are 512 specially designed VLSI message-router chips, interconnected in a two-dimensional mesh. The router chip was designed at Caltech by Seitz and others. Its channels are byte-wide, unidirectional. It is capable of an 80 Mbyte/sec data transfer rate.

Attached to each router chip is a processor node built around an Intel 80860 microprocessor. Each of these microprocessors integrates over 2 million gates and is capable of over 10 Mflops. The data bus is 64 bits wide. The power of the Delta machine resides primarily in the individual power of these processors, and in the innovations of the message-routing network.

6.7   BIBLIOGRAPHICAL NOTES AND FURTHER READING

An excellent book presenting many aspects of software and examples of multiprocessors is [Almasi and Gottlieb 1989]. Several papers in

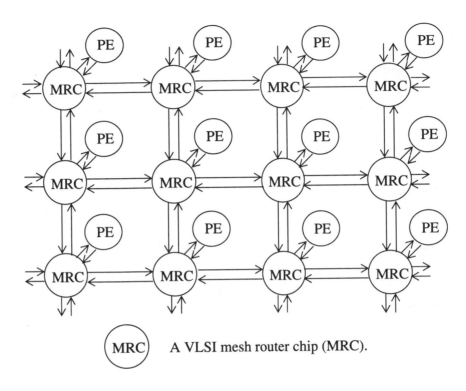

A VLSI mesh router chip (MRC).

Figure 6.23 The interconnection network in the Delta supercomputer.

[Hwang and DeGroot 1989] are good tutorials on multiprocesors. A review of important issues in multiprocessors can be found in [Gajski and Peirr 1985].

The cache coherence problem has been studied in [Dubois and Briggs 1982], [Archibald and Baer 1986], and others. A survey of cache coherence methods for multiprocessor memories can be found in [Stenstrom 1990]. Directory-based cache coherence schemes are presented in [Chaiken, Fields, Kurihara, and Agarwal 1990]. Software-oriented cache coherence is presented in [Cheong and Veidenbaum 1990]. Snoopy cache controllers for multiprocessors have been investigated in [Goodman and Woest 1988]. Synchronization methods in multicache systems are presented in [Dubois, Scheurich, and Briggs 1988].

Methods for partitioning and scheduling programs on multiprocessors were developed by Sarkar [Sarkar 1989] and by Polychronopoulos [Polychronopoulos 1988]. The Paraphrase compiler, developed at the University of Illinois in the early 1980s, was one of the first multiprocessor compilers [Kuck et al. 1981]. The Bulldog compiler was developed by Ellis [Ellis 1986], and the multiflow trace compacting compiler by Fisher [Fisher 1987]. The MACH operating system project was conducted at Carnegie-Mellon University, and one of the first papers describing MACH is [Accetta, Baron, Bolosky, and Golub 1986].

Interconnection networks for multiprocessors have been studied extensively. One of the early books on the subject is [Siegel 1984]. Surveys of multistage interconnection networks are found in [Feng and Wu 1979] and [Adams, Agrawal, and Siegel 1987]. Properties of interconnection networks and routing algorithms are presented in [Leighton 1992].

The Ultracomputer project at New York University was based on the work of Schwartz, described in [Schwartz 1980]. A version of the actual machine is presented in [Gottlieb, Grishman, Kruskal, McAalifte, Randolf, and Smir 1983]. The Cedar project at the University of Illinois, under the leadership of David Kuck, is described in [Kuck, Davidson, Lawrie, and Sameh 1986]. A survey of commercially available hypercube systems is [Shih and Fier 1989]. The NCUBE/ten is presented in [Hayes, Mudge, Stout, Colley, and Palmer 1986]. The wormhole message-routing technique used in the Intel Touchstone Delta and other supercomputers was developed at Caltech by Dally and Seitz [Dally and Seitz 1987].

6.8   PROBLEMS

6.1.A. An MIMD algorithm has the task dependence graph shown in Figure 6.24. The number next to each task indicates the amount of time needed to process that particular task. For example, task T_5 requires 4 time units.

(a) Derive the permissible task initiation table; that is, the earliest and the latest time for each task.

(b) What is the minimum number of processors needed for this algorithm in order not to introduce unnecessary delays? Explain.

(c) Propose a general algorithm to find the minimum number of

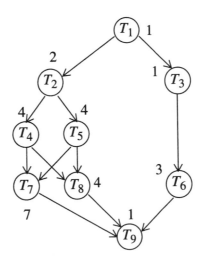

Figure 6.24 The dependence graph for Problem 6.1.A.

processors for any arbitrary task graph.

Solution.

(a) Permissible task initiation table:

Task	Earliest time	Latest time
1	1	1
2	2	2
3	2	11
4	4	4
5	4	4
6	3	12
7	8	8
8	8	11
9	15	15

(b) Two processors; one for the critical path, $T_1 \rightarrow T_2 \rightarrow T_4 \rightarrow T_7 \rightarrow T_9$, and the other for T_3, T_5, T_6 and T_8.

(c) Algorithm:

1. Find all tasks in which the earliest and the latest time are the same, and allocate one processor to these tasks. Add more pro-

cessors as necessary. E.g.: $T_1, T_2, T_4, T_5, T_9, \ldots$ Since T_4 or T_5 is in the critical path, pick only one.

2. After step 1, we know the smallest number of processors needed.

3. Fill in time slots by allocating tasks to processors as per step 1.

4. Fill in the time slots that are still available with other tasks. If there is no time slot that can be used for a task, add a new processor, until all tasks are allocated. Give priority to the slots with the smallest difference between the earliest and the latest time.

6.2.A. [Prasanna 1991] What is the minimum number of crosspoints in a 3-stage rearrangeable nonblocking Clos network? Provide an asymptotic bound.

Solution.

$$O(n\sqrt{n})$$

6.3.A. Prove that mesh connections and trees of all dimensions can be embedded in a hypercube so that neighboring nodes are mapped to neighbors in the hypercube.

Solution.

(a) *Mesh.* Let M_{ij} be a node in row i, column j of an $N \times N$ mesh $(1 \le i \le N,\ 1 \le j \le N)$, and let $g(k)$ be the kth word of the gray code with $n = \log_2 N$ bits.

Then M_{ij} can be mapped to the node $g(i) \cdot g(j)$ of the 2^{2n}-node hypercube, where $g(i) \cdot g(j)$ means the concatenation of two binary numbers $g(i)$ and $g(j)$.

Since $g(k)$ and $g((k \pm 1) \bmod N)$ differ in a single bit, the neighbors of M_{ij} will also be neighbors in the hypercube.

For example, if $N = 8$, the node M_{22} is mapped to node (001001) of the 2^6-node hypercube.

(b) *Tree.* Let d be the depth of the tree and b be the maximum number of branches per node. Let T_{lm} be a node in the tree where l is

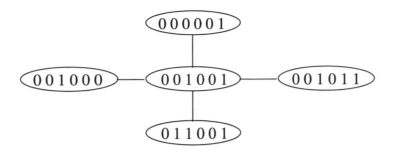

Figure 6.25 Figure illustrating Problem 6.3.A.

the level of the node (root = level 0) and the node is the mth child of its parent.

$$(1 \le l \le d, \quad 1 \le m \le b)$$

Then T_{lm} can be mapped to the node

$$(A_b^d A_{b-1}^d \ldots A_1^d, A_b^{d-1} A_{b-1}^{d-1} \ldots A_1^{d-1}, \ldots A_m^l \ldots, A_b^1 A_{b-1}^1 \ldots A_1^1)$$

of the 2^{db}-node hypercube, where

$A_i^j = 0$ for all $i, d \ge j > l$
$A_i^l = 0$ for $i \ne m$
$A_i^l = 1$ for $i = m$

and

A_i^j is same as its parent for all $i, l > j \ge 1$.

In other words, the root of the tree is mapped to $(000...0)$ and a child node and its parent node differ in a single bit only.

Therefore, all the child nodes of a parent node in the tree will also be neighbors in the hypercube.

For example, a binary tree $(b = 2)$ of depth $2(d = 2)$ can be mapped to a 2^4-node hypercube, as in Figure 6.26.

6.4.A.

(a) For the execution graph shown in Figure 6.27, write the control flow using fork/join constructs.

(b) Can this be expressed using parbegin/parend? Explain.

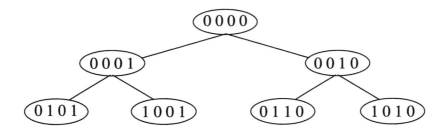

Figure 6.26 Figure illustrating Problem 6.3.A.

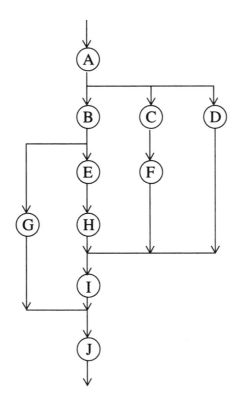

Figure 6.27 Execution graph for Problem 6.4.A.

Solution.

$$A$$
$$j_1 = 3$$
fork b
fork c
fork d
$$J$$
exit

c: C
$$F$$
join j_1, exit

d: D

(a)   join j_1, exit

b: B
$$j_2 = 2$$
fork g
fork e

g: G
join j_2, exit

e: E
$$H$$
join j_1
$$I$$
join j_2, exit

(b) This execution graph cannot be expressed with parbegin/parend because loops are not nested.

6.5.A.

```
for     i = 1, 6
        fork next
end i
next: for j = 1, 4
```
$$a(i,j) = a(i-1, j-1) + b(i, j-2)$$
$$b(i,j) = a(i-1, j) * b(i-1, j-1)$$
```
        end j
join 6
```

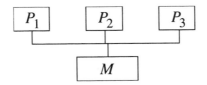

Figure 6.28 A 3-processor system for Problem 6.5.A.

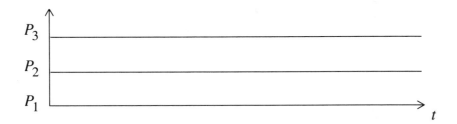

Figure 6.29 Scheduling diagram for Problem 6.5.A.

This program is to be executed on a 3-processor shared-memory multiprocessor as shown in Figure 6.28.

(a) Explain how processes are spawned, how many there are, and how they are to be executed.

(b) Identify the dependencies between processes and propose either a hardware or a software solution to handle these dependencies.

(c) Schedule the execution of processes on the 3-processor system. Show the load of each processor. For this, use the diagram in Figure 6.29. Assume that processor P_1 is running the original program and that it is the one that spawns processes.

Note: Write down whatever assumptions you make.

Solution.

(a) Each i loop represents a process. The address "next" is passed to the processor as the process is being spawned for an i. Six processes are spawned.

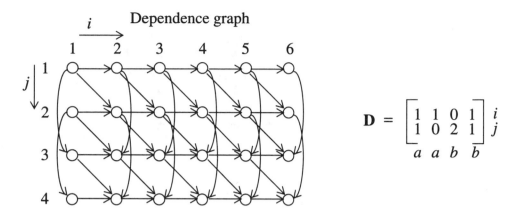

Figure 6.30 Dependencies for Problem 6.5.A.

(b) Dependencies are shown in Figure 6.30. There are dependencies between i loops. Dependencies between j loops of the same i loop can be neglected because they are executed by the same processor. The jth loop of process P_i ($1 \leq i \leq 6$) cannot execute until the jth loop of P_{i-1} has finished. Therefore, synchronization is needed. Synchronization can be performed by using shared variables as flags. Define flag (i, j) as a shared variable for process i, loop j. Flag (i, j) is initialized as false and is set to true by process $i - 1$ by an atomic instruction when it finishes loop j.

(c) The scheduling of processes to processors is shown in Figure 6.31.

6.1.B. The following recursive equation is to be executed on a message-passing multiprocessor with three processors interconnected as shown in Figure 6.32:

$$\mathbf{x}(k) = \mathbf{A}\mathbf{x}(k-1) + \mathbf{B}\mathbf{x}(k-2)$$

where $\mathbf{x}$ is a 3×1 vector, and $\mathbf{A}$ and $\mathbf{B}$ are 3×3 matrices.

(a) Partition the problem (i.e., form processes) and schedule.

(b) Describe the features of an operating system appropriate for performing this job, in as much detail as you can.

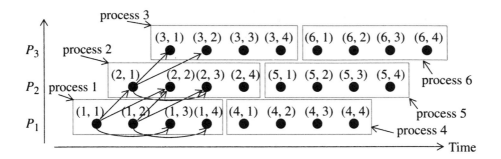

Figure 6.31 Scheduling processes to processors in Problem 6.5.A.

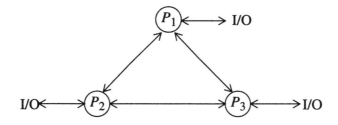

Figure 6.32 Message-passing multiprocessor for Problem 6.1.B.

6.2.B. Suppose that programs A and B from Problem 4.5.B are executed now on a shared-memory multiprocessor with $N/2$ processors. Explain briefly the key issues in each case. Write a high-level MIMD program, including comments, to perform the computations. Discuss the processing time for cases A and B in relation to the interconnection network, the memory structure, and the operating system controls.

6.3.B. Consider the loop

```
for i = 1 to n
    P(i) = A(i) * B(i)
    S(i) = P(i) + S(i − 1)
end i
```

Determine the execution time of this loop for each of the following computer systems. Briefly explain your answers.

(a) An SIMD system with n PEs and a ring interconnection network.

(b) An SIMD system with $((n/2) - 1)$ PEs and a perfect-shuffle interconnection network.

(c) An MIMD system with $(n-2)$ processors in which each processor can communicate with all other processors.

Addition and multiplication require one and two time units, respectively. Memory access time is ignored, and data transfer time from one PE to another PE is assumed to take one time unit.

6.4.B. The task graph for a MIMD algorithm is given by the connectivity matrix

	1	2	3	4	5	6	7	8	9	10	11
1	0	1	0	0	0	0	0	0	0	0	0
2	0	0	1	0	0	1	0	0	1	0	0
3	0	0	0	1	1	0	0	0	0	0	0
4	0	0	0	0	1	0	0	0	0	0	0
5	0	0	0	0	0	0	0	0	0	0	1
6	0	0	0	0	0	0	1	1	0	0	0
7	0	0	0	0	0	0	0	1	0	0	0
8	0	0	0	0	0	0	0	0	0	1	0
9	0	0	0	0	0	0	0	0	0	0	1
10	0	0	0	0	0	0	0	0	0	0	1
11	0	0	0	0	0	0	0	0	0	0	0

(a) Find the permissible task execution time for each task.

(b) Provide a task scheduling table showing the allocation of tasks to processors.

6.5.B. [Prasanna 1991] One of the important problems in a multistage network is to determine the switch settings to realize a permutation P through the network. A simple procedure to route a permutation through a Benes network is as follows: Assume the Benes network has N inputs. This network can be looked upon as a three-stage network, as shown in Figure 6.12. Construct a bipartite graph G with N vertices, in which each vertex represents a switch in the input or output stage.

An edge (i, j) is present in this graph if an input of box$_i$ is to be routed to the output of box$_j$. Thus the graph has N edges. A complete matching in G is a collection of $N/2$ edges, such that no two edges are incident on the same vertex. Given P, construct G and find two disjoint complete matchings M_1 and M_2. Select switch settings for input and output boxes such that the connections in M_1 (M_2) are routed through the upper box (lower box) in the middle stage. Repeatedly apply the above idea to the permutations to be realized by the upper and lower boxes in the middle stage.

Now consider the eight-input Benes network shown in Figure 6.12, and obtain the switch settings to realize the shuffle permutation on eight inputs.

6.6.B. [Prasanna 1991] One of the important problems to be solved for parallel implementation of algorithms is packet routing. Consider an $N \times N$ mesh in which each PE has a packet of data to be routed to a PE in the mesh. Assume that the routing is a permutation. Show how the three-stage Clos network can be emulated to perform the routing in $3(N - 1)$ routing steps. List three applications for the above data routing question.

6.7.B. Design a parallel algorithm to find the maximum of an array of n elements on a shared-memory multiprocessor. What is the time complexity, assuming that communication time is negligible?

6.8.B. For the execution graph shown in Figure 6.33, write the control flow using fork/join and parbegin/parend constructs.

6.9.B. The problem of matrix-matrix multiplication is to be performed on a shared-memory multiprocessor and a message-passing multiprocessor. The number of processors is n and the size of each matrix is $n \times n$. Describe the implementation of this problem on the two multiprocessors. Be specific about data allocation, synchronization, and program control.

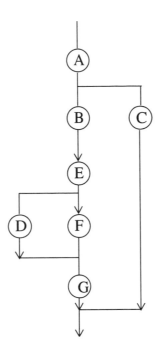

Figure 6.33 Execution graph for Problem 6.8.B.

6.10.B. Show which connections in permutation P may be implemented simultaneously on the Omega network shown in Figure 6.13. Draw the connections on the network.

$$P = \begin{pmatrix} 0 & 1 & 2 & 3 & 4 & 5 & 6 & 7 \\ 2 & 3 & 1 & 4 & 5 & 7 & 6 & 0 \end{pmatrix}$$

Hint: An algorithm for routing messages on an Omega network is: The switch box looks at the bit i of the destination address. If it is 0, it uses the output to the upper port; if it is 1, it uses the output to the lower port.

6.11.B. Write a simulation program to simulate the circuit shown in Figure 6.34 on a four-processor hypercube. Assume $1\text{-}\mu s$ time increments.

6.12.B. Demonstrate that a 4×4 mesh array with wraparound can be embedded into the 16-node hypercube shown in Figure 6.35.

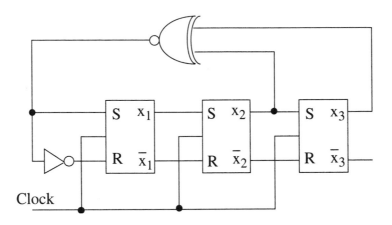

Figure 6.34 Logic circuit for Problem 6.11.B.

(a) Draw the hypercube and label its nodes with binary digits from 0000 to 1111. Show how to map the array nodes to the hypercube nodes.

(b) How many hypercube edges, if any, are not used?

6.13.B. Provide a mapping of a ring interconnection into a hypercube.

6.14.B. *(a)* Derive an algorithm to route a message between any two nodes in an n-hypercube. Provide a bound for the shortest path between two nodes.

(b) Derive another algorithm to broadcast a message from a node to all other nodes in a hypercube. How many time steps are required?

6.15.B. Provide a mapping of the matrix multiplication problem into a hypercube. The matrices are $m \times m$ and the hypercube is of order n.

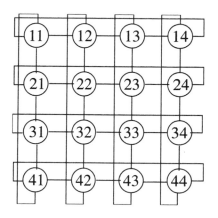

Figure 6.35 Sixteen-node hypercube for Problem 6.12.B.

Chapter 7

DATA-FLOW COMPUTING

The data-flow processing model is based on the idea that computations take place when data are available. The central control unit is replaced by other, more distributed, data-moving mechanisms. Data-flow computing is capable of fine-grain parallelism, and has the potential of reducing the synchronization overhead. However, it introduces some problems of its own, such as construction and management of memories for efficient data matching, balancing the load in a large system, programming, and others. Several data-flow computers have been built, but their performance is not yet in the supercomputer range. A current trend in data-flow research is to combine the idea of pure data flow with that of control flow and to implement "hybrid" data-flow computers. Doubts about the practicality of data-flow computers are being dispelled as more extensions of data-flow become mainstream parallel processing.

7.1 DATA- AND DEMAND-DRIVEN MODELS OF COMPUTATION

7.1.1 Basic Models

As the computer field matured and some major deficiencies in the von Neumann computational model became more visible, efforts were made to develop computer architectures based on principles other than those of the von Neumann model. The goal was to find new instruction execution orderings and new ways of manipulating data. Two computational models that are significantly different from the von Neumann model are the *data-driven* and *demand-driven* models. In data-driven computers, the availability of operands triggers the execution of operations, whereas in demand-driven computers the demand for a result triggers the operation that will generate it. Trelevan, Brownbridge, and Hopking [Trelevan, Brownbridge, and Hopking 1982] have suggested that practical computer models can be examined from two points of view: the *control mechanism,* which defines the order of execution, and the *data mechanism,* which defines the way in which arguments are used by an instruction. The basic control mechanisms are:

1. *Sequential.* Control is passed from one instruction to another, as in the traditional von Neumann model.

2. *By dependence.* Control is directed by the availability of arguments, and an instruction is executed after all its arguments become available.

3. *By demand.* Control is directed by the need for arguments, and an instruction is executed when the output argument is required by another instruction. After execution, control is returned to the invoking instruction.

The basic data mechanisms are:

- *By value.* An argument carries actual data used in computations.

- *By reference.* An argument points to a storage location where the data resides.

If these control and data mechanisms are combined, several distinct computer models result, as indicated in Figure 7.1.

Notice that dependence-driven models are more general than data-driven models, in the sense that *dependence-driven* means that computations can be started any time after all arguments have been generated, whereas *pure data-driven* means that computations start as soon as their arguments are available. This is why in Figure 7.1 the data-driven (or data-flow) model is part of a dependence control mechanism.

Control	*Data mechanisms*	
mechanisms	By value	By reference
Sequential		von Neumann
Dependence	Data flow	Parallel control flow
Demand	String reduction	Graph reduction

Figure 7.1 Computer models based on control and data mechanisms [Trelevan, Brownbridge, and Hopking 1982].

One can say that dependence is based on *availability* and demand is based on *need*.

From the control and data mechanisms, two basic principles for the data-flow model follow:

- *Principle of asynchrony.* A data-flow operation is executed when all its operands have become available.

- *Principle of functionality.* A data-flow operation is purely functional and produces no side-effects. This functionality is due to the fact that instructions operate directly on values (or tokens), rather than on addresses of variables.

Some advantages of data-flow are that scheduling is less of a problem, program organization is simpler, and abundant parallelism at fine granularity can be exploited. Data-flow program organization is very efficient for the evaluation of simple expressions and functions with call-by-value parameters. However, where shared data structures are to be manipulated or where specific patterns of control, such as sequential or conditional, are required, data-flow seems to be at a disadvantage. Implementation of data-flow program organizations often separates the storage for data tokens and instructions, which makes compilation at least conceptually difficult.

As mentioned above, by demand-driven computation we mean a computing scheme in which instructions are selected when the value they produce is needed by another, already selected, instruction. The instruction is executed only when its result is demanded by some other instruction and the arguments may be recursively evaluated where necessary. If the inputs have not been completed, the operation demands the inputs that it needs. These inputs will obviously be the outputs of some other operations, and hence this demand chain will propagate until the external inputs are demanded. At this point the values will be available, so the operation that requested them will be able to continue. When it completes the computation, this operation sends the resulting value to all the other operations that have requested it.

Let us consider the expression $z = (x + y) * (x - y)$. In order to calculate this expression using demand-driven control, first z is demanded, which triggers the need for the two multiplication terms $(x + y)$ and $(x - y)$, which in turn demands fetching values x and y and performing the two operations, after which the results are passed back and the multiplication is performed. Demand-driven control coincides with reducing expressions following the outermost order of operations; that is, first multiplication, then addition and subtraction. Thus, demand-driven computation is called *reduction in outermost order,* or simply *reduction.* By in-place replacement of expressions by their values, expressions are reduced, such that at the end, the whole program is reduced, leaving only the result behind. Notice that reduction of expressions is possible following the usual order, or the innermost order; that is, first addition and subtraction, then multiplication. When control proceeds in this order, the computation is not demand-driven, but dependence-driven.

There are two types of reductions, depending on how the instruction arguments are handled: string reduction and graph reduction.

In *string reduction,* a different copy of a value has to be sent to each of the operations that use it. Thus common subexpressions, if any, will be evaluated separately. This leads to inefficient use of resources, but excludes an addressing scheme. The string reduction computation of $z = (x + y) * (x - y)$ is shown in Figure 7.2. The value of z is demanded. This causes the node containing the identifier z to be replaced by a copy of its definition. Next, identifiers x and y are also replaced by copies of

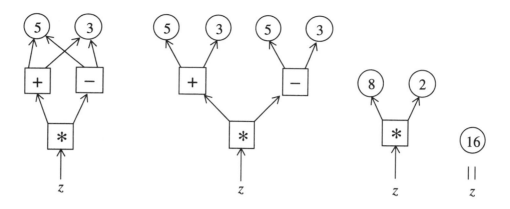

Figure 7.2 Computing $z = (x + y) * (x - y)$ using string reduction.

their respective definitions. This is a reduction process. The addition and subtraction are replaced by their corresponding values, and finally the multiplication is replaced by the value of z.

Graph reduction is another way of implementing a demand-driven computation. Instead of copying each identifier definition, after the demand pointers have reached the data, the pointers are simply reversed. This is shown in Figure 7.3. Once the pointers have been reversed, the reduction of the subexpression in the definition starts with the rewriting of the addition and the subtraction. This proceeds until the definition of z is replaced by the value 16, and then a copy is returned to the computation originally demanding z. Any subsequent request for value z will immediately receive the constant 16. The fact that once the value of an expression has been computed it can be used by some other operation represents a major benefit of graph reduction over string reduction, in which this is not possible. However, pointers, and hence memory addressing, are now required for the ability to reference already-computed values. Thus if we refer back to Figure 7.1, it should be clear now that string reduction has a by-value data mechanism with minimal addressing overhead,indexoverhead whereas graph reduction uses by-reference data mechanisms allowing sharing and manipulation of unevaluated objects. String and graph reduction are both efficient

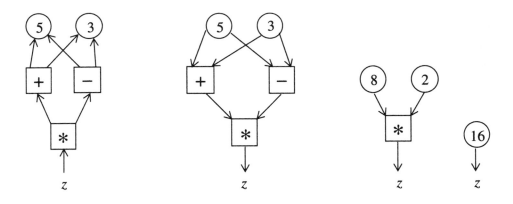

Figure 7.3 Computing $z = (x + y) * (x - y)$ using graph reduction.

computational models for functional programming languages such as Lisp.

Demand-driven computation is superior only for "nonstrict" operators, such as "if-then-else," which do not require all their arguments. The advantage of demand-driven computation is that only instructions whose results are needed are executed. A procedure-calling mechanism is built in, by allowing the operator of an instruction to be defined as a block of instructions. Demand-driven computations are not suitable for arithmetic expressions, in which instructions always contribute to the final result.

7.1.2 Data-Flow Graphs

Data-flow programs are usually described in terms of directed graphs. Consider the statement $z = (x + y) * (x - y)$. In the data-flow program representing this statement, each instruction consists of an operator and two inputs, which are either literal operands or "unknown" operands. Figure 7.4(a) shows the data-flow graph for the expression of z; Figure 7.4(b) shows a different representation, emphasizing the instructions, or templates, and the dependencies between instructions. The fields for each instruction are: type of operation, first operand,

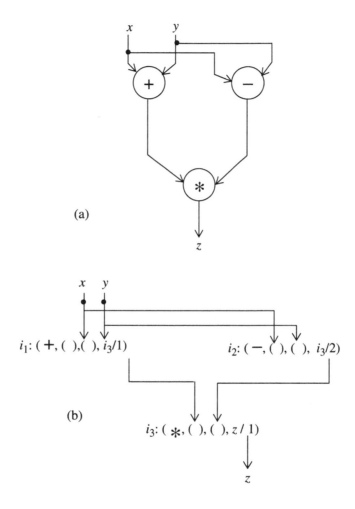

Figure 7.4 (a) Data-flow graph; (b) data-flow graph implemented with instructions (or templates).

second operand, and the instruction and operand for which the result is needed.

The unknown operands are defined by empty parentheses (); a reference, such as the $i_3/1$ argument, defines the position of the result, in this case instruction 3, operand 1. A reference is a unidirectional arc linking the producer instruction to the consumer. Data tokens are passed between instructions.

An instruction is enabled for execution when all operands are known; that is, when they have been replaced by partial results made available by previous instructions. The operator then executes (or "fires"), which consists of removing the input tokens from storage, performing the specified operation, and using the embedded reference to store the result in one of the operands of the successor instruction. When one variable is used as the operand in more than one instruction, copies of the variable are generated and stored in corresponding locations in each instruction (for example, variable y).

As can be seen from this example, the data-flow model deals only with values and not with names of value containers (i.e., addresses). This is the concept of purely functional or applicative language; these languages have no built-in notion of global updatable memory. An operator in these languages produces a value that is used by other operators. The data-flow model has nothing to do with an instruction counter; an instruction is enabled if and only if all the required input values have been computed. These are the reasons why it is said that an instruction in the data-flow model has no side-effects.

The data-flow programs are constructed from actor nodes and arcs, or links. The actors perform simple operations and the arcs represent channels through which tokens flow, carrying values from each actor to other actors. Notice that there are data and control tokens traveling on data and control links. Data links that have no source operator are input links; data links that have no destination operator are output links. In the case of control arcs, the token values are either "true" or "false". Data tokens are integers, real numbers, or strings. The execution of a data-flow program is carried out by firing the actors eligible to fire. An actor is said to be enabled if tokens are present on all input arcs and no token is present on any output arc. Figure 7.5 shows a library of typical actors before and after firing. Figure 7.5(a) and (b) indicate that a data or control token arriving at a bifurcation is replicated such that each link has its own token. The operator from Figure 7.5(c) could be any arithmetic or logic function. The operator is executed only when all input arcs have their tokens and when there is no token on the output arc. Figure 7.5(d) shows a decision actor. When expression p is satisfied, the input tokens are removed and a boolean token is placed on the output arc, provided that there is no other token on that arc. For example, p may represent $p = v_1 - v_r > 0$. The next two actors are control actors. They require proper control tokens on their control arcs (oriented horizontally) to fire. For example, a T-gate (true gate) in Figure 7.5(e) will fire when the control arc has "true token" and there is a data token in the input arc and no data token on the output arc. The actor in Figure 7.5(f) is used to control the merging of two data streams.

Next, we show the data-flow representation of an elementary program, expressed as follows:

> input (x, y)
> while $x < y$ do
> $z = 0$
>   if $z < 10$
>   then $z = z + 1$
>   else $z = z - 5$
> $x = x + 1$
>   end
> output (z)

A data-flow graph corresponding to this program is shown in Figure 7.6.

It is easy to verify that data-flow programs are equivalent in expressive power to formal programs written using assignment statements "while", "do", "if-then-else", and so on.

As shown in Figure 7.4(b), a data-flow graph may be implemented on a computer as a collection of activity templates, each corresponding to one or more actors of the data-flow graph. Each template has four fields: an operation code specifying the operation to be performed, two operands, and the destination, which specifies where the result will be

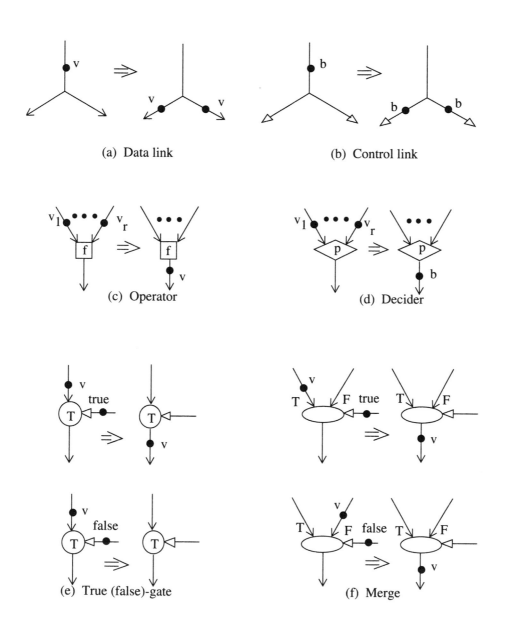

Figure 7.5 Examples of firing rules.

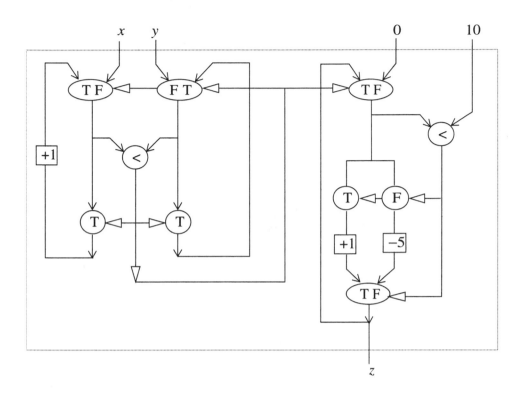

Figure 7.6 A data-flow program.

used. The activity templates are linked to represent a program graph. Activity templates are actually stored in the data-flow computer as files:

> instruction: < opcode, operands, destination >

The destination field specifies the address of the template receiving that result and an input integer specifying which operand needs that result:

> destination: < address, input >

Execution of a machine program consisting of activity templates is viewed as follows: The contents of a template activated by the presence of an operand value in each receiver take the form

> operation packet: < opcode, operands, destinations >

Such a packet specifies one result packet of the form

result packet: < value, destination >

for each destination field of the template. Generation of a result packet causes the value to be placed in the receiver designated by its destination field.

7.2 STATIC DATA-FLOW COMPUTERS

The basic operation of a static data-flow computer, proposed by Jack Dennis [Dennis 1979], is illustrated in Figure 7.7. The data-flow program describing the computation to be performed is held as a collection of activity templates in the activity store. Each activity template has a unique address, which is entered in the instruction queue unit (a FIFO buffer store) when the instruction is ready for execution. The fetch unit takes an instruction address from the instruction queue and reads the activity template from the activity store, forms it into an operation packet, and passes it on to the execution unit. Here the instruction is actually processed, and a result packet is generated for the destination field of the operation packet. The send and receive units connect this processor with other similar modules. A result packet may be sent to the communication network or kept locally.

The update unit receives result packets and enters the values they carry into operand fields of activity templates as specified by their destination fields. The update unit also tests whether all operand packets required to activate the destination instruction have been received and, if so, enters the instruction address in the instruction queue. During program execution, the number of entries in the instruction queue measures the degree of concurrency present in the program. The basic mechanism shown in Figure 7.7 can exploit this potential to a limited but significant degree: once the fetch unit has sent an operation packet off to the execution unit, it may immediately read another entry from the instruction queue without waiting for the previously fetched instruction to be completely processed. Thus a continuous stream of operation packets may flow from the fetch unit to the operation unit so long as the instruction queue is not empty.

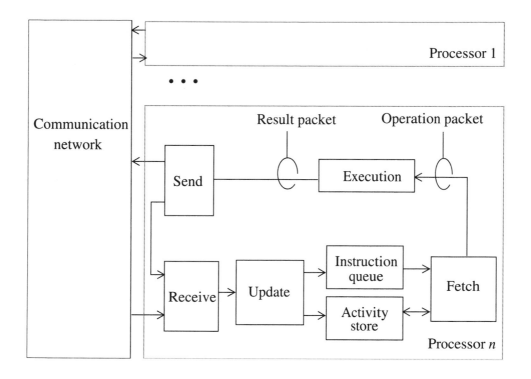

Figure 7.7 Basic instruction execution mechanism.

This execution mechanism forms a circular pipeline within each processor. A number of packets may be flowing simultaneously in different parts of the processor ring on behalf of different instructions. The degree of concurrency is limited by the number of units on the ring and by the degree of pipelining within each unit. Additional concurrency may be exploited by splitting any unit on the ring into several units operating in parallel. Ultimately, the level of concurrency is limited by the capacity of the data paths connecting the units on the ring.

Data-flow models that allow one token to exist on an arc at any given time are called *static data-flow models*. The reason why only one token is allowed is that otherwise it would not be clear which set of tokens belonged to which set of inputs.

Now consider a *multiiteration process*. There is nothing to stop further iterations from proceeding even though one iteration is not totally completed. This causes tokens to accumulate on certain arcs of the data-flow graph. It is then no longer possible to declare a node executable because of the presence of any two tokens on its input, because they might belong to totally different parts of the computation.

There are several possible solutions to this problem:

1. Replicate the data-flow graph such that each stage of the iteration must be described by a separate graph. This solution requires large amounts of program storage. It also requires dynamic code generation if the loop's iteration depth is only known at run time. Both of these deficiencies can result in significant overhead in practical systems.

2. The use of a reentrant graph is allowed, but an iteration is not allowed to start before the previous one has finished. This approach does not allow for parallelism between iterations and requires extra instructions or hardware to test the completion of an iteration.

3. The use of a data-flow graph is limited by allowing only one token to reside on each arc of the graph at any time. This is accomplished by allowing an operation to be executable only when all its input tokens are present and no tokens exist on its output arc. This approach, which implies sequential but pipelined use of the data-flow graph, allows exploitation of more parallelism than do the previous two solutions. A single token per arc is implemented through the use of "acknowledge" signals, which are returned to the nodes in the graph that generated those values by the nodes that consumed the values. These "acknowledge" signals approximately double the number of arcs in the corresponding data-flow graph, and therefore double the traffic through the data-flow machine.

4. Each token is assumed to carry its index and iteration number as a label. This label is usually referred to as the token's *color*. A node is executable only if all input tokens have the same color. The labeling method permits the use of pure static code and enables maximum use of any parallelism that exists in the problem

specification. This is clearly achieved at the cost of the extra information that must be carried by each token and the extra instructions necessary for labeling and delabeling. The penalty for this approach is obviously extra time spent for processing labels and additional storage.

5. The tokens are queued on arcs in the order of their arrival. This solution can deliver as much parallelism as the labeling approach, but requires large queues, which are very costly.

The static data-flow model has some serious drawbacks. The feedback interpretation of data-flow programs using acknowledgment arcs allows only a limited amount of parallelism to be explored. This is because consecutive iterations of loops can only partially overlap in time; they can never proceed concurrently, even in the absence of interloop dependencies. Another drawback is the overhead caused by acknowledgment signals as the token traffic is roughly doubled! In addition, the static data-flow model cannot efficiently support programming constructs such as procedure calls, recurrences, and arrays.

7.3   DYNAMIC DATA-FLOW COMPUTERS

7.3.1   The Tagged-Token Principle

Considerable parallelism is achieved when loop iterations are processed in parallel. To achieve this, each iteration should be able to execute as a separate instance of a reentrant subgraph. In order to distinguish between activities related to different iterations, the basic activity names are extended: each carries an iteration count and also the procedure context within which it executes. Thus each node is replicated for every loop iteration and every procedure invocation. This replication is only conceptual. When implemented, only one copy of any data-flow graph is actually kept in memory, but each instruction being processed is associated with a respective iteration number and procedure context.

This leads to a significant modification in the operation of data-flow graphs. With this approach, an arc may have several tokens, each token carrying a different tag. The *firing rule for tagged-token data-*

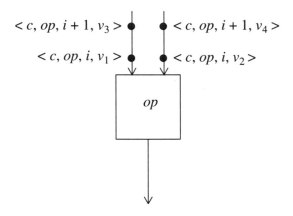

Figure 7.8 Example of a tagged-token data-flow graph.

flow actors is: An actor is enabled as soon as tokens with identical tags are present at each of its input arcs.

A major benefit of the tagged-token principle is that it eliminates the need for acknowledgment signals, thus decreasing the amount of token traffic. Data-flow systems that employ this method are called *dynamic data-flow machines*.

The tagged tokens are of the form $< c, op, i, v >$, where c is the context or the subroutine performed; op is the operation performed; i is the iteration number; and v is the value carried by the token.

When the node marked op fires, it consumes two tokens of the same iteration, $< c, op, i, v_1 >$ and $< c, op, i, v_2 >$, and produces a result token $< c, op, i, v_{12} >$. In order for operands to constitute a pair and to participate in a computation, their contexts, operation types, and iteration numbers must match. Note that the result token carries the same tag as the input tokens. An example is shown in Figure 7.8.

7.3.2   The Manchester Data-Flow Computer

The first implementation of the tagged-token data-flow model was carried out at the University of Manchester, England [Watson and Gurd 1982]. The structure of the Manchester data-flow computer is shown

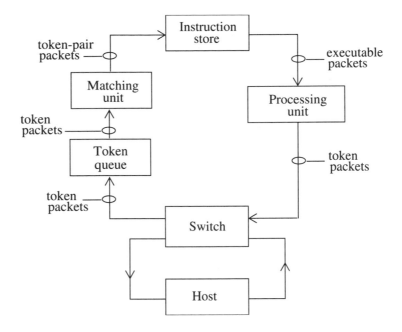

Figure 7.9 Structure of the Manchester data-flow computer [Watson and Gurd 1982].

in Figure 7.9. It consists of four units: a token queue, a matching unit, an instruction store, and a processing unit. Each unit is internally synchronized, but they communicate asynchronously via token packets.

The role of the matching unit is to pair tokens that are intended for the same operation. Token-matching implements synchronization and communication between instructions. Matching may fail, in which case tokens are stored in the matching unit, whose storage capacity is 1M tokens. If the match is successful, a token-pair packet is formed and sent to the next unit in the pipeline.

The instruction store receives the token-pair packets and forms executable packets by adding to them information such as the instruction to be performed and the destination address for the result token. This unit has a capacity of 64K instruction nodes. The processing unit executes complete packets. For fast processing it has 20 ALUs. Result tokens are passed to the I/O switch, where, depending on their address, they either leave to pipeline for the host or continue, in which case they are placed in a token queue. This unit is a 32K-token FIFO whose role is to regulate the token flow through the pipeline.

The pipeline has the capacity to process about 30 token packets simultaneously. This parallelism results from multiple ALUs and overlapping of the pipeline units. The pipeline rate is 200 ns. The data paths are 166 bits wide, which is more than enough to transmit one packet in parallel.

In this architecture, the matching unit is the critical area. The rate at which the destination and label fields are matched dictates the maximum data flow around the ring. A limitation of the Manchester computer is its inability to handle complex structures. It has been used successfully only for simple applications, and its performance is limited. Nevertheless, it has demonstrated the feasibility of tagged-token data flow and it has constituted an inspiration for other data-flow computers.

7.3.3   The SIGMA-1 Data-Flow Computer

The SIGMA-1 computer, built in 1988 at the Electrotechnical Laboratory in Japan, is the most powerful data-flow computer to date. Its performance is between 200 and 400 Mflops. The system organization is shown in Figure 7.10. It consists of 128 processing elements (PEs), 128 structure elements (SEs), 32 local networks, a global network, 16 maintenance processors, and a host computer. The local network is a 10×10 packet-switching crossbar interconnecting four PEs, four SEs, one port of the global network, and a maintenance processor. The global network is a two-stage Omega network. The entire system operates synchronously from a single 10-MHz clock.

The structure of one processing element is shown in Figure 7.11. It operates as a two-stage pipeline. The first stage is the firing stage, consisting of a FIFO input buffer, an instruction-fetch unit accessing a program memory, and a matching unit with memory. The input buffer can store 8K packets. The instruction-fetch unit reads the instruction memory according to the address provided by the input packet, and also reads immediate operands from the instruction memory. The second stage contains the execution unit, which produces the addresses for the result tokens.

Each packet has 88 bits: 8 bits for processor destination, 8 bits for

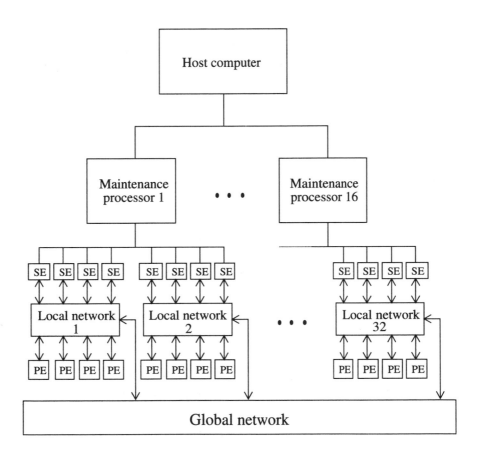

Figure 7.10 Overall structure of SIGMA-1 [Hiraki, Sekiguchi, and Shimada 1991].

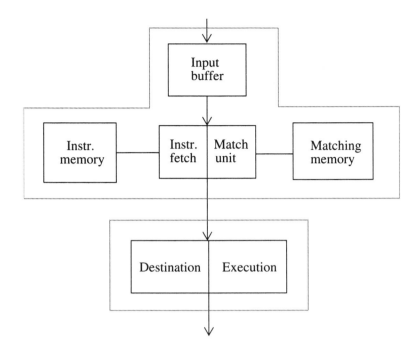

Figure 7.11 Structure of a processing element of SIGMA-1.

the packet type, 32 bits for instruction information, 8 bits for the data tag, and 32 bits for actual data.

A packet fetched from the input buffer is processed simultaneously in the match unit and the instruction-fetch unit. The match unit attempts to match the data in the packet with that of other packets stored in the matching-unit memory to form two input packets. At the same time, the instruction-fetch unit reads from its memory information pertaining to the type of instruction. If the match is successful, an executable packet is formed and sent to the next pipeline stage; if not, the instruction-fetch activity is aborted and the packet is stored in the match memory to wait for its match to arrive.

The second pipeline stage is dedicated to executing the instruction and preparing the destination address of the result packet. The execution unit contains an integer ALU, a floating-point ALU, and other hardware. The destination unit forms the result packet and provides the destination address.

The role of the structure processing elements is to handle complex data structures and to provide I/O interface. Simple data structures for scalar variables are stored in the matching memory. In order to avoid a potential bottleneck in the matching unit, which is constantly busy and is a precious resource, functions such as array management, garbage collection, and memory allocation are performed in the structure processing elements.

A larger data-flow computer is in progress at the Electrotechnical Laboratory in Japan. The newer EM-4 system has 1,024 processors and builds upon the experience of the SIGMA-1.

7.4 COMBINING DATA FLOW AND CONTROL FLOW

Data flow and control flow are two extremes of a spectrum on which a variety of architectures may be designed. While the data-flow model is elegant and appealing, it has not produced cost-effective machines. A recent trend in the data-flow community is to combine the data-flow and control-flow models and to take advantage of improvements in conventional computers, such as pipelining, vectorization, compiler optimization, hierarchical memories, RISC architecture, and many others. The new hybrid data-flow models aim at retaining the advantages of pure data flow connected with memory latency and synchronization, while using efficient von Neumann processors.

7.4.1 Hybrid Data-Flow Computers

A hybrid data-flow computer is a multiprocessor that uses both data flow and control flow. One possibility is to provide the scheduling and synchronization using data flow while the instruction execution uses control flow. In a proposed implementation of this idea [Gao 1991], data never flows and there are no tokens. The threads of instructions are synchronized via data-driven methods, while the instructions within a thread are executed sequentially under control flow. Ideally, we would

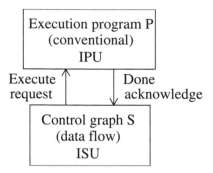

Figure 7.12 Structure of a hybrid data-flow model.

like to change the granularity of threads even within the same application. This so-called *argument-fetching model* does not use tokens; instead, a storage area is created at run time and instructions operate on values stored there.

A data-flow program is seen as a tuple {P, S}, where P is a set of instructions forming a process, and S is a directed graph, called a signal graph.

The architecture for this model, shown in Figure 7.12, has two parts: an instruction scheduling unit (ISU) and instruction processing unit (IPU). The ISU operates on a data-flow graph; the IPU is an instruction processing unit that uses conventional architecture, including argument-fetching. The P code resides in the IPU; the S code, in the ISU.

The operands and results of the instructions are stored in the IPU. After an instruction is executed, a signal is sent to the ISU via a "done" link. The scheduling of instructions takes place in the ISU. The S code contains a set of instructions interconnected via arcs. Each S node receives signals from other enabled nodes, and when all input signals are received it is scheduled for execution. A signal is sent via an "execute" link to the IPU, where the instruction is actually stored, and then operands are fetched and the instruction is executed.

The movement of tokens is replaced by signals. The S node is identified by an S-node address. The granularity of the modules being signaled to fire may vary from instructions to sequences of instructions.

One aspect of these systems is multiple invocation of the same code in the IPU. To support multiple invocations, the system allocates a frame of locations for each invocation. The actual address of the instruction is calculated from a base address generated at run time.

Once a P instruction in executed, by providing a mechanism to start another P instruction without the ISU, a hybrid data flow is achieved. This may be simply realized by providing a program center for each sequence of P instructions (or process). Each instruction in the IPU may have a tag field that indicates whether or not it needs ISU support. Under this model any instruction can be set to one of the two modes, IPU or ISU. This enables the change of granularity that is highly desirable in multiprocessors. Moreover, various process sizes are possible and can be active concurrently.

7.5 BIBLIOGRAPHICAL NOTES AND FURTHER READING

Much of the early data-flow research was done at MIT by a group led by Jack Dennis [Dennis and Misunas 1975, Dennis 1979]. The first operational data-flow processor was built by Al Devis [Devis 1977]. Tagged-token architecture was proposed independently by Arvind and Gostelow [Arvind and Gostelow 1982] and by Watson and Gurd [Watson and Gurd 1982]. The Manchester machine project was led by Ian Watson [Watson and Gurd 1982].

The SIGMA-1 project in Japan is described in [Hiraki, Sekiguchi, and Shimada 1991]. Hybrid data-flow architectures were proposed in [Iannuci 1988], [Gao 1991], [Evripidou and Gaudiot 1991], and others. A new book on data-flow computers, which contains recent papers and results, was edited by Gaudiot and Bic [Gaudiot and Bic 1991].

7.6 PROBLEMS

7.1.A. Provide a data-flow graph for the solution of the equation

$$ax^2 + bx + c = 0$$

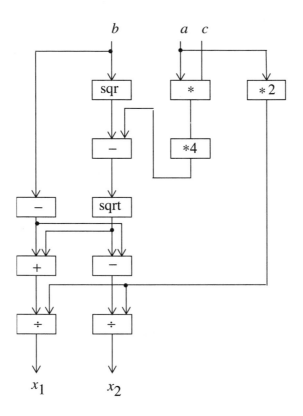

Figure 7.13 Data-flow graph for Problem 7.1.A.

Solution.

$$x_{1,2} = \frac{-b \pm \sqrt{b^2 - 4ac}}{2a}$$

The graph is shown in Figure 7.13.

7.2.A. Derive the data-flow graph for the nested if-then-else program

> if $x > y$
>   then if $a = b$
>   then $z = c + d$
>   else $z = e * f$

endif
else $z = g + h$

Solution.

The graph is shown in Figure 7.14.

7.3.A. For a typical dynamic data-flow machine with a tagged-token, circular pipeline, operating at instruction-level granularity:

(a) indicate the main sources of parallelism; and

(b) indicate the main obstacles for achieving high performance.

Solution.

(a) Parallelism may be provided by:

- Spreading executable packets to several PEs;

- Using pipelined PEs;

- Overlapping token-matching, instruction-fetch, packet transfers, and execution; and

- Using a parallel interconnection network for packet transfers.

(b) Some problems are as follows:

- Matching time is large and instruction prefetch and token pre-matching are difficult;

- Packet-based operations do not take advantage of fast processor architectures;

- Units on the pipeline are different, so a constant high pipeline rate is difficult to achieve;

- Overhead is required for data preparation and transfer; and

- Variable granularity and complex data structures are difficult to handle.

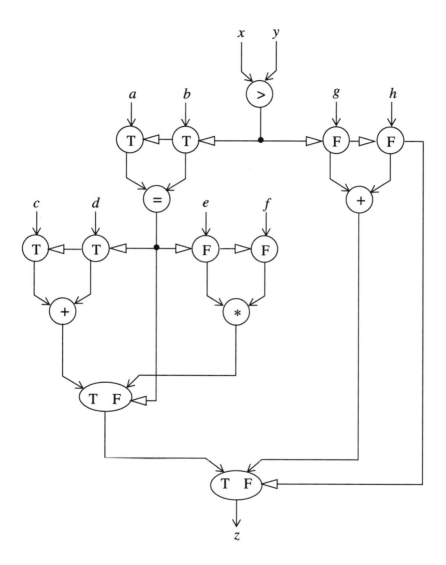

Figure 7.14 Data-flow graph for Problem 7.2.A.

7.4.A. [Gajski, Padua, Kuck, and Kuhn 1982]

> input d, e, f
> $c_0 = 0$
> for i from 1 to 8 do
>   begin
> $a_i := d_i / e_i$
> $b_i := a_i * f_i$
> $c_i := b_i + c_{i-1}$
>   end
> output a, b, c

We want to study the execution time of this loop program on a hypothetical data-flow machine with four processors, assuming the following modes of operation:

1. One token-per-arc strategy without acknowledgment;

2. One token-per-arc strategy with acknowledgment; and

3. Tagged-token strategy.

Assume that division takes three time units, multiplication takes two time units, and addition takes one time unit. All other memory or intercommunication delays are ignored.

Solution.
The solution is shown in Figure 7.15.

7.1.B. Draw a data-flow graph to evaluate the expression

$$\cos x \approx 1 - \frac{x^2}{2!} + \frac{x^4}{4!} - \frac{x^6}{6!}$$

7.2.B. Draw data-flow graphs to represent the following computations:

(a) if $(a = b)$ and $(c < d)$ then
        $c \leftarrow c - a$
    else
        $c \leftarrow c + a$

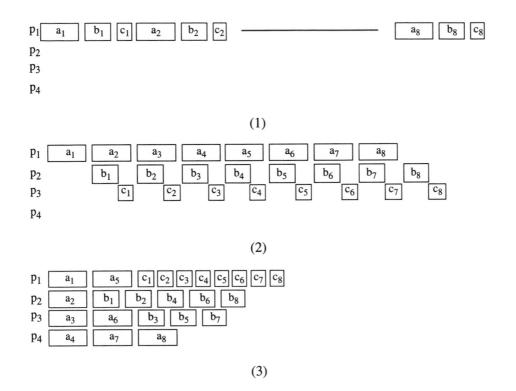

Figure 7.15 Time performance for the program in Problem 7.4.A
[Gajski, Padua, Kuck, and Kuhn 1982].

(b) for $i \leftarrow 1$ until m do
    begin
        $c(i) \leftarrow 0$
        for $j \leftarrow 1$ until n do
            $c[i] \leftarrow c[i] + a[i,j] * b[j]$
    end
(c) $Z = N! = N \times (N-1) \times (N-2) \times \cdots \times 2 \times 1$

You are allowed to use the *merge operator*, the *true gate*, the *false gate*,
the *multiply operator*, the *add* or *subtract operator*, the *logical operator*,
and the *compare operator* in your graph construction.

7.3.B. Show how to compute the conditional expression

if $x > y$ then
$$x - y$$
else
$$x + y$$

(a) using the data-flow model of computation;
(b) using the graph reduction model of computation.

7.4.B.

for $i = 1, 2$
  for $j = 1, 2$
    for $k = 1, 3$
      $c_{ij}^k = c_{ij}^{k-1} + a_{ik}b_{kj}$
    end k
  end j
end i

Study the time performance for this matrix multiplication problem on a hypothetical data-flow machine with two processors.

(a) Draw the time-space diagram and show all the templates and the arcs linking them under the following assumptions:

1. One token-per-arc-strategy with acknowledgement.

2. Tagged-token strategy.

(b) Show the content of a tag at bit level that will work for this problem.

7.5.B. Draw a data-flow graph for this program:

input(w, x)
$y := x$; $t := 0$;
while $t \neq w$ do
begin
    if $y > 1$ then $y := y/2$
    else $y := y * 3$;

$$t := t + 1;$$
   end
   output y

7.6.B. Derive the data-flow graph of the matrix multiplication

$$c(i, j) = \sum_{k=1}^{n} a(i, k)b(k, j)$$

7.7.B. Explain how to calculate a factorial number $n!$ using the reduction mode of computation. Calculate the factorial number by the divide-and-conquer method.

7.8.B Consider again the dynamic programming algorithm in Section 2.3.2. Propose a hybrid mode of operation in which the control flow is provided by a signal-flow graph and the actual instruction execution is performed in a conventional von Neumann manner. This system does not have tokens; its operation is based on signal exchanges between control and execution units.

Chapter 8

PARALLEL PROCESSING OF RULE-BASED SYSTEMS AND SEMANTIC NETWORKS

Rule-based systems and semantic networks are among the most important paradigms for knowledge representation and processing. Knowledge processing is a fast-growing area of computer science and engineering. It includes applications such as natural language understanding, machine translation, planning, image understanding, and many other areas normally associated with artificial intelligence. Realistic knowledge-processing systems require huge amounts of storage and processing power. Parallel processing techniques not only can improve the processing speed, but can also make possible the tackling of large, realistic applications that are often difficult if not impossible to handle on sequential machines. In this chapter, our goal is to analyze parallelism and to identify specific processing requirements for two important AI paradigms. In rule-based systems, the sources of parallelism are identified, and several parallel execution models are presented. Rule-based systems have been used to build expert systems.

For some AI applications it is preferable to use semantic networks to represent knowledge. Marker propagation on semantic networks represents a viable approach to implementing parallel reasoning engines. An application area to which the parallel techniques described in this chapter apply well is natural language processing. Both general-purpose parallel computers and special-purpose parallel architectures may be used for knowledge processing. The design of a massively parallel computer, the SNAP, specialized for semantic network processing, is discussed below.

8.1 PARALLELISM ANALYSIS IN RULE-BASED SYSTEMS

8.1.1 Rule-Based Systems

Rule-based systems (RBS) are one of the most important ways of modeling knowledge and building expert systems. *Expert systems* are AI systems with the ability to perform at the level of a human expert within a specific task domain. RBS differ from conventional programming in very profound ways. They are suitable for manipulating knowledge bases, but are computation-intensive. The applicability of sequential RBS has been limited by their slow execution speed. To solve real and complex knowledge-base problems often requires tens of thousands of rules, which cannot be realistically implemented on sequential computers.

The processing speed of RBS may be increased by using parallel processing. Special parallel processing techniques are required for this rather new computational paradigm. One of the first problems that must be solved is parallelism detection. Parallelism analysis may be done at compile time, or at run time, or both. Several parallel execution models can be designed. Once the parallelism analysis is completed and an execution model is selected, the problem remains of mapping the RBS into a multiprocessor, or designing specialized architectures for parallel RBS.

A rule-based system, or production system (PS), is a general knowledge representation and processing mechanism widely used in many AI applications where the problem can be expressed as a set of rules (or productions) and an initial condition. A pure PS is composed of: (1) declarative knowledge, or database; (2) procedural knowledge, or rules; and (3) control knowledge, or interpreter of rules.

The *database*, also called the *working memory*, contains objects and relations. It stores the current state of knowledge. It is a collection of symbols representing facts about the domain world. The items in data memory are sometimes referred to as *elements*.

The *set of rules* represents the knowledge of the PS, and is called *production memory*. A production rule is a statement of the form

$$\text{if } C_1 \And C_2 \And \ldots \And C_n \text{ then } A_1, A_2, \ldots, A_m$$

where C_1 through C_n are conditions that constitute the left-hand side (LHS), and A_1 through A_m are actions that constitute the right-hand side (RHS). If the conditions match the database, then the rule is applicable; that is, the database is modified according to actions A_1 through A_m.

The *control knowledge* constitutes an inference engine that guides the operation of the PS. This part is responsible for matching production conditions to the database, and deciding which rules should be activated in order to bring the system closer to the solution. The basic RBS model of computation is shown in Figure 8.1. The application of a production rule to a database brings that database into a new state. A solution is reached when the database is in a state that satisfies a goal condition. Typically, the problem is to find any, some, or all solutions, and the paths to the solution(s). The path from the initial condition to the goal is nondeterministic. The behavior of a PS depends not only on the received inputs that are added to the database, but also on its current state of knowledge. The state of a PS is completely determined by data memory and by the state of the inference engine.

The first operation, called *match*, starts when the inference engine selects relevant rules for the problem domain. Then the problem is to find the set of rules that match the working memory. This is done by comparing the rule conditions against the elements of the database. Rule conditions may call for either the presence or the absence of data elements in the working memory. As a result of this operation, rules whose conditions match the working memory are marked as eligible to fire.

The next operation, called *resolve*, or *conflict resolution*, consists of determining which rules it will actually make sense to execute. The criterion is to drive the system toward the goal state. As a result of the conflict-resolution operation, one rule is selected from all eligible rules.

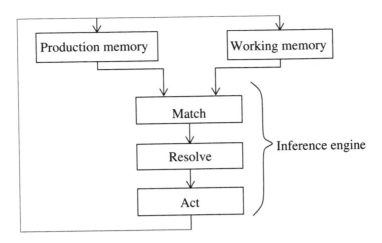

Figure 8.1 Sequential RBS model of computation.

The selection of rules to be executed from all possible applicable rules is a difficult step; it lies at the core of AI research.

The last operation in a cycle is the *act,* or *execute,* phase. Once the rule selection has been completed, the actual execution follows. The execution usually consists of modifying, adding, or removing elements from the knowledge base. Also, in some cases, the application of a rule may modify the production memory (metaknowledge) or even influence the behavior of the inference engine.

The production-system style of computation is different from those of conventional programming languages. PS are more suitable for ill-defined or difficult-to-express problem domains. They are used when the problem domain is complex, with many independent states and variations; when system responses depend on many factors and there are no fixed procedures for handling them; and when there is no fixed or apparent order in which the subproblems or behaviors must be solved. In such cases, procedural programs would require complex control of switching between appropriate parts of the program.

Production systems are suitable for applications in which changes in the database trigger computations. In procedural languages, computations are driven by instructions. In contrast, many of the computations in PS are driven by data rather than by instructions. For example, in a PS, when a subproblem becomes the focus of attention, a subset of the rules dedicated to that subproblem will be triggered, which in turn may trigger other rules, and so on. The presence of new knowledge in the knowledge base makes the application of appropriate rules possible.

OPS5

For some of the examples in this chapter, we use OPS5 as a PS language. OPS5, developed at Carnegie-Mellon University [Brownston, Farrel, Kant, and Martin 1985], is suitable because: (1) it allows testing for both the presence and the absence of data elements in rule preconditions; (2) it allows variables; and (3) it has been used in several expert systems.

In OPS5, a data element in the working memory is called a *working memory element* (wme). OPS5 views each data object as a collection of properties and represents the data object with a wme. Each data object is typed by a *class name* and its properties are represented by an *attribute-value* list in a wme. A production rule tests for the presence or absence of a wme in its condition part by specifying the class name of the wme and the desired attribute-value items. We will illustrate these OPS5 constructs using the monkey-and-bananas production program.

Example 8.1. (Working Memory Elements.)

wme_1: *(phys-object ↑name bananas ↑weight light ↑at 9-9 ↑on ceiling)*
wme_2: *(phys-object ↑name couch ↑weight heavy ↑at 7-7 ↑on floor)*
wme_3: *(phys-object ↑name ladder ↑weight light ↑at 9-9 ↑on floor)*
wme_4: *(phys-object ↑name blanket ↑weight light ↑at 7-7)*
wme_5: *(monkey ↑on ladder ↑at 9-9 ↑holds null)*
wme_6: *(goal ↑status active ↑type holds ↑object − name bananas)*

The first item of each wme is its class name. We know that bananas are physical objects because the class name for the wme_1 is phys-object. Each phys-object has four properties: its name (↑*name*), its weight (↑*weight*), its location (↑*at*), and its support (↑*on*). The symbol ↑ placed in front of a property type is used to distinguish the property from its value. Therefore wme_1, as a whole, means that physical objects

— bananas — are hanging from the ceiling at location 9-9 and that their weight is light.

Next, we show the representation of a production rule in OPS5.

Example 8.2. (Production Rule.)

(P holds_object_ceiling
       { (goal ↑status active ↑type holds ↑object-name <o1>) <goal>}
       { (phys-object ↑name <o1> ↑weight light ↑at <p> ↑on ceiling)
           <object1>}
       { (phys-object ↑name ladder ↑at <p> ↑on floor) <object2>}
       { (monkey ↑on ladder ↑holds null) <monkey>}
       −(phys-object ↑on <o1>)

⟶

      (modify <monkey> ↑holds <o1>)
      (modify <object1> ↑on null)
      (modify <goal> ↑status satisfied)

The production rule "holds_object_ceiling" tells the monkey to grasp an object from the ceiling if the monkey is standing on the ladder, under the object, and is holding nothing. As will be seen below, this production rule is satisfied by the working memory in Example 8.1.1.

Production rules may contain variables. They are denoted by < *variable_name* >. Variables are used in a production rule in order to generalize the knowledge captured in that rule. When rules containing variables are matched to working memory, variables are bound or unified to constants provided that consistency is satisfied. In the example above, the inference engine binds variable <o1> to "bananas", <p> to "9-9", <goal> to "wme$_6$", <object1> to "wme$_1$", <object2> to "wme$_3$", and <moneky> to "wme$_5$". The rule "holds_object_ceiling" modifies wme$_5$, wme$_1$, and wme$_6$ such that the new wmes are (monkey ↑on ladder ↑at 9-9 ↑holds bananas), (phys-object ↑name bananas ↑weight light ↑at 9-9 ↑on null), and (goal ↑status satisfied ↑type holds ↑object-name bananas).

For the purpose of parallelism analysis, it is convenient to represent production rules in the form

$$(type \ name \ CE^+, CE^- \longrightarrow AE^+, AE^-)$$

where

- CE^+ is the set of condition elements that must be present in the working memory for the rule to fire (a member of this set will be identified as CE_i^+).

- CE^- is the set of condition elements that must not be found in the working memory.

- AE^+ is the set of actions that add elements to the working memory when the rule is fired.

- AE^- is the set of actions that remove elements from the working memory when the rule is fired.

Forward and Backward Chaining

Production systems have been used in a variety of AI domains. The way in which rules are applied to the knowledge base is influenced by the nature of the AI problem. Sometimes it is appropriate to consider the left-hand side to be the condition and the right-hand side to be the action; at other times, vice versa.

For example, for purposes of *generation*, such as constructing a plan of action to move a robot from point A to point B, the LHS of the rule is matched against the database and the RHS is executed to perform the actions. This rule application is called forward application, or *forward chaining*. In this case, the starting point is the initial data, and the PS works toward a solution or a goal. This reasoning is sometimes called *bottom-up reasoning*.

The nature of production rules makes PS an ideal model for classification or recognition problems; for example, finding possible causes of illnesses, or possible therapy treatments. In recognition problems, the starting point is a desired goal and the problem is the attempt to find a solution. Matching the RHS against desired goal states and using the LHS to match the data in data memory or to establish subgoals is referred to as *backward-chaining propagation*. Another example of a recognition problem is parsing sentences. Here, the starting point is the sentence and the solution is finding a single parse of the sentence, all parses, or a subset of legal parses. This reasoning is sometimes called *top-down reasoning*.

Parallelism Analysis

There are several levels of parallelism in a PS. These include:

1. Parallelism within a rule, namely simultaneous matching and processing of the elements forming a rule;

2. Parallelism between rules, including simultaneous matching of production rules on the database and simultaneous execution of rules; and

3. Overlap between phases of the production system cycle.

The first form of parallelism is obvious and well understood. Parallelism within rules provided by simultaneous processing of condition elements CE_i or action elements AE_i does not have any side-effects and is easy to implement. At the second level, while parallel rule matching does not create any problem, parallel rule application may. As we will see, only mutually independent rules may be applied in parallel. These sets of rules will result from the study of rule interdependencies. When rules fire in parallel, intermediate database states are skipped. The controller determines the rule application strategy based on the state of the database, the goal, and possibly some context knowledge that may not be part of the knowledge base. Thus, even when many parallel rules are eligible to fire, it is not always advantageous to fire them all at once. The third form of parallelism, obtained from overlapping phases of processing cycles, is rather complex; little experience of it has been gained so far.

Potentially, other forms of parallelism in PS may be exploited. For example, a hierarchy of production systems may be conceived for the purpose of operating at several levels of abstraction in large knowledge bases. Also, parallelism may be implemented in the control portion of PS. These ideas have not yet been thoroughly investigated.

To fully explore the inherent parallelism in PS, an analysis of rule interdependencies is necessary. It is possible to smooth the growth of the search space by eliminating redundant paths. The approach is to study the dependencies between rules at compile time, and then to provide this information to the controller.

8.1.2 Parallelism in the Match Phase

There are two types of match algorithms: state-saving and non-state-saving algorithms. In a non-state-saving algorithm, each rule is matched with every working memory element in each match-resolve-act cycle. As a result, performance for non-state-saving algorithms is very slow. Matching each rule with every working memory element is redundant because only changes in the working memory would produce new bindings. In a state-saving match algorithm, the state of the match is stored. Then by updating the changes to the match state caused by the changes to the working memory, a new set of eligible rules is easily determined without redundant matching. An example of a state-saving algorithm is the Rete algorithm.

Rete Algorithm

The Rete algorithm, developed at Carnegie-Mellon University by Forgy [Forgy 1982], is an efficient match algorithm used for OPS5 and other implementations of production systems. The algorithm achieves its high efficiency by exploiting two facts: (1) that only a small fraction of working memory changes during each cycle, which allows results from previous cycles to be stored and used subsequently; and (2) that the similarity between condition elements reduces the number of tests.

The basic idea of the Rete algorithm is to construct a common network from the conditions of all productions and then to perform the match operation by sending working memory elements, in the form of tokens, over this network. The state match is stored in the network nodes. To generate a Rete network for all precondition elements, test nodes are constructed for each attribute. Common nodes corresponding to the same class and the same attribute appear only once in the network. All attributes in a class appear as sequential nodes. At the top of the network there is a common node, called the root, which is followed by the constant nodes corresponding to different classes. The sharing of variables between attributes is marked by merging two inputs at a time into an *and-node*. The memory nodes corresponding to the same class of attributes are called α-*memory nodes*, and the memory nodes corresponding to a sequence of condition elements in the left-hand side of a production are called β-*memory nodes*. In addition, there are terminal nodes, one for each production. Whenever a terminal node has a match, the corresponding production becomes eligible to fire.

An example of a Rete network for two productions is shown in Figure 8.2. Information flows from the top down along the paths. The single-input nodes are concerned with constants or individual condition elements. The nodes with two inputs perform variable bindings between condition elements.

The working memory elements are assembled as tokens and pass through the network for the purpose of matching. A token consists of a tag: either +, meaning addition to the working memory, or −, meaning deletion from the working memory and from the list of attributes.

The Rete algorithm stores the results of the match between the working memory element and the network as states of the nodes. The changes in the working memory are presented to the network as new tokens, which in turn change the states of appropriate nodes.

8.1.3   Rule Interdependencies

The analysis of rule interdependencies is fundamental to parallel processing of PS, just as data dependencies are essential to parallel processing of deterministic programs. For a pair of rules, several dependencies can be defined. Dependencies for RBS were proposed independently in [Tenorio and Moldovan 1985] and in [Ishida and Stolfo 1985].

There are three important types of interrule dependencies: *inhibit* dependence, *output* dependence, and *enable* dependence. Inhibit dependence occurs when the firing of one production rule deletes or adds working memory elements such that the condition part of another production rule is no longer satisfied. Output dependence occurs when the working memory elements that are added by the firing of one production rule are deleted by the firing of another production rule. Enable dependence occurs when the firing of one production rule deletes or adds working memory elements such that the condition part of another production rule may then be satisfied. Recall from the previous section

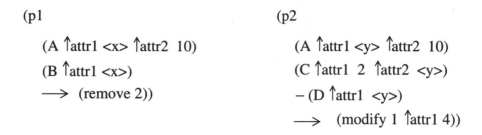

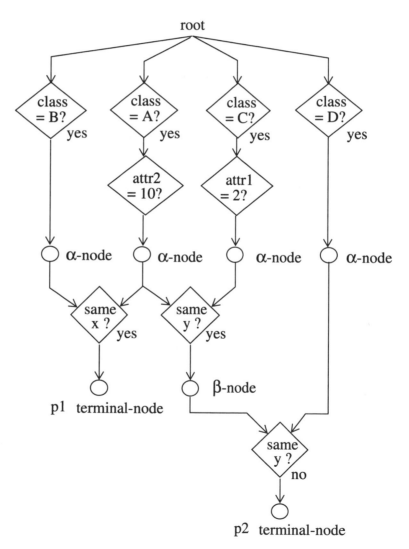

Figure 8.2 An example of a Rete network.

that CE_i^+ and CE_i^- denote the working memory elements that match the positive and negative condition elements of rule R_i, and AE_i^+ and AE_i^- denote the working memory elements to be added or deleted by rule R_i.

Definition 8.1 In an OPS5 production system, R_2 is said to be *inhibit-dependent* on R_1 when the firing of R_1 deletes or adds working memory elements such that the condition part of R_2 is no longer satisfied, written $R_1 \overset{i}{\rightarrow} R_2$:

$$(AE_1^- \cap CE_2^+) \cup (AE_1^+ \cap CE_2^-) \neq \emptyset$$

Definition 8.2 In an OPS5 production system, R_2 and R_1 are said to be *output-dependent* when the firing of R_1 adds working memory elements that are deleted by R_2, or the firing of R_1 deletes working memory elements that are added by R_2, written $R_1 \overset{o}{\leftrightarrow} R_2$:

$$(AE_1^- \cap AE_2^+) \cup (AE_1^+ \cap AE_2^-) \neq \emptyset$$

Notice that output dependence is symmetric.

Definition 8.3 In an OPS5 production system, R_2 is said to be *enable-dependent* on R_1 when the firing of R_1 deletes or adds working memory elements such that the condition part of R_2 may become satisfied, written $R_1 \overset{e}{\rightarrow} R_2$:

$$(AE_1^- \cap CE_2^-) \cup (AE_1^+ \cap CE_2^+) \neq \emptyset$$

The analysis of dependencies between all pairs of rules in the production system is used to construct a parallelism matrix $\mathbf{P} = [p_{jk}]$. The parallelism matrix is constructed such that an element $p_{jk} = 0$ if rules R_j and R_k can be fired in parallel, and $p_{jk} = 1$ if they cannot. Two rules can be fired in parallel and are said to be compatible if they are neither inhibit- nor output-dependent.

Definition 8.4 The *parallelism matrix* $\mathbf{P} \in \{0,1\}^{r \times r}$ for a production system with r rules is constructed such that for an element p in row j and column k,

$$p_{jk} = \begin{cases} 1 & \text{if } R_j \overset{i}{\rightarrow} R_k \vee R_k \overset{i}{\rightarrow} R_j \vee R_j \overset{o}{\leftrightarrow} R_k \\ 0 & \text{otherwise} \end{cases}$$

For the purpose of executing a PS on a multiprocessor, it is important to indicate how the firing of one production affects other productions in the system. For example, when two rules are inhibit-dependent, the firing of one production may destroy the conditions for firing the other production, and when two rules are enable-dependent, the firing of one production brings elements into the database that may make the other production fire. Let us form a square matrix $\mathbf{C}$, called the *communication matrix*, whose dimensionality is equal to the number of rules. The communication matrix is constructed such that an element $c_{jk} = 0$ if, when fired, rule R_j does not exchange any messages with rule R_k. Conversely, an element $c_{jk} = 1$ if they exchange messages. Two rules in different processors can be fired simultaneously without communicating changes to working memory if they are not inhibit-dependent or enable-dependent.

Definition 8.5 The *communication matrix* $\mathbf{C} \in \{0,1\}^{r \times r}$ for a production system with r rules is constructed such that for an element c in row j and column k,

$$c_{jk} = \begin{cases} 1 & \text{if } R_j \overset{i}{\to} R_k \vee R_j \overset{e}{\to} R_k \\ 0 & \text{otherwise} \end{cases}$$

Example 8.3. A small example of a six-rule PS, including the starting database and the goal, is shown in Figure 8.3. This example has been discussed in [Moldovan 1989]. The elements of the productions and database are of the form R(A,B), where A and B are objects or nodes and R is a relation or predicate between the objects. This is another possible representation of production systems much weaker than OPS5, because it lacks the capability of expressing variables and negative (or missing) elements. However, for our purpose of illustrating interdependencies it provides the advantage of visualizing the dependencies by intersecting some graphs. For each production rule, it shows the left-hand side represented as a graph, and the right-hand side separated into a deleted graph and an added graph. For example, the color graph representation of production rule p_1 may correspond to the following English sentence:

p_1 : *if*   Adam owns a car and

car was purchased in California and
car has color green
then Adam lives in California and
it does not matter that car was purchased in California.

The following notation is used:

A	Adam	P	owns
B	car	Q	was purchased
C	California	R	has color
D	green	S	lives

As shown in Figure 8.3, the right-hand side consists of removing "Car was purchased in California," and adding "Adam lives in California."

For this example, the parallelism matrix **P** and the communication matrix **C** are

$$\mathbf{P} = \begin{bmatrix} 1 & 0 & 1 & 0 & 0 & 0 \\ 0 & 1 & 1 & 0 & 1 & 0 \\ 1 & 1 & 1 & 0 & 1 & 0 \\ 0 & 0 & 0 & 1 & 1 & 0 \\ 0 & 1 & 1 & 1 & 1 & 1 \\ 0 & 0 & 0 & 0 & 1 & 0 \end{bmatrix} \qquad \mathbf{C} = \begin{bmatrix} 1 & 0 & 0 & 0 & 0 & 0 \\ 0 & 1 & 1 & 1 & 1 & 1 \\ 1 & 1 & 1 & 0 & 1 & 1 \\ 0 & 0 & 0 & 1 & 0 & 0 \\ 0 & 0 & 1 & 1 & 1 & 1 \\ 0 & 0 & 0 & 0 & 0 & 0 \end{bmatrix}$$

Unfortunately, the use of variables in OPS5 sometimes prevents a definite analysis of dependencies for a pair of production rules because the bindings of variables are not known until run time. We can still construct **P** and **C** matrices at compile time to eliminate as much run-time computation as possible. The uncertainty of parallelism between two rules may be represented by a * in the **P** matrix, and similarly the uncertainty of communication between two rules may be represented by a * in the **C** matrix. These are resolved at run time. Because it is easier to implement message-passing between processors than to resolve the interrule communication uncertainty within each processor, the interrule communication uncertainty may be represented as a 1 in the **C** matrix instead.

Definition 8.6 Two rules p_1 and p_2 are said to be *compatible* (or commutative) if they are neither inhibit-dependent nor output-dependent in both directions.

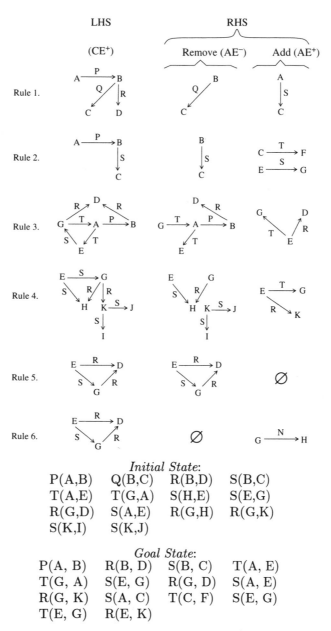

Initial State:

P(A,B)	Q(B,C)	R(B,D)	S(B,C)
T(A,E)	T(G,A)	S(H,E)	S(E,G)
R(G,D)	S(A,E)	R(G,H)	R(G,K)
S(K,I)	S(K,J)		

Goal State:

P(A, B)	R(B, D)	S(B, C)	T(A, E)
T(G, A)	S(E, G)	R(G, D)	S(A, E)
R(G, K)	S(A, C)	T(C, F)	S(E, G)
T(E, G)	R(E, K)		

Figure 8.3 A six-rule production system [Moldovan 1989].

Lemma 8.1 For any two compatible rules applicable to a database, the following derivations are equivalent:

1. $p_1 p_2$ (p_1 followed by p_2);

2. $p_2 p_1$ (p_2 followed by p_1); and

3. $p_1 \| p_2$ (p_1 in parallel with p_2).

The proof of this lemma is shown in Problem 8.4.A.

The equivalent derivations of three compatible productions are shown in Figure 8.4. It is assumed that these sequences are applicable to the respective database states. There are thirteen possible derivations, of which six are sequential, six are partially parallel, and one is fully parallel.

8.1.4   Search Space Reduction

The P matrix carries important information about the concurrent application of rules in the search space. According to Lemma 8.1, when $p_{ij} = p_{ji} = 0$, rule i is commutative with rule j. This is important in situations when sequences i, j and j, i are applied to the same database; only one sequence needs to be applied, as shown in Figure 8.4. The idea of compatibility can be extended to the entire set of rules. It is useful for the partitioning of a production system. By inspecting the P matrix, it is possible to identify the largest sets of compatible rules (which may be fired in parallel if applicable). The following sets were obtained in the case of the example shown in Figure 8.3:

$$
\begin{aligned}
S_1 &= \{3, 4, 6\} \\
S_2 &= \{1, 2, 4, 6\} \\
S_3 &= \{1, 5\}
\end{aligned}
$$

These sets are useful for reducing the search space of the PS by eliminating redundant derivations. Figure 8.5 shows the original search space for the example PS. It is easy to verify that the goal state indicated in Figure 8.3 is reached by one of the following production sequences: 142, 124, 241, 214, 412, or 421. Figure 8.6 shows the reduced sequential search space after eliminating redundant search states.

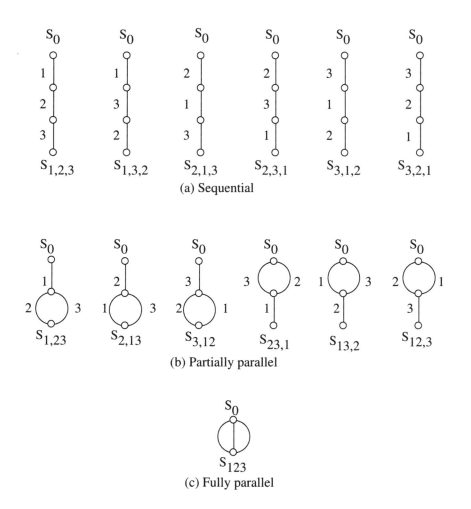

Figure 8.4 Equivalent derivations of three compatible rules [Moldovan 1989].

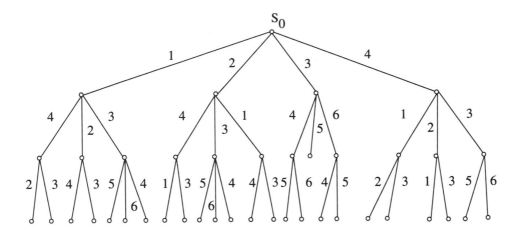

Figure 8.5 Original search space.

Notice that while they are equivalent, the reduced sequential space has considerably fewer nodes than the original one. When the depth becomes larger, the reduction factor can be very significant. Figure 8.7 shows the equivalent parallel search space; that is, all the states reached either by sequential derivation or by parallel derivation. Notice that the goal is now reached in a single step, 124.

It is possible to design an algorithm for constructing the reduced parallel search space; moreover, it can be demonstrated that by using the parallelism matrix, a minimum search space is achieved (see Problem 8.1.B).

8.2   MULTIPLE-RULE FIRING

8.2.1   Compatibility and Convergence

There are two basic problems in multiple-rule firing: the *compatibility* problem and the *convergence* problem. The compatibility problem is concerned with finding a set of eligible rules in an inference cycle that are allowed to fire simultaneously. A set of rules is allowed to fire simultaneously if they reach the same state both sequentially and in

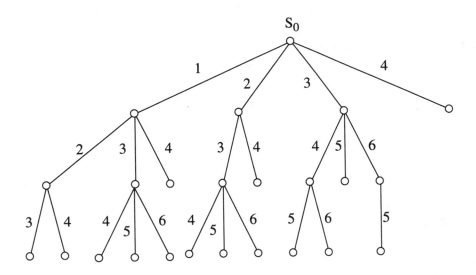

Figure 8.6 Reduced sequential search space.

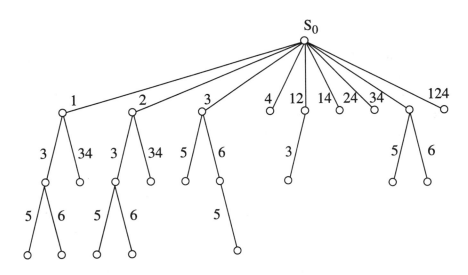

Figure 8.7 Reduced parallel search space.

parallel; that is, if the resulting working memories from sequential firing and multiple-rule firing are the same. In the previous section these were called compatible rules. The data dependence analysis is sufficient to determine compatible rules.

The convergence problem is concerned with firing only rules that achieve correct solutions; that is, rules that drive the system to the goal states. Unfortunately, correct solutions are not always reached when multiple compatible rules are fired. This is because not all compatible rules in an inference cycle should be fired if they are to produce correct solutions. For example, consider the case of the parallel search space in Figure 8.7. If the goal is reached by rule combination 12, by firing all compatible rules 1, 2, 4, the goal is skipped and the system may not converge.

Contexts in Production Programs

A classical way to solve a complex problem is to divide it into smaller and smaller subproblems until the subproblems are small enough to be easily solved. A large and complex rule-based system may be divided into smaller subproblems, called *contexts*. Each context is marked by the presence of a unique context working element, such that the rules applicable to that context contain this context working element in their preconditions. The contexts and the rules applicable to each context are determined by the knowledge engineer based on the nature of the application. In addition to the regular production rules that fire within each context, it is necessary now to introduce *control* rules that transfer program control from one context to another. A context is activated when a control rule adds a context working memory element to the database.

Firing compatible rule instantiations in parallel within a context C_i does not always reach the correct goal states for context C_i, even though executing them concurrently is equivalent to executing them in some sequential order. This is because not every sequential rule firing sequence for context C_i reaches the correct goal states. In sequential production system, conflict resolution strategy is used to select the correct rule firing sequence. However, since conflict resolution only selects one rule instantiation per cycle, potential parallelism between rule instantiations is lost.

A condition for eliminating conflict resolution for a context C_i is that every rule firing sequence for C_i reaches the correct goal states. Such contexts are called *converging* contexts. Nonconverging contexts are called *sequential* contexts.

For a sequential context, conflict resolution must be used to reach the correct solution. By dividing contexts into converging and sequential contexts and applying the correct execution model for each type, the convergence problem can be resolved at the context level. The designer, who understands the nature of the application domain, may be able to partition the application into contexts. The next step is to construct a control flow diagram that indicates the interaction between concepts.

Let us consider the rules given in Figure 8.8. The context working memory elements are the first condition elements, and are of the class (goal ↑name ↑object). Because rules 11 and 12 have the same context condition elements, they are in the same context, holds_object. Rule 0 is in a different context, on_floor. Because rule 12 modifies the context working memory element so that rule 0 is matched, given that its second condition element is also matched, rule 12 deactivates the context holds_object and activates the context on_floor. This is represented in the control flow diagram by an arrow pointing from the context holds_object to the context on_floor. The control flow for the entire production system, Monkey and Bananas, is derived by repeating these steps.

The control flow diagram of a production program is important because it shows possible sequences of context calls in problem-solving. Since the control flows from one context to the next, not all contexts can be active at the same time. Available parallelism is to be found among active contexts. Therefore, one does not have to look at the entire set of rules, but need only consider the interactions between contexts, which is much simpler.

Compatible Contexts

Two contexts C_i and C_j are compatible if executing them in parallel does not cause incompatible rule instantiations to fire or violate the control flow. This requires that rule instantiations in C_i and C_j do not have data dependencies and that the control flow is such that C_i is not

(p 0.monkey_on_floor
{ (goal ↑ name monkey_on ↑ object floor) <goal>}
{(monkey ↑ on <> floor) <monkey>}
⟶
(modify <monkey> ↑ on floor)
(remove <goal>))

(p 11.holds_object_on_floor
{ (goal ↑ name monkey_holds ↑ object <o>) <goal>}
{(object ↑ name <o> ↑ weight light ↑ on floor) <object>}
{(monkey ↑ on floor) <monkey>}
⟶
(modify <monkey> ↑ holds <o>)
(modify <object> ↑ on null)
(remove <goal>))

(p 12.call_on_floor
{ (goal ↑ name monkey_holds ↑ object <o>) <goal>}
{(object ↑ name <o> ↑ weight light ↑ on floor)}
{(monkey ↑ on floor)}
⟶
(modify goal ↑ name monkey_on ↑ object floor))

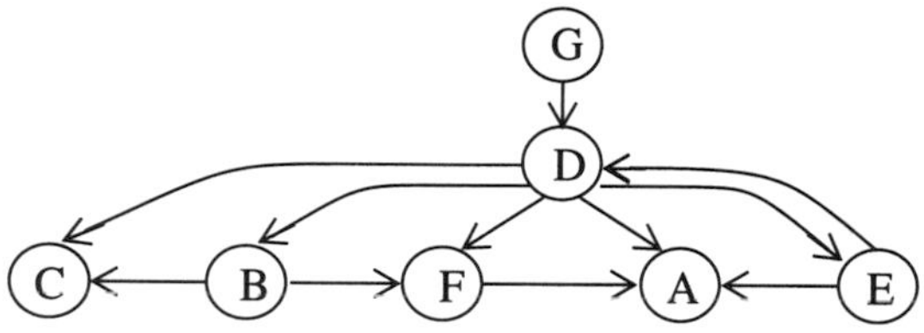

CONTEXT	REACHABLE SET
A: on...floor	{A}
B: on...phys-object	{A, B, C, F}
C: holds...null	{C}
D: holds...object	{A, B, C, D, E, F}
E: at...object	{A, B, C, D, E, F}
F: at...monkey	{A, F}
G: initialization	{A, B, C, D, E, F, G}

Figure 8.8 Contexts and control flow diagram for monkey-and-bananas problem.

in the reachable set of C_j, or (vice versa), C_j is not in the reachable set of C_i.

The reachable set RS_i for a context C_i is a set of contexts whose elements are reachable by following the directed arcs in the control flow diagram starting from C_i. C_i is included in its own reachable set. For the context C_i, the contexts in its reachable set RS_i are the contexts that may be activated as a result of its execution.

Definition 8.7 Context C_j is in the reachable set RS_i of context C_i if there is a sequence $S = C_i \rightarrow \cdots \rightarrow C_n$ such that $C_j \in S$.

We can define a context activation matrix $\mathbf{CA} = [ca_{ij}]$ such that $ca_{ij} = 0$ if $C_i \cap RS_j = \emptyset$ and rule instantiations in C_i and C_j do not have data dependencies; otherwise, $ca_{ij} = 1$. Contexts C_i and C_j are compatible if $ca_{ij} = ca_{ji} = 0$. If $ca_{ij} = 1$, they are incompatible and are not allowed to execute concurrently. In this case, if C_i and C_j are both active, C_i must wait until C_j completes its execution.

Parallel execution converges to the correct solution by firing only compatible rule instantiations concurrently for converging contexts, and sequential rule instantiations serially for sequential contexts, and executing only compatible contexts simultaneously.

8.2.2 Multiple-Rule Firing Models

In this section, we present three multiple-rule firing models: the rule dependence model (RDM), the single-context multiple-rules (SCMR) model, and the multiple-contexts multiple-rules (MCMR) model. The RDM resolves the compatibility problem by data dependence analysis, but it does not address the convergence problem. The SCMR and MCMR models address both the compatibility problem and the convergence problem. The difference between the SCMR and the MCMR models is that only one context at a time is active for the SCMR model, whereas multiple contexts may be active simultaneously for the MCMR model.

A new parallel inference cycle, shown in Figure 8.9, is needed for multiple-rule firings. It consists of four phases: the *match* phase, the *conflict resolution* (CR) phase, the *compatibility determination* (CD) phase, and the *act* phase. The three models follow this new parallel cycle with some modifications, depending on how contexts are handled.

Rule Dependence Model

In the rule dependence model, some or all compatible rules that match the database are allowed to fire simultaneously. Compatibility between rules is based on interrule dependencies, as defined previously. This dependence analysis is performed at compile time when the parallelism matrix $\mathbf{P}$ and the communication matrix $\mathbf{C}$ are constructed.

As shown in Figure 8.9, an inference cycle starts with the match phase. This is performed in parallel using an efficient Rete-like algorithm. The next phase, conflict resolution, is necessary in order to select a dominant rule according to some conflict resolution strategy. This selection is problem-specific, and the selection criterion is based on bringing the system closer to the goal. In some instances, when such a criterion is not available, the dominant rule is selected at random. At the next phase, compatibility determination, a set of rules is selected from the eligible rules, provided by the match phase, that are compatible with the dominant rule. This is determined by inspecting the $\mathbf{P}$ matrix. In some instances, all compatible eligible rules are incorporated into the compatibility set. Finally, at the act phase, the compatible rules selected previously are fired concurrently. This inference cycle is repeated.

Since the RDM fires rules in different contexts, it may activate rules in incompatible contexts, which may create a convergence problem. This model works well when all contexts are compatible with each other, and a correct solution is guaranteed. When this is not the case, the RDM fails.

Single-Context Multiple-Rules Model

The SCMR model resolves the convergence deficiency of the RDM by allowing only one context to be active at a time. The contexts are activated sequentially, but compatible rules within each context are fired in parallel. By activating contexts in a correct sequence, this model leads to correct solutions. Since only one context is active at a time, there is a loss of potential parallelism.

The inference cycle for the SCMR model is slightly different from that for the RDM. The match phase is the same. However, instead of

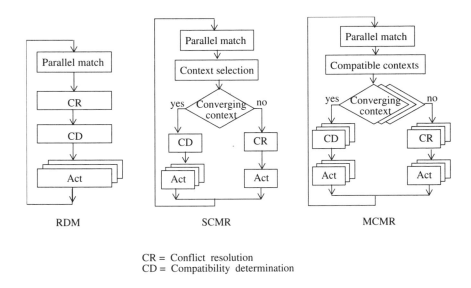

CR = Conflict resolution
CD = Compatibility determination

Figure 8.9 Inference cycles for multiple-rule firing models.

analyzing dependencies between all rules, here it is necessary to analyze interactions between rules only if they belong to the same context. This reduces processing time as well as storage space.

A context activation matrix may be generated to prestore inter-context dependencies. This is done at compile time, in the same way as for the parallelism matrix. After the match phase, a context is selected; it is from all active contexts. The contexts may be sequential or converging. For a sequential context, the compatibility determination is skipped. During the conflict resolution phase a dominant rule is selected and fired at the act phase. For a converging context, the conflict resolution phase is skipped. A set of compatible rules is formed from the eligible rules that belong to that context, then they are fired in parallel.

Multiple-Contexts Multiple-Rules Model
In order to gain more parallelism, the SCMR model may be extended to allow simultaneous activation of compatible contexts. Compatible

contexts are detected at compile time. The inference cycle is similar to the SCMR cycle. Each active context proceeds independent of the others. It passes either through a conflict resolution phase if it is a sequential context, or through a compatibility determination phase if it is a converging context. The concurrent creation of multiple conflict sets and compatible sets speeds up the processing time, yet brings the overall system to correct solution.

8.2.3   Mapping RBS into Multiprocessors

Some of the first attempts to implement RBS using parallel processing dealt with the mapping of the Rete match algorithm into multiprocessors. This was because most of the time used in the match-resolve-act cycle is spent in the match phase. The mapping of a multiple rule firing model on a message-passing multiprocessor is also discussed below.

The hardware model described below for the parallel execution of PS with multiple-rule firing has been studied by Moldovan [Moldovan 1989] and extended by Kuo and Moldovan [Kuo and Moldovan 1991]. The hardware consists of a message-passing multiprocessor, as shown in Figure 8.10. The multiprocessor is attached to a host computer through a common bus. Before the operation starts, the PS is preprocessed by an interpreter in the host computer. As a result, parallelism matrix $\mathbf{P}$ and communication matrix $\mathbf{C}$ are generated. Then the set of rules is partitioned into disjoint subsets, and each set is allocated to one processor. The partitioning and allocation scheme will be explained later. The database is also partitioned as the intersection of the original database with the union of the preconditions of each rule subset. As a result, elements in the database, coded as tokens, will fill in the corresponding rule preconditions distributed over the processing elements. The remaining part of the database is stored in the host computer.

Each PE's memory is functionally separated into three modules: program memory, data memory, and control memory. The program memory contains the rules assigned to the PE. The data memory contains the corresponding database subset and is comparable in size to the program memory. The control memory contains the addresses of the rules that are inhibit- and enable-dependent on the rules assigned

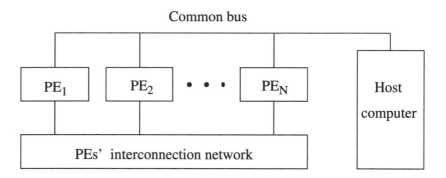

Figure 8.10 A message-passing multiprocessor for RBS.

to the PE, and the variable assignment that can take place during the matching phase.

The interconnection network is the only medium through which interprocessor communication takes place. Associated with each processor are some memory queues that store messages that cannot be directly routed through the network.

The left-hand side of each rule can be interpreted as a template whose tokens are relations forming preconditions. A rule fires when all tokens in its precondition are present and the outside controller allows that rule to fire. Then, after a rule fires, the tokens generated by the left-hand side of that rule go to the precondition templates of other rules, residing either in the same PE node or in other PE nodes.

For every $c_{ij} = 1$ in the communication matrix $\mathbf{C}$, there is either an inhibit dependence or an enable dependence between rule i and rule j. In the case of inhibit dependence, the link between the processors hosting rules i and j is used by the processor whose rule fires to inform the other processor that its common input tokens should be removed from the precondition template of that processor. This operation can be thought of as a processor's sending some antitokens over the communication link that annihilate existing tokens in other processors.

In the case of enable dependence, the link between processors hosting rules j and i is simply used to send tokens generated by the postcondition of j to the precondition of i. In the case in which two or more

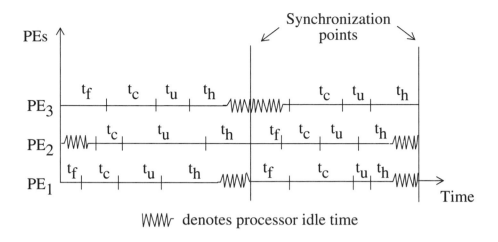

Figure 8.11 A timing example for three processors [Moldovan 1989].

rules become eligible to fire at the same time, the outside controller becomes aware of this and arbitrates, deciding which rule should fire, based on a parallelism analysis and some optimization criteria.

A timing diagram for rule processing is shown in Figure 8.11. The operation of a rule-based system consists of a number of rule firing cycles. Control is centralized in the host, and the beginning of a rule firing cycle is synchronized by the host. Each cycle includes rule firing time t_f, interprocessor communication time t_c, precondition update time t_u, communication with host time t_h, and possible idling time. Note that not all these times need be present in a rule firing cycle in each processor. For example, if one processor does not fire any rule in a cycle, it idles until messages arrive. The duration of each time component varies. The operation of PEs within each firing cycle is asynchronous, but the beginning of each cycle is synchronized by the host. Schmolze [Schmolze 1991] has derived some constraints that a rule-based system must satisfy in order to eliminate the synchronization at the end of a multirule firing cycle.

In local memory, incoming messages are checked to determine whether they are intended for that respective PE (in which case they are advanced into the shared memory queue), or are intended for some

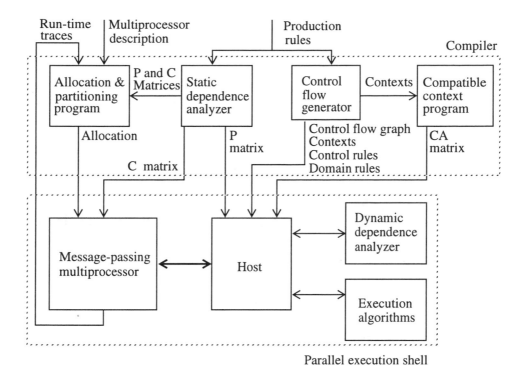

Figure 8.12 The RUBIC architecture.

other PE (in which case they are placed in an output queue). Figure 8.12 shows a block diagram of the RUBIC system, which implements this approach.

Rule Allocation

An important problem is the proper allocation of r rules to n processors when $r >> n$. The objective is to decrease the overall communication cost while maintaining the inherent parallelism as much as possible. The difficulty in determining good partitioning and allocation schemes for PS is their nondeterminism. In this section, the allocation problem is formulated as a performance optimization problem. Let the production system be characterized by its parallelism and communication matrices $\mathbf{P}$ and $\mathbf{C} \in \{0,1\}^{r \times r}$. Let $\mathbf{D} \in R^{n \times n}$ be the distance matrix characterizing the interconnection network. Elements d_{ij} represent the cost of communicating a unit message from processor i to processor j. Let $\mathbf{X} \in \{0,1\}^{r \times r}$ be the assignment matrix, where $x_{ij} = 1$ if production i is assigned to processor j and $x_{ij} = 0$ otherwise.

Communication Cost. For the sake of simplicity, the communication matrix may be assumed to represent not just the communication requirement but the actual cost of communication; the nonzero entries in the communication matrix may be modified to reflect the actual costs if necessary. Such a cost may be a function of the "amount of dependence," which is measured by the number of common elements that cause the dependence. This is justified because the length of the communication packet, and the time required to encode and decode it, may depend on the common elements. The costs incurred at the transmitting and the receiving processors may not be equal; however, they are considered equal to keep matters simple.

The cost of communication between the productions p_i and p_j is $x_{ik}c_{kl}x_{jl}d_{ij}$; in other words, the cost of communicating between processors PE_k and PE_l provided p_i is assigned to PE_k, i.e., $x_{ik} = 1$; p_j is assigned to PE_l, i.e., $x_{jl} = 1$; and the two productions communicate, i.e., $c_{ij} = 1$. The total communication cost of the allocation can be compactly written as

$$E_c = \Sigma_{row}\Sigma_{col}(\mathbf{X}^t\mathbf{C}\mathbf{X}) \cdot \mathbf{D}$$

where $\cdot$ represents the product of respective matrix elements.

Parallelism Loss. When two parallel productions are assigned to the same processor, there is a potential loss of parallelism. The parallelism loss between two productions i and j is some multiple of $x_{ik}x_{jk}\bar{p}_{ij}$; that is, the productions are parallel ($\bar{p}_{ij} = 1$) and are assigned to the same processor. The total parallelism loss of allocation can be written compactly as

$$E_p = \Sigma_{row}\Sigma_{col}\mathbf{X}\mathbf{X}^t \cdot \bar{\mathbf{P}}$$

Several improvements could be made to make the loss of parallelism E_p a bit more realistic. If m parallel rules are assigned to the same processor, the time required to execute them is $O(m)$; if they are assigned to different processors, then the time required to execute is $O(1)$ in the best case. Thus, the potential loss of speedup or parallelism is $O(m)$, and not $O(m^2)$ as given by the above formula. Also, some productions are executed more than others. These differences can be easily modeled by modifying the communication and parallelism matrices. Simply replace each element c_{kl} in $\mathbf{C}$ by $w_k c_{kl}$, and each element p_{ki} in $\mathbf{P}$ by $w_k p_{kl}$, where w_k is the execution frequency of the production p_k.

The Constraints. Obviously, every production must be assigned to some processor. In addition, let every rule be assigned to one and only one processor. In order to avoid trivial solutions and load imbalances, such as assigning all rules to just one processor, assume that each processor is capable of handling only a few productions. Let the production capacity of the processor i be R_i, meaning the processor cannot handle more than R_i rules. This limitation may arise because of limited local memory. These constraints are reasonable and effectively restrict the range of solutions.

The allocation problem can now be formulated as follows:

Find an $\mathbf{X}$ that minimizes

$$E = E_c + E_p = \Sigma\Sigma(\mathbf{X}^t\mathbf{C}\mathbf{X}) \cdot \mathbf{D} + \Sigma\Sigma\mathbf{X}\mathbf{X}^t \cdot \bar{\mathbf{P}}$$

subject to

$$\sum_{j=l}^{n} x_{ij} = 1 \quad 1 \le i \le r$$
$$\sum_{i=l}^{n} x_{ij} \le R_j \quad 1 \le j \le n$$

As formulated, the problem is quadratic and is very difficult to solve. By taking advantage of the fact that the variables are boolean, the problem can be reduced to $0-1$ linear programming, at the cost of introducing more variables.

Example 8.4. Consider a PS with four rules, which is to be mapped into a three-processor message-passing multiprocessor with an interconnection as shown in Figure 8.13. The parallelism matrix and the communication matrix derived from the rule interdependencies are given:

$$\mathbf{P} = \begin{bmatrix} 1 & 0 & 1 & 0 \\ 0 & 1 & 1 & 0 \\ 1 & 1 & 1 & 0 \\ 0 & 0 & 0 & 1 \end{bmatrix} \qquad \mathbf{C} = \begin{bmatrix} 1 & 0 & 1 & 0 \\ 0 & 1 & 1 & 0 \\ 1 & 1 & 1 & 0 \\ 0 & 1 & 0 & 1 \end{bmatrix}$$

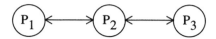

Figure 8.13 Message-passing multiprocessor system.

The problem is to compute the allocation cost, consisting of the communication cost and the parallelism cost, given by the following two allocation matrices:

$$\mathbf{X}_1 = \begin{bmatrix} 0\ 1\ 0 \\ 1\ 0\ 0 \\ 0\ 1\ 0 \\ 1\ 0\ 0 \end{bmatrix} \qquad \mathbf{X}_2 = \begin{bmatrix} 1\ 0\ 0 \\ 0\ 1\ 0 \\ 1\ 0\ 0 \\ 0\ 0\ 1 \end{bmatrix}$$

Rules	Processor
1	2
2	1
3	2
4	1

Rules	Processor
1	1
2	2
3	1
4	3

Decide which allocation scheme is better.

The allocation cost is

$$E = \sum_{col}\sum_{row} \mathbf{E}_c + \frac{1}{2}\sum_{col}\sum_{row} \mathbf{E}_p$$

$$\mathbf{E}_c = (\mathbf{X}^t\mathbf{C}\mathbf{X}) \cdot \mathbf{D}$$

$$\mathbf{E}_p = \mathbf{X}\mathbf{X}^t \cdot \bar{\mathbf{P}}$$

(i) In the case of $\mathbf{X}_1$, the cost is

$$\mathbf{E}_c = \begin{bmatrix} 0\ 1\ 0\ 1 \\ 1\ 0\ 1\ 0 \\ 0\ 0\ 0\ 0 \end{bmatrix} \begin{bmatrix} 1\ 0\ 1\ 0 \\ 0\ 1\ 1\ 0 \\ 1\ 1\ 1\ 0 \\ 0\ 1\ 0\ 1 \end{bmatrix} \begin{bmatrix} 0\ 1\ 0 \\ 1\ 0\ 0 \\ 0\ 1\ 0 \\ 1\ 0\ 0 \end{bmatrix} \cdot \begin{bmatrix} 0\ 1\ 2 \\ 1\ 0\ 1 \\ 2\ 1\ 0 \end{bmatrix}$$

$$= \begin{bmatrix} 0\,2\,1\,1 \\ 2\,1\,2\,0 \\ 0\,0\,0\,0 \end{bmatrix} \begin{bmatrix} 0\,1\,0 \\ 1\,0\,0 \\ 0\,1\,0 \\ 1\,0\,0 \end{bmatrix} \cdot \begin{bmatrix} 0\,1\,2 \\ 1\,0\,1 \\ 2\,1\,0 \end{bmatrix}$$

$$= \begin{bmatrix} 3\,1\,0 \\ 1\,4\,0 \\ 0\,0\,0 \end{bmatrix} \cdot \begin{bmatrix} 0\,1\,2 \\ 1\,0\,1 \\ 2\,1\,0 \end{bmatrix}$$

$$= \begin{bmatrix} 0\,1\,0 \\ 1\,0\,0 \\ 0\,0\,0 \end{bmatrix}$$

$$\mathbf{E}_p = \begin{bmatrix} 0\,1\,0 \\ 1\,0\,0 \\ 0\,1\,0 \\ 1\,0\,0 \end{bmatrix} \begin{bmatrix} 0\,1\,0\,1 \\ 1\,0\,1\,0 \\ 0\,0\,0\,0 \end{bmatrix} \cdot \begin{bmatrix} 0\,1\,0\,1 \\ 1\,0\,0\,1 \\ 0\,0\,0\,1 \\ 1\,1\,1\,0 \end{bmatrix}$$

$$= \begin{bmatrix} 0\,0\,0\,0 \\ 0\,0\,0\,1 \\ 0\,0\,0\,0 \\ 0\,1\,0\,0 \end{bmatrix}$$

Thus, the total cost is

$$E(\mathbf{X}_1) = 2 + 1 = 3$$

(ii) In the case of $\mathbf{X}_2$, the cost is

$$\mathbf{E}_c = \begin{bmatrix} 1\,0\,1\,0 \\ 0\,1\,0\,0 \\ 0\,0\,0\,1 \end{bmatrix} \begin{bmatrix} 1\,0\,1\,0 \\ 0\,1\,1\,0 \\ 1\,1\,1\,0 \\ 0\,1\,0\,1 \end{bmatrix} \begin{bmatrix} 1\,0\,0 \\ 0\,1\,0 \\ 1\,0\,0 \\ 0\,0\,1 \end{bmatrix} \cdot \begin{bmatrix} 0\,1\,2 \\ 1\,0\,1 \\ 2\,1\,0 \end{bmatrix}$$

$$= \begin{bmatrix} 2\,1\,2\,0 \\ 0\,1\,1\,0 \\ 0\,1\,0\,1 \end{bmatrix} \begin{bmatrix} 1\,0\,0 \\ 0\,1\,0 \\ 1\,0\,0 \\ 0\,0\,1 \end{bmatrix} \cdot \begin{bmatrix} 0\,1\,2 \\ 1\,0\,1 \\ 2\,1\,0 \end{bmatrix}$$

$$= \begin{bmatrix} 4\,1\,0 \\ 1\,1\,0 \\ 0\,1\,1 \end{bmatrix} \cdot \begin{bmatrix} 0\,1\,2 \\ 1\,0\,1 \\ 2\,1\,0 \end{bmatrix}$$

$$= \begin{bmatrix} 0 & 1 & 0 \\ 1 & 0 & 0 \\ 0 & 1 & 0 \end{bmatrix}$$

$$\mathbf{E}_p = \begin{bmatrix} 1 & 0 & 0 \\ 0 & 1 & 0 \\ 1 & 0 & 0 \\ 0 & 0 & 1 \end{bmatrix} \begin{bmatrix} 1 & 0 & 1 & 0 \\ 0 & 1 & 0 & 0 \\ 0 & 0 & 0 & 1 \end{bmatrix} \cdot \begin{bmatrix} 0 & 1 & 0 & 1 \\ 1 & 0 & 0 & 1 \\ 0 & 0 & 0 & 1 \\ 1 & 1 & 1 & 0 \end{bmatrix}$$

$$= \begin{bmatrix} 1 & 0 & 1 & 0 \\ 0 & 1 & 0 & 0 \\ 1 & 0 & 1 & 0 \\ 0 & 0 & 0 & 1 \end{bmatrix} \cdot \begin{bmatrix} 0 & 1 & 0 & 1 \\ 1 & 0 & 0 & 1 \\ 0 & 0 & 0 & 1 \\ 1 & 1 & 1 & 0 \end{bmatrix}$$

$$= \begin{bmatrix} 0 & 0 & 0 & 0 \\ 0 & 0 & 0 & 0 \\ 0 & 0 & 0 & 0 \\ 0 & 0 & 0 & 0 \end{bmatrix}$$

Thus, the total cost is

$$E(\mathbf{X}_2) = 3 + 0 = 3$$

Therefore, the total costs are the same for the two allocations.

8.3 KNOWLEDGE REPRESENTATION AND REASONING USING SEMANTIC NETWORKS

8.3.1 Semantic Networks

Semantic networks are used for knowledge representation and reasoning. The value of semantic networks resides in the fact that knowledge is represented associatively and structurally. Hierarchically structured knowledge is organized as a parallel network memory scheme. Node units represent concepts and entities in the knowledge base. They are numerous but very simple. The links represent relations between nodes and allow the exchange of information between nodes. The knowledge represented by the network is stored partly inside the nodes, but mostly in the pattern of interconnections among the nodes.

In this section we will discuss some of the important issues in the construction of semantic network knowledge bases.

Knowledge Structuring

One of the most important issues in knowledge processing is how to structure the knowledge at hand. The organization of knowledge is often driven by two goals:

1. The desire to store knowledge in a compact manner, while also being able to derive as much implicit knowledge as possible; and

2. The desire for fast access to information in an arbitrarily large knowledge base.

The human brain meets these goals. When we speak, we say only enough for others to understand our intent. We are also able to recall and manipulate loosely related facts in a fraction of a second.

Many researchers working in knowledge representation agree that *hierarchical structuring* of knowledge contributes toward both goals. Hierarchies imply some ordering. A primary ordering criterion is generality, or level of abstraction: more general or abstract concepts are at the top of the hierarchy, while more specific ones are placed lower in the hierarchy. The ordering relation is called *subsumption,* or the *is_a* relation. For example the concept `person` subsumes the concept `father`, which further subsumes the concept `grandfather`. They can be written as `person` > `father` > `grandfather`, where > represents the ordering relation is_a.

A primary advantage of hierarchical structuring is its efficient method of representation. This efficiency is derived from the fact that hierarchies provide a powerful mechanism for property inheritance. The properties of concepts may be derived based on the inheritance mechanism from the concepts above them in the hierarchy. For example, the properties of the concept `person`, such as two arms, two legs, two eyes, and so on, need not be repeated for the concepts below it, because the properties are inherited by all the subsumees. However, exceptions (one arm instead of two) or specific values (weight equals 160 pounds) may need to be specified for a particular person which is an instantiation of concept **person**.

The hierarchical organization of knowledge makes knowledge retrieval faster, similarly to the way the lexicographical ordering of words in a dictionary makes possible the finding of words.

Knowledge Base Maintenance

In order for an intelligent system to perform tasks such as natural language processing, its knowledge base must be populated with vast amounts of information. The construction of a huge, hierarchically structured knowledge base is not a trivial task. The maintenance of such an entity also raises serious computational problems. New knowledge constantly becomes available and needs to be integrated into the existing knowledge base. Inconsistencies between new and previous knowledge must be resolved; this requires considerable processing.

Computational Effectiveness

Intelligent interactive systems must be capable of responding within a specified time frame. Machine processing time can often be compared to the time humans take to produce similar results. Many human activities, such as recognizing objects, or understanding speech or text, require only hundreds of milliseconds. This should be the target for future intelligent systems. Today's computers are far from this target.

There are also applications in which a machine must even outperform humans. Consider, for example, an AI system designed for helping fighter pilots during a mission. Such systems must integrate a considerable amount of information very fast to be able to assist pilots in making split-second decisions.

Set Operations

Set operations, such as intersection and union, are essential for knowledge processing. Set intersection, for example, may be used to identify concepts that share two or more features, to identify features common to several concepts, and in general to restrict the members of a set by imposing a new condition. Sets can be represented in many ways. Simple ways to represent sets explicitly are listing members or using a set membership flag. Another, more complex, representation can be achieved implicitly, by generator functions or predicates. Since we postulate large knowledge bases, it follows that the operation described here is the intersection of large sets. Clearly, we would like this operation to be done in constant time, independent of set cardinalities. Quite often, sequential AI algorithms avoid set intersections for the very reason that this operation is time-consuming on sequential machines.

Global Broadcasts

Broadcast operations are performed on knowledge bases to collect results, set initial conditions, and provide the capability for a global controller to communicate with the networks. Parallel knowledge bases should not needlessly depend on the step-by-step operation of a central controller. We want the nodes to have some autonomy for deciding how to route messages and how to react to various conditions. While such local asynchronous processing is desirable, there are, however, some operations that require simultaneous access to many nodes. These latter operations can be achieved via broadcasts from the central controller.

An example of a semantic network is shown in Figure 8.14. Notice the subsumption relation between the concepts linked by the `isa` relation. Since there are no standards for ways of constructing semantic networks, many possibilities exist. For example, we choose to have two nodes called `birthdate`, one attached to the concept `parent` and another one attached to the concept `grandparent`. In this case, `birthdate` is the color of the nodes with the same label; however, each node may store different instant values. The inheritance property can also be seen in Figure 8.14. The concept `breathes air` is attached to `mammal` via property link. All concepts subsumed by `mammal` inherit the property `breathes air`.

8.3.2   Marker/Value Propagation Model

What makes knowledge processing networks distinct from other multiprocessors is their ability to support reasoning mechanisms. Knowledge processing is communication-intensive and highly nondeterministic. The nature of knowledge is such that a slight perturbation of some concepts or relations sends waves of messages to numerous other

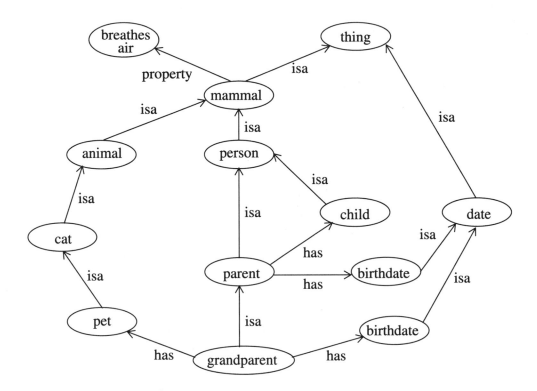

Figure 8.14 An example of a semantic network.

destinations. The nondeterministic behavior derives from the requirement that the knowledge base adapts to new situations and, moreover, performs learning. This implies the need for interconnection networks with high bandwidths. In the brain, each neuron has on the order of 10^4 individual connections with other neurons. Present technology is far from offering the ability to build so many dedicated links between processors. We must overcome this obstacle by cleverly controlling the flow of data on more modest, but realistic, interconnection networks.

Traditional interconnection networks use centralized control to reconfigure, whereas in this case there is a need for reconfiguration based on decisions at local nodes.

One possible communication mechanism that can be useful for knowledge processing is *marker propagation*. Markers are bit patterns that replace addresses. They indicate which nodes are active for a particular computation. Markers may satisfy many functions, and their identities may be coded in bit patterns. The presence of some markers at a node may guide the utilization of information at that node. Markers may also be used to enable links, or to inhibit the passage of other markers. Markers may be used to color messages, and thus to represent different waves of activations that simultaneously advance through the network. Each such wave may be connected to a hypothesis, or to a part of a hypothesis.

Another use of markers is to construct temporary connections between different nodes in the network. For example, the simultaneous presence of a marker on node A and node B may be regarded as a *virtual link* between nodes A and B. If one wants to assign specific properties to such a link, one can associate some node M with that link by assigning it the same marker.

The propagation of messages through the network must not be controlled by an outside controller; instead, it should be guided by the nature of the messages via some propagation rules. Complex reasoning mechanisms can be implemented by controlling the movement of messages according to the hypothesis at hand.

Marker propagation is a technique that was developed for using parallelism to find connections between concepts in semantic networks while avoiding many of the irrelevant facts. Essentially, two nodes, representing the concepts to be connected, are "marked." The neighbors of these nodes are then also marked, usually with a pointer that shows where the mark derives from. The neighbors of these nodes are then marked, and so on. At some point, some nodes may be marked from two different origins, and the algorithm then uses the back pointers to compute a "path" consisting of the set of nodes and links that connect the two originally marked nodes in the semantic network. Many variants of this basic process have been used.

As an example, consider the network in Figure 8.15. We want to find out the semantic relationship between the concepts john and today_menu. First, these two concepts are marked as shown in Figure 8.15(a). Then markers are allowed to pass along all links from these nodes to others, although some implementations treat some links as

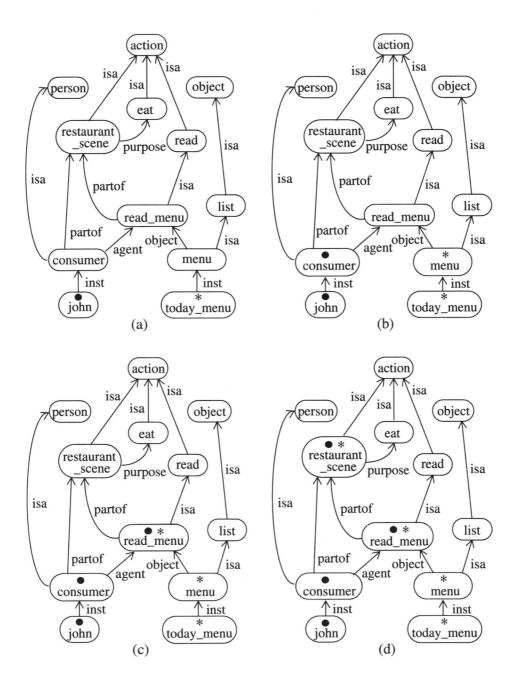

Figure 8.15 Marker propagation in a semantic network.

special. Thus, in Figure 8.15(b), we see that respective markers pass from `john` to `consumer` and from `today_menu` to `menu`.

The algorithm continues by propagating the markers further. Of particular interest is the node `read_menu`, which has now been marked from both origins as shown in Figure 8.15(c). This would cause the path `john` → `consumer` → `read_menu` → `menu` → `today_menu` to be found by following the back pointers. This represents one relationship between `john` and `menu`: they are both used in a particular reading event. Again, reporting such paths is the purpose of the marker-passing process.

Most marker-propagation algorithms do not stop upon encountering a path, but rather continue propagation until all paths within some attenuation limit are encountered. Thus, in our example, Figure 8.15(d) shows that the markers continue to propagate. In this snapshot, the node `restaurant_scene` is marked from both origins, permitting the path `john` → `consumer` → `restaurant_scene` → `read_menu` → `menu` → `today_menu` to be found. This represents the information that `john` is reading a menu in a restaurant. At this point, marking could continue, allowing other paths to be found. Note that the concept `read` was not marked at this step because it subsumes a concept that has already been marked by both markers, and we are interested in the most specific node concepts.

As one can see, this technique has two inherent problems. First, some of the paths found may meet at nodes that are not relevant to a particular problem. For example, in the cycle following Figure 8.15(d) a path from `john` to `today_menu` through the node `action` will be found. Second, the number of nodes marked can grow exponentially as time goes on, and soon all nodes will be marked. These important issues are related to the control of marker propagation, which will be addressed shortly. Before that, we will enhance the meaning of markers by attaching some numerical values to them and allowing them to participate in computations.

Value-Passing

By adopting the brain model and replacing discrete marker-passing with more complex markers containing value-passing, a whole new computational dimension is opened. Many properties associated with concepts can be quantified now, instead of simply indicating their binary presence or absence. The values of a property may indicate the relative likelihood of occurence of these values. Value-passing represents a good mechanism for resolving ambiguities. Values may be used to indicate the strength of a hypothesis; that is, a measure of belief of that hypothesis. Consider for example an application in which a sentence is parsed; several interpretations may be possible, and each interpretation represents a hypothesis with its own value.

Value-passing may be used to indicate how long a mark has been present on a node. Such age counters may be used to perform garbage collection in a distributed manner.

Another possible application of value-passing is to act as a speed regulator for spreading waves of markers through the network. It is feasible to have implementations that allow different markers to propagate at different speeds, depending on the marker category.

In terms of implementation, value-passing implies the transfer of numbers between processing cells. The probability-based marker-passing algorithms show the most promise in controlling the number of paths found. They require hardware support not provided in many current systems.

Controlling Marker Propagation

The problem of winnowing out those paths that are of no use has been attacked in several ways. The first approach is to use *constrained* marker-propagation techniques. Under this approach, the markers are allowed to traverse only some types of links, which need to be specified prior to marker-passing. During the propagation stage, tests are performed to determine which links could be traversed. A variant of this technique is to propagate markers under external control, rather than in parallel, to allow more discrimination in the constraints.

The second approach to eliminating bad paths is to use a *path evaluator* mechanism that can filter out paths violating certain restrictions. This usually consists of developing of a set of heuristic "filters" that weed out those paths which cannot satisfy some set of conditions.

To achieve massive parallelism, marker-passing systems have generally been formulated using "local algorithms," or programs in which each node being marked can decide whether to propagate markers to its neighbors.

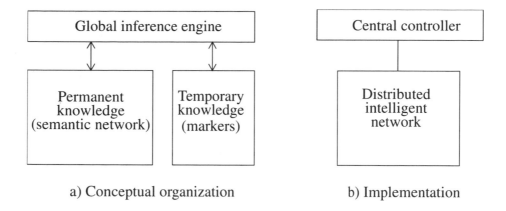

a) Conceptual organization   b) Implementation

Figure 8.16 Marker-passing model.

Among the first issues to be considered in designing AI systems are (1) how to represent knowledge and (2) which reasoning paradigm to use. Next, we describe a marker-passing model that addresses these questions.

A Marker-Passing Model

This model integrates permanent knowledge, temporary knowledge, and a reasoning mechanism, as shown in Figure 8.16.

1. *Permanent knowledge* is represented as a semantic network. The network nodes represent concepts and their properties, whereas the network arcs represent interrelations among the nodes. The network has a hierarchical structure, with more general or abstract nodes at the top subsuming more specific nodes below. The inheritance property that results from the subsumption ordering saves memory because the properties of more general nodes are inherited by more specific nodes, and thus need not be repeated.

2. *Temporary knowledge* is represented by markers and by values attached to node data. We will assume that markers are complex bit patterns that may incorporate values as necessary. Thus, temporary knowledge physically overlaps with permanent knowledge.

3. *Reasoning* is achieved by changing the states of both temporary and permanent knowledge. Originally, markers are assigned to nodes by a global inference engine to indicate a specific knowledge state. Stimulated by the inference engine, markers move from node to node; while moving, they interact with selected markers in some other nodes along the path, changing the state of the knowledge base. The movement of markers is guided by some propagation rules embedded in the network. The controller may change the marker propagation rules.

In Figure 8.16 it is shown that this model may be implemented as a distributed intelligent network working under the supervision of a controller. Permanent and temporary knowledge are mapped into the intelligent network and the inference engine into the controller. The controller broadcasts instructions and collects results. However, in order to support the movement of markers and other local processing, the processor nodes should be capable of running their own programs. The model presented above is rather general; it may lead to a number of possible implementations depending on the technology, the mode of operation, and other aspects.

Next we discuss some important reasoning techniques and indicate how the marker-propagation model may be used to implement them.

8.3.3 Reasoning on Semantic Networks

Reasoning is the process through which new information is extracted from a knowledge base. A characteristic of knowledge bases is that only a small portion of the knowledge is stated explicitly; much more is implicit and could be made explicit via an inference mechanism. Some important reasoning techniques for semantic network knowledge bases are recognition, inheritance, classification, generalization, and unification.

Recognition

One of the most important forms of reasoning on a knowledge base is the recognition of concepts or situations on that knowledge base. The *recognition problem* may be described as follows: Given a description of a set of properties, find a concept or a pattern of concepts that best matches the description. For example, the description "large animal, has trunk, and lives in a cage" may correspond to `circus elephant`.

Although similar to ordinary pattern-matching, this problem is far more complex because concept properties are not available locally, and may have to be extracted via inheritance mechanisms. Moreover, the exact pattern commonly does not exist and the closest corresponding match must be determined.

Locating entities in knowledge bases that best match a set of features is perhaps the most important operation carried out on knowledge bases, because it is the "inner loop" operation used in reasoning schemes. The operation varies in complexity from a trivial word (or key) search to locating the best match among properties dispersed through the knowledge base. An example of this latter case occurs when we try to find a situation similar to an existing problem, but with some modifications. Thus, features need to be sorted out and those which are most significant must play a larger role, while some less important features might be ignored. Such a requirement rules out fixed pattern-matching techniques, hashing, or indexing schemes.

Situation recognition is a fundamental AI operation used in recognizing scenes, parsing sentences, recognizing the intents of utterances, planning, learning, and other applications. As we will see, marker propagation is a useful technique for implementing complex recognition applications.

Inheritance

Inheritance is another form of reasoning, the dual of recognition. The *inheritance problem* may be defined as follows: Given a concept or a pattern of concepts in a hierarchical structure, find the most likely properties inherited by that concept (or pattern) from the properties of other, ancestor concepts. For example, the input pattern may be "`Clyde is an elephant`." We would like the system to conclude rather rapidly that most likely `Clyde` is a large animal, has four legs, has a trunk, and much more. Inheritance reasoning is the mechanism that locates properties attached to concepts within a certain "distance."

Finding the implicit properties of any concept in a knowledge base is possible due to the inheritance properties that link it with its ancestors.

The main problem in such an operation is that the paths can bifurcate into multiple computation paths, which increases the computational complexity. Often, conflicting information may be gathered by inheritance reasoning because of multiple inheritance channels. Resolving these conflicts may be quite difficult.

Unification and Generalization

The *unification problem* may be stated as follows: Given two descriptions x and y, find an object z that fits both descriptions. For example, let $x = f(u, v)$ and $y = f(g(v, a), h(a))$. These expressions are unifiable because replacing

$$u \leftarrow g(h(a), a)$$

$$v \leftarrow h(a)$$

will make both x and y look like $f(g(h(a), a), h(a))$. Unification is normally done using unification substitutions; it requires many computations.

In semantic networks, unification produces a new pattern that will match whatever both input patterns would have matched. This operation may be used, for example, to match an inference rule with a knowledge base to determine the applicability of that inference rule. It is also used to place a pattern within a context domain by unifying the pattern concepts with the rest of the knowledge base.

Generalization is the dual of unification. The *generalization problem* can be stated as follows: Given two objects x and y, find a third object z of which both x and y are instances. The operation used to perform generalizations is antisubstitution, which is a mapping from terms into variables.

As an example of generalization, let x be the sentence "John is playing a string instrument," and y be the sentence "The boy's violin is new." A generalized pattern z might be "The boy is playing his new string instrument," since both x and y are instances of z.

The generalization process seeks more abstract patterns, whereas unification seeks more specific patterns. They proceed in opposite directions in the knowledge base hierarchy.

8.4   PARALLEL NATURAL LANGUAGE PROCESSING

8.4.1   Memory-Based Parsing

A modern approach to natural language processing (NLP) is to perform parsing directly in the knowledge base memory. This is compatible with massively parallel architectures. Unlike other NLP approaches, which are based on time-consuming search operations or clever heuristics, this approach relies on marker-passing techniques to achieve inferencing. Parsing becomes a pattern-recognition problem.

The idea of viewing natural language processing as a memory activity was proposed by Riesbeck and Martin in their Direct Memory Access Parsing (DMAP) [Riesbeck and Martin 1985]. Memory-based parsing considers understanding to be a process of recalling a relevant portion of memory. This idea differs from most other traditional parsing methods. In the memory-based approach, time complexity is traded for space complexity; this trend is consistent with the availability of massively parallel computers and large memories.

A memory-based parsing algorithm basically works as follows: Words from the input sentence activate nodes in the knowledge base by creating some markers. These are passed up through inheritance links. Some nodes in the knowledge base contain *prediction* markers, as a result of some prediction mechanism performed in the beginning. The nodes where *activation* markers meet prediction markers have a chance of being accepted. Their level of relevance is increased. Costs are updated and constraint satisfaction conditions are tested. The process of acceptance and prediction spreads throughout the network.

In addition, the acceptance of some nodes connected to other, distant nodes through context links sends out markers to their relevant contexts. Thus the inference process is guided toward regions of interest in the knowledge base. Eventually, some nodes remain marked as accepted; this is the result of parsing activity.

The basic idea behind memory-based parsing may be explained using Figure 8.17. This figure shows a knowledge base consisting of several layers. The lexical layer is the lowest one; it contains lexical item nodes. These are connected to the concepts of a semantic network. The semantic network layer captures the semantic and syntactic relationships and constraints. The top nodes of the semantic layer are connected to some *concept sequence element* nodes. The nodes at the concept sequence element (CSE) layer, together with the root node in the *concept sequence root* (CSR) layer, form a *concept sequence,* a pattern that is designed to fit a large number of sentences.

The parsing algorithm is based upon repeated applications of top-down *expectations* and bottom-up *activations.* At first, all the CSRs are expected as possible hypotheses, and accordingly their first CSEs and all the subsumed concepts in the knowledge base are also expected. This is implemented by placing some expectation (or prediction) markers on these nodes. When an input word is read, bottom-up activation is propagated up to the corresponding subsuming nodes in the knowledge base. Even though many nodes are initially expected, only a small number of them are verified by activations as input words are processed. Therefore, candidate hypotheses are quickly narrowed down to the correct ones. In this way, multiple hypotheses are handled in parallel without using backtracking, which is not the case in some other sequential parsing algorithms.

For example, when the word **they** is received from an input sentence, markers are moved up, activating the concept **experiencer**, which has been expected as the first element of a concept sequence [*experiencer, see, determiner, object*]. The activation of this element triggers the expectation of the next element in the sequence, **see**. The arrival of the word **saw** moves markers up to the concept **see**. Since it was already expected, it is accepted, after which it triggers the expectation of the next concept sequence element, and so on. The CSR is activated when all its elements are accepted. As a parsing result, a new *concept sequence instance* (CSI) **seeing-event#1** is created. It is an instantiation of the concept sequence **seeing-event** that existed in the knowledge base. The new CSI is linked to the accepted instances of the most specific concepts in the knowledge base. For example, in Figure 8.17, the experiencer of **seeing-event#1** is **concept-they#1**, and the object is **concept-log#1**.

Parallelism is abundant in this form of parsing. For example, when the word **they** occurs, it sends markers to many concept sequences, such as **seeing-event, eating-event, cutting-event,** and so on,

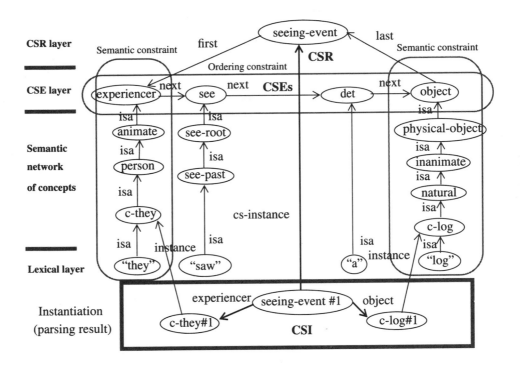

Figure 8.17 Concept sequence [*experiencer see determiner object*] for processing *"They saw a log."*

most of them not shown in the figure. This is because we don't know yet what the next word is going to be. With each new word, the system *filters out* wrong interpretations. As more words occur, fewer and fewer hypotheses remain, and eventually the correct interpretation may be formed. Realistic linguistic knowledge bases are very large, with hundreds of thousands of concepts. It may be obvious by now that sequential processing of such large knowledge bases is impractical, whereas parallel marker propagations are not directly affected by the size of the knowledge base.

8.4.2   Parallel Linguistic Processing

The scalability of this concept-sequence knowledge representation is severely limited. Too many concept sequences are needed to process even a very simple sentence with syntactic variations, because of the inflexibility of the representation discussed above and the lack of syntactic analysis. For example, consider the recognition of the concept seeing-event in sentences such as:

> They saw a log.
> They saw logs.
> They saw a big log.
> They saw a log yesterday.
> They saw a big brown log yesterday.

Many separate concept sequences such as [*experiencer see determiner object*], [*experiencer see object*], [*experiencer see determiner modifier object*], [*experiencer see determiner object time*], and [*experiencer see determiner modifier1 modifier2 object time*] are required, and it could be even worse with more syntactic variations.

In order to increase the expressiveness of the representation while maintaining the high performance provided by searching for patterns, we break a concept sequence into a *basic* concept sequence (BCS) and an *auxiliary* concept sequence (ACS) as shown in Figure 8.18, and use an integrated syntactic and semantic analysis for memory-based parsing. In general, BCSs form case frame interpretations with obligatory cases, including agent, object, experiencer, beneficiary, location, and others. ACSs form optional cases such as time and manner, which surround a basic case frame interpretation. Based on these definitions, many linguistic templates may be created.

Nodes in the knowledge base are classified as AND nodes with ordering constraint, AND nodes without ordering constraint, and OR nodes. An AND node without ordering constraint is used to combine syntactic and semantic constraints on the CSE node, and is accepted if all its child nodes are accepted. For example, the concept experiencer in Figure 8.18 is accepted only if it is an animate (semantic constraint) and a noun phrase (syntactic constraint). A CSR node is an AND node with an ordering constraint that is accepted only if all of its child

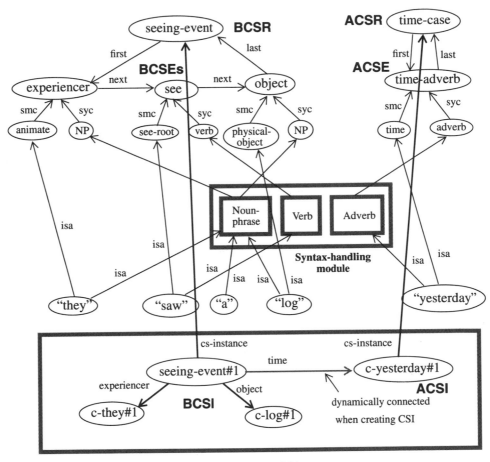

Figure 8.18 Basic concept sequence [*experiencer see object*] and auxiliary concept sequence [*time*] for processing "*They saw a log yesterday.*"

nodes are accepted in the prespecified order. For example, the concept
seeing-event is accepted only after **experiencer, see**, and **object**
have been accepted. All other nodes are OR nodes that are accepted
when any of their child nodes are accepted. If an expected node with an
activation satisfies its acceptance condition, a specific action is taken.
For example, an accepted CSE sends expectation to the next CSE until
all CSEs under a CSR are accepted. When a BCSR or ACSR is accepted, then a BCS instance (BCSI) or ACS instance (ACSI) is created,
respectively.

At the end of the parsing process, the BCSI is dynamically combined
with ACSIs to form a CSI. The resulting CSI is a concept sequence with
both obligatory and optional cases. The gain from breaking up a large
concept sequence into BCSs and ACSs is the increased flexibility and
expressiveness of knowledge representation. For example, as shown in
Figure 8.18, we need only one BCS [*experiencer see object*] and one
ACS [*time*] to handle several variations of seeing-events and time. Increased flexibility is obtained because memory-based parsing is done
with integrated syntactic and semantic analysis. Using these ideas, the
knowledge base can be extended to cover a much wider class of English
sentences.

Understanding Complex Sentences

Complex sentences with embedded clauses can be interpreted by combining the CSI of the main clause with the CSIs of embedded clauses.
Repeated use of the same concept sequence is easily handled, as in

`John loves Mary, who loves Fred.`

We need to avoid the cycle phenomenon in the knowledge representation and marker propagations. At the end of an embedded clause, BCSI
or ACSIs of the embedded clause are created, and are dynamically combined to form a CSI of the embedded clause. The resulting CSIs for
embedded clauses are also dynamically combined with the CSI of the
main clause to form an extended CSI (ECSI) when all input words are
processed. This ECSI represents the meaning of the input sentence.
Figure 8.19 illustrates this idea.

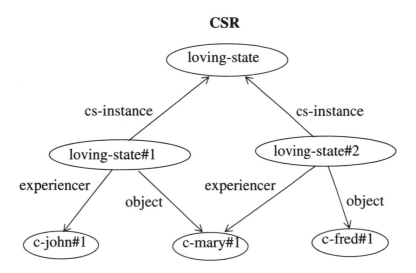

Figure 8.19 ECSI resulting from *"John loves Mary, who loves Fred."*

The definitions of BCS, ACS, CSI, and ECSI are summarized in Figure 8.20. The ECSIs capturing the meaning of a complex sentence are shown in Figure 8.21.

```
Yesterday they saw Mary, who gave a small red car phone to
John.
```

The syntactic complications in this sentence include a relative clause, adverb-preposing, dative movement of the indirect object of *gave,* and a complex noun phrase with a compound noun. Despite these complications, memory-based parsing performs a sound analysis because of the integrated syntactic and semantic feature of the algorithm and the flexible basic concept-sequence knowledge representation.

Understanding Ambiguous Sentences

Many sentence ambiguities are resolved by checking syntactic and semantic constraints. High-precision parsers check a large number of syntactic and semantic rules. In the memory-based parser presented

BCS = BCS root (BCSR) + BCS elements (BCSEs)

BCSE = concept, lexical item, or obligatory case role name

ACS = ACS root (ACSR) + ACS elements (ACSEs)

ACSE = concept, lexical item, or optional case role name

CSI = BCSI + ACSIs

ECSI = CSI of main clause + CSIs of embedded clauses

Figure 8.20 Definitions of BCS, BCSE, ACS, ACSE, CSI, and ECSI.

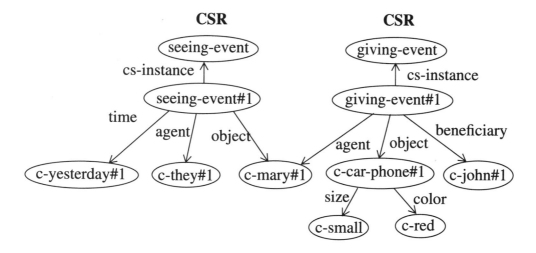

Figure 8.21 CSI resulting from *"Yesterday they saw Mary, who gave a small red car phone to John."*

here these constraints are encoded as part of the semantic network, and their verification is done in parallel via marker propagation. Consider the following sentences:

(1) John saw a log.
(2) They saw a log.
(3) They saw a log yesterday.

In these examples, because of the lexical ambiguity in `saw`, both `seeing-event` and `sawing-event` can be valid hypotheses. Of course,

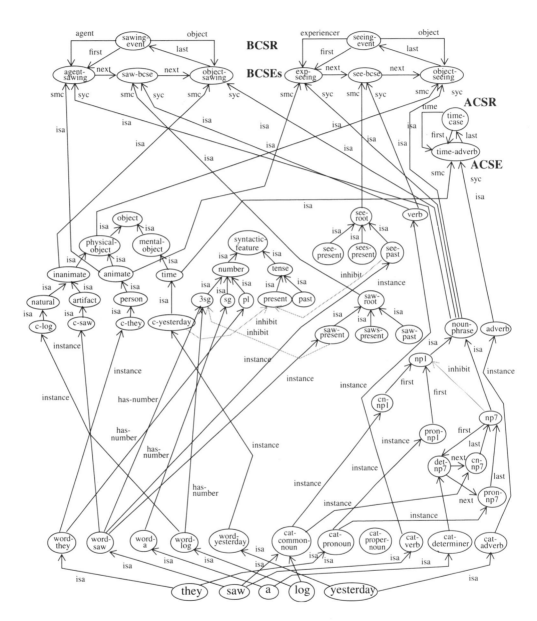

Figure 8.22 Part of the knowledge base used for processing *"They saw a log yesterday."*

the noun meaning of saw is rejected since it is not expected when saw is processed. In (1), although both see-past and saw-present satisfy semantic constraint, only see-past is accepted. Saw-present is rejected because it violates subject-verb agreement. Therefore, only a CSI of seeing-event is created. In (2), both seeing-event and sawing-event are valid interpretations because both syntactic and semantic constraints are satisfied by both. In order to disambiguate this sentence, more contextual information is needed. In (3), saw-present cannot be verified because of yesterday. Therefore, only seeing-event creates a CSI. Figure 8.22 shows how constraints are implemented and used. This kind of analysis is performed in parallel through memory search using markers, and as a result, disambiguated interpretation is obtained and a CSI is formed.

8.5   SEMANTIC NETWORK ARRAY PROCESSOR

8.5.1   Conceptual SNAP Architecture

The Semantic Network Array Processor (SNAP) computer system, developed at the University of Southern California, is based on the marker-passing model of computation. We shall first present the main ideas of the SNAP computer by using a conceptual model, and then describe an actual SNAP prototype constructed with off-the-shelf components.

As shown in Figure 8.23, a SNAP system consists of an array of specialized processors, one or more controllers, an interconnection network, and disks. SNAP's functionality is based on two underlying concepts: *marker-passing* and *associative memory*. Each processor, indicated in the figure as a SNAP processor, contains memory, control logic, and communication logic. A semantic network is distributed over the SNAP processors, such that each processor holds many semantic network nodes and their associated relations. Although a SNAP is globally driven by an outside controller, processors perform most of the functions independently, making this architecture a "smart memory." The knowledge base, represented as a semantic network, is distributed

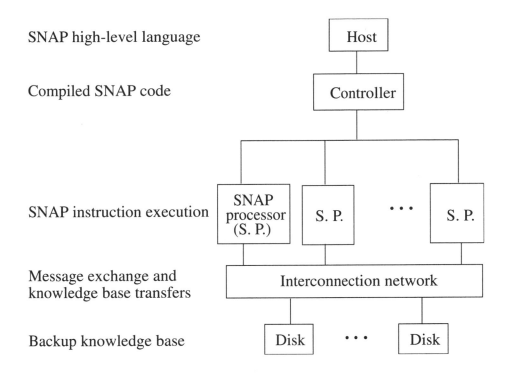

SNAP high-level language

Compiled SNAP code

SNAP instruction execution

Message exchange and
knowledge base transfers

Backup knowledge base

Figure 8.23 SNAP system.

throughout the SNAP array. As we have seen in the previous section,
the marker-propagation model provides a viable alternative for reasoning on knowledge bases, whereas associative processing offers fast
retrieval of data stored in local memories. In order to provide adequate
storage space, a set of disks is attached to the array. The interconnection network facilitates marker communication and interfaces the disks
with the array.

SNAP Processor
The SNAP processor shown in Figure 8.24 consists of four units: an
instruction unit (IU), a relation memory (RM), a marker control unit
(MU), and a communication unit (CU). The IU controls the operation
of the SNAP processor. Its function is to decode the intructions received from the controller and to provide the necessary commands to

the other units. The RM provides the main local memory. It stores semantic network nodes and relations. In order to provide a high degree of
parallelism within a chip, the RM is built around a content-addressable
memory (CAM). The MU provides storage and processing capabilities
for markers associated with semantic network nodes. The inferencing
power of the SNAP system rests on marker processing. The CU interfaces the processor with the interconnection network. It inspects
incoming messages and determines their type and destination.

Knowledge Representation on a SNAP

There are two forms of knowledge in a SNAP. Permanent knowledge
is stored as a semantic network, and temporary knowledge is encoded
as markers within the semantic network. Both forms of knowledge are
stored within the SNAP processors and it is easy to convert from one
to the other.

Permanent Knowledge. Permanent knowledge is constructed by the
user at the beginning of processing and is stored in the relation memory. Each SNAP processor may hold a number of semantic network
nodes, and each node may have several relations (or links). Basically,
the application program running on the controller generates a series
of CREATE instructions to build a semantic network knowledge base.
The controller takes these CREATE instructions, performs transformations and node assignment, and then broadcasts commands to specific
SNAP processors to store the knowledge.

Figure 8.25 shows how the creation of USC is in Los Angeles is
performed. First, the program executes the CREATE(USC,<is-in>,Los
Angeles) instruction. The controller checks to see if the concepts USC
and Los Angeles have been assigned to SNAP processors. Let us say
that USC has already been assigned to processor 9, node 2, but Los
Angeles is a brand-new concept, unassigned yet. Using a partitioning
algorithm, the controller creates a new table entry and assigns Los
Angeles to processor 16 as node 7. Next, the controller converts the
is-in relation to a number. Thus, the instruction becomes CREATE
((9,2), <14>, (16,7)), where (9,2) and (16,7) correspond to the
(processor, node) locations for USC and Los Angeles, respectively, and
14 is the number code for the relation is_in. This command is then sent

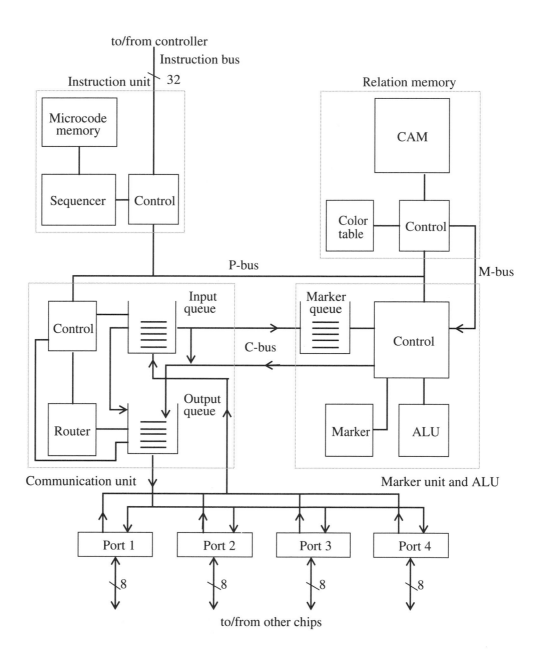

Figure 8.24 Structure of a SNAP processor.

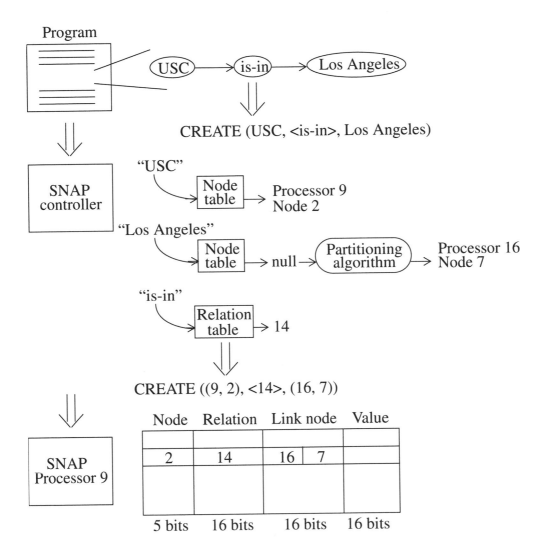

Figure 8.25 Storing permanent knowledge in a SNAP [Moldovan, Lee, Lin, and Chung 1992].

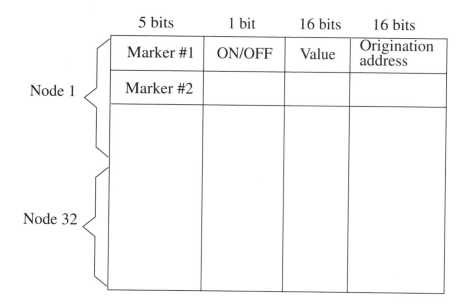

Figure 8.26 SNAP marker storage.

to the SNAP processors. Each SNAP processor determines whether any action is needed. Here only processors 9 and 16 are involved, and the other processors can continue with the next instruction. In processor 9, a new relation entry is placed in the relation memory to link node 2 with processor 16, node 7. The relation memory has a field for associating values to relations. The user has a choice of ways to take advantage of this. One possible use is to regard the relation value as a measure of belief, or of how "true" we think a relation is.

The notion of coloring (or grouping) nodes is useful when we need to refer to a set of nodes collectively. For example, we may want to refer to all people whose name is John, such as John 1, John 2, and so on. For this purpose there is a color table in the relation memory unit that associates a color with each node. Thus, semantic network nodes may be identified individually by their names or collectively by their color (or type).

Temporary Knowledge. Markers are used to store and evaluate different hypotheses in the semantic network. To each semantic network node stored in the relation memory, a memory space is allocated in the marker unit to store the markers corresponding to that node. In SNAP, each node is capable of simultaneously having simple markers and complex markers. A simple marker consists solely of an ON/OFF bit, while a complex marker (shown in Figure 8.26) consists of an ON/OFF bit plus a value register and a pointer register. The value register can store either data, the current strength of the marker, or a probability. The pointer register identifies the node that originated the marker. The marker pointer allows the same marker to be used for different hypotheses. The pointer "colors" the marker so that it is possible to identify which hypothesis it refers to. The marker pointer also enables the easy creation of new relations between nodes.

SNAP Instruction Set

The SNAP instruction set consists of powerful instructions specific to knowledge processing. These are listed in Figure 8.27. These instructions are executed by the SNAP processors and are divided into seven groups: node maintenance, marker node maintenance, search, logical, propagate, marker-supplemental, and data retrieval. The instructions in these seven groups have been used to program a number of knowledge-processing applications on a SNAP and it has been discovered that they represent the core functions required for semantic network processing. Each instruction consists of an operational code and a field of arguments. The arguments may refer to semantic network nodes, relations, markers, node types (or colors), rules governing the propagation of markers, or functions initiated by markers. The arguments that are consequences of an instruction are marked by the brackets < >.

Node maintenance instructions (CREATE, DELETE, SET-COLOR) are used for loading and modifying the knowledge base. For example, (CREATE A <R> <W> B) sets up in node A a new relation R, with weight equal to W, from node A to node B. If either A or B is new, the controller assigns it to a new node. Initially, the array is loaded with nodes and links by the controller. This allocation procedure is built upon the function CREATE. Conceptually, this procedure employs as many CREATEs as the number of links in the semantic network.

Instruction	Argument	Type
CREATE	s-node, <relation>, <weight>, e-node	node
DELETE	s-node, <relation>, e-node	maintenance
SET-COLOR	node, <color>	
MARKER-CREATE	marker, <s-relation>, e-node, <e-relation>	marker
MARKER-DELETE	marker, <s-relation>, e-node, <e-relation>	node
MARKER-SET-COLOR	marker, <color>	maintenance
TEST	marker-1, <marker-2>, <value>, <cond>	
AND	marker-1, marker-2, < marker-3>, <func>	logic
OR	marker-1, marker-2, < marker-3>, <func>	
NOT	marker-1, <marker-2>	
SEARCH	node, <marker>, <value>	
SEARCH-COLOR	color, <marker>, <value>	search
SEARCH-RELATION	relation, <marker>, <value>	
PROPAGATE	marker-1, <marker-2>, <rule>, <func>	propagate
SET-MARKER-VALUE	marker, <value>	
CLEAR-MARKER	marker	marker supplemental
FUNC-MARKER	marker, <func>	
COLLECT-MARKER	marker	
COLLECT-COLOR	marker	retrieval
COLLECT-RELATION	marker, relation	

Figure 8.27 SNAP instruction set [Moldovan, Lee, and Lin 1992].

Marker node maintenance instructions (MARKER-CREATE, MARKER-DELETE, MARKER-SET-COLOR) are used for parallel creation, deletion, and color setup in the knowledge base. For example, (MARKER-CREATE #1 <R1> B <R2>) creats a new relation R1 to B in every node that has marker #1 set. The weight of the relation is equal to the value of marker #1. If the argument R2 is missing, no relation will be created in node B. Otherwise, each of the nodes with marker #1 on will send a message to node B to inform it of the node address for creating a new relation R2 from node B to that node.

Logical functions (TEST, AND, OR, NOT) are used to manipulate the markers within a node. For example, AND (#1, #2, <#3>, ADD) will set marker #3 in those nodes where both markers #1 and marker #2 are set. The value of marker #3 is the sum of the values of markers #1 and #2. The mathematic functions available for AND and OR are addition, subtraction, multiplication, division, maximum, minimum, and no-operation. The condition checking functions available for TEST are greater-than, less-than, and equal.

Search instructions (SEARCH, SEARCH-COLOR, SEARCH-RELATION) are used to select a node or a group of nodes in the array. The instruction SEARCH (USC, <#4>, <N>) will locate the processor and the node corresponding to the semantic node USC and will set marker #4 in that node to a value equal to N. The instruction SEARCH-COLOR (A, R1, <#1>, <N>) means to search for nodes with color A and relation R1, and set marker #1 in those nodes to a value equal to N. The color of each semantic network node is stored in the color table inside the relation memory unit of each processor.

The *propagate* instruction (PROPAGATE) is used to propagate markers in parallel. A propagation rule is associated with it to provide decentralized marker-propagation control. For example, PROPAGATE (#1, <#2>, <SEQ(R_1, R_2)>, <NOP>) causes all nodes with marker #1 set to propagate marker #2 once along the R_1 relation of the affected nodes, and then once through the R_2 relation. In addition, an arithmetic function can be associated with a marker to enable manipulation of the numeric values in the marker value and the relation weight registers. In other words, a marker that propagates along some relations has the ability to modify the values of these relations. This enables a SNAP to support a wide range of applications, including natural language parsing and generation. The arithmetic functions available for PROPAGATE are addition, subtraction, multiplication, and division.

Marker-supplemental functions (CLEAR-MARKER, FUNC-MARKER, SET-MARKER-VALUE) are used to modify the operation of marker instructions. The CLEAR-MARKER instruction is to clear a marker and its content. FUNC-MARKER specifies the operation of a node for incoming markers. For example, the instruction FUNC-MARKER (#1, <max>) will set the function compute maximum in all nodes with marker #1 set. This node function will be used to compare the value of each incoming marker, say marker #3, with the value of the existing marker #3 already stored in the node, and to keep the maximum of the two as the future value for marker #3. The functions available for FUNC-MARKER are no-operation, stop, maximum, minimum, addition, subtraction, multiplication, and division. Only one operation can be specified for a node at one time. SET-MARKER-VALUE is designed to update the values of markers.

Finally, *data retrieval* functions (COLLECT, COLLECT-RELATION, COLLECT-MARKER) are used to obtain information from nodes. They are used to retrieve results from a node and to save its state. For example, COLLECT-RELATION (#1, R1) gets all the weights and destination node addresses stored in a node that has relation R1 and has marker #1 set.

Marker Propagation

Markers are assigned to certain semantic network nodes. These markers are then propagated to other nodes by way of messages. The way markers propagate is dictated by a set of propagation rules. The formats of propagation rules are Rule, Relation1, and Relation2, where Relation1 and Relation2 are the types of links (relations) in which we are interested. The following propagation rules have been defined for a SNAP:

1. SEQ(R1, R2): The SEQuence propagation rule allows the marker to propagate through R1 once, then to R2 once.

2. SPREAD(R1, R2): The SPREAD propagation rule allows the marker to travel through a chain of R1 links. For each cell in the

R1 path, if there exist any R2, the marker switches to the R2 link and continues to propagate until it reaches the end of the R2 link.

3. COMB(R1, R2): The COMBine propagation rule allows the marker to propagate to all R1, R2 links without limitation.

4. END-SPREAD(R1, R2): This propagation rule is the same as SPREAD, except that it marks only the last cells in the paths.

5. END-COMB(R1, R2): This propagation rule is the same as COMB, except that it marks only the last cells in the paths.

8.5.2   Marker Processing on a SNAP

Markers are used in a SNAP to perform inferencing. The application program generates a marker at one or more nodes. These markers then propagate independently and mark other nodes. At the end of the marking process, the application program can perform arithmetic and set operations to manipulate the various markers in the knowledge base.

Figure 8.28 shows the process of marker propagation along a chain of is-in relations. Consider the statements: USC is in Los Angeles. Los Angeles is in California. California is in USA. First, the program issues the SEARCH (USC,<1>) to set marker #1 in node USC. Then the program sends PROPAGATE (1,<2>, <SPREAD(is-in)>, <NOP>) to the SNAP processors. When each SNAP processor executes the PROPAGATE instruction, it places the SPREAD propagation rule in a propagation rule table. This table resides in the SNAP processor and holds the propagation rules for all of the markers circulating in the system. In the processor that holds the node USC, a search is performed in the relation memory to find all of the nodes that are linked to USC by the relation is_in. In this example, one node is found: Los Angeles. The processor puts together a marker message with the destination Los Angeles and sends it into the interconnection network. A marker message has the format of:

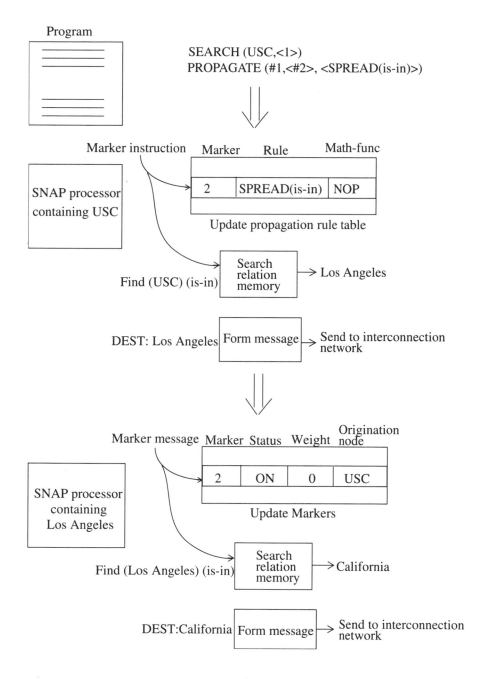

Figure 8.28 SNAP marker processing [Moldovan, Lee, Lin, and Chung 1992].

Destination processor (14 bits)
Marker (ON/OFF, value, pointer) (36 bits)
Propagation phase (2 bits)

The propagation phase indicates the stage of the propagation when more than one relation are involved. For example, in a SEQ(isa, has-part) propagation rule, phase 1 indicates propagation along the isa relation and phase 2 indicates has-part propagation. At the processor that contains Los Angeles, marker #2 is set. Then the processor checks the propagation rule and determines whether any more nodes should be marked. If so, the cycle continues.

SNAP-1 Prototype

The SNAP-1 prototype is a microprocessor implementation of the conceptual system described above. It was built in the Parallel Knowledge Processing Laboratory at USC in 1991. Five Texas Instruments TMS320C30 microprocessors, memories, and other logic were used to implement a SNAP processor. We will refer to this as a *cluster*. Each cluster stores up to 1,024 semantic network nodes, and each node may have an average of 10 relations. As shown in Figure 8.29, the instruction unit and communication unit are each implemented with a microprocessor and local memory. Since simulations have shown that the marker unit tends to create a bottleneck, three microprocessors and three local memories were dedicated for the MU. The microprocessors within a cluster communicate via two four-port memories. Semaphores and cycle stretching techniques are used to maintain data coherence.

Interconnection Network

The SNAP-1 consists of 32 clusters, interconnected as shown in Figure 8.30. The entire system is packaged on eight array boards and one controller board. Message routing is performed using the address of the destination cluster. A five-bit address is used for each cluster. The lower two bits encode one of the four clusters in a board, the next two bits encode the four boards along the Y direction, and the most significant bit separates the boards along the X direction.

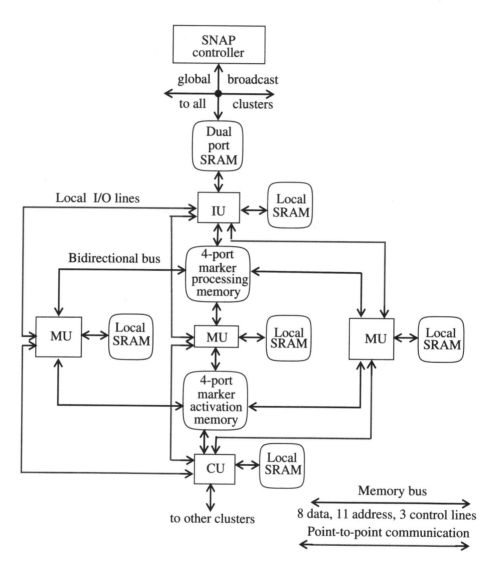

Figure 8.29 The structure of a SNAP cluster.

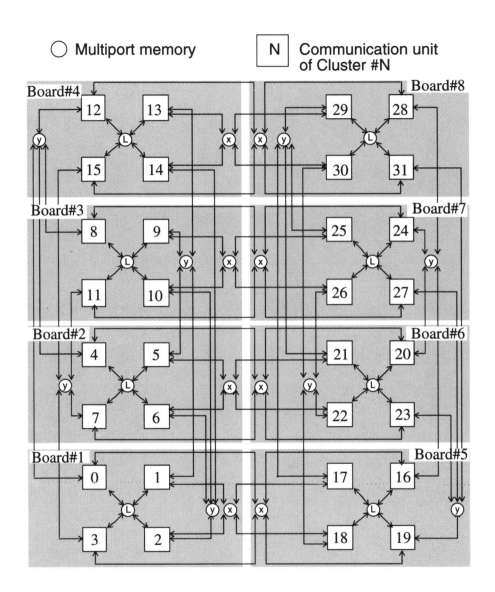

Figure 8.30 Interconnection network for the SNAP prototype.

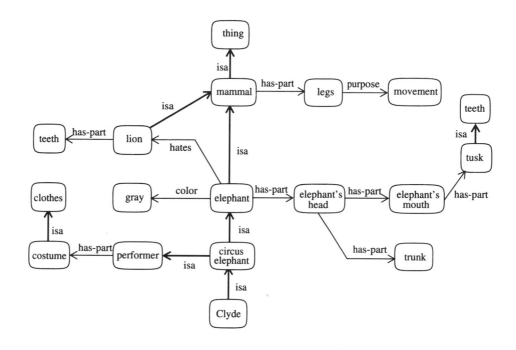

Figure 8.31 Semantic network for Clyde.

8.5.3   Examples of Knowledge Processing on a SNAP

Several SNAP application examples are presented in this section. These examples are typical of semantic network processing. The programs are written in SNAP instructions.

Many queries are based on establishing an inheritance link between two nodes. However, in many cases the inheritance is not obvious, yet given the facts a human can easily see the connection. In the following example, it is shown how a nonobvious query is processed in SNAP.

Example 8.5.   Property Inheritance. Clyde, the circus elephant, is a famous figure in the AI literature. This example on inheritance includes Clyde and the semantic network in Figure 8.31. With this semantic network, the following query is processed on the SNAP:

Does Clyde have teeth?

The SNAP program to answer this query is very simple. It relies on the guiding of markers from `Clyde` toward the destination `teeth`. Only valid relations are allowed to propagate markers. Thus, markers cannot travel from `elephant` through `hates` to `lion` and further to `teeth`. The program is shown below:

1. SEARCH (Clyde, #2, 0)
   sets marker #2 in node Clyde
2. SEARCH (teeth, #3, 0)
   sets marker #3 in node teeth
3. PROPAGATION (#2, #2, COMB(isa, has-part), NOP)
   causes marker #2 to be propagated from Clyde
4. WAIT-COMM-END
   (this is a controller instruction)
   wait until markers finish propagating
5. AND (#2, #3, #4, NOP)
6. COLLECT (#4)
   If the node teeth gets marker #2, then marker #4
   is set. Otherwise, marker #4 gets reset. If
   we are able to collect a node with marker #4 set,
   then the answer to the query is yes. Otherwise,
   the answer is no.

Thus SNAP is able to respond to the query using just six instructions.

Example 8.6. Recognition with Multiple Properties. We now consider an example that requires the propagation of multiple markers. A semantic network is shown in Figure 8.32. The query is:

> Among the graduate students, who meets the description:
> single, male, Ph.D. student, living on campus, has
> research assistantship, and has a car?

The idea for answering this query is to mark with different markers all properties specified in the query and then to let markers propagate along appropriate relations; the nodes where all markers intersect are the ones we are looking for. The SNAP program is:

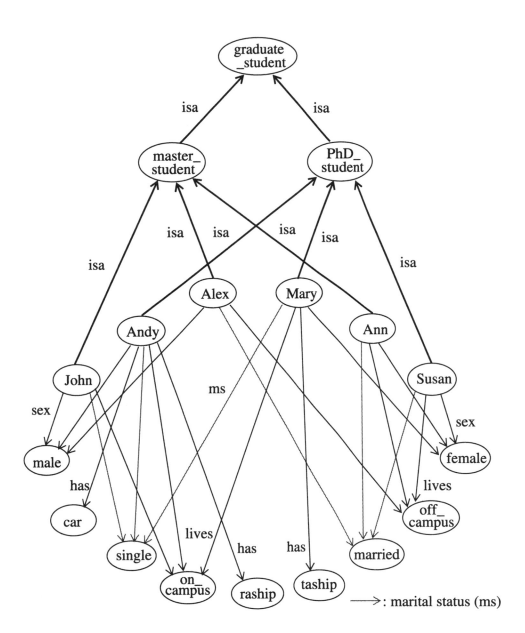

Figure 8.32 Semantic network for the recognition example.

0. SEARCH (PhD_student, #0, 0)
    select PhD_student and set marker #0
1. SEARCH (male, #1, 0)
    select male and set marker #1
2. SEARCH (single, #2, 0)
    select single and set marker #2
3. SEARCH (on_campus, #3, 0)
    select on_campus and set marker #3
4. SEARCH (raship, #4, 0)
    select raship and set marker #4
5. SEARCH (car, #5, 0)
    select car and set marker #5
6. PROPAGATE (#0, #6, SPREAD(r_isa), NOP)
    causes marker to be propagated
    in reverse isa direction
7. PROPAGATE (#1, #7, SPREAD(r_sex), NOP)
    causes marker to be propagated from male
    to all the people that are male
8. PROPAGATE (#2, #8, SPREAD(r_ms), NOP)
    causes marker to be propagated from single
    to all the people that are single
9. PROPAGATE (#3, #9, SPREAD(r_role), NOP)
    causes marker to be propagated from on-campus
    to all the people living on-campus
10.PROPAGATE (#4, #10, SPREAD(r_role), NOP)
    causes marker to be propagated from raship
    to all the people who have a raship
11.PROPAGATE (#5, #11, SPREAD(r_role), NOP)
    causes marker to be propagated from car
    to all the people who have a car
12.WAIT-COMM-END
    wait until markers finish propagating
13.AND (#6, #7, #12, NOP)
14.AND (#8, #9, #13, NOP)
15.AND (#10, #11, #14, NOP)
16.AND (#12, #13, #15, NOP)
17.AND (#14, #15, #16, NOP)
18.COLLECT (#16)
    If any node has all of the properties, then
    collect will return non-nil.

This is a recognition problem with multiple properties, which requires multiple marker propagations. The length of the critical path is

1 and no major marker propagation chains exist. However, the query contains six types of marker propagations. In this type of query, the SNAP can propagate multiple markers simultaneously.

8.6 BIBLIOGRAPHICAL NOTES AND FURTHER READING

The OPS5 production language, developed at Carnegie-Mellon University, is described in [Brownston, Farrel, Kant, and Martin 1985]. The Rete match algorithm was proposed and implemented by Forgy [Forgy 1982]. Some of the most notable improvements to Rete are the Treat algorithm, proposed in [Miranker 1987], the Yes/Rete algorithm, proposed in [Schor, Daly, Lee, and Tibbitts 1986], and the DRete algorithm, in [Kelly and Seviora 1989].

Interrule dependencies and the idea of parallelism and communication matrices were developed by Moldovan [Moldovan 1989]. The search space reduction material is from [Dixit and Moldovan 1989]. Multiple-rule firing was studied in [Moldovan 1989], [Ishida and Stolfo 1985], [Schmoltze 1988], [Miranker 1987], and others. The ideas of contexts and SCMR and MCMR models were proposed in [Kuo and Moldovan 1991]. The mapping of Rete into a shared-memory multiprocessor was investigated by Gupta [Gupta 1987], and the mapping of Rete into a message-passing multiprocessor was studied by Acharya and Tambe [Acharya and Tambe 1989].

The RUBIC parallel inference environment was developed at USC by Kuo and Moldovan [Kuo and Moldovan 1991]. The allocation of rules to message-passing multiprocessor was studied by Dixit and Moldovan [Dixit and Moldovan 1990] and subsequently implemented on a hypercube by Kuo and Moldovan [Kuo and Moldovan 1991].

Semantic networks were used by Quillian to model human memory [Quillian 1966]. Quillian has introduced the idea of marker-spreading activation as a reasoning mechanism. Woods extended the idea of marker-passing to parallel knowledge processing, and in particular to natural language processing [Woods 1979]. One of the first architectures implementing Quillian's spreading activation idea was proposed in [Fahlman 1979]. The NETL system envisioned by Fahlman constituted the intellectual framework for the Connection Machine project and the SNAP project.

Several knowledge representation languages were developed to model semantic networks and frames. Most notable is KL-ONE, originated by Brachman and subsequently extended by many other researchers at BBN, Standford, and USC/ISI. KL-ONE is described in [Brachman and Schmoltze 1985]. An early knowledge classification algorithm for KL-ONE is described in [Lipkis and Schmolze 1983] and extends Wood's work in concept subsumption.

The application of marker-passing technique to natural language processing and the idea of direct memory parsing started with work done at Yale by Schank [Schank 1982], Rieseback, and others. DMAP is one of the early systems of this kind [Riesbeck and Martin 1985]. Kitano at CMU has implemented a system for speech-to-speech translation, called ΦDMDIALOG [Kitano 1991]. Other important work in marker passing was reported in [Hendler 1988], [Charniack 1983], [Norvig 1989], and others.

The SNAP project at USC, under the leadership of Dan Moldovan, is an example of massively parallel marker-passing architecture intended for knowledge processing. Among the early papers describing the conceptual SNAP machine are [Moldovan 1983a] and [Moldovan and Tung 1985]. A more recent paper describing SNAP architecture, software, and applications is [Moldovan, Lee, Lin, and Chung 1992].

8.7   PROBLEMS

8.1.A. Find the inhibit, output, and enable dependence matrices and from these derive the parallelism and communication matrices for the following production system:

P1: (P 1   {(Class1 ↑A a1) < $X1$ > }
              {(Class2 ↑B b1 ↑C < c1 >) < $Y1$ > }
              {(Class3 ↑D d1) < $Z2$ > }

$\longrightarrow$

              (remove < $X1$ >)
              (remove < $Y1$ >)
              (remove < $Z2$ >))

P2: (P 2   (Class1 ↑A a2)
⟶
          (make Class2 ↑B b2))

P3: (P 3   (Class1 ↑A a1)
          (Class3 ↑D d2)
⟶
          (make Class3 ↑D d4))

P4: (P 4   (Class3 ↑D d5)
          { (Class2 ↑B b1) < Y2 > }
⟶
          (remove < Y2 >))

P5: (P 5   (Class1 ↑A a2 ↑F < f1 >)
          (Class2 ↑B b1 ↑C < c2 >)
⟶
          (make Class4 ↑E e1))

P6: (P 6   (Class1 ↑A a2)
          { (Class3 ↑D < d3 >) < Z1 > }
⟶
          (remove < Z1 >))

Solution.

$$
I \;=\; \begin{bmatrix}
1 & 0 & * & * & * & * \\
0 & 0 & 0 & 0 & 0 & 0 \\
* & 0 & 0 & 0 & 0 & * \\
* & 0 & 0 & 1 & * & * \\
* & 0 & 0 & * & 0 & 0 \\
* & 0 & * & * & 0 & 1
\end{bmatrix}
$$

$$
O \;=\; \begin{bmatrix}
0 & 0 & 0 & 0 & 0 & 0 \\
0 & 0 & 0 & 0 & 0 & 0 \\
0 & 0 & 0 & 0 & 0 & * \\
0 & 0 & 0 & 0 & 0 & 0 \\
0 & 0 & 0 & 0 & 0 & 0 \\
0 & 0 & * & 0 & 0 & 0
\end{bmatrix}
\quad
E \;=\; \begin{bmatrix}
0 & 0 & 0 & 0 & 0 & 0 \\
0 & 0 & 0 & 0 & 0 & 0 \\
0 & 0 & 0 & 0 & 0 & 1 \\
0 & 0 & 0 & 0 & 0 & 0 \\
0 & 0 & 0 & 0 & 0 & 0 \\
0 & 0 & 0 & 0 & 0 & 0
\end{bmatrix}
$$

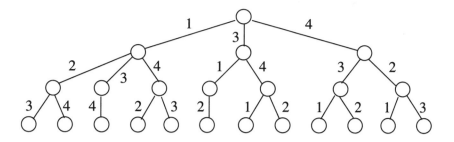

Figure 8.33 A four-rule search space for Problem 8.2.A.

$$P = \begin{bmatrix} 1 & 0 & * & * & * & * \\ 0 & 0 & 0 & 0 & 0 & 0 \\ * & 0 & 0 & 0 & 0 & * \\ * & 0 & 0 & 1 & * & * \\ * & 0 & 0 & * & 0 & 0 \\ * & 0 & * & * & 0 & 1 \end{bmatrix} \quad C = \begin{bmatrix} 1 & 0 & * & * & * & * \\ 0 & 0 & 0 & 0 & 0 & 0 \\ * & 0 & 0 & 0 & 0 & 1 \\ * & 0 & 0 & 1 & * & * \\ * & 0 & 0 & * & 0 & 0 \\ * & 0 & * & * & 0 & 1 \end{bmatrix}$$

8.2.A. The search space of a rule-based system with four rules is shown in Figure 8.33.

The parallelism matrix is

$$P = \begin{array}{c} \\ 1 \\ 2 \\ 3 \\ 4 \end{array} \begin{array}{c} \begin{array}{cccc} 1 & 2 & 3 & 4 \end{array} \\ \begin{bmatrix} 1 & 0 & 1 & 0 \\ 0 & 1 & 1 & 0 \\ 1 & 1 & 1 & 0 \\ 0 & 0 & 0 & 1 \end{bmatrix} \end{array}$$

(a) Using the information from the P matrix, find the compatible sets of rules and draw the reduced search space by eliminating all redundant paths.

(b) Suppose now that compatible rules are fired in parallel. Draw the reduced parallel search space by showing all the states that could be reached; that is, sequential rule firings and parallel rule firings.

Solution.
The maximum compatible sets are $\{1, 2, 4\}, \{3, 4\}$.

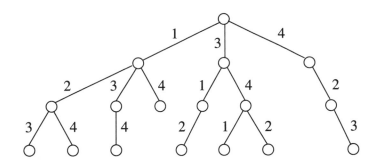

Figure 8.34 Reduced search space for Problem 8.2.A.

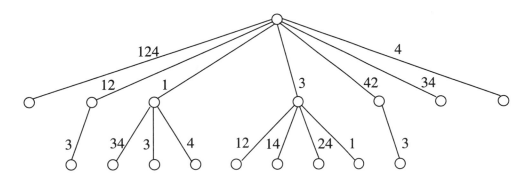

Figure 8.35 Parallel search space for Problem 8.2.A.

The reduced search space is shown in Figure 8.34.
The parallel search space is shown in Figure 8.35.

8.3.A. The semantic network in Figure 8.36 is stored in a SNAP array. Construct a data structure that shows the contents of the Marker Memory for processors 1 through 4, and of the Relation Memory. The markers and relations values are "don't-care" (X).

(a) From the semantic network above fill in the Relation Memory table.

(b) Update the Marker Memory after the execution of the following marker-propagation instruction on the semantic network loaded in the

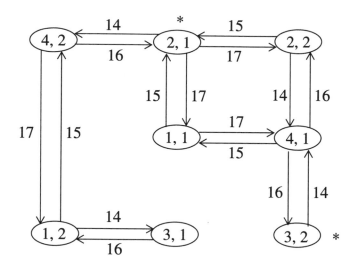

$(1, 2)$ means that this semantic network node is allocated to processor 1, node 2.

Figure 8.36 Semantic network for Problem 8.3.A.

SNAP array:

```
PROPAGATE (#1, <#2>, <SEQ(14, 17)> <NOP>).
```

The presence of marker #1 is indicated in Figure 8.36 by a * attached to some nodes.

Solution.
    Shown in Figure 8.37.

8.4.A. Prove that whether a set of compatible rules in a production cycle is executed either sequentially or in parallel, the same changes to the working memory are produced.

Relation memory   Marker memory

Proc.

Node	Relation	Link node Proc.	node	Value
2	15	4	2	X
2	14	3	1	X
1	15	2	1	X
1	17	4	1	X

Node	Marker	ON/OFF	Value	Originating address
1	1		X	
1	2		X	
1	3		X	
2	1		X	
2	2	ON	X	2, 1
2	3		X	

1

Node	Relation	Proc.	node	Value
1	17	1	1	X
1	14	4	2	X
1	17	2	2	X
2	14	4	1	X
2	15	2	1	X

Node	Marker	ON/OFF	Value	Originating address
1	1	ON	X	—
1	2		X	
1	3		X	
2	1		X	
2	2		X	
2	3		X	

2

Node	Relation	Proc.	node	Value
1	16	1	2	X
2	14	4	1	X

Node	Marker	ON/OFF	Value	Originating address
1	1		X	
1	2		X	
1	3		X	
2	1	ON	X	—
2	2		X	
2	3		X	

3

Node	Relation	Proc.	node	Value
1	16	2	2	X
1	15	1	1	X
1	16	3	2	X
2	16	2	1	X
2	17	1	2	X

Node	Marker	ON/OFF	Value	Originating address
1	1		X	
1	2	ON	X	3, 2
1	3		X	
2	1		X	
2	2	ON	X	2, 1
2	3		X	

4

Proc. node

Figure 8.37 SNAP data structure for Problem 8.3.A.

Solution [Kuo 1991].

Let wm_i^s and wm_i^p be the initial working memories for the sequential and parallel derivations, and wm_f^s and wm_f^p be the final working memories after the sequential and parallel executions. If $\{R_1 \cdots R_n\}$ is a set of compatible rules, we have to prove that $wm_f^s = wm_f^p$.

Assume that $wm_i^s = wm_i^p$. The rules are of the form
$$R_1 = \text{if } (CE_1^+, CE_1^-) \text{ then } (+AE_1^+, -AE_1^-)$$
$$R_2 = \text{if } (CE_2^+, CE_2^-) \text{ then } (+AE_2^+, -AE_2^-)$$
$$\vdots \qquad \vdots$$
$$R_n = \text{if } (CE_n^+, CE_n^-) \text{ then } (+AE_n^+, -AE_n^-)$$

In sequential firing, the working memory wm_{i+1}^s after firing R_1 is

$$wm_{i+1}^s = wm_i^s + AE_1^+ - AE_1^-$$

After R_1 is fired, R_2 is eligible to fire if

$$CE_2^+ \cap (wm_i^s - AE_1^-) = CE_2^+ \cap wm_i^s$$
$$\text{and}$$
$$CE_2^- \cap (wm_i^s + AE_1^+) = CE_2^- \cap wm_i^s$$

which implies

$$(CE_2^+ \cap AE_1^-) + (CE_2^- \cap AE_1^+) = \emptyset$$

Because R_1 and R_2 are compatible, this equation is satisfied. As a result, R_2 is eligible to fire after R_1 is fired. The working memory wm_{i+1+2}^s after R_2 is fired is

$$wm_{i+1+2}^s = wm_i^s + AE_1^+ - AE_1^- + AE_2^+ - AE_2^-$$

By induction, the final sequential working memory wm_f^s is

$$wm_f^s = wm_i^s + \sum_{j=1}^n AE_j^+ - \sum_{j=1}^n AE_j^-$$

In parallel mode, the set of rules $\{R_1 \cdots R_n\}$ is fired simultaneously, and wm_f^p is

$$wm_f^p = wm_i^p + \sum_{j=1}^{n} AE_j^+ - \sum_{j=1}^{n} AE_j^-$$

Because $wm_i^s = wm_i^p$, it follows that $wm_f^s = wm_f^p$.

8.5.A. What are the main differences between a typical database (DB) and a typical knowledge base (KB)?

Solution.

(1) The complexity of the facts recorded in a KB is far greater than that of the facts in a DB. Facts stored in a DB must conform to a rigid format. In contrast, KB systems usually have a wide range of inhomogeneous knowledge. (2) KB deals with incomplete information, whereas DB has almost no mechanism for inference—every field must be filled with an individual value. In a DB there is no notion of entailment, and thus of inference about domain, though databases may allow complex queries to be answered. The computations are only about data structures. (3) Knowledge bases represent generic descriptions in a way that allows new classes or instances to be recognized, or classified. Databases are merely representations of facts, and do not include conditions for recognizing new items as members of classes to which they have not been explicitly stated to belong. (4) The part of a DB that might correspond to concepts or classes in a KB, namely scheme, stays fixed, whereas the class structure in a typical KB changes fairly often. Typical AI applications have more classes (relations) than instances, whereas databases are intended for problems in which the instances to be stored greatly outnumber the relations, usually by orders of magnitude.

8.6.A. For a KL-ONE semantic network, design an algorithm that provides the necessary conditions for a concept **A** to subsume another concept **B**. As an example, consider Figure 8.38; concept **A** may be **parent** and concept **B** may be **grandparent**. Perform a piece-by-piece comparison of the components of **A** with those of **B**, including inherited components.

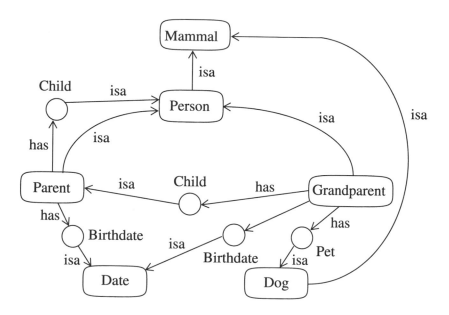

Figure 8.38 Example of a KL-ONE network.

Solution [Lipkis and Schmolze 1983].

In a KL-ONE representation, there is a distinction between primitive nodes (denoted as rectangles), and role nodes (denoted as circles). The role node `pet` for example can be interpreted as: `grandparent` has a `pet` and the `pet` is a `dog`. The node `dog` is called the value description of role node `pet`.

A concept `A` (`parent`) subsumes a concept `B` (`grandparent`) if:

- All primitive concepts that subsume `A` also subsume `B`. (Both `person` and `grandparent` have some primitive subsumers, namely `person` and `mammal`.)

- For each role node of `A`, there is a role node of `B` that denotes the same relation (both `parent` and `grandparent` have just two role nodes, namely `birthdate` and `child`), and for those corresponding role nodes, the value descriptions of `A`'s role nodes subsume those of `B`'s. For example, for the role node `birthdate`, both `parent` and `grandparent` have the same value description,

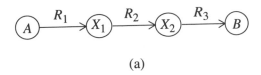

(a)

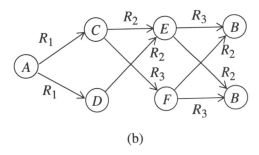

(b)

Figure 8.39 (a) The pattern; (b) the knowledge base.

namely date. For child, parent's value description subsumes grandparent's, i.e., person subsumes parent.

Thus, the hypothesis "parent subsumes grandparent" is true.

8.8.A. Using SNAP instructions, write a program to determine whether or not the pattern shown in Figure 8.39(a) matches the knowledge base shown in Figure 8.39(b).

Solution.
SEARCH (A, #1, NULL)
PROPAGATE (#1, #2, SEQ (R1, NULL), NOP)
WAIT-COMM
PROPAGATE (#2, #3, SEQ (R2, NULL), NOP)
WAIT-COMM
PROPAGATE (#3, #4, SEQ (R3, NULL), NOP)
WAIT-COMM
SEARCH (B, #5, NULL)
AND (#4, #5, #6, NOP)
COLLECT (#6)

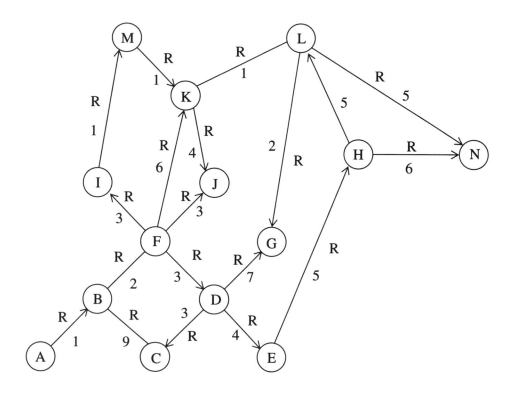

Figure 8.40 Find the distance from node A to any node.

If there is a node with marker #6, the knowledge base contains the input pattern.

8.9.A. Write a SNAP program to find the semantic distance from node A to all other nodes for the directed graph in Figure 8.40.

Solution.

```
/* Relations */
#define R 0
/* Markers */
#define Mborder 1
#define Mdist 2
#define Mnew 3
```

```
#define Mdiff 4
#define Mworse 5

#define INFINITY 0x7FFF

SEARCH(A,Mborder,0)
SEARCH(A,Mdist,0)
do
    {
    CLEAR_MARKER(Mnew)
    PROPAGATE(Mborder,Mnew,SEQ(R,NULL),NOP)
    WAIT_COMM
    FUNC_MARKER(Mnew,MIN)
    SET_MARKER_VALUE(Mnew,INFINITY)
    PROPAGATE(Mborder,Mnew,SEQ(R,NULL),ADD)
    WAIT_COMM
    CLEAR_MARKER(Mdiff)
    AND(Mnew,Mdist,Mdiff,SUB)
    CLEAR_MARKER(Mworse)
    TEST(Mdiff.GT.0,Mworse)
    TEST(Mdiff.EQ.0,Mworse)
    CLEAR_MARKER(Mborder)
    AND(Mnew,Mnew,Mborder,MIN)
    CLEAR_MARKER(Mworse,Mborder)
    AND(Mborder,Mborder,Mdist,MIN)
    COLLECT_MARKER(Mborder,&n)
    }
while (n!=0)
COLLECT_MARKER(Mdist)
```

8.1.B. Below are four OPS5 rules and an initial database.

(a) For these four rules, find the inhibit, output, and enable dependence matrices, and from these derive the P matrix and the C matrix.

(b) Using the initial database and the rules, develop a search space (of only depth 3).

(c) Find compatible sets of rules and, based on compatibility be-

tween the rules, find the simplified parallel search space for the search
space you found above.

Working Memory
(class A ↑ α 0)
(class B ↑ β 1)
(class C ↑ γ 0 ↑ δ 1)
(class D ↑ α 1)
(class E ↑ α 0)

(P 1
    {(class A ↑ α 0) <A> }
    (class B ↑ β 1)
    -(class C ↑ γ 1)
⟶

    (remove <A>)
    (make class A ↑ α 1)
    (make class D ↑ α 0))

(P 2
    {(class C ↑ γ 0 ↑ δ 1) <C> }
    (class D ↑ α 1)
⟶

    (remove <C>)
    (make class C ↑ γ 1 ↑ δ 1)
    (make class E ↑ δ 1))

(P 3
    {(class D ↑ α 1) <D> }
    {(class B ↑ β 1) <B> }
    -(class E ↑ γ 1)
⟶

    (remove <D>)
    (remove <B>)
    (make class B ↑ β 0))

(P 4
    (class A ↑ α 1)
    {(class E ↑ δ 0) <E> }

$\longrightarrow$

(remove <E>)
(make class E ↑ δ 1))

Hint: For example, "remove <A>" means to remove from the database the working memory element that satisfies the conditions of that rule, namely {(class A ↑ α 0) <A> }.

8.2.B. Based on the analysis of data dependencies in RBS, propose a procedure (algorithm) that eliminates visiting duplicate states during the search space. Such an algorithm may be useful when an RBS is executed on a multiprocessor. Can you prove that your proposed algorithm produces a "complete minimal tree"? By *complete* it is meant that the addition of a legal path to the tree produces a state that is already in the tree.

8.3.B. The parallelism matrix for a five-rule production system is

$$
P = \begin{array}{c|ccccc}
 & 1 & 2 & 3 & 4 & 5 \\
\hline
1 & 1 & 1 & 0 & 0 & 0 \\
2 & 1 & 1 & 0 & 1 & 1 \\
3 & 0 & 0 & 1 & 0 & 1 \\
4 & 0 & 1 & 0 & 1 & 1 \\
5 & 0 & 1 & 1 & 1 & 1 \\
\end{array}
$$

Find all possible (parallel and sequential) derivation sequences equivalent to the sequence $p_1 p_3 p_4 p_5$.

8.4.B. Write an OPS5 program and derive the inhibit, output, and enable interrule dependencies for the production system shown in Figure 8.41.

8.5.B. Study the allocation of the six-rule production system from Example 8.3 on the message-passing multiprocessor shown in Figure 8.42 by computing the allocation cost.

1. If animal A has hair then animal A is a mammal.

2. If animal A gives milk then animal A is a mammal.

3. If animal A has two legs, stands upright, and is warm-blooded then animal A is a mammal.

4. If animal A is a mammal, has two legs, stands upright, and communicates with written language then animal A is a human.

5. If animal A is a mammal, and animal A lives in water, then animal A is an aquatic mammal.

6. If animal A lives in water and gives milk then animal A is an aquatic mammal.

7. If animal A is an aquatic mammal and has a dorsal fin then animal A is a dolphin.

8. If animal A lives in water and breathes air then animal A is an aquatic mammal.

9. If animal A is an aquatic mammal and has a snout then animal A is a dolphin.

10. If animal A is an aquatic mammal and weighs one ton then animal A is a whale.

11. If animal A is a mammal and has two legs and stands upright and eats bananas then animal A is an ape.

12. If animal A eats meat then animal A is a carnivore.

13. If animal A is a mammal, and a carnivore, and has stripes, and has a tawny, color then animal A is a tiger.

Figure 8.41 RBS for Problem 8.4.B.

8.6.B. Consider the four-rule production system

r_1: if P(A, B) & N(B, C) then M(A, B)
r_2: if R(C, D) & N(B, C) then Q(C, D)
r_3: if R(C, D) & N(D, A) then P(D, E)
r_4: if M(B, D) & Q(A, C) then N(B, C)

(a) Derive the parallelism matrix and the communication matrix.

(b) Design the interconnection network among four PEs that minimizes the communication cost. (Assign one rule per processor.)

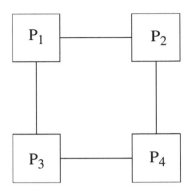

Figure 8.42 A message-passing multiprocessor.

8.7.B. For the rule-based system shown in Figure 8.41,
  (a) Find the set of rules that may fire in parallel.
  (b) For an initial database

HAS(A,HAIR)	GIVES(A,MILK)	LIVES(A,WATER)
BREATHES(A,AIR)	HAS(A,DORSAL-FIN)	

show the search space leading to the goal state that is to classify the animal corresponding to the initial database.
  (c) Using the set of compatible rules found in *(a)*, reduce the search space found in *(b)*.

8.8.B. Outline the most important operations in knowledge processing and identify computer architecture features that provide efficient implementations of these operations.

8.9.B. Consider an imaginary network as shown in Figure 8.43. We present the query:

Does node 0 have node 99?

Write a SNAP program for processing this query.

8.10.B. Provide a SNAP-like semantic network representation of the sentence "The Eiffel Tower is located in Paris and the Statue of Liberty in New York City."

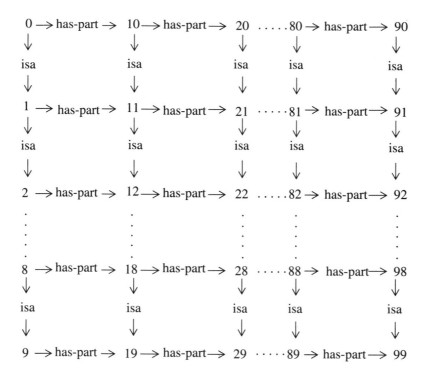

Figure 8.43 Imaginary two-dimensional 10 × 10 network.

8.11.B. Construct a semantic network for the world description:

Lions are mammals. Lions have-part lion's-head. Lion's-head has-part lion's-mouth. Lion's-mouth has-part lion's-teeth. Lion's teeth are teeth. Lion's-teeth-counts are counts. Typical lion's-teeth-count is equal to 10.

Elephants are mammals. Elephants have-part elephant's-head. Elephants hate lions. Elephant's-head has-part elephant's-mouth. Elephant's-mouth has-part tusk. Tusks are teeth. Tusk has-part tusk-count. Tusk-counts are counts. Typical elephant's tusk-count is equal to 2.

Clyde is circus-elephant. Clyde has-part Clyde's-tusk. Clyde's-tusk is tusk. Clyde's-tusk has-part Clyde's-tusk-

Figure 8.44 The graph for Problem 8.14.B.

count. Clyde's-tusk-count is tusk-count. Clyde's-tusk-count is equal to 1.

Provide a marker-passing solution to the query (recognition):

    Is there an animal with 1 tooth? What is it?

Be specific about the propagation of markers.

8.12.B. Write a SNAP program for the subsumption algorithm in Problem 8.8.A.

8.13.B. Devise a semantic network marker propagation scheme that will allow multiple markers to propagate at different speeds when they originate in the same node.

8.14.B. Write a SNAP program to demonstrate that the graph in Figure 8.44 can be drawn in one continuous line without overlapping any two edges.

Bibliography

Accetta, M., R. Baron, W. Bolosky, and D. Golub (1986). "MACH: A New Kernel Foundation for UNIX Development," *Proc. USENIX Conf.*, Atlanta, Ga., pp. 93–113.

Acharya, A., and M. Tambe (1989). "Production Systems on Message-Passing Computers: Simulation Results and Analysis," *Proc. International Conf. on Parallel Processing*, Vol. II, 246–54.

Adams, G.B., D.P. Agrawal, and H.J. Seigel (1987). "A Survey and Comparison of Fault-Tolerant Multistage Interconnection Networks," *Computer*, **20**(6):14–27.

Aho, A. V., J. E. Hopcroft, and J. D. Ullman (1974). *The Design and Analysis of Computer Algorithms*, Addison-Wesley, Reading, Mass.

Almasi, G. S., and A. Gottlieb (1989). *Highly Parallel Computing*, Benjamin-Cummings, Redwood City, Calif.

Annaratone, M., E. Arnould, T. Gross, H.T. Kung, M. Lam, O. Menzilcioglu, and J.A. Webb (1987). "The Warp Computer: Architecture, Implementation, and Performance," *IEEE Trans. on Computers*, C**36**(12):1523–38.

Archibald, J., and J.L. Baer (1986). "Cache Coherence Protocols: Evaluation Using a Multiprocessor Simulation Model," *ACM Trans. on Computer Systems*, **4**(4):273–98.

Arvind, and K.P. Gostelow (1982). "The U-Interpreter," *Computer*, **15**(2):42–50.

Baer, J.L. (1980). *Computer Systems Architecture*, Computer Science Press, Rockville, Md.

Batcher, K. E. (1968). "Sorting Networks and Their Applications," *Proc. AFIPS Spring Joint Computer Conf.*, **32**:307–15.

Berman, F., and L. Snyder (1987). "On Mapping Parallel Algorithms into Parallel Architectures," *J. Parallel and Distributed Computing*, **4**(5):439–58.

Bitton, D., D. J. DeWitt, D. K. Hsiao, and J. Menon (1984). "A Taxonomy of Parallel Sorting," *ACM Computing Surveys*, **16**(3):287–318.

Bokhari, S.H. (1987). *Assignment Problems in Parallel and Distributed Computing*, Kluwer Academic Publishers, Boston, Mass.

Brachman, R.J., and J.G. Schmolze (1985). "An Overview of the KL-ONE Knowledge Representation System," *Cognitive Science*, 9:171–216.

Brent, R.P. (1973). "The Parallel Evaluation of Arithmetic Expression in Logarithmic Time," in *Complexity of Sequential and Parallel Numerical Algorithms,* ed. J.F. Traub, Academic Press, San Diego, Calif., pp. 83–102.

Brownston, L., R. Farrel, E. Kant, and N. Martin (1985). *Programming Expert Systems in OPS5: An Introduction to Rule-Based Programming*, Addison-Wesley, Reading, Mass.

Cappelo, P.R., and Steighitz, K. (1983). "Unifying VLSI Array Designs with Geometric Transformations," *Proc. 1983 International Conf. on Parallel Processing*, Vol. II, pp. 448–57.

Carpenter, R.J. (1987). "Performance Measurement Instrumentation for Multiprocessor Computers," Technical Report NBSIR 87-3627, National Bureau of Standards, Washington, D.C.

Chaiken, D., C. Fields, K. Kurihara, and A. Agarwal (1990). "Directory-Based Cache Coherence in Large-Scale Multiprocessors," *Computer*, **23**(6):49–59.

Chandy, K.M., and J. Misra (1988). *Parallel Program Design*, Addison-Wesley, Reading, Mass.

Charniak, E. (1983). "Passing Markers: A Theory of Contextual Inference in Language Comprehension," *Cognitive Science*, **7**(3):171–90.

Chen, S. C., and D. J. Kuck (1975). "Time and Parallel Processor Bounds for Linear Recurrence Systems," *IEEE Trans. on Computers*, C**24**(7):701–17.

Cheong, H., and A. Veidenbaum (1990). "Compiler-Directed Cache Management in Multiprocessors," *Computer*, **23**(6):39–47.

Connection Machine Model CM-2 Technical Summary (1989), Technical Report, Thinking Machines Corporation, Cambridge, Mass.

Dally, W.J., and C.L. Seitz (1987). "Deadlock-Free Message Routing in Multiprocessor Interconnection Network," *IEEE Trans. on Computers*, C**36**(5):547–553.

Davis, A. L. (1977). "Architecture of DDM1: A Recursively Structured Data-Driven Machine," Department of Computer Science Technical Report, Univ. of Utah, Salt Lake City, Utah.

DeCegama, A. L. (1989). *Parallel Processing Architectures and VLSI Hardware*, Prentice-Hall, Englewood Cliffs, N.J.

Dennis, J.B. (1979). "The Varieties of Data Flow Computers," *Proc. First International Conf. on Distributed Computing Systems*, 430–9.

Dennis, J.B., and D.P. Misunas (1975), "A Preliminary Architecture for a Basic Data Flow Computer," *Proc. Second Annual Symposium on Computer Architecture*, ACM 1975.

Dixit, V.V., and D. Moldovan (1989). "Minimal Search Space in Production Systems," *Proc. 1989 International Conf. on Parallel Processing*, Vol. II, pp. 254–59.

Dixit, V.V., and D. Moldovan (1990). "The Allocation Problem in Parallel Production Systems," *J. Parallel and Distributed Computing*, **8**(1):20−9.

Dubois, M., and F. A. Briggs (1982). "Effects of Coherency in Multiprocessors," *IEEE Trans. on Computer*, C**31**(11):1083−98.

Dubois, M., C. Scheurich, and F. A. Briggs (1988). "Synchronization, Coherence and Ordering of Events in Multiprocessors," *Computer*, **20**(2):9−21.

Ellis, J.R. (1986). *Bulldog: A Compiler for VLIW Architectures*, MIT Press, Cambridge, Mass.

Evripidou, P., and J.L. Gaudiot (1991). "The USC Decoupled Multilevel Data-Flow Execution Model," in *Advanced Topics in Data-Flow Computing*, eds. J.L. Gaudiot and L. Bic, Prentice-Hall, Englewood Cliffs, N.J.

Fahlman, S.E. (1979). *NETL: A System for Representing and Using Real-World Knowledge*, MIT Press, Cambridge, Mass.

Fahlman, S.E., and G.E. Hinton (1987). "Connectionist Architectures for Artificial Intelligence," *Computer*, **20**(1):100−09.

Feng, T.Y., and C. Wu (1979). "Interconnection Networks in Multiple-Processor Systems," Technical Report, Wayne State Univ., Detroit, Michigan.

Finnila, C. A., and H. H. Love, Jr. (1977). "The Associative Linear Array Processor," *IEEE Trans. on Computers*, C**26**(2).

Fisher, J. A. (1987). "VLIW Architecture Supercomputer via Overlapped Execution," *Proc. Second International Conf. on Supercomputing*, May 1987.

Forgy, C.L. (1982). "RETE. A Fast Algorithm for the Many Pattern/Many Object Pattern Problem," *AI Journal*, 19:17–37.

Fortes, J.A.B. (1983). "Algorithm Transformations for Parallel Processing and VLSI Architecture Design," Ph.D. thesis, Dept. of Electrical Engineering—Systems, Univ. of Southern Calif., Los Angeles.

Fortes, J.A.B., and D.I. Moldovan (1985). "Parallel Detection and Transformation Techniques Useful for VLSI Algorithms," *J. Parallel and Distributed Computing*, **2**:277–301.

Fortes, J.A.B., and F. Parisi-Presicce (1984). "Optimal Linear Schedules for the Parallel Execution of Algorithms," *Proc. 1984 International Conf. on Parallel Processing*, pp. 322–29.

Foster, C.C. (1976). *Content Addressable Parallel Processors*, Van Nostrand Reinhold Co., New York.

Franklin, M.A. (1978). "Parallel Solution of Ordinary Differential Equations," *IEEE Trans. on Computers*, C**27**(5):413–20.

Gajski, D.D. (1981). "An Algorithm for Solving Linear Recurrence Systems on Parallel and Pipeline Machines," *IEEE Trans. on Computers*, C**30**(3):190–206.

Gajski, D.D., D.A. Padua, D.J. Kuck, and R.H. Kuhn (1982). "A Second Opinion on Data Flow Machines and Languages," *Computer*, **15**(2):58–69.

Gajski, D.D., and J.K. Peir (1985). "Essential Issues in Multiprocessor Systems," *Computer*, **18**(6):9–27.

Gao, G.R. (1991). "A Flexible Architecture Model for Hybrid Data-Flow and Control-Flow Evaluation," in *Advanced Topics in Data-Flow Computing*, eds. J.L. Gaudiot and L. Bic, Prentice-Hall, Englewood Cliffs, N.J.

Gaudiot, J.L., and L. Bic (1991). *Advanced Topics in Data Flow Computing*, Prentice-Hall, Englewood Cliffs, N.J.

Goodman, J.R., and P. Woest (1988). "The Wisconsin Multicube: A New Large-Scale Cache-Coherent Multiprocessor," *Proc. 15th Annual Symposium on Computer Architecture*, 422–31.

Gottlieb, A. (1987). "An Overview of the NYU Ultracomputer Project," in *Experimental Parallel Computing Architectures*, ed. J. Dongarra, North-Holland, Amsterdam.

Gottlieb, A., R. Grishman, R. Kruskal, C. P. McAalifte, K. P. Randolf, and M. Smir (1983). "The NYU Ultracomputer—Designing an MIMD Shared Memory Parallel Computer," *IEEE Trans. on Computers*, C**32**(2):175–89.

Gupta, A. (1987). *Parallelism in Production Systems*, Morgan Kaufmann, Los Altos, Calif.

Hayes, J. P. (1978). *Computer Architecture and Organization*, McGraw-Hill, New York.

Hayes, J. P., T. N. Mudge, Q. F. Stout, S. Colley, and J. Palmer (1986). "Architecture of a Hypercube Supercomputer," *Proc. 1986 International Conference on Parallel Processing*, pp. 653–60.

Hendler, J.A. (1988). *Integrating Marker-Passing and Problem-Solving*, Lawerence Erlbaum Associates, Hillsdale, N.J.

Hillis, W.D. (1985). *The Connection Machine*, MIT Press, Cambridge, Mass.

Hiroki, K., S. Sekiguchi, and T. Shimada (1991). "Status of SIGMA-1: A Data-Flow Supercomputer," in *Advanced Topics in Data Flow Computing*, eds. J.L. Gaudiot and L. Bic, Prentice-Hall, Englewood Cliffs, N.J.

Hockney, R.W., and C.R. Jesshope (1981). *Parallel Computers: Architecture, Programming and Algorithms*, Adam Hilger Ltd., Bristol, England.

Hwang, K., and F.A. Briggs (1984). *Computer Architecture and Parallel Processing*, McGraw-Hill, New York.

Hwang, K., and D. DeGroot, eds. (1989). *Parallel Processing for Supercomputers and Artificial Intelligence*, McGraw-Hill, New York.

Iannucci, R.A. (1988). "Towards a Data-Flow / Von Neumann Hybrid Architecture," *Proc. 15th Annual Symposium on Computer Architecture*, pp. 131–40.

Ishida, T., and S. Stolfo (1985). "Toward the Parallel Extension of Rules in Production System Programs," *Proc. International Conf. on Parallel Processing*, pp. 568–75.

JaJa, J. (1992). *An Introduction to Parallel Algorithms*, Addison-Wesley, Reading, Mass.

Karp, R.M., and V.A. Ramachandran (1990). "A Survey of Parallel Algorithms for Shared Memory Machines," in *Handbook of Theoretical Computer Science*, ed. J. Van Lecuwen, North-Holland, Amsterdam.

Kelly, M., and R. Seviora (1989). "An Evaluation of DRete on CUPID for OPS5," *Proc. 11th International Joint Conference on Artificial Intelligence*, pp. 84–90.

Kitano, H. (1991). "ΦDm-DIALOG: An Experimental Speech-to-Speech Dialog Translation System," *Computer*, **24**(6):36–51.

Knuth, D. (1973). *Searching and Sorting*, Vol. 3 *The Art of Computer Programming*, Addison-Wesley, Reading, Mass.

Kronsjö, L.I. (1979). *Algorithms: Their Complexity and Efficiency*, John Wiley and Sons, Chichester, England.

Kuck, D.J. (1978). *The Structure of Computers and Computations*, Vol. **1**, John Wiley and Sons, New York.

Kuck, D.J., E.S. Davidson, D.H. Lawrie, and A.H. Sameh (1986). "Parallel Supercomputing Today and the Cedar Approach," *Science*, **231**:967–74.

Kuck, D.J., R.H. Kuhn, D.A. Padua, B. Leasure, and M. Wolfe (1981). "Dependence Graphs and Compiler Optimizations," *Proc. 8th ACM Symp. Principles Programming Languages*, pp. 207–18.

Kuck, D.J., and Y. Maruyama (1975). "Time Bounds on the Parallel Evaluation of Arithmetic Expressions," *SIAM J. Comp*, **4**:147–62.

Kuck, D.J., Y. Muraoka, and S.C. Chan (1972). "On the Number of Operations Simultaneously Executable in FORTRAN-like Programs and Their Resulting Speed-up," *IEEE Trans. on Computers*, C**21**:1293–1310.

Kuck, D.J., and A. Sameh (1971). "Parallel Computation of Eigenvalues of Real Matrices," *IFIP Congress* 1971, North-Holland, Amsterdam, **2**:1266–72.

Kuck, D.J., and A. Sameh (1987). "A Supercomputing Performance Evaluation Plan," *Proc. International Conf. on Supercomputing*, Springer-Verlag, New York, LNCS Vol. 297.

Kung, H.T. (1979). "Let's Design Algorithms for VLSI Systems," *Proc. Caltech Conf. on VLSI*, pp. 65–90.

Kung, H.T. (1980). "The Structure of Parallel Algorithms," *Advances in Computers*, **19**:65–111.

Kung, H.T. (1982). "Why Systolic Architectures?," *Computer*, **15**(1):37–46.

Kung, H.T., and C.E. Leiserson (1980). "Systolic Arrays for VLSI," in *Introduction to VLSI Systems,* eds. C.A. Mead and L.A. Conway, sec. 8.3., Addison-Wesley, Reading, Mass.

Kung, H.T., and D. Stevenson (1977). "A Software Technique for Reducing the Outing Time on a Parallel Computer with a Fixed Interconnection Network," in *High Speed Computer and Algorithm Organization,* eds. D. Kuck et al., Academic Press, San Diego, Calif.

Kuo, S. (1991). "A Parallel Asynchronous Message-Driven Production Systems," Ph.D. thesis, Dept. of Electrical Engineering—Systems, Univ. of Southern Calif., Los Angeles.

Kuo, S., and D.I. Moldovan (1991). "Implementation of Multiple Rule Firing Production Systems on Hypercube," *J. Parallel and Distributed Computing*, **13**(4):383–94.

Kuo, S., and D.I. Moldovan (1992). "The State-of-the-Art in Parallel Processing for Production Systems," *J. Parallel and Distributed Processing*, **15**(1):1–26.

Lamport, L. (1974). "The Parallel Execution of DO Loops," *Comm. of the ACM*, **17**(2):83–93.

Lawrie, D.H. (1975). "Access and Alignment of Data in an Array Processor," *IEEE Trans. on Computers*, C**24**(12):1145–55.

Leighton, F.T. (1992). *Introduction to Parallel Algorithms and Architectures: Arrays, Trees, Hypercubes*, Morgan Kaufmann, San Mateo, Calif.

Li, G.J., and B.W. Wah (1985). "The Design of Optimal Systolic Arrays," *IEEE Trans. on Computers*, C**34**(1):66–77.

Lin, T.C., and D.I. Moldovan (1986). "Mapping of Algorithms into Mesh Connected Computers," Technical Report CRI 86-18, Dept. of Electrical Engineering—Systems, Univ. of Southern Calif., Los Angeles.

Lipkis, T.A., and J.G. Schmolze (1983). "Classification in the KL-ONE Knowledge Representation System," *Proc. Eighth International Joint Conference on Artificial Intelligence*, 1:330–32.

Lipovski, G.J., and M. Malek (1987). *Parallel Computing: Theory and Comparisons*, John Wiley and Sons, Chichester, England.

Little, M.J., and J. Grinberg (1988). "The Third Dimension," *Byte*, November, pp. 311–19.

Malony, A. (1986). "Cedar Performance Measurements," CSRD report No. 579, Univ. of Ill. Press, Urbana-Champaign, Ill.

Miller, R., and Q. Stout (1989). "Mesh Computer Algorithms for Computational Geometry," *IEEE Trans. on Computers*, **38**(3):321–40.

Miranker, D.P. (1987). "TREAT: A Better Match Algorithm for AI Production Systems," *Proc. of National Conf. on Artificial Intelligence,* pp. 42–7.

Moldovan, D.I. (1983a). "An Associative Array Architecture Intended for Semantic Network Processing," Technical Report PPP 83-8, Dept. of Electrical Engineering—Systems, Univ. of Southern Calif., Los Angeles.

Moldovan, D.I. (1983b). "On the Design of Algorithms for VLSI Systolic Arrays," *Proc. IEEE,* **71**(1):113–20.

Moldovan, D.I. (1984). "Partitioned QR Algorithm for Systolic Arrays," *VLSI Signal Processing,* 350–62, IEEE Press, New York.

Moldovan, D.I., and G.R. Nudd (1984). "A VLSI Algorithm and Architecture for Subgraph Isomorphism," *Proc. 1984 Phoenix Conf. on Computers and Communications,* Phoenix, Ariz.

Moldovan, D.I., and Y.W. Tung (1985). "SNAP: A VLSI Architecture for Artificial Intelligence Processing," *J. Parallel and Distributed Computing,* **7**(2):43–8.

Moldovan, D.I., and J.A.B. Fortes (1986). "Partitioning and Mapping Algorithms into Fixed Size Systolic Arrays," *IEEE Trans. on Computers,* C**35**(1):1–12.

Moldovan, D.I. (1987). "A Systolic Array for Optimal Binary Search Tree Algorithm," *Proc. 20th Hawaii International Conf. on Systems Sciences.*

Moldovan, D.I., W. Lee, and C. Lin (1992). "SNAP: A Marker-Propagation for Knowledge Processing," *IEEE Trans. on Parallel and Distributed Systems,* **3**(4):397–410.

Moldovan, D.I., W. Lee, C. Lin, and M. Chung (1992). "SNAP: Parallel Processing Applied to AI," *Computer,* **25**(5):39–50.

Moldovan, D.I. (1989). "RUBIC: A Multiprocessor for Rule-Based Systems," *IEEE Trans. on System, Man and Cybernetics,* **19**(4):699–706.

Muller, D.E., and F.P. Preparata (1976). "Restructuring of Arithmetic Expressions for Parallel Evaluation," *JACM*, **23**(3):534–43.

Norvig, P. (1989). "Marker Passing as a Weak Method for Text Inferencing," *Cognitive Science*, **13**:569–620.

O'Leary, D.P., and G.W. Stewart (1985). "Data-Flow Algorithms for Parallel Matrix Computations," *Comm. ACM*, **28**(8):840–53.

Padua, D.A., D.J. Kuck, and D.H. Lawrie (1980). "High-Speed Multiprocessors and Compilation Techniques," *IEEE Trans. on Computers*, C**29**(9):763–76.

Padua, D.A., and M.J. Wolfe (1986). "Advanced Compiler Optimizations for Supercomputers," *Comm. ACM* **29**(12):1184–1201.

Patterson, D.A., and J.L. Hennessy (1990). *Computer Architecture: A Quantitative Approach*, Morgan Kaufmann, San Mateo, Calif.

Polychronopoulos, C.D. (1988). *Parallel Programming and Compilers*, Kluwer Academic Publishers, Norwell, Mass.

Prasanna, V.K. (1991). "Parallel Processing Course," class notes, Dept. of Electrical Engineering—Systems, Univ. Southern Calif., Los Angeles.

Preparata, F. (1978). "New Parallel Sorting Schemes," *IEEE Trans. on Computers*, **27**(7):669–73.

Quillian, M.R. (1966). *Semantic Memory*, Ph.D. diss., Carnegie Institute of Technology (now Carnegie-Mellon Univ.), Pittsburgh. Appeared as Report AFCRL-66-189.

Quinn, M.J. (1987). *Designing Efficient Algorithms for Parallel Computers*, McGraw-Hill, New York.

Quinn, M.J., and N. Deo (1984). "Parallel Graph Algorithms," *ACM Computing Surveys*, **16**(3):319–48.

Quinton, P. (1984). "Automatic Synthesis of Systolic Arrays from Uniform Recurrent Equations," *Proc. 11th Annual International Symposium on Computer Architecture*, pp. 208–14.

Raghavendra, C.S., and P. Kumar (1984). "Permutations on Illiac-IV Type Networks," *Proc. 1984 International Conf. on Parallel Processing*.

Raveche, H.J., D.H. Lawrie, and A.M. Despain (1987). "A National Computing Initiative," Report on SIAM workshop, Leesburg, Va.

Riesbeck, C.K., and C.E. Martin (1985). "Direct Memory Access Parsing," Technical Report YaleU/DCS/RR 354, Yale Univ., New Haven, Conn.

Sameh, A.H. (1971). "On Jacobi and Jacobi-like Algorithms for a Parallel Computer," *Math. Comp.*, **25**:579–90.

Sameh, A.H. (1977). "Numerical Parallel Algorithms—a Survey," in *High Speed Computer and Algorithm Organization*, Academic Press, New York, pp. 207–28.

Sameh, A.H., and R.P. Brent (1977). "Solving Triangular Systems on a Parallel Computer," *SIAM J. Numer. Anal.*, **14**(6):1101–13.

Sameh, A., and D. Kuck (1977). "A Parallel QR-algorithm for Symmetric Tridiagonal Matrices," *IEEE Trans. on Computers*, C**26**:147–153.

Sarkar, V. (1989). *Partitioning and Scheduling Parallel Programs for Multiprocessors*, MIT Press, Cambridge, Mass.

Schank, R.C. (1982). *Dynamic Memory: A Theory of Learning in Computers and People.* Cambridge University Press, New York.

Schmolze, J. (1991). "Guaranteeing Serializable Results in Synchronous Parallel Production Systems," *J. Parallel and Distributed Computing*, **13**(4):348–65.

Schor, M., T. Daly, H.S. Lee, and B. Tibbitts (1986). "Advances in Rete Pattern Matching," *Proc. AAAI-86*, pp. 226–32.

Schwartz, J.T. (1980). "Ultracomputers," *ACM Trans. Programming Languages and Systems*, **2**(4):484–521.

Shih, Y., and J. Fier (1989). "Hypercube Systems and Key Applications," in Chapter 6 of *Parallel Processing for Supercomputers and Artificial Intelligence*, eds. K. Hwang and D. DeGroot, McGraw-Hill, New York.

Siegel, H.J. (1984). *Interconnection Networks for Large-Scale Parallel Processing*, Lexington Books, Boston, Mass.

Stenstrom, P. (1990). "A Survey of Cache Coherence Schemes for Multiprocessors," *Computer*, **23**(6):12–25.

Stewart, G.W. (1974). *Introduction to Matrix Computations*, Academic Press, San Diego, Calif.

Stolfo, S.J. (1987). "Initial Performance of the DADO2 Prototype," *Computer*, **20**(1):75–83.

Stone, H.S. (1971). "Parallel Processing with the Perfect Shuffle," *IEEE Trans. on Computers*, C**20**(2).

Stone, H.S. (1980). "Parallel Computers," in *Introduction to Computer Architecture*, ed. H.S. Stone, Science Research Associates, pp. 363–425.

Tenorio, F., and D. Moldovan (1985). "Mapping Production Systems into Multiprocessors," *Proc. 1985 International Conf. on Parallel Processing*, pp. 56–62.

Towle, R. (1976). "Control and Data Dependence for Program Transformation," Ph.D. diss., Technical Report 71-788, Dept. of Comp. Sci., Univ. of Ill. Press, Urbana-Champaign, Ill.

Treleaven, P.C., D.R. Brownbridge, and R.P. Hopkins (1982). "Data-Driven and Demand-Driven Computer Architecture," *ACM Computing Surveys*, **14**(1):93–143.

Ullman, J.R. (1976). "An Algorithm for Subgraph Isomorphism," *JACM*, **23**(1):31–42.

Waltz, D.L. (1987). "Applications of the Connection Machine," *Computer*, **20**(1):85−97.

Watson, I., and J. Gurd (1982). "A Practical Data Flow Computer," *Computer*, **15**(2):51−7.

Woods, W.A. (1979). "Research in Knowledge Representation for Natural Language Understanding," Technical Report No. 4785, Bolt Beranek and Newman Inc., Boston.

Worlton, J. (1986). "Toward a Science of Parallel Computation," *Computational Mechanics*, New York, pp. 23−35.

Wos, L. (1988). *Automated Reasoning: 33 Basic Research Problems*, Prentice-Hall, Englewood Cliffs, N.J.

Index